TOBAGO IN WARTIME 1793-1815

K.O. LAURENCE

THE PRESS UNIVERSITY OF THE WEST INDIES
Barbados ● Jamaica ● Trinidad and Tobago

The Press University of the West Indies
1A Aqueduct Flats Kingston Jamaica W I

© 1995 by Keith Ormiston Laurence
All rights reserved. Published 1995
Printed in Canada

99 98 97 96 95   5 4 3 2 1

Illustrations (pp. 56, 95, 122, 202) reproduced by permission of The Main Library, The University of the West Indies, St Augustine; (p.32) by permission of Prof. B. W. Higman (UWI, Mona)

CATALOGUING IN PUBLICATION DATA

Laurence, K. O.
   Tobago in wartime, 1793-1815 / K. O. Laurence.

   p. cm.
   Includes bibliographical references.
   ISBN 976 640 003 2
   1. Tobago – History. 2. Tobago – Politics
   and government. 3. Slavery – Tobago.
   4. Tobago – Economic conditions.
   5. Tobago – Social conditions. I. Title.
   F 2116.L38 1995   972.983–dc - 20

Book design by Orville Bloise
Set in 10.5 / 12.5 Garamond x 27
This book has been printed on acid-free paper

CONTENTS

Illustrations / iv

Tables / v

Abbreviations / vi

Preface / vii

1. Introduction / 1
2. The Population of Tobago / 10
3. Politics, Administration, and the Constitution / 45
4. The Slave System / 94
5. The Economy / 133
6. The Christian Churches / 182
7. The Organization of Defence / 197
8. Conclusion / 224

   Notes / 229

   Bibliography / 270

   Index / 275

ILLUSTRATIONS

MAPS

1.1 Plantations in Tobago, 1793-1815   /   *viii*

2.1 Slave population per square mile, 1819   /   *32*

6.1 Estates visited by missionaries, 1798-1813   /   *185*

7.1 Communications and fortifications circa 1800   /   *198*

PLATES

North Front of Government House, Mount William   /   *56*

Betsy's Hope Estate, Queensvale   /   *95*

Slave House in Tobago   /   *122*

Fort King George   /   *202*

TABLES

1.1 Exports from Tobago   / 3

2.1 French and white free persons   / 10

2.2 Free population of Tobago   / 13

2.3 Garrison mortality figures 1808-1815   / 19

2.4 Free male population of Tobago, white and free coloured   / 24

2.5 Slave imports, 1795-1807   / 30

2.6 Slave population of Tobogo   / 31

2.7 Slave occupations, 1811   / 38

4.1 Slave mortality and birth rates in Tobago, 1819-1821   / 125

5.1 Exports from Tobago, 1794-1815   / 136

5.2 Ships reaching Tobago from the United States, 1794-1801   / 165

5.3 Quantities of goods imported into Tobago, 1805-1807   / 171

5.4 Quantities of lumber imported from the USA and BNA, 1812-1815   / 171

ABBREVIATIONS

B.L.	British Library
B.N.A.	British North America
C.O.	Colonial Office Records
L.M.S.	London Missionary Society
M.H.A.	Minutes of the House of Assembly
M.L.C.	Minutes of the Legislative Council
M.M.S.	Moravian Missionary Society
M.P.C.	Minutes of the Privy Council
N.L.S.	National Library of Scotland
S.O.A.S.	School of Oriental and African Studies
S.R.O.	Scottish Record Office
T.P.L.	Tobago Public Library

PREFACE

This study of a short period in the history of one of the least known of the West Indian islands from a scholarly point of view began as a limited probe and its ultimate shape became visible but slowly. It was influenced by an interest in the surviving fortifications of Tobago and in the important eighteenth century maps which survive, and this is reflected in the emphases of the finished product. It is my hope that the work will contribute something to redressing the imbalance which exists between the two islands of the state of Trinidad and Tobago in the context of historical study and that it will stimulate other scholars to be more attentive to the experience of the latter.

My thanks are due to the staffs of the Public Record Office in London, the British Library, the Scottish Record Office and the National Library of Scotland, the Tobago Public Library as well as the Library of the St Augustine Campus of the University of the West Indies, who rendered valuable assistance. I am particularly indebted to the Herman Dunlap Smith Centre at Chicago's Newberry Library, which awarded me a short-term fellowship to assist me in using its valuable map collection, without which the maps in this book would not exist.

Finally, I am grateful to Dr Bridget Brereton for her valuable comments on a draft of the manuscript and to Mrs Janice Edwards, who transformed an often barely legible mass of jottings into a polished typescript.

K.O. LAURENCE
University of the West Indies
St. Augustine

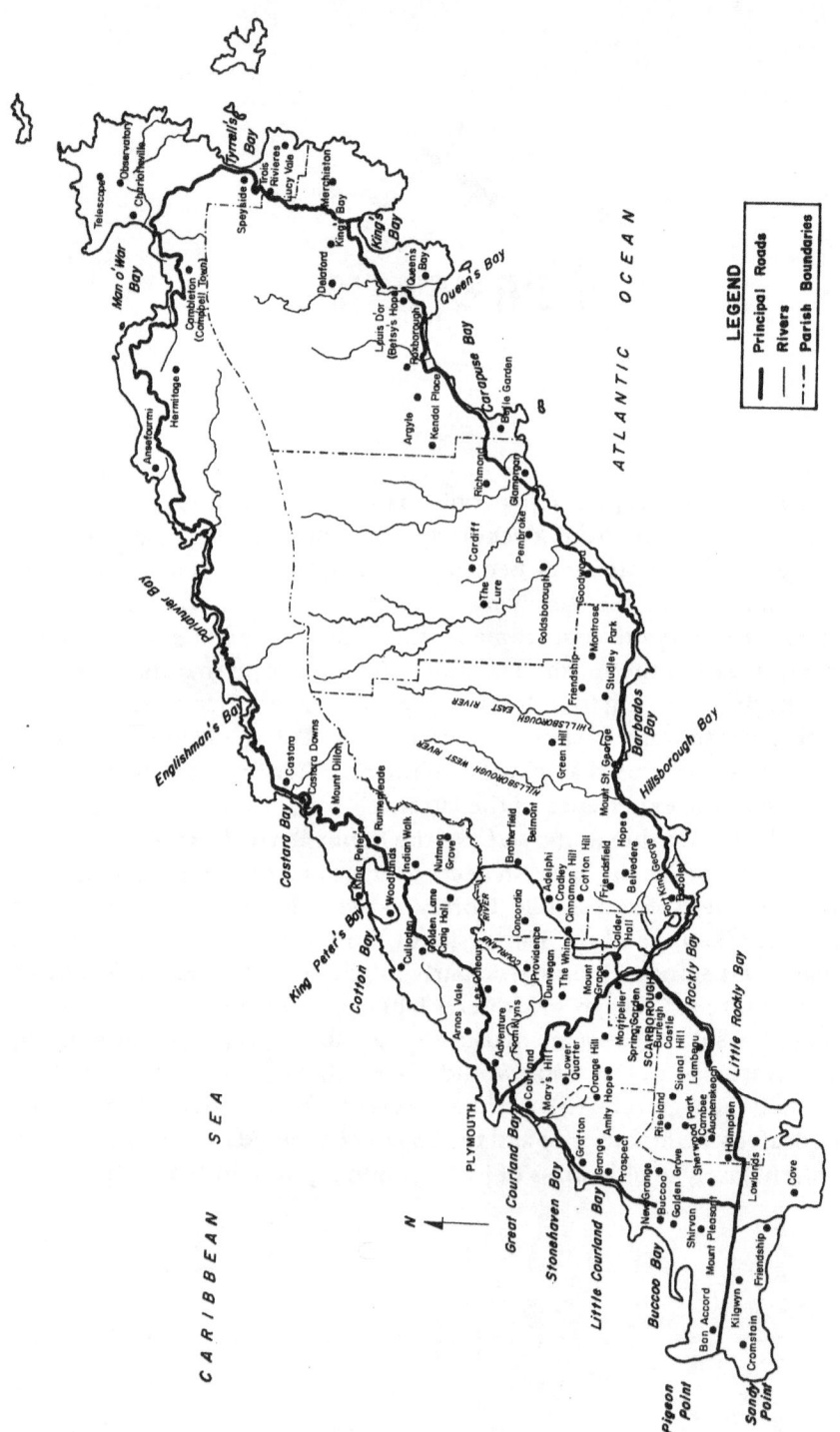

Fig. 1.1 Plantations in Tobago, 1793–1815

INTRODUCTION

The island of Tobago was the object of rivalry and dispute between European powers for more than a century, and changed hands so frequently that it is difficult to keep count of the incidents, until in 1763 France agreed to acknowledge Britain's claim as one of the terms of the Treaty of Paris which ended the Seven Years War. A normal British colonial constitution was then established, Tobago being accorded a representative Assembly and administered under the Governor-in-Chief of the Windward Islands who had his headquarters in Grenada. At this time, Europeans had settled the island only in very small numbers and its economic potential remained almost wholly unexploited. In the 1750s some dozens of Europeans lived there, together with perhaps as many as 300 Amerindians. Though the few settlers had experimented with cocoa, cotton, tobacco, sugar and provisions, Tobago produced no significant quantities of these crops and it attracted the attention of the Great Powers because of its strategic value as a possible base for attacks on or the defense of the neighbouring commercially active islands and the activities of transient Europeans who cut timber and dyewoods or hunted turtles.[1]

The "cession" to Britain in 1763, however, abruptly and completely changed the picture. In 1764 the government began to sell land to private purchasers as the first step in promoting economic development. The terms of these sales stimulated the early exploitation of the land and penalized those who held tracts in idleness, and an effort was also made to stimulate the growth of a white population. Significant numbers of British settlers soon began to arrive and they at once began to import slaves. Sugar, cotton and cocoa were soon being produced in noticeable quantities, and cotton production in particular grew rapidly. When, in

1781, Tobago was captured by the French during what had begun as the War of American Independence, it was as important an economic unit as many other West Indian colonies.

Tobago was ceded to France in 1783 by the Treaty of Versailles on terms which preserved its British character. It was agreed that the practice of the Protestant religion should not be disturbed and that the British inhabitants should retain their property on the existing terms or be free to sell their estates and depart, provided they were sold to French subjects, at any time during the following eighteen months. The constitution and laws of the colony were to remain unaltered.[2]

New elections in 1784 left the membership of the Assembly much the same as it had been under the British. In 1785, however, it refused to vote money for the government's local expenses on the ground that the island's proprietors were in serious financial straits, and the French administration responded by demanding that the Assembly agree to provide an annual sum known as *les grâces du roi*, an imperial impost which was clearly in breach of the British-style constitution. In December 1785 came royal instructions that the island should provide an annual sum of 200,000 livres tournois, about £5,500 sterling. This the Council and Assembly eventually accepted with effect from 1786,[3] imposing a poll tax of 22s. 6d. on slaves and an 8 per cent tax on house rents.[4]

It may be this dispute which, despite the legislature's eventual capitulation, prompted the French, with a measure of sleight of hand, to abrogate the old constitution. In October 1787 an order was promulgated establishing a Colonial Assembly and a Council, with each parish having two seats in the Assembly rather than one, and Scarborough now renamed Port Louis, being represented for the first time, also by two members. In addition to these sixteen members the new Assembly also included the governor, ordonnateur, the commandant particulier and the oldest administrative official, the four most senior officials. The Assembly was to endure for four years, but half its members were to be elected every second year. The first task of the Assembly at its annual session was to be the provision of the *grâces du roi* and money for local expenses; the second, a review of the economy and the public works.[5]

Thus the old Assembly was simply suppressed, its successor enjoying far less independence and authority, and the Council was henceforth to act only as a Chamber of Registration for edicts from Paris, under the name of Privy Council. Under new elections in October 1787 fifteen Englishmen and a single Frenchman, Louis Delgré representing Port Louis, were elected. The new Assembly performed as the French authorities required and approved a 4 per cent export duty, a 6 per cent tax on jobbing slaves, a capitation tax of 50 livres on domestic slaves, and a 6 per cent tax on house rents.[6] If the legislature remained full of Englishmen, the administration was exclusively French and was patterned on the model of the other French colonies so that the ordonnateur in effect shared power with the governor.[7]

The coming of French rule was followed by the emigration of a number of English residents, though most plantation owners remained as they were unable to sell their property to advantage. There was, however, no significant French immigration, and the economic picture presented by Tobago remained much the same.[8] In terms of the nominally cultivated area cotton was easily the dominant crop, occupying 12,491 acres in 1785 against 4,241 in sugar; but the quantity produced was tending to fall and did so abruptly after 1789, while sugar production was rising to take its place. Sometimes sugar and cotton were grown on the same estate, but some 38 were devoted essentially to sugar and 107 to cotton in 1785. The figures in Table 1.1 tell their own story.[9]

TABLE 1.1 EXPORTS FROM TOBAGO

Year	Sugar (tons)	Rum (gallons)	Cotton ('000 lb)
1785	1 102	133 600	1 584
1786	1 257	189 600	1 201
1787	1 338	121 275	1 360
1788	929	95 730	1 226
1789	1 119	129 809	1 205
1790	1 863	250 873	811
1791	1 991	261 840	516

Sugar production was clearly rising to replace the declining cotton, though the overall result was probably a declining economy. Very small quantities of indigo and an infinitesimal amount of cocoa and coffee were also exported in the late 1780s, while one planter, Joseph Robley, experimented with turmeric but could not find a market for it.

The spectacular decline of cotton has been ascribed to two factors: the depredations of the caterpillar and the difficulty of finding markets in France or through French merchants for goods which had invariably been sold in Britain. The latter problem, of course, affected all Tobago's exports and helps to explain the economic difficulty apparent under the French. Also relevant is the extremely restrictive French mercantilist policy, which led to a clandestine trade that has prompted one writer to suggest that the existing export statistics understate reality by about 30 per cent.[10]

Tobago's commerce had been practically free in the years just before and after the French conquest because of wartime relaxations of restrictive laws and the terms of the capitulation. After peace was established in 1783, however, the French *Exclusif* system took effect, requiring Tobago to trade only with French ports. The establishment of a free port at Scarborough in 1784 was a very limited step and hardly affected exports. The Minister of Marine attempted to press the Chambers of Commerce of Bordeaux, Nantes and Marseilles to pay more attention to trading with Tobago, but the merchants at those ports were fully occupied with the business of St Domingue, Martinique and Guadeloupe while Tobago's inhabitants were accustomed to getting their manufactured goods from England rather than France and were disinclined to change.[11]

So Tobago failed to develop new commercial contacts after 1783. In fact its commerce was increasingly concentrated in the hands of a small number of shipowners centred at Havre and Dunkirk whose operations were in fact branches of British firms with long standing Tobago connections. They practised a new form of triangular trade: Britain/France/Tobago/France/Britain. They imported from Britain goods which their customers in Tobago wanted, paying duties of 10 per cent to 12 per cent when they entered France, re-exported them to Tobago, and then re-exported the island products which they received in return, usually to Britain. The ships employed were mostly of British origin, necessarily naturalized in France. The system was in fact a carefully organized contraband trade, more or less disguised, which France was forced to tolerate as the only means of keeping Tobago's economic life afloat.[12]

In December 1786 two new administrators arrived in Tobago: Count Dillon as governor and Roume de St Laurent, who had been responsible for setting in train an emigration of French settlers from Grenada to Trinidad, as ordonnateur. They were charged specifically with liquidating the debts of the colonists and easing the path of mortgagees who wished to foreclose on a defaulting mortgagor, provided French subjects were given preference in the sale of such properties. This was calculated to promote economic development.[13] Some creditors had complained that they were having trouble with their debtors even though it sometimes seemed that almost all Tobago's produce was going to Britain to service old loans dating from before the conquest. St Laurent proposed to enquire into the legal status of these debts and the possibility of reducing, or even confiscating them, in cases where the interest charged appeared excessive. A Special Commission was appointed in 1786 consisting of the two administrators and three judges, and it began work in June 1787. All the colonists and their creditors were required to present relevant documents for inspection by a given date.[14]

The Commission determined that a Tobago Act which had fixed interest at 8 per cent was invalid and agreed that all loans effected before

1774 at a rate exceeding 5 per cent should be invalidated. After 1774, when an Act of Parliament had permitted 6 per cent interest, that would be taken as the lawful limit. Creditors who had charged 8 per cent in good faith on the strength of the Tobago Act would have their interest rates reduced to the legal limit, but in cases of manifest usury the loan would be forfeit to the Crown and interest reduced appropriately.[15]

The Commission sat until February 1789, examining 159 cases and finding 49 loans to be usurious and accordingly forfeit. These involved a total of at least 8M livres. It is difficult to pass a balanced judgement on its proceedings for the heavy criticism aimed at it blurs the issue. Some of its judgements certainly reduced debts in a very arbitrary fashion but it was of great help to many who had been hopelessly indebted. In the end it probably profited the Crown rather than the debtor colonists it had been set up to relieve. The latter were not always pleased at the relief they obtained, for it antagonized creditors on whom they remained dependent for necessary finance,[16] and the outcome did nothing to attach their allegiance to France. As the political situation in France deteriorated with the outbreak of revolution and the colonists began to see a chance of being returned to British rule, they did not hesitate to welcome it.

Meanwhile the dispossessed creditors complained bitterly to France through the British government, and in 1791 the Order of 1786 which set up the Special Commission was declared illegal. A scheme was put forward for the retrocession of Tobago to Britain in return for an indemnity sufficient to cover the cost of the fortifications erected by the French and the property of any French subjects who chose to leave, possibly 50M francs with Britain perhaps compensating the creditors. Tobago's Agent in Paris argued that the creditors would no longer make advances to Tobago's planters and alternative finance could not be found from the French, who did not understand the British system of financing. Thus the creditors would foreclose and sell off the slaves and the island would collapse. France thus could have no interest in keeping it. In April 1792 the French mission in London was authorized to cede Tobago on reasonable terms, including her neutrality in Europe in the new war, but Britain showed little interest in such a transaction.[17]

Despite the economic difficulties during the period of French rule the population of Tobago was rising. The available figures put the number of whites at 541 in 1790 against 405 in 1782 but probably the latter figure is an underestimate. The free coloured population was increasing at a constant and fairly rapid rate, from 118 in 1782 to 185 in 1787 and 303 in 1790, as manumission proceeded year by year, while the number of slaves rose from 10,530 in 1782 to 14,171 in 1790. This increase was the result of new importations, as the death rate among the slave population, estimated at about forty per thousand, far exceeded births.[18]

The outbreak of the French Revolution in 1789 seems to have left the slaves in Tobago largely unmoved, despite the potentially inflammatory nature of its ideology. This was not the case, however, with the few French planters and merchants, the officials or the soldiers of the garrison, among whom it created a cleavage. Then Count Dillon returned to France in 1789 and the interim governor, the chevalier de Jobal, was soon at odds with St Laurent, who remained as ordonnateur until 1790. The French officials took sides in this personal dispute, thus adding to the friction caused by the news from France. Then the lesser French whites, who were largely concentrated in Port Louis, followed the revolutionary activities of St Pierre in Martinique. A patriotic assembly was held in the capital, almost certainly involving only a handful of lesser whites and a small group of patriotic volunteers was set up, which came to be known in France as the Tobago National Guard, led by an Irish interpreter called St Léger.[19]

Serious trouble did not develop, however, until the garrison let its resentment over the conduct of some of its officers boil over. It is difficult to say how far the troops were affected by revolutionary fervour, but both in 1789 and in 1790 there was some trouble among them. On 2 May 1790 a fire which was certainly a case of arson broke out in Scarborough and the patriotic volunteers and the troops accused each other of starting it. The town was completely burnt out save for a few warehouses and the island was threatened with a grave shortage of supplies in consequence. Then in August 1790 came a severe hurricane, the first in the eighteenth century to damage Tobago seriously. Twenty vessels were lost and many buildings destroyed, and there was much damage to crops. These events, added to the backlash caused by the activities of the Special Commission, led France to take a new interest in Tobago, and in 1791 the colony was placed under commissioners sent to restore government authority in Martinique.[20]

Revolutionary feeling remained strong, however, and when a new French governor arrived in 1792 his calls for loyalty to the royalist government did not go down well; in January 1793 both the governor and the ordonnateur removed themselves to Grenada to join the royalist Governor General of the French Windward Islands who had also fled his post. A new, revolutionary, governor arrived soon afterwards.[21]

The island which was attacked by the British soon after they entered the war with France was thus still very British in outlook after twelve years of French rule. Commerce with France was largely a cover for a continued relationship with Britain, and only in the capital town was there a noticeable number of white Frenchmen, mostly officials and soldiers and perhaps two or three dozen others. The gallicization of the colony, to which Dillon and St Laurent certainly aspired, could have made substantial progress only over a long period. Even the replacement of English law by French law had by 1793 been the subject only of proposals but no effective action. The overwhelmingly British white population had during twelve years of French rule seen their constitutional privileges largely destroyed, and despite increasing sugar production had suffered considerable economic and financial woes. The period of British rule took on a rose-coloured hue in retrospect and the planters desired nothing so much as the restoration of the island to Britain. Some of them indeed, notably the prominent Gilbert Petrie, were already in touch with the British government with a view to achieving that end.

War between Great Britain and Revolutionary France broke out on 1 February 1793. Since this development had been clearly in the offing for several months, it is no matter for surprise that within a few days instructions for an immediate offensive were being sent to the British forces in the West Indies. On 10 February 1793 Secretary of State Henry Dundas addressed a secret despatch to Major General Cornelius Cuyler at Barbados with orders to attack Tobago as soon as he should judge the forces under his command to be adequate.[22]

Dundas had a special reason for selecting Tobago for such early attention. Apart from the fact that the island had broken away from the Republican government in France in 1792 and the subsequent reversal of fortune, ending in the flight of the royalist governor in January 1793 was not yet known to him, Dundas was convinced that most of the colonists disliked French rule and would welcome, and indeed assist, a British invasion. Dundas was even able to instruct Cuyler to discuss the terms of any capitulation with Gilbert Petrie.

Cuyler decided to attack Tobago in the event that and as soon as an expected naval squadron under Vice-Admiral Sir John Laforey should arrive.[23] Laforey reached Barbados on 10 April and two days later the expedition sailed, two warships escorting a number of schooners hired at Barbados to transport equipment and a troop-carrying merchantman, with some 500 men.[24]

On 14 April the force arrived at Great Courland Bay and disembarked before the French were aware of their presence.[25] Having made contact with Petrie who supplied the invaders from his estate,[26] Cuyler advanced "within sight of the Enemy's Post", Fort Castries (later Fort King George), then two or three miles distant, and called upon the island's commandant to surrender. But the French, though heavily outnumbered, had been anticipating an attack, and decided to resist. Cuyler determined upon an immediate assault at night. At 1:30 a.m. on 15 April the men again began to move forward. They reached Scarborough before being detected and proceeded at once to the fort. In the darkness the attacking force became divided into two as it climbed the hill. One group moved up the vulnerable northwest flank, while the other seized the main approach road and made a frontal attack. The French, with their fire divided, surrendered after the troops on their flank pushed their way into the fort against "a heavy fire of round and grape shot musquetry".[27] The British losses in this action were 3 killed and 24 wounded; the French 6 killed and 7 wounded. Ninety six French prisoners were taken at the fort and about 100 sailors and militiamen were also captured.[28] Cuyler at once restored the British colonial constitution which the French had found in 1781.

It is convenient here to complete the story of Tobago's shifting allegiance. At the Peace of Amiens in 1802, which ended the war temporarily, Great Britain agreed to return Tobago to France. Thus when war broke out again in 1803 the recapture of the island was a fairly obvious stratagem. On 16 May 1803 the Secretary of State wrote to General Grinfield, the British Commander-in-Chief in the Eastern Caribbean, based in Barbados, with instructions that he should prepare for a renewal of the war with France by collecting the largest possible force. He was directed to make arrangements to seize Martinique, St Lucia and Tobago, or such of them as his force was equal to, as soon as hostilities should be resumed. No attack was to be mounted without a reasonable prospect of success, but

> From the amount of British property connected with the island of Tobago, the uniform attachment of the Inhabitants to His Majesty's Person, and the importance of its position, I am induced to recommend that the earliest steps should be taken for placing it under the King's Government; and the more so, as from the Accounts I have received of the State of the French Force upon the Island, there is no probability of any Serious Resistance.[29]

It was a month before this despatch reached Grinfield who, meanwhile, had reached much the same conclusion himself. On 7 June, anticipating war, he had reported that his force was ready for service at a moment's notice, and he began to discuss possible moves with the commodore, Sir Samuel Hood.[30] Grinfield believed that his force was inadequate for an attack on Martinique but equal to the conquest of St Lucia and Tobago in that order.[31] Tobago, he thought, would be easily taken since his information was that its garrison numbered only 70, with 43 seamen aboard an armed brig in Scarborough harbour, though repair work was in progress at Fort King George.[32] He continued preparations to embark his army.[33] Deeming it wholly unequal to an attack on the strongly held Martinique, he captured St Lucia on 22 June[34] and, leaving 1100 of his 4200 men there, he then set out for Tobago.[35]

On 30 June 1803 Grinfield arrived off Tobago with Commodore Sir Samuel Hood, landed his troops and marched towards Scarborough.

When they were about two miles from Fort King George he called on the French commander, General César Berthier, to surrender, since his forces were vastly inferior. Terms of capitulation were agreed next morning and the British entered the fort. The French garrison of only 228 men marched out "with the honours of war" and laid down their arms. There had in fact been no attempt at resistance.[36]

Under the terms of capitulation the French were to abandon their arms but all their officers and men, and others in the service of the Republic, together with their wives and children, were to be despatched to France within one month, sick and wounded to follow when fit. The colony was to retain all existing laws, in effect those prevailing when the British had departed in 1802, and all rights of property were to be respected. French merchant shipping in Scarborough harbour was permitted to depart and any inhabitant who wished to leave the island would be permitted to do so within two years, taking with him the sale price of his property.[37] The last of the French capitulants actually sailed for home on 25 July 1803.[38]

Once more, Tobago had passed from French to British sovereignty and Grinfield reported that, as was to be expected, the inhabitants were very pleased. At the same time, however, apprehension that this might once more turn out to be a temporary change was very evident.[39] For the present, Grinfield, as Cuyler had done in 1793, restored the constitution and institutions which Britain had first bestowed on the island in 1763 and Tobago embarked or what was to be the final phase of its history as an outpost of empire.

THE POPULATION OF TOBAGO, 1793-1815

The Free Population

Numbers and national allegiance

The population of Tobago at the time of its conquest in 1793 is impossible to determine with accuracy, but a census of 1790 recorded 15,019 persons of whom 14,170 were slaves; 541 were whites of whom 434 were men; and 303 were free coloured of whom 105 were men.[1] The term "free coloured" is used to include both blacks and persons of mixed blood. A survey conducted through the district militia commanders at the end of 1794 shows a total of 631 free persons comprising the groupings in Table 2.1.[2]

TABLE 2.1 FRENCH AND WHITE FREE PERSONS IN TOBAGO, 1794

	Men	Women	Total
British			
Whites	304	41	345
Free coloureds	52	113	165
French			
Whites	24	22	46
Free coloureds	16	59	75

While the militia figures are probably too low, they are enough to indicate that while the majority of whites were of British origin and orientation, there was a significant minority of French people at a time when war between England and France was in progress. The obvious political problem thus posed to the new British administration was further complicated by the conflict between revolutionaries and royalists among the French in the West Indies, and by the impact on the free coloureds, to say nothing of the slave population, of the ideas of revolution which had been emanating from France since 1789 and from St Domingue since 1790-91. Even before the outbreak of war French refugees had begun to arrive in the British Windward Islands from neighbouring French colonies, and British colonists had become very suspicious of the new egalitarian ideas.[3] In August 1793 a letter from John Balfour, a prominent member of the Council in Tobago, warned the British Government that French emissaries were busy not only in that island but all over the West Indies, and that their activities were likely to provoke revolt by the blacks.[4] News also reached London from France that Jacobin emissaries had been despatched to foment revolutionary discord among the slaves in the British islands, and on 29 August 1793 the Jacobin Commissioner in St Domingue proclaimed the abolition of slavery there.[5] In 1794 with the formal capture of Martinique, Guadeloupe and St Lucia, and fighting in St Domingue, all four colonies saw fighting between British troops and blacks inspired largely by French revolutionary doctrines.

In these circumstances the new administration in Tobago became increasingly concerned with the "fifth column" potential of the French minority as well as with the possible arrival of enemy agents. After the capture in 1793 the French garrison had been removed from the island as prisoners of war, together with a few French persons who claimed to be resident proprietors but were for one reason or another lumped together with the prisoners.[6] But the continuing presence of a French minority gravely disturbed the English whites and early in January 1795 Joseph Robley, President of the Council, administering the island in the absence of a governor, issued a proclamation requiring all the free inhabitants to take the oaths of allegiance and fidelity to the British Crown. Many of the remaining French inhabitants refused to do this and declared themselves to be republicans who wished to be considered as prisoners of war,[7] in notable contrast to the readiness of so many French planters elsewhere in the West Indies at this time to throw in their lot with Britain. An Act was then passed declaring those who refused the oaths to be prisoners of war and authorizing their removal from the island, "as their remaining might disturb our internal peace, and be the means of diffusing their horrid principles among the lower and weaker class of people".[8] The problem posed by their presence appeared critical when on 2 March 1795 the slaves at Grenada rose, and began to rampage through that island,[9] a rising which may have been inspired by French agents and certainly sought to promote French revolutionary doctrines. News of it caused great alarm in Tobago and two weeks later a vessel was hired to take twenty-four French residents under guard to Martinique.[10]

Not all of the French population were thus disposed of, however, and two weeks later the newly arrived Governor Lindsay became convinced that an insurrection similar to that in Grenada was on the point of breaking out, fomented by dissident Frenchmen.[11] John Franklyn, a member of the Council, had been told of a meeting, supposedly attended by twenty-nine people, at which the French Republic had been toasted. Some of those involved had English names.[12] Lindsay set out to find an opportunity to deport the remaining French. Meanwhile some of them were confined within the limits of Scarborough.[13]

The political problem of the French minority was thus diminished, but it had not disappeared. Indeed it was at this time that four French emissaries, believed to be sent "to corrupt the Negroes", were arrested in Tobago after landing in an open boat from St Vincent.[14] In July 1795 the Secretary of State warned the governor to be on his guard to prevent the landing of new French emissaries.[15]

The French inhabitants themselves now helped the British authorities to move closer towards a homogeneous national orientation. They were, of course, being made most unwelcome, and later in 1795 a number of French free coloureds moved at their own expense to Trinidad, where an open invitation to Catholic settlers, first made in 1783, still endured. These appear to have been a mixed collection, and probably not all were republicans anxious to quit an alien government like those deported to Martinique earlier in the year.[16] By October 1795 the remnant French population, never more than a few score, was so insignificant that a false report of an impending French attack produced no noticeable evidence of disaffection.[17] Indeed, the evidence suggests that only two or three French whites were left in the island, though there were possibly a few more free coloureds. A Frenchman whose name appears to have been Deugue owned a small estate;[18] while another, Dinet de Monteron, may have done the same.[19] No other Frenchman appears ever to have owned an estate in Tobago, which may help to explain why the French were so simply and yet so conclusively displaced in 1795: not being owners of estates they were relatively mobile. More generally, their small numbers and short lived presence explain why the French left so little lasting influence on the island.

After the island was restored to France in 1802 a number of Frenchmen arrived and took up commercial activities and a very few stayed on after the British reconquest, though prisoners of war were repatriated to France. At first they were regarded with intense suspicion by the Lieutenant Governor, who kept them under close scrutiny;[20] but in 1804 one John Prosper De Bruille, very probably a Frenchman, was appointed Colony Surveyor.[21] In 1816 President Balfour claimed that not more than five foreigners had been in Tobago since its reconquest in 1803.[22] After 1795 the French presence may for all practical purposes be disregarded save for the short period of occupation in 1802-03.

While it might be expected that in the course of time the departing French would be replaced by at least an equivalent number of British immigrants, the uncertainty as to the future of the island which persisted down to 1815 meant that no significant number of British people arrived to take up residence; and by the time the uncertainty had been removed the abolition of the slave trade and the resulting difficulty in obtaining labour for the plantations had destroyed the incentive to any material measure of white immigration. On the contrary, some English colonists left when Tobago was restored to France in 1802 and never returned,[23] while there was a continuing tendency for the whites to drift back to England. One would therefore expect to find a small and gradual but definite fall in the white population, but the available figures do not confirm this beyond dispute. See Table 2.2.[24]

TABLE 2.2   FREE POPULATION OF TOBAGO

	Whites				Free coloureds			
	Men	Women	Children	Total	Men	Women	Children	Total
1790	434	-	-	541	105	-	-	303
1794	328	63	-	-	68	172	-	-
1808	389	48	10	437	92	96	65	253
1810	497	64	31	592	111	137	104	352
1811	501	49	41	591	92	153	105	350

These figures must obviously be used with caution since no adequate explanation is available for the sudden rise in population which they posit between 1808 and 1810. In 1813 Governor Sir William Young was quite sure that there had been a substantial fall in the adult male population since 1808 which he ascribed to the decline in the opportunities which the island offered after the prohibition on the importation of new slaves, the clue to most economic advancement. He estimated that the white population had fallen to 440.[25] Young may possibly be accused of producing estimates to fit his theories. On the other hand, his record as a compiler of statistics is generally a good one and it is unlikely that he would indicate a decline of 25 per cent unless there really had been a significant fall in numbers. Ultimately it is clear that the free population, both white and coloured, was to be numbered in hundreds.

The whites

Compostion

By late 1795, therefore, the white population was almost wholly English. This meant that the political problem of divided national loyalties had been eliminated. It did not mean, however, that the whites were a homogeneous group. Within the white population there were significant differences not only of wealth but also of status. While Tobago was certainly ruled by and for the whites, not all whites by any means were members either of the social or of the political elite. In 1810 Sir William Young, attempting to compile a list of the "principal inhabitants", counted only thirty "gentlemen" in Scarborough including eight military officers, and twenty-five in the country areas, out of a total of 497 white men. Attached to these fifty-five gentlemen's households were twenty-four "ladies".[26] Here, then, was a small elite group atop the social pyramid. Then there was a larger group of second rank whites, who might have been politically influential and even loosely classed as elite, but whom Young would not accept as "gentlemen". Both groups qualified to vote through ownership of real property. Planters by definition qualified to vote, and so did merchants, who owned shops, town houses and domestic slaves. Professional men owned town houses and slaves and sometimes invested in sugar estates as did Dr George Cumine who eventually became a member of the island's Council. Managers and attorneys operated similarly and likewise sometimes qualified both for elite society and for political rights.

Less certain was the position of white overseers, shopkeepers, clerks, bookkeepers and artisans. Such people, who may conveniently be described as lesser whites, were not prima facie even of the second rank much less of the gentlemanly elite, and they might be expected to lack the property qualification for voting. They might, however, come to qualify on both counts if they acquired enough property; and the institution of slavery provided excellent opportunities for whites of lesser status to do just that, beginning with the fact that slaves were real property and, until the slave trade was abolished in 1807, easily acquired. At the bottom of the hierarchy there were a few white "servants", but even they had some chance of upward social and economic mobility if they could save a little money.²⁷ Finally we must notice the presence of a military garrison of anything from 300 to 800 men, all of whom were white in the 1790s and in the majority even in later years, when some black troops were usually present. The garrison might include anything up to perhaps two dozen white officers whose relationship with the local elite was not always cordial. The variety of occupations alone was enough to ensure that social integration among the whites had its limits, though they would stand together if threatened from below by non-whites or from without by foreigners.

All whites and all free coloureds of any economic consequence aspired to the ownership of slaves. Apart from the practical fact that a slave or two could insulate them from onerous menial tasks and help them towards a better economic position by enhancing their capacity to earn, distancing oneself from menial tasks would secure on the social ladder a place which was clearly removed from the ground. As more slaves were acquired, so could that ladder be climbed and one's economic status improved. White and even free coloured artisans were accustomed to equip themselves with slaves whom they would train to assist them in their trades and crafts.²⁸ However, the acquisition of personal or domestic slaves came most easily to managers and overseers, who were in a good position to acquire the small sums of capital required to start the process because they had the opportunity to exploit the labour of the estate slaves to their personal advantage. Such personal slaves could then be hired out and their earnings reinvested by their owners in the advantageous business of owning slaves for hire. In this way, many men who began as overseers on arriving from Britain were able to begin rising in the economic and social scale later to become managers and later still, when they had acquired a close knowledge of sugar production and if they were able to accumulate enough capital, to acquire plantations. In 1811 Governor Young claimed that two-thirds of the proprietors of estates in Tobago had either started life as overseers or were the sons of men who had done so.²⁹

Slavery, then, provided a ready made opening to social and economic mobility and white society was in consequence strikingly fluid. This was true in all the smaller colonies of the British West Indies where the means of such mobility coincided with great pressure on white society to present a united and cohesive front to the massive numbers of slaves who might be expected to regard any obvious fissure in the society of their masters as an invitation and an opportunity to revolt. The fluidity of white society was also enhanced by the fact that as absentee ownership grew – by 1819, fifty-three of eighty-one active estates were in the hands of managers or attorneys[30] and, in the later years of the period under consideration, the lesser whites too began to drift away from the island – the dwindling white community came under increasing pressure to preserve its unity. As members of the elite group moved out it was necessary to replace them both in social terms and to keep the political system operational. So there arose a tendency to pay little attention to the property qualifications for membership of the Assembly and for voting at elections, and lesser whites began to play a part in spheres from which they had once been excluded. The mobility of white society however was almost wholly in an upward direction. People moved upwards to fill vacancies in the structure or in response to their own achievements. To move downwards in the scale was scarcely known, though whites did emigrate if their fortunes became bleak.

The maintenance of an adequate population of whites in the face of so large a number of black slaves was inevitably a matter of serious concern to the colonists and even to the British Government. It was, as the preamble to an Act of 1797 stated, "most essentially necessary for [the] peace, safety and preservation" of the colony, as of any slave colony; and there was also a feeling that a larger white population would enhance the colony's capacity to defend itself against external attack.

The usual course in the British West Indian colonies was to seek to promote the importation of white immigrants through a series of "deficiency laws" which imposed penalties on plantation owners who failed to employ a fixed proportion of whites to slaves. Thus Tobago in 1797 passed "an Act to Encourage the Further Introduction of White Inhabitants into this Island" which required all planters to employ one able bodied white man between the ages of 16 and 60 years for every 50 slaves up to 300, and then one for every 100 more, or pay a fine of £100 currency (approximately £50 sterling) per year for each white man short of the required complement. Deficiencies of fewer than fifty slaves were to be calculated at 25s. per slave. All white slave owners resident on the plantation, and their wives, could be counted towards the tally. Conversely, estates which employed more than the required quota of white men were to be paid a bounty of £60 currency per man in excess and £40 for each woman. Importers of white servants who entered indentures for at least three years and any voluntary immigrants who entered such indentures were also to be paid a bounty of £40, repayable if the indenture was prematurely terminated.[31]

The Act of 1797 was to remain in force for three years and lapsed in 1801, but it was revived in 1804.[32] Thereafter the law was maintained with minor changes in the formula in 1808 in favour of the deficient planter.

Thus in 1808 wives of managers, overseers and white servants and relatives of the proprietor over 15 years of age were allowed to be counted in the complement of whites.[33] We do not know how many planters were compelled to pay the deficiency tax or how far they failed in practice to employ the required number of whites, but the fact that the law was regularly renewed suggests that there was need for it. Without it many of the jobs held by whites might have been taken by free coloureds who, as we shall see, were now entering almost every field of employment. Indeed the deficiency tax was in part a measure designed to restrict the competition which coloureds offered to whites in the economic sphere.

These deficiency laws were especially onerous when applied to the odd free coloured planter. The general effect of the law however was to exclude free coloureds from supervisory or management jobs on the estates, which were the only estate jobs they were willing to accept, since all those jobs which could possibly be held by whites in a slave society were needed to enable the estate to employ its quota of whites. Free coloured planters, moreover, were compelled to pay the deficiency fines in practice, since no whites would agree to work for a free coloured employer.

Health

The state of health of the white population of Tobago during this period is difficult to ascertain. In general the subject occupied public attention only in so far as the military garrison was concerned or when some unusual sickness or epidemic was experienced. The local population, even the whites, were usually noticed only in the context of exceptional sickness. However, up to half of the garrison could be unfit at any given time in the middle 1790s.[34] The rate of sickness began to fall about 1797 and by 1800 was generally unspectacular, while the mortality rate could be as low as 5 per cent.[35] The only statistics which have come to light show the following numbers of deaths among the garrison in this period:[36]

1799	1800	1801	1802
65	33	111	21

It is impossible to determine a mortality rate since the size of the garrison is given for 1801 only, as 800, which is significantly higher than normal.[37] It is clear, however, that while the rate fluctuated it could be disturbingly high.

Indeed, in the late eighteenth century the health of British troops in the West Indies was a matter of considerable concern to the army. That concern was greatly intensified by the spectacular mortality among the troops sent to St Domingue in 1793-98, where it has been estimated that 40,000 died of yellow fever.[38] In this general period garrison mortality in all the West Indian islands fluctuated widely, being especially high during wartime because the arrival of troops unused to the area almost invariably brought increased sickness and campaign conditions, where they existed, tended to lower standards of sanitation.[39] In the British Windward and Leeward Islands Command, of which Tobago was a part, garrison mortality fluctuated between 1 per cent in 1812 and 27.5 per cent in 1805.[40] In Tobago itself garrison mortality was a matter of special concern during the wars of 1793-1815.

Theories of epidemiology centred on the relative importance of the constitution of the atmosphere, the miasmas of the area, and contagion.[41] Contemporaries believed that the high mortality rate among Europeans in the West Indies, civilians no less than troops, especially high among the newly arrived, was a matter of the unaccustomed climate to which those who survived for a while became to some extent "seasoned" or "acclimated". The experience of the troops sent from Europe seemed to bear this out and even to suggest that such "seasoning" should bear reference not only to the West Indies as a whole but to each particular locality.[42]

The concept of "seasoning" to local climatic conditions as a protection against disease died very hard; but modern medical science suggests that the problem was not simply a matter of climate, but rather one of an unfamiliar disease environment. The heat and, in places, the marshes of the region were always there, but mortality fluctuated; neither did rainfall in practice correlate with the rate of disease or death.[43] "Seasoning" therefore related to the specific environment of each locality rather than to climate, but it explains why a garrison which was rotated at intervals suffered more than the settled population.

The most common cause of death among West Indian garrisons was "fevers", including "remittent fever" (malaria), "intermittent fever" (yellow fever), and "continual fevers" (often typhoid or typhus). Tobago was in fact an island specially associated with malaria, like nearby Trinidad and Grenada. Yellow fever was less common, being altogether less prevalent in the Eastern than in the Western Caribbean.[44] In the Windward and Leeward Islands Command in the period following 1815 malaria accounted for 90 per cent of the deaths from "fevers".[45] Second came diseases of the lungs, and third diseases of the stomach and/or bowels, mostly dysentery. These three categories between them accounted for about 90 per cent of all the deaths from disease in early nineteenth century British garrisons.[46]

Whites and blacks in the West Indies showed different disease patterns. Whites were affected principally by malaria and yellow fever, both of which probably originated in Africa. Blacks, of similar geographical origin, possessed an innate immunity to both. They were much less affected than whites and, when they were, did not usually die. Creole whites commonly acquired a measure of immunity to both. Newly arrived whites were therefore the principal victims.[47]

If black troops were largely immune from malaria and yellow fever and were on that account increasingly used after 1796, they were vulnerable to other prevalent diseases, and also suffered increased illness when moved to unfamiliar places. For this reason the death rate among them was commonly higher than among the plantation slaves.[48] In the West Indies generally they were troubled chiefly by diseases of the lungs and by dysentery. "Fevers" came third, but at only half the rate for whites.[49]

By the middle of the eighteenth century it was strongly suggested by medical men that malaria was assisted by the presence of trees, shrubs and marshes and by vapours rising from stagnant water (miasmas). Avoidance of bad air and stagnant water was strongly recommended.[50] The role of the mosquito was not then recognized, but stagnant water on swampy land was of course a vital factor. In Tobago one factor in the often high mortality among the (white) garrison troops in the 1790s was undoubtedly the presence of the Bacolet swamp just to the east of the fort. At some times of the year the swamp was said to be "offensive",[51] and the authorities were conscious that it was "prejudicial to the health of the garrison".[52]

When Tobago was recaptured from the French in 1803 General Grinfield initiated a plan to drain the swamp, hoping to improve conditions in Fort King George and more widely in Scarborough.[53] The attorney of Bacolet Estate, George Morison, agreed to provide the labour of 120 slaves and under military direction three areas totalling sixteen acres were drained and/or filled between December 1803 and March 1804, free of charge to the colony's government.[54] At once Tobago began to figure as an island where the troops were relatively healthy and governors were quite convinced that here was a case of cause and effect.[55] Table 2.3 shows the garrison mortality figures after 1807.[56]

TABLE 2.3   GARRISON MORTALITY FIGURES, 1808-1815

	1808	1809	1810	1811	1812	1813	1814	1815
Garrison (avg.)	360	350	370	351	313	262	319	
Deaths	15	14	16	3	12	5	2	
				(4 mths)	(5 mths)	(9 mths)	(1 mth)	
Rate % (annual)	4.2	4.0	4.3	2.6	9.2	2.6	7.5	

Unsatisfactory as these figures are, especially those for 1811, 1812 and 1814 which cover only a few months in each case, they nevertheless suggest strongly that by contemporary standards mortality was low. They do not however distinguish between white and black troops. In the subsequent period 1817-36 mortality among black troops was only 3.4 per cent against 15.3 per cent for white troops, the highest rate among British islands in the Eastern Caribbean.[57] The apparent improvement after 1807 may be related to the increasing use of black troops with their superior resistance to the prevailing diseases, and it was certainly assisted by the more effective clearing of the bush around the fort; but it seems more than probable that the principal factor was a decreased incidence of malaria and perhaps yellow fever, called Bulam fever in Tobago, following the draining of the swamp.[58]

For the most part there is little evidence that the resident white population was particularly affected by the sickness which so often troubled the garrison. In these years however specific outbreaks of epidemic disease were always a danger. In 1794 a "contagious distemper" which broke out in several islands appeared in Tobago,[59] where it was recognized as smallpox, and many people sought vaccination. The troops were as badly affected as any and the legislature discussed unspecified measures for the public safety.[60] In 1804 there was an outbreak of "fever" which wrought havoc among the white colonists but, strangely, not among the troops.[61] It was ascribed locally to prolonged "very dry weather".[62] In 1811 an "almost universal sickness" appeared, again coincidentally with the dry season.[63] These however were exceptional episodes. The absence of further comment from official sources suggests strongly that the whites in Tobago were normally healthy by the admittedly low standards of the West Indies in the early nineteenth century. Sir William Young after two and a half years in Tobago claimed never to have been ill and he always asserted that it was a very healthy island.[64]

Cultural practices

The whites in Tobago, as elsewhere in the West Indies, sought to live as nearly as possible as they would have done in Europe. They wore European clothing with few concessions to the heat of the tropics, used European types of music, and remained nominally Christian even while opportunities for religious observance were unavailable for long periods and their own behaviour departed widely from Christian patterns. In part this was a reflection of their conviction that European culture and civilization were inherently superior to all others, but in part it was also a means of boosting European morale and solidarity in the face of overwhelmingly superior numbers who came from an altogether different culture.

It was not possible, of course, to preserve the European culture undiluted. The environment itself saw to that. European foods were often not available regularly if at all, even without the wartime shortages which persisted during the period under review. The use of slave attendants in the household brought Africa too close to be kept altogether at bay, especially where children were cared for by slave nurses who told them African-derived tales or taught them African amusements. The easy availability of durable tropical hardwoods close to any building site combined with the greater expense of working and transporting bricks and stone led nearly all the whites, even the wealthiest planters, to build wooden houses. As Sir William Young put it, "a House framed with Hardwood and planked with Cedar will last an Age. There are Houses in Tobago of forty years standing with no sign of Decay". Water mills too were usually built of wood in the early 1800s. Only the sugar works and boiling houses, where there was a danger of fire and wood was obviously inadequate, were of stone or brick as would have been the case in Europe.[65]

The free coloureds

Composition

The free coloured population meanwhile had clearly grown since 1794, though the fact that there were ninety-one coloured militiamen in the island in 1813 against ninety-four in 1808 suggests that the number of coloured males was fairly stable. Women normally outnumbered men by about 3 to 2, specifically 153 to 92 in 1811.[66] The increase in the number of coloured women may be accounted for by the fact that twice as many females as males were manumitted – between 1808 and 1816 inclusive 85 males and 176 females.[67] Probably a large proportion of the females was made up of the concubines of white men. As Sir William Young put it in 1811 when reporting the manumission in one year of six females but only one male slave:

> The Greater Number of free coloured women, in proportion to free coloured men, is a consequence of the planters and other Europeans, being deprived of any opportunities of tender intercourse with white ladies, connecting themselves with handsome negresses, to whom in a kind hour, and from a desire that their offspring may be born free (the freedom of the child being dependent on that of the mother and not the father) they give freedom.[68]

It may be questioned whether the number of female slaves manumitted before the birth of their children was not exceeded by those manumitted later in life after more or less lengthy periods of concubinal relationship, but Young's ascription of the superior numbers of females manumitted to the favour of their white male connections admits of no doubt.

The most striking fact about the available figures for both white and free coloured population is undoubtedly the small numbers which they indicate. Both whites and free coloureds amounted to a very few hundreds. Barry Higman suggests that in 1810 the white and free coloured populations together amounted to 1600, accounting for 4.1 per cent of the total population.[69] These are significantly higher figures than those provided by Young, but even so slave outnumbered free by 11 to 1. The present writer believes that Higman overestimates the free population.

As was usual in the West Indian islands the free coloureds in Tobago were found mostly in and around the towns. In 1808, of a total of 253 free coloured people 28 lived in Plymouth and the parish of St David, and 140 in Scarborough and the adjourning parish of St Andrew; 28 in the parish of St George which itself contained an urban sector in the old Georgetown, and only 57 in the four really rural parishes. In 1811, of 350 free people, 163 lived in Scarborough and St Andrew, 78 in Plymouth and St David, 32 in St George and only 77 elsewhere.[70] The fact is, though, that the distribution of the white population was not dissimilar though less extreme. As in all the Windward Islands a large proportion of whites, 126 out of 439, was concentrated in the capital town and the parish of St Andrew, a further 92 in Plymouth and St David and 53 in St George.[71] In 1811, 167 white men out of 501 lived in Scarborough and Plymouth and a further 183 in the three urban parishes leaving 151 in the four really rural parishes. In addition there were 49 white women and 33 children scattered through the island.[72]

Occupations

Table 2.4 indicates the occupations pursued by the free adult males of Tobago, white and coloured, in 1810-11. It does not seem that more than a very occasional white woman was gainfully employed but more will be said later about the free coloured women. The figures were painstakingly put together by Sir William Young in response to a request for information by the House of Commons and while the ascription of persons to particular occupations may sometimes be challenged, notably the distinction between merchant and shopkeeper, Young was certainly in a position to get reasonably accurate information. In so small a community the senior white officials and principal planters would have had personal knowledge of most of the white inhabitants and a fairly good idea of who was doing what among the free coloured population most of whom lived in the two towns. Moreover, the militia rolls, which Young used, would have included almost all the free adult males over the age of fifteen. While there are occasional anomalies, the figures may be taken as substantially accurate.

The first point to be noticed is the white monopoly of professional jobs and public office. Indeed in all the Windward Islands at this time only one coloured man is known to have practised a profession, a Dr Bermingham in Dominica, and that not until the 1820s.[73] No doubt the necessary professional training was generally speaking out of reach. Ten or eleven doctors for roughly 800 free people and 16,000 slaves appears a pretty fair proportion and, strikingly, each town and each parish had at least one.[74] Four lawyers seems a striking figure for so small a community.

Agriculture, too, was dominated by the whites, though not so completely. There was at least one coloured planter (another source mentions two)[75] though the prohibitive deficiency tax which faced them had only been modified in 1808, and eight or ten coloured overseers among the hundred plus estates. Coloureds had also begun to penetrate into the largely white preserve of commerce and there was one such shopkeeper and four clerks in 1811, with an indication elsewhere that the former figure was not comprehensive.[76] It is not surprising that no free coloured had yet achieved the status of merchant, even allowing for some vagueness of definition.

The missing figures for free servants and shopkeepers in 1810 would no doubt make up the shortfall in the actual total. See Table 2.4.

The number of clerks, sixty-six whites and four free coloureds in 1811 or 12 per cent of the employed male population, provides a proportion exceeded only by that for the expectedly large group of managers and overseers (37 per cent), the size of which reflects the growing incidence of absenteeism among the owners of estates.

Activities of lesser status than the professions, estate management and commerce attracted both whites and coloureds in substantial proportions though in most cases the actual numbers employed were small in a community itself limited to a few hundred adult males. The solitary tavern keeper and the lone watchmaker were both white as were the two printers, people with a technical skill which coloureds not surprisingly found it difficult to acquire; it is more surprising to find a coloured silversmith alongside a white one but there were no white barbers. However bakers, butchers, gardeners, fishermen, tailors, shoemakers, sadlers, plumbers, smiths, carpenters and masons were all drawn from both races. There were seven white and ten coloured domestic servants

TABLE 2.4 FREE MALE POPULATION OF TOBAGO, WHITE AND FREE COLOURED

Professional	Whites 1810	Whites 1811	Free Coloureds 1810	Free Coloureds 1811	Total 1810	Total 1811	Whites in Scarborough 1810	Whites in Scarborough 1811	Whites in Plymouth 1810	Whites in Plymouth 1811
Public Officers	32	31	0	0	32	31	30	28	0	1
Clergymen	3	2	0	0	3	2	3	2	0	0
Lawyers	4	4	0	0	4	4	4	4	0	0
Doctors	10	11	0	0	10	11	2	3	1	1
Agriculture										
Planters	52	27	2	1	54	28	2	0	1	0
Managers & Overseers	242	220	8	10	250	230	2	0	1	0
Gardeners	4	7	4	0	8	7	4	3	1	0
Trade										
Merchants	22	12	3	0	25	12	20	10	2	2
Shopkeepers	n.a.	22	n.a.	1	n.a.	23	n.a.	20	n.a.	2
Clerks	51	66	2	4	53	70	26	40	2	6
Provisioning										
Bakers	1	1	3	2	4	3	1	1	0	0
Butchers	1	2	3	2	4	4	1	2	0	0
Tavern keepers	1	1	0	0	1	1	1	1	0	0
Sea										
Mariners/Fishermen	5	14	10	6	15	20	5	3	2	0
Handicraft										
Barbers	0	0	3	1	3	1	0	0	0	0
Tailors	4	5	5	2	9	7	4	5	0	0
Shoemakers	2	2	3	2	5	4	2	2	0	0
Sadlers	1	2	4	2	5	4	1	2	0	0
Silversmiths	1	1	1	1	2	2	1	1	0	0
Upholsterers	n.a.	1	n.a.	0	n.a.	1	n.a.	1	n.a.	0
Watchmakers	1	1	0	0	1	1	1	1	0	0
Printers	2	2	0	0	2	2	2	2	0	0
Plumbers	5	5	1	1	6	6	2	0	0	1
Smiths	6	11	2	2	8	13	3	3	1	1
Masons	4	5	4	1	8	6	2	1	2	0
Carpenters	31	36	34	44	65	80	6	7	0	3
Miscellaneous										
School teachers	0	1	0	0	0	1	0	1	0	0
Auctioneers	n.a.	2	n.a.	0	n.a.	2	n.a.	2	n.a.	0
Domestics	n.a.	7	n.a.	10	n.a.	12	n.a.	0	n.a.	0
Total Free Men	497	501	111	92	608	593	125	145	13	17

in 1811. If the smiths and plumbers were mostly white, their numbers were too small to support the conclusion that coloureds had difficulty in entering those trades. The very large and increasing number of carpenters, thirty-six whites and forty-four free coloureds in 1811, reflected the overwhelming preponderance of building in wood. Baking and butchering each supported one white and three coloureds in 1810, but by 1811 one additional white butcher had appeared while one coloured disappeared from each trade unless perhaps he was overlooked at the later count. The handicraft and artisanal trades, including silversmiths and watchmakers, supported fifty-seven whites and fifty-seven coloureds in 1810, seventy-one and fifty-six respectively in 1811.

The figures for coloured employment as tailors, sadlers and carpenters declined sharply over this period, but the numbers involved were too small to permit of any clear conclusion even if the figures could be taken entirely at their face value. It does not seem that any non-professional occupation was closed to the free coloureds, though they found it very difficult to penetrate into agriculture or commerce. On the other hand there was no occupation which they dominated to the exclusion of the lesser whites. The figures are not adequate to suggest any trend in one direction or another, though the apparent fall in the white population as people moved out for lack of opportunity suggests that the free coloureds were beginning to find that more doors were opening to them. But it may also be that as the free coloureds and, as we shall see, the skilled slaves penetrated more deeply into the trades and skills, the poorer whites and their children gradually deserted them, preferring to find occupations more clearly identified with their own community even at the cost of emigrating. In the West Indies, generally, there was a certain social odium attached to a white holding the same job as his free coloured or, worse, slave neighbours.[78]

To look at the matter of occupations in another way, of the 501 white men 49 may be classed as professionals if one includes the schoolteacher, 247 as planters, managers or overseers, 34 ran commercial establishments, 57 were artisans. Of the 92 coloureds none were professionals, 11 were planters managers or overseers, only one ran a shop and 52 were artisans.

The figures cited above, however, give an incomplete picture of the activities of the free coloureds because they apply only to men who accounted for only about 40 per cent of the free coloured population. White women were generally expected not to take paid employment, and there was only the odd exception; but coloured women were often employed in non-domestic occupations which need to be taken into account. In particular, many made a living as hucksters, travelling from plantation to plantation selling goods by retail both to the managerial staff plantation to plantation selling goods by retail both to the managerial staff and, perhaps more largely, to the slaves. Young believed that such hucksters accounted for at least one-third of the island's retail trade. It brought them a steady flow of cash and as Young remarked "They are the only people who have any quantities of Gold or Silver Money; little in the higher Circles is to be seen". Such women were said to have goods specially ordered from England for them by their white "sleeping partners".[79] It is also probable that free coloured women were sometimes employed as seamstresses or laundresses though no specific cases have been identified.

Interaction between whites and coloureds

The free coloured population operated under legal restrictions which were designed to prevent them from offering economic competition to the whites. Such restrictions would also reinforce the social distance between the groups and diminish the chances of any free coloured pushing his way into white elite society. Indeed the whole complex of relationships between the two groups was determined principally by the mutually reinforcing factors of colour and legal status. Until 1808, when a coloured estate owner was allowed to count himself as the "white" servant required to balance the first fifty slaves under the Deficiency Acts,[80] a free coloured who sought to acquire an estate was faced from the outset with the deficiency tax since no white man would work for him. There were of course very few free coloureds who had any chance of becoming planters, so that this disability was largely academic; but to the few the £100 deficiency tax must have been an overwhelming barrier.[81]

The law governing the Assembly, originating in the 1760s, also prevented coloured persons from becoming members of the Assembly or voting in elections. They were required to serve in the militia but could not hold a militia commission. In 1804 the free coloureds of Scarborough were grouped into a separate militia company, of course under white officers.[82]

The fact that the free coloureds in this period almost never contracted formal marriage, so that pretty well all their children were illegitimate, brought further, perhaps inadvertent, disabilities in relation to the law of inheritance. It meant that they could not inherit at all unless their parents made wills, and free coloured people seldom did that. When they did, the will was often upset for lack of the proper form. Their estates therefore had commonly to be handled through the medium of letters of administration for which any interested person seems to have been free "petty European shopkeepers or pretended creditors" would obtain letters of administration for his or her estate. The newly instituted administrator was then in a position to appropriate much of the estate. Governor Young in 1809 was moved to interfere. He did not, of course, contemplate altering the English law of inheritance, but he revived the office of Escheator to the Crown, charged with pressing the Crown's claims to doubtful estates, as a means of subjecting the estates of free coloureds to closer scrutiny.[84]

In the first session of the new Court of Escheat two of the five cases proved to involve attempts at fraudulent administration. In three cases, after the estate was escheated to the Crown for lack of lawful heirs the claims of a mulatto heir were then admitted by grace.[85] All five cases would probably have involved loss of a free coloured inheritance but for Young's intervention and it may be assumed that many such cases had occurred during the preceding years.

Even less evidence has been found relating to the health of the free coloured population specifically than to that of the whites. It may be assumed that the periodic outbreaks of epidemic disease already mentioned did not spare the free coloureds, but otherwise it is not possible to say anything specific about their physical well being.

In the late eighteenth century the European culture was generally assumed by many, perhaps most, of the free coloured people in the West Indies to be "superior" to that of the slaves. Thus, while social ties between the recently manumitted and the slaves were certainly maintained in at least some cases, the evidence suggests that most free coloureds tried to disassociate themselves from the slaves and so from their African heritage. They tried to cultivate European habits and customs, beginning with European clothing and the English language.[86] Clothing was easy to adopt, of course, though the coloured women tended to dress in a specially ostentatious fashion, which was doubtless an attempt to demonstrate that they had crossed a culture line which separated them from Africa and placed them closer to the Europeans. Language was more difficult. While the language of the free coloureds tended to approximate more closely to English than that of the slaves, and to show less obvious signs of their African origin, it was none the less clearly Creole, involving a mixture of English and African elements. Music and religion were other aspects of the coloureds' quest for respectability in European eyes. They were generally unlikely to engage with open enthusiasm in African-derived drumming and were more receptive to the preachings of Christian missionaries than were the slaves. In all these matters the free coloureds on the whole sought to put Africa behind them and to move closer to

European norms, though there could be no hope that they would ever enter the social circle of the Europeans or even achieve practical equality with them.

Among the elite of the free coloureds were a number who themselves owned slaves and so were clearly identified with the white-dominated slave society. Thirteen of them, apparently all female, can be identified in 1819; but this number seems much too small[87] and it can be safely assumed that some free coloured men also owned slaves by this time.

Direct evidence of the everyday relationship between whites and free coloureds in Tobago during this period is not easy to find. The indirect evidence, while not abundant, supports the view of the missionary Isaac Purkis that the free coloured "very highly respect white people and treat them in the most obliging manner".[88] The view that they were, at least outwardly, respectful and co-operative towards the whites is supported by the fact that when the deficiency laws were being amended in their favour in 1808 the amending Act itself recorded that this was a gesture in recognition of "the exemplary good conduct of the free coloured inhabitants" which "deserves every encouragement that is proper".[89] A recent study of the work of the missionaries confirms the view that the free coloured were generally loyal to the status quo, content to be held inferior to the whites provided that their own superiority to the blacks was acknowledged,[90] and we have seen how commonly they sought to imitate the habits of the whites. It is not surprising that they came to accept the view that things Africans were generally inferior. They were surrounded by it and the leaders of the society thrust it at them. Even the missionaries, who sought their welfare, believed that intelligence went with whiteness. Even Purkis, who befriended them, believed that the blacks were the least intelligent group, being unable to surmount the obstacles posed by their lack of English.[91]

Thus the free coloureds generally co-operated with the white elite and the Assembly thought that, at least in some contexts, they deserved encouragement. The 1802 Slave Law provided a public flogging at the discretion of a single Justice of the Peace for any slave who insulted, abused or treated contemptuously any free coloured person, a protection previously reserved for whites; but this probably represents a desire for solidarity against slave revolt rather than a gesture towards the free coloured as such.[92] There was also the matter of the deficiency laws. On the other hand, the free coloureds must know their place in the society and the lesser whites in particular were prone to react swiftly to any indication that free coloured competitors were gaining on them, especially in the economic sphere. In 1797, the fact that a number of licenses to sell liquor had been granted to coloured persons who employed only slaves prompted a petition from white liquor sellers against the issue of licenses to "improper persons" which led to a change in the licensing law.[93] In 1803, representations about "the improper conduct of some of the free people of colour" led Lieutenant Governor Macdonald to ask the legislature to consider amending the laws, accusing the coloured community of a lack of "decency and decorum".[94] What they had been doing has not been discovered, but there is other evidence of active white hostility, which is easily intelligible in view of the obvious competition which they had begun to offer to the lesser whites in the skilled occupations. There was also the fact that many coloureds were passably well off and often held their wealth in cash which even the white proprietors found hard to raise.

It is also instructive that in the extremely few cases where a white man would agree to work for a coloured planter, Governor Robinson claimed in 1819 that "their white brethren would laugh them out of [it], so that the owners of such estates had not remedy and were compelled to pay the penalties in spite of their utmost endeavours to obtain white men".[95]

But if the whites resented the coloureds' success, the latter, for all their apparent respect and what missionary Purkis called their "generosity", clearly reacted. As Purkis wrote in 1809 "They are despised and rejected by the white people which operates on them as a constant stimulus to render themselves independent".[96] This constant quest for independence was seen as a major element in the coloureds' success.[97] It is noteworthy that Purkis concentrated his work among the free coloureds and probably knew them as well as any other white in this period. It is difficult not to credit his view that there was another side to the seeming respectfulness of coloureds towards whites.

The relationship between the two communities was also affected in a complex variety of ways by the practice of white concubinage with coloured women. Granted the common inclination of free coloured women in the West Indies to seek the material advantages of a personal alliance with the whites and the equally common tendency of male white colonists in a colony where white men far outnumbered white women and planters preferred unmarried overseers to seek coloured or slave concubines, the incidence of concubinage, sometimes short term, sometimes stable for long periods, was certainly very great. In 1811 there were 501 white men in Tobago but only 49 white women, and a total of 153 free coloured women, to only 92 men. The evidence which is specific to Tobago consists of generalizations, but the experience of other islands suggests that the great majority of the 153 free coloured women were probably kept by white men while the free coloured men often had to turn to slave women. This situation created an enduring if capricious link between white and free coloured society and a situation of constant between white and free coloured society and a situation of constant culture contact on an individual level which in the long run could not fail to affect both the white and the coloured communities generally. This process had of course begun with the settlement of Tobago in the 1760s and in the early nineteenth century the limits on the socioeconomic activities of the free coloured people and the pattern of their cultural movement were fairly well understood. But they were flexible limits, and as the free coloureds became more numerous and the whites less so, the former would encroach further on the preserves of the latter.

The Slaves

Numbers, gender and distribution

The number of slaves in Tobago when the British recovered the island in 1793 is impossible to determine accurately, but a census of 1790 showed a slave population of 14,170,[98] which is probably an underestimate since such counts were seldom completely comprehensive. The subsequent return of the British coincided with the boom in the international sugar market which followed the slave revolt in St Domingue in 1791 and the destruction of that colony's export trade, and sugar production in Tobago began to accelerate as it did elsewhere. New estates were opened up on hitherto uncultivated land, of which Tobago had a good supply, and existing estates sought to increase their cultivated area. This situation naturally created pressure for the importation of new slaves during the 1790s and by 1797 there were 16,190 in the island despite the fact that deaths substantially outnumbered births.[99] Sugar production rose from 5,300 tons in 1794 to 8,890 in 1799[100] before the natural consequences of overproduction in the British colonies brought the boom to an end. Simultaneously, in 1798-99, the average price of slaves in the British West Indies rose sharply from less than £60 to about £70 and subsequently remained very high.[101] After 1799 there was no more incentive to any further expansion of production and imports of slaves declined sharply as Table 2.5 shows.[102]

TABLE 2.5 SLAVE IMPORTS, 1795-1807

1 July 1795 to 1 July 1797	1797	1798	1799	1800	1801 to 5 July	1802	1803	1804 to 1807
1533	323	721	1463	38	255	172	n.a.	830

With births still failing to keep pace with deaths, the slave population can hardly have grown significantly between the end of 1799 and the end of the slave trade in 1807, after which it began to decline slowly but steadily as Table 2.6 shows. [103]

TABLE 2.6   SLAVE POPULATION OF TOBAGO

1802	1803	1804	1805	1806	1807	1808	1809	1810	1811	1812	1813
17,037	16,846		17,168	18,153	17,142	16,981	16,712	16,489	16,265	16,080	

These figures were compiled by Governor Sir William Young between 1811 and 1813 with great care and attention to detail, but they are between 5 per cent and 8 per cent lower than a recent calculation by Barry Higman.[104] Fig 2.1 looks more closely at Tobago's slave population by parish.

The sharp rise in the slave population during 1806 was occasioned by new importations, while the subsequent fall during 1807 was partly the result of an epidemic of whooping cough.[105]

In the 1790s it is probable that Tobago's slave population, with a large proportion, probably a majority, of Africans, contained a substantial majority of males. Male slaves were generally regarded as more valuable workers than females and at the end of the eighteenth century the sex ratio among consignments of new slaves varied from 150 to 180 males per 100 females,[106] while before 1807 there was no great interest in breeding a self-sustaining slave population. However, as the Creole slave population grew, more normal sex ratios were achieved and by the early 1800s males only narrowly outnumbered females. In 1811 the 15,084 slaves recorded as residing on estates comprised 5,931 men, 5,714 women and 3,439 "children", or 103.8 men to 100 women, while by 1819 there were 97.4 male slaves in the island to every 100 females.[107]

Like the white and free coloured people the slaves were unevenly distributed among the several parishes, the distribution of the slaves being determined by their suitability for the production of sugar. In only one parish, St Andrew, which contained the urban area of Scarborough, were there more than 400 slaves to the square mile at the end of this period (1819). Next came St David, containing the urban area of Plymouth and the well developed area along the Courland River, with a density of 200-300 to the square mile, and then the generally flat parish of St Patrick and the parish of St George, another well developed area, with between 100 and 200 slaves to the square mile. These four parishes together made up the easily accessible western half of the island. In none of the three

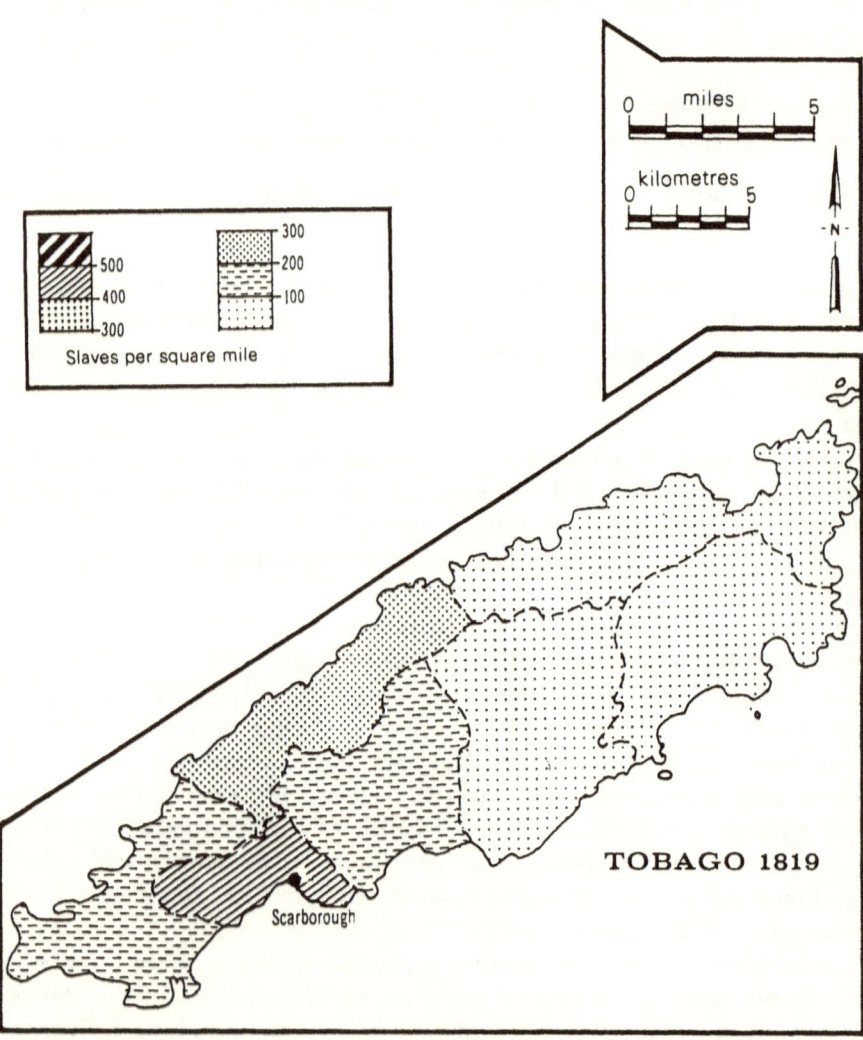

FIG. 2.1 SLAVE POPULATION PER SQUARE MILE, TOBAGO 1819

Reproduced from B.W. Higman, *Slave Populations of the British Caribbean 1807-1834*, p 89.

eastern parishes, St Mary, St Paul and St John, were there more than 100 slaves per square mile. This distribution precisely reflects the intensity of sugar cultivation, in which about 90 per cent of the slaves were engaged.[108]

Within this spatial distribution the slaves were concentrated on large plantations to a greater extent than in most other islands. In 1819, 81.7 per cent were located on holdings which employed more than 100 slaves, 30.3 per cent on holdings with more than 200.[109] In 1811 there were eighty-nine estates of which only twenty employed less than 100 slaves and twenty-seven over 200.[110] While no figures have been found, it is likely that as cotton and coffee, normally cultivated on smaller holdings than sugar, declined in the 1790s the concentration of slaves in large units was increased. In the urban areas slaves were normally owned in much smaller, often very small units, where most were engaged in essentially domestic work. In 1819, 55 per cent of the slave owners in Scarborough were women, none of whom owned more than fifty slaves.[111]

Demographic patterns

The slave population, for all the evening out of the sex ratio, was never able to maintain itself. In the first place we have noticed that deaths normally exceeded births. Sir William Young's statistical returns show that in the three years to 1 October 1811 there were 1,224 births and 1,533 deaths on the estates in a slave population averaging 15,038, which produces a birth rate of 27 per cent against a death rate of 33 per cent and a natural decrease of 6 per cent per annum.[112] Whatever error there may be in Young's figures it is clear that this relationship is absolutely typical. Higman's calculations show that in 1819-21 the birth rate varied from 23.8 per cent to 26.9 per cent, the death rate from 49.5 per cent to 56.8 per cent,[113] a rate which incidentally was the highest in the British West Indies among both sexes and all age groups and which varied little between Africans and Creoles.[114] The average rate of natural decrease he calculated as 26.2 per cent in 1819-21, the highest in the British West Indies at that time.[115]

The slave population was also diminished by the loss of those who ran away successfully or were manumitted and those who were taken out of the island, but it is clear that these difficulties affected only very small numbers. In Tobago, as in other islands, the failure of the process of natural reproduction remains as a striking fact. This failure was of course due to an excess of mortality over fertility and theoretically the cause may lie in either. Recent scholarship has suggested that while the rates of both are of roughly equal importance in explaining what happened in the West Indies, the mortality rate is in fact the more crucial.[116] It was the rate of mortality rather than that of fertility which determined the difference between one locality or estate and another.

Fertility in Tobago was certainly unusually low, for a variety of reasons, including the fact that the island had one of the larger proportions of "aged" slaves among the British colonies, at least in the later years of this period.[117] Contemporaries were quite convinced that the problem was one of fertility, in Tobago as in the other islands, recognizing that the birth rate was unusually low, and inadequate to maintaining the population, and that in a colony where the sex ratio was almost even. It is probable that the fertility of the slave population was actually declining because the old African element was aging and no longer being replaced quickly after 1799, or at all after 1807.

Sir William Young sought to explain the problem with reference to the fact that when Tobago was first developed in the 1760s and 1770s a disproportionately large number of men had been imported, thus disrupting African family patterns. In West Africa polygamy was widely practised, but the polygamous marriage was expected to endure and unfaithfulness in the wife was not tolerated. As Young put it "In Africa . . . the Husband is the Despot of his Household"; but when he was enslaved and transported to the West Indies he found that the woman was the property of the master and he himself of little consequence.[118] Indeed, the male slave could not even "check infidelity or be assured of his offspring", so that he "revolted at a Connection so little conformable to the Usages of his nation and to [his] right of command over [his] women". "Hence the slaves who first came to Tobago rarely settled in families, but indulged in promiscuous intercourse little favourable to population".[119] The failure of the slaves to engage more often in some kind of formal marriage and family life, Young recognized to be a product of slave conditions, but it may well have tended to reduce the birth rate. The women for their part adopted habits of their own, like abortion, which militated against a high birth rate. Some neglected their children while "the better mothers, suckling their infant for two years or more, could not be very prolific",[120] a potentially significant factor.

Writing in 1811, Young thought that things had probably begun to improve, noticing that the planters, while the slave trade persisted, had been accustomed to take the view that it was more economical to buy new slaves from Africa than to attempt to breed their own.[121] Since 1807, however, they had, according to Young, set out to "foster domestic affection" in a deliberate effort to promote the birth rate. He saw the allowance of abundant provision grounds as an opportunity for the slave to provide for his children himself which should be an encouragement to him to beget a family.[122] Female slaves had been relieved of labour in respect of each pregnancy and mothers of six living children had been relieved of labour altogether since before 1793.[123] Infant and child mortality rates made this a very rare achievement, but Young now believed that the planters had begun to show

> humane Attentions to the Instruction, Encouragement, Rewards and a Care of Mothers and Children on their Estates and for which the Mothers at least are become grateful and conform to the Advice & Directions they receive from their Master, or from the Physician at the Hospital of the Plantation.

> A settled union of Man & Woman is anxiously encouraged and fostered on each Estate and on Intimation given by the Parties they are allowed time and materials to build or enlarge and furnish their Hut.[124]

There is evidence that in the West Indies generally fertility levels did increase after 1807 as the living conditions of the slaves improved;[125] but Young was over-optimistic. The planters were still often inclined to see attempts at breeding slaves as uneconomical, even with the price of slaves exceeding £100.[126] Rearing slave children was, after all, expensive. The process involved the loss of much if not all of the mother's labour for a long period, the waiting time before return on the investment was possible was several years, and with it all the survival rate was low. Higman's calculations suggest that as late as 1819-21 the infant mortality rate in Tobago in the first twelve months of life was more than 50 per cent while not more than 30 per cent of births reached the age of 15.[127] Only an acute shortage of labour was likely to make the breeding of slaves seem a really attractive proposition and this was certainly not the case in Tobago by 1815.

Low fertility, however, while undeniable, was not the crucial factor in the persistent natural decrease in the slave population. That role must go to the high mortality rate, inflated by the presence of unusual numbers of aging slaves. Barry Higman has shown that the high mortality among the slaves was caused essentially by the nature of the work regime on the sugar plantations. Throughout the West Indies mortality rates on sugar estates were higher than those on plantations growing cocoa, coffee or cotton, rearing livestock or cultivating provisions, for reasons lying in the internal organization of the different crops rather than in differences of terrain or climate, though these could play a part.

The close connection between sugar production and high mortality was well known at the time, being too obvious to miss.[128] The mortality was in fact caused, as Richard Pares long ago suggested, primarily by the combination of overwork and underfeeding, and was highest in that occupation which involved the hardest toil.[129] The most important factors were "the extreme hours of heavy labour and the brutality of the gang-driving system" on the sugar estates.[130] And in Tobago roughly 90 per cent of the slaves worked on sugar estates by 1800. Secondly, large sugar plantations contained large slave populations whose quarters were commonly cramped and insanitary. Such conditions were an important cause of diarrhoeal diseases, the major recorded cause of deaths.[131] And in Tobago about 80 per cent of the slaves worked on estates employing gangs in excess of 100. Moreover, the slave mortality in Tobago reached a peak each year in the months following the extreme exertion of the crop, as during the crop itself the availability of cane juice provided a source of sustainment which postponed the effects of the labour regime.[132] Similarly, urban mortality rates were generally rather lower than rural,[133] again because the work regime was less arduous.

Health

While the health of the free coloureds and slaves generally excited little comment in official circles, the high mortality rate was of course a reflection of problems of health. In several respects the health of the slave population was subject to special stress. The planters' desire to maximize the profits of sugar production meant that, especially after 1800 when profit margins were falling and soon to become generally very low, while the cost of maintaining the slaves was tending to rise, the allowances of food and clothing which the slaves received were invariably small. Even where they were allowed liberal provision gardens, as was the case in Tobago, the field slaves had a very low standard of living, significantly lower than that of the skilled slave elite who received larger allowances and had better opportunities to earn money. In Tobago there was a period of perhaps three months each year, after the end of the crop, when the slaves were overwhelmingly dependent on their small allowances.

In consequence the general health of the field slaves, hard worked and minimally fed, was always likely to be poor, and it was among the field slaves that mortality was most severe. The health of the slaves was also likely to be affected by the nature of their diet and the availability of food, and as we shall see the diet was often questionable and serious shortages were quite common. In May 1815, for instance, Dr George Cumine, who claimed, probably with some exaggeration, that with one partner he was responsible for the health of over 10,000 slaves, suggested that a recent "sickly period" had occurred because drought had forced the estates to fall back on issuing dry provisions in place of the usual produce of the provision grounds.[134] Drought was a recurring problem, and so were shortages of imported goods due to the interference of warfare with normal patterns of trade and other vicissitudes. Slaves certainly did suffer from periodic interruptions of the food supply which affected other sections of the population less seriously.[135]

The generally poor standard of nutrition was glaringly evident in the high rate of child mortality. This factor must be added to the effects of the harsh work regime and, most importantly, the insanitary living conditions on the estates which have already been noticed. Indeed wartime shortages and price rises sometimes put the planters under severe financial pressure and this was likely to lead to increased pressure on the slaves as they sought to economize. On the one hand, work regimes were likely to become more rigorous; on the other, the provision of clothing and medical attention and the repair of houses were likely to see economies. Rations of salt meat and fish were also likely to be reduced. Ultimately this situation would be reflected in a rise in the rate of slave mortality.

The years 1819-21, for which the slave registration returns provide much information, illustrate the general pattern of disease. The most commonly fatal afflictions were diarrhoeal diseases, which accounted for 20.1 per cent of deaths, followed by dropsy (12.1 per cent), fever, generally malaria and yellow fever (10.6 per cent), and tuberculosis (8.8 per cent). Next came diseases of the digestive and nervous systems and leprosy. Worms and tetanus were also well known.[136]

Occupations

The overwhelming majority of the slaves worked in the fields as manual labourers, cultivating sugar cane and a little cotton or coffee but by 1800 the latter were declining to the point of disappearance. Field workers numbered upwards of two thirds of the estate slaves or about 85% of those capable of work. In his 1811 statistical survey Sir William Young put the number of field labourers on the estates at 9,865 out of a total of 15,122 slaves, with 2,190 children under 7 and 1,350 aged or infirm.[137]

On each estate there was also a group of privileged slaves who enjoyed a considerably higher standard of living than the field slaves based on the performance of some skilled or supervisory task. These were the headmen or "drivers", who were responsible for seeing that the slaves maintained a certain rate of labour and did their work satisfactorily, and the practitioners of artisanal or trade skills, and the domestics. Young in 1811 estimated that a typical estate of 200 slaves, which would be among the largest 30 per cent of the estates in Tobago, would normally employ eight house servants (butler, footman, stableman, cook, housekeeper, washer and two maids) as well as a gardener, stockkeeper, cattle keeper, midwife, sick nurse, children's nurse, five carpenters, five coopers, one mason, and it would share the services of a smith with two other estates.[138] By an extrapolation of these proportions Young suggested that among the 15,122 "attached" slaves on the island's estates in 1811 there were 600 house servants, 225 nurses and midwives, 225 muleteers, stockkeepers and cattle keepers, 365 carpenters, 365 coopers, 73 masons and 24 smiths. He further calculated that in Scarborough's 230 houses there were about 700 domestic slaves, engaged in assorted tasks, 200 employed as assistants by 80 master carpenters and coopers, 100 similarly employed by masons, smiths, tailors, shoemakers, sadlers and other tradesmen, and 100 seamen. Altogether he suggested that Tobago supported 1,650 slaves not attached to plantations, described as "unattached" slaves.[139] See Table 2.7.[140]

TABLE 2.7 SLAVE OCCUPATIONS, 1811

	"Attached" to Estates	"Unattached" in Scarborough	Total
House servants	600	700	1,300
Hospital and children's nurses and midwives	225	25	250
Muleteers, stockkeepers, cattle keepers	225	25	250
Carpenters	365	} 200	} 930
Coopers	365		
Masons	73	} 100	} 220
Smiths	24		
Mariners (fishermen)		100	100
Superannuated and sick in hospital	1,350		1,100
Field and boiling house labourers	9,865		[10,422]
For hire to estates		400	400
Children under 7	2,190	100	2,300

Young does not distinguish a number of specific trades. Sugar boilers and rum distillers were usually slaves, though they worked as such only during the crop season and were no doubt otherwise classified. The skill of the head boiler could be crucial to an estate's performance in production. Seamstresses and tailors would be expected to be present in Scarborough in significant numbers. Shoemakers, bakers and butchers, catering to the public at large and not specifically to their masters, might also have been mentioned.[141] But in so small a society as Tobago these functions may have been seldom performed as specialities, and all involved occupations which might also be found among the free coloured. Several urban slaves will have been employed in transportation, sometimes driving carts, but usually carrying items on their heads or backs, the hardest physical labour of all urban tasks.[142] But these together with the urban general labourers were no doubt comprehended either as domestics or as slaves for hire, the number of which is surprisingly high.

Specialist slaves were also often employed to tend the estate animals and as watchmen over livestock, crops, provision grounds, or as fishermen. Hucksters and other sellers of their owners' goods might also be separately identified.[143] The domestic slaves performed a variety of functions including many which were far removed from housecleaning or cooking or attendance on planters and their families. They ranged from emptying the chamber pots of their owners, as Higman puts it, to buying food in the market and cooking and serving it, to functioning as messengers, valets or ladies' maids or selling their owners' goods in the streets.[144] As Higman puts it, they were responsible for "making bread and butter as well as beds".[145] Of the specialist domestics the most important were cooks and washerwomen. Housekeepers, butlers or footmen were seldom found on the plantations, more often in town. Nurses, separately identified by Young, were quite numerous, but they often watched over the children of slaves as well as those of their masters. Some estate domestics served elite slaves rather than overseers or managers. It is noteworthy that most urban slave owners owned very small numbers of slaves. This meant that urban slaves were less specialized in function than rural slaves. Each slave would have to perform many different kinds of tasks so that his or her classification could only be a general one. But as Sir William Young wrote in 1810 in relation to the plantations:

> Adam Smith's principle of the 'Division of Labor' was never more comically insisted upon than in the mansion House of the West India Planter. "What, Me One, do Two Something!" - is the exclamation of the Negroe Boy, who having Blacked his Masters shoes, is told to help in the Stable: - the Sempstress wont wash; - and the Washerwoman cant sew. Add the consequent multiplication of servants, in a Country, the habits in which are so indolent, that scarcely any white Person, or even free Mulatto, will for Him or Herself, open a window, shut a door, or snuff a Candle, - *and with this observe that every Overseer has a favourite Black Girl under his protection* ...[146]

Cultural tradition and practices

The slaves who were employed in Tobago from the 1790s appear to have come mostly from that area of the West African coast between Senegambia and Northern Angola. While their origins are not known precisely, the

Africans brought to the British West Indies in the period came principally from Senegambia, the Bight of Biafra and Central Africa. In the Southern Caribbean the Bight of Biafra was the most important source.[147] But each colony contained a heterogeneous mixture of Africans since each region of Africa contained many tribal or ethnic groups. In the southern Caribbean generally the most numerous were Malinke (Mandingo), Igbo, Kongo and Moco.[148] Thus Tobago contained people of many diverse origins and habits but they shared a set of common beliefs and traditions which were distinctively African in origin.[149] African tradition can, for instance, be traced in the music, dancing and dress of the slaves as in their religious beliefs and customs. The slave culture of course embraced many beliefs and practices which came from non-African sources. Many were the product of the conditions of slavery itself. Together they created a slave culture which was quite different from the culture of the whites and from which the free coloureds were generally concerned to distance themselves.

It has been possible to find only a little evidence of the slave culture relating to Tobago specifically in the years before 1815 but there is no reason to doubt that the slaves behaved in much the same way as in the other Windward Islands and the following account draws to some extent on those nearby islands.

While Sir William Young's remarks about "promiscuous intercourse" certainly reflected the style of many slaves, that pattern of sexual activity was far from being universal. The incidence and structure of the West Indian slave family is a complex issue about which there has been much scholarly controversy, but the slave system certainly disorganized the African family patterns from which they came. This resulted from the separation of relatives first by seizure and then by sale or transfer, and the elimination of the formal rights of the slave father -- though in practice father-child links may often have been significant, for the relationship between the parents frequently enjoyed some stability -- and the interpolation into the family structure of the rights of the slave-master. In very many cases, probably a majority, the link between mother and child became paramount, if not the only family link of real substance. Yet there is good evidence that strong family ties existed among the slaves and that family patterns of African origin persisted or were recreated in modified form. No specific evidence of any significance relating to the slave family in Tobago has yet emerged, but in both Trinidad and St Lucia slaves were more likely to live in family groups in large holdings than in small, and hence in the country rather than in town.[150]

Slave family households were however of different types. Many, perhaps most, were mother-children units; but there was a noticeable number of nuclear families in both town and country, most often on the larger plantations; and in many matrifocal families the father may have had a stable "visiting" status, though living outside the household, very possibly on another estate. Extended families and polygamous units were also known, especially on large plantations where the chances of forced separation were smaller than on lesser holdings. Higman suggests that slave families were much more common in older than in newer slave communities and it is likely that in Tobago slave families of one sort or another were considerably more common than in Trinidad where according to one calculation 56 per cent of slaves were living in family units in 1813, or in the similarly less developed St Lucia where 69 per cent were doing so in 1815.[151] Drivers and skilled slaves seem to have been more likely than the unskilled to live in family units.[152] However, Africans were less likely to do so than Creoles perhaps because enslavement had disrupted their family life, and the incidence of family households seems to have increased as the Creole population did, though in a sugar colony like Tobago the nuclear family was more often found among Africans.[153]

The formal legal marriage of slaves was of course out of the question but they frequently maintained enduring sexual connection with one partner, and the frequency of the matrifocal family pattern is not an index of sexual promiscuity nor even of the supposedly marginal status of the male partner. Where, as happened not infrequently, slave parents had different owners and so necessarily resided separately, it may have been the only possible form of family organization.

It is clear that the slaves held a variety of religious beliefs derived from their ancestors in Africa. Just what those beliefs were is difficult to ascertain precisely but West African religions appear to have been polytheistic, though positing a belief in a supreme being generally conceived as the father and creator of all men and all things, and in the spirits of departed ancestors.[154] Modern scholarship has confirmed the contemporary views that they had "some notion of the immortality of the soul" as well as the opinion expressed by a Methodist missionary in Tobago in 1822 that they had "some belief in the doctrine of transmigration of souls". This missionary believed that the principal reason for the slaves' resistance to Christianity was their belief that accepting it would prevent the return of their souls to Africa, which was otherwise assured.[155] Such a belief was perhaps related to the recognition of ancestors as active spirits and to a belief in duppies and ghosts and jumbies, all spirits of the departed.[156] These spirits and the native gods associated with water, sea and land had an important influence on the fortunes of every individual and here the way was open for religious practitioners to mediate between the individual and the spirit world.

In this context African tradition was also reflected in the persistent influence of obeah, especially among those born in Africa. The practice of obeah involved the preparation and use of potions and spells designed to protect the user and his property or to inflict harm on his enemies, or both. Obeah men and women were also skilled in the use of herbal medicines and very familiar with the use of poisons. To most whites, obeah was the same as witchcraft and those indulging in it were seen as merely evil. In fact, apart from the obeah man's activities as medicine man, his supposed influence with the spirit world had an important function in the society. In Africa the obeah man was priest and philosopher, as well as doctor, and some sought to fill the same dual role in the West Indies. Some achieved very considerable influence over the slaves among whom they practised, even those who became Christians.[157]

Slaves tended to have their own funeral rights largely derived from Africa. It was common for them to return to the graveside on the first anniversary to pay their respects in a ceremony which would include a feast:

> On these occasions, the relatives of the deceased often go to a considerable expense in providing a feast, and invite a number of their friends to partake with them. A fowl, which they select with some caution, and which their superstition dictates must be either a black or white one, is prepared in a peculiar manner, as being intended entirely for the benefit of the dead. Previous to their sitting down to feast themselves, this fowl is, with a good deal of ceremony, thrown out at the door of the hut, and with a quantity of rum and water, it being supposed that their departed friends must needs want to drink as well as eat.
>
> All this being done under the cover of night, the negro easily brings his superstitious mind to conclude, that what he throws away in the dark is actually devoured by the hungry ghost of his long lost relative. This momentous rite being thus duly performed, and the craving appetite of their invisible guest perfectly satisfied, they immediately turn their attention to eating and drinking; after which, when the maddening fumes of liquor begin to ascend they 'rise up to play' and spend the night in performing their wild barbarous dances to the savage din of the African tom tom.[158]

The African tradition also endured in the patterns of music and dancing found among the slaves. Dancing was the characteristic form of social and artistic expression and had a religious as well as a secular importance. As President Balfour said to the Council in 1815, "there is not one of us that does not know the rage the negroes have for dancing, and that is their principal enjoyment".[159] Not only was it used at funeral rites and ceremonies honouring the deceased, but also for recreation, entertainment and the relief of tension. The end of crop was often celebrated with music and dancing – a kind of relief from the long period of toil as well as a celebration of success. Dancing was also part of the Christmas festivities and the slaves also arranged dances on casual occasions to suit themselves.[160] Both European and African-derived music might be encountered, or the styles might mingle; but much of it was what one Methodist missionary described as "purely African". African-derived dances were commonly seen by the whites as conducive to sexual license but occasionally their grace was appreciated, as when Sir William Young described one dance at one of his estates in St Vincent in 1792, performed by about a dozen slave girls as "curious and most lascivious ... with much grace as well as action".[161] Elaborate and expensive dress was sometimes worn at slave dances.[162]

Both European and African instruments were used by the slaves. The fiddle was widely used, as were various African drums, the balaso ("pieces of hard wood of different diameters, laid on a row over a sort of box") and triangles. But the cardinal instrument was the drum at any dance intended principally for slaves.[163]

Language, cooking and dress were also much influenced by African tradition. The slaves spoke a Creole which combined English and African words and speech patterns. They used highly spiced foods and in many islands African head-dresses were common among the women.[164]

The skilled or elite slaves were often, perhaps usually, of mixed blood, offspring of white fathers who had neglected or omitted to free their slave children. Because of their white blood, they were usually protected from the field which was seen as the preserve of the blacks, and were therefore pushed into the elite ranks and placed in positions in which they could acquire skills, if only those of the domestic slave, which enabled them to hold the less arduous, better rewarded positions on the estates. White blood helped the skilled slave to fill a distinctive position.[165] As for those who were black, it was the more intelligent blacks who were singled out for these skilled and responsible tasks. It is not surprising that the London Missionary Society (LMS) missionary Roger Elliot should have claimed that the house slaves were more intelligent that those in the field.[166]

The widespread practice of concubinage between white men and slave women, many of whom would be black, meant that the mixed blood, elite group tended to grow larger. It has been calculated that in Tobago in 1819 the number of mixed blood slaves was 3.3 per cent of the total, which may well be an underestimate.[167] In the nature of things mixed blood slaves were well placed to achieve manumission at the hands of their planter relatives, and so the free coloured population was constantly augmented by a trickle of recruits from among the coloured slaves and there was a standing link of ancestry between the two groups. It is not surprising, then, that generally speaking the elite slaves in the West Indies tended to share the attitudes of the free coloureds and to look down on the mass of black field slaves as an inferior group. They commonly avoided labour in the fields and regarded demotion to it as a considerable punishment.[168] The mixed blood slaves in Tobago will have shared this general attitude.

Such was the importance of colour among the slaves themselves that a slave who appeared to come from a given racial or sub-racial category might well describe himself as belonging to another.[169] Thus a Black might seek to pass as a mulatto or a mulatto as a mustee. It is unlikely that any one would seek to pass as belonging to a category ranked lower than his appearance suggested. Many appear to have been described locally as "yellow" or "yellowish",[170] though the line between that and a simple brown or mulatto must have been difficult to draw.

The slave population of Tobago at the end of the eighteenth and in the early nineteenth century, then, was not a cohesive group. The African majority which was almost certainly present in 1793 had shrunk to a large minority by 1815 (about 40 per cent)[171] but was still of fundamental importance. Yet long residence in Tobago was gradually "creolizing" many of the Africans in varying degrees. The Creoles were culturally removed from them in further varying degrees and those of mixed blood could sometimes be closer to a white that an African culture. The result was a cultural continuum which, while it no longer contained the new arrival who was scarcely removed from Africa, ranged over a very wide spectrum of Africanness which overlapped with the cultural spectrum of the free coloured. At the same time, the free coloured was trying hard to move along that spectrum in the general direction of white creole culture.

POLITICS, ADMINISTRATION AND THE CONSTITUTION

The Structure of Government

The Council

When Tobago was recaptured in 1783 General Cuyler at once nominated a Council of ten members and appointed a number of officials from among the local inhabitants of British origin whom he believed to be both loyal to the Crown and possessed of local influence. Joseph Robley, a prominent planter who had lived in Tobago since the 1760s and had been a member of the Council in the 1770s, was appointed President of the Council. Cuyler then appointed Lt Colonel William Myers, his Deputy Quartermaster General, to act as Lieutenant Governor and left the island. It is clear that in taking these decisions he relied heavily on the advice of Gilbert Petrie, another prominent planter of long standing whom Henry Dundas, the Secretary of State, had recommended to him as likely to promote the return of British rule.[1]

The appointment of a Council was to become the first step towards the restoration of a representative constitution on the lines of that first granted in 1763, a typical example of the Old Representative System as known in the British colonies. The establishment of a Council, to act both as advisers to the Governor in his capacity as head of the administration, when it came to be referred to as the Privy Council, and as the upper chamber of the legislature, was confirmed in the Royal Instructions to the first Governor, George Poyntz Ricketts, in September 1793. It was the starting point of a new administrative and representative system, followed as it was by the election of an Assembly at the beginning of 1794. The planters clearly welcomed this development, and the early minutes of the Council are full of reiterated comment about the blessings of the new system of government as compared with the late French administration.[2]

In addition to the formal restoration of a Council, in 1793 the Royal Instructions to Governor Ricketts required him to call an Assembly of fifteen members, one for Scarborough and two for each of the seven parishes. The Assembly was to last during the governor's pleasure and voting and membership qualifications were taken over from the old constitution of 1763, though the House was empowered to amend those qualifications and to regulate elections by local Acts. It had full legislative powers under the governor, but as was usual, specific instructions were given to the governor concerning classes of legislation to which he should not consent, or consent only with the condition of a clause delaying implementation until the Crown's pleasure be signified.[3]

Ricketts took office as governor on 4 January 1794 and at once issued an Ordinance with the advice and consent of the Council to provide for the holding of elections. This provided for sixteen members, the town of Plymouth being created a new constituency. The new Assembly was convened on 10 February.[4] Subsequently the maintenance of active and effective political institutions, more particularly the Council, was to be a significant problem for successive governors. For various reasons it was seldom possible to assemble all the members of the Council. Members were ill, or away from the island with or without formal leave, or seats were vacant because their holders died and governors found it difficult to identify persons for membership among the small population. Although substantive appointments to the Council were made by the Crown, Governors were empowered to nominate up to three persons to the Council if vacancies occurred, as well as to fill any vacant seats necessary to provide a minimum of seven active members, the quorum being five. Such was the difficulty of keeping an active Council in being, however, that in 1805 it frequently met and did business with only four members present including the President, then acting as governor. It does not appear that any attention whatever was paid to the lack of a quorum on these occasions.[5] As early as March 1794 two members were no longer resident in Tobago and two others were ill. Attendance was then reduced to three of the ten originally appointed and Governor Ricketts decided to fill the two critical vacancies himself.[6] A year later two members had died, one had resigned, and two more had left the island at least temporarily.[7]

In April 1798 six of the twelve were absent and three had been away more than two years.[8] The governor's Instructions provided that while any period of absence from Tobago by a councillor required his permission, councillors absent for more than one year without special leave should vacate their seats;[9] but not until 1801 was any action taken on this score and that was ineffective.[10]

Matters of health not infrequently led members to go on leave for a year or more and such periods of leave were sometimes extended. Then there were normal visits to Britain or to other islands for business or pleasure. Of the twelve councillors nominated by Grinfield on the recovery of the island in July 1803, only six were available a year later.[11]

Subsequently the movements of members were more tightly monitored and in 1804 Richard Robertson was suspended for leaving the island without leave,[12] but it remained very difficult to sustain an adequate Council. In 1810 Governor Young reported that "some little embarrassment" had been caused to his government because of "the contingency, so repeatedly occurring of privy councillors, on the plea of ill health, or of business leaving this island for Europe". Once more Young had been left with only five councillors, a bare quorum, so that if one fell ill business would have to stop. At the same time there was a full quota of members on the roll so that additional ones could not be appointed. Young decided to make two new appointments despite the fact that they might possibly be deemed illegal,[13] and then at last attacked the problem head on by suggesting that the two who had been absent from the colony for four years should be deemed to have vacated their seats.[14] Another two who had been absent for well over a year without proper leave were similarly treated a few months later.[15] Young filled the vacancies thus created and by July 1811 had achieved an almost complete Council, eleven of the twelve members being resident. But this situation could not be expected to last: within weeks three went on leave.[16] Young determined never to allow more than five to go on leave at any one time,[17] and while it is unlikely that he could do better this merely returned the situation to normal – seven active members at any time. Within three months five were on leave and a sixth was refused permission to go to England. It is instructive that he merely departed without the required leave, apparently with impunity.[18] In 1814 four of the eight resident members applied for leave simultaneously and the status quo had returned.[19]

Thus membership of the Council was very unstable, a situation which could not make for good government in relation to its executive functions, and emergency nominations by governors or officiating presidents to bring it up to its minimal strength of five or perhaps seven members were commonplace.

The difficulty facing the governor in achieving an adequate Council was much accentuated by the attitude of the imperial government, which alone could revoke the substantive appointments of absent members and so create vacancies. Seldom was any effort made on this score and we have noticed two who still remained members four years after leaving the island. Neither did the Secretary of State make any effort to fill the vacancies in the Council, though he invariably confirmed the temporary appointments by which the governor brought numbers up to seven. The governor was very commonly left with a reduced membership of between five and seven members, the limit of his authority to nominate, which with a quorum of five left him no room to manoeuvre.

More important, however, was the difficulty of finding suitably qualified nominees. Respectability and property were the cardinal points.[20] Beyond that, the terms in which President Robley recommended two temporary appointments in 1795 were typical of the criteria governors sought to apply in making their selections: gentlemen "of good understanding, of good fortune and well affected to His Majesty's Government".[21] Long residence in the island and familiarity with its current problems were not essential: James Campbell who arrived there after its recapture in 1793 was a member within a few months and President three months later.[22] His swift appointment to the Council was not unique. In 1796 Drury Ottley was appointed although he was already a member of the Council of St Vincent, in the hope that he was likely to stay in Tobago for some time.[23] In fact he was back in St Vincent in less than two years.[24]

After the reconquest of the island in 1803 it was observed that "there is literally no person, qualified as to property, to sit in Council but those already in". In these circumstances governors took to nominating "some respectable individuals, who are otherwise extremely well qualified". Such a man was Dr George Cumine, a well known medical man who had been living in Tobago for many years and who served in the Council for several years although he possessed no landed or "other" property.[25] Likewise Coll Turner, "a most respectable character", but without landed property, served for many years after he was appointed in 1805.[26] Both were gubernatorial appointments subsequently confirmed by the Secretary of State.[27] Another non-propertied person appointed was Revd William Terrill, Rector of Scarborough, in 1806.[28] The number of residents of property was small and selection was complicated by the need to staff a House of Assembly and a number of offices as well as a Council. President Campbell once nominated Charles Franklyn from the Assembly in order to find a suitable landed proprietor, but such a translation was regarded as undesirable.[29]

Yet councillors frequently held public appointments simultaneously with their membership of the Council. In 1803 Charles Wightman and Thomas McKnaight, and in 1806 Charles Franklyn were appointed Assistant Justices of Common Pleas while Members of Council,[30] while in 1808 Attorney General John Glanville was appointed a member.[31] No one seems to have questioned such duality of function.

Some light is thrown on the manner in which permanent councillors were appointed on the rare occasions when imperial authority did take an initiative by the fact that when Joseph Robley died in 1807, his heir, his nephew John who had held his power of attorney as his principal agent in Britain,[32] on setting out from London to take over the ancestral estates, wrote to the Secretary of State asking to be appointed to the Council.[33] Lord Castlereagh deemed him "perfectly qualified", despite his lack of personal acquaintance with Tobago, and authorized the governor to make the appointment. In the light of the chronic shortage of suitable members he was naturally appointed at once.[34] His concern for Tobago and its business may be judged from the fact that he left the island temporarily less than a year later.[35]

On the other hand, Tobago during this period was able to find in Joseph Robley and James Campbell, both already mentioned, two men who held the office of President of the Council, administering the government during periods when no governor was present. Robley was left in charge for more than a year in 1794-5 and Campbell for a similar period in 1796-7, when Robley was suspended from the Council on the initiative of Governor Lindsay specifically in order to prevent him from taking charge, after allegations that he had previously attempted to pack the Council with ill qualified men who would do his bidding,[36] and used his position for the financial advantage of his nephew.[37] The real facts remain obscure and Robley eventually was restored to his seat in 1798 and to the Presidency,[38] in which office he served until the arrival of Governor Master in January 1800. He served again after Master's death in October 1800 for another two years until Tobago was returned to France. Robley won the approbation of the Secretary of State, and of the Council and Assembly.[39] The two houses commented on his "wisdom and firmness",[40] and presented him with 100 guineas worth of plate in recognition of his guidance in 1794-5, and later passed a unanimous resolution of thanks for "the able and upright manner in which he governed this colony" in 1798-1800.[41] Robley appears to have been generally popular among the white inhabitants,[42] and in 1802 the Secretary of State decided to pay him the full salary of the governor in respect of periods when he had been in charge of the government although only half that salary was the normal emolument in such cases.[43] Campbell, who returned to the presidency after the British recaptured Tobago in 1803, did no less well.

The Council's executive functions were clearly not very demanding. The executive and legislative business was separated to the point of being subject to different sets of minutes, but legislative sessions occurred with the same regularity as those of the Assembly, while executive sessions were decidedly erratic. The minute book of the Privy Council for the period 1806-14 suggests, from the total absence of minutes, that no meetings were held in November 1806, or February 1807, or between 18 August and 8 December 1807, though the meeting of 18 August ended without a decision on the important question of the importation of provisions. No minutes exist between 26 October 1808 and 19 September 1809 or between 19 December 1909 and 24 March 1810 or between 24 March and 4 June 1810. The Privy Council's minutes thereafter record only one meeting, in August 1813, between 29 December 1812 and 12 April 1814 and that in an incomplete minute, suggesting that the minute book now extant may not tell the whole story.

The atmosphere in Council however, at least where executive business was concerned, was very largely determined by the attitude and personality of the governor, or the president when he was called upon to take charge of the administration. Sir William Young was an able governor, not dependent on the Council's advice where he was not required by his instructions to seek it. At the same time he was a relatively easy going man, often content to see the colony move peacefully along. So long as there was enough food and supplies in the island and the slaves were quiet and apparently not discontented, he was unlikely to want to meet his Privy Council too often. No doubt this attitude had much to do with the long periods of seeming inactivity in 1807, 1808-09, 1810 and 1813-14. Young consulted his Council when something exceptional happened or his instructions required it. The work of the Council in its legislative capacity was, of course, closely related to the actions of the Assembly and will be considered in that context.

The Assembly

Under the Ordinance of 1794 the qualification for membership of the Assembly was fixed at freehold or lifetime leasehold tenure of fifty acres of land or town property with a rental value of £50 currency per annum. Members were also required to be white, Protestant, British subjects aged at least 21. The voting qualification was ten acres of land or town property to the value of £20 currency (£10 sterling), or alternatively an assured lifetime income from real property of £20 per annum. The Assembly was empowered to decide disputed elections.[44]

It did occasionally happen that the Assembly had to adjudicate in an election dispute. In 1810, for instance, Archibald Napier, a member of the Assembly, brought a petition in his capacity as a voter in St Paul to unseat the member for St Paul parish, Matthew Hood, on the ground that he was not duly qualified. The Assembly appointed a committee to consider the matter and endorsed its view that the petition must fail.[45]

In addition to its statutory right to determine disputed elections the Assembly in Tobago inherited from its predecessor in the 1770s all the privileges which were normally granted to the assemblies of other British colonies, and this was commonly confirmed whenever a new Speaker took office. The principal privileges were freedom of speech during debate and freedom from arrest on civil process while a session was in progress.[46]

Like the Council, and to some extent for similar reasons, the Assembly was soon found to suffer from problems of personnel. Not only was it difficult to find suitably qualified candidates to stand for election; some duly elected members would decline to take their seats after the election because of the demands made on their time by the Assembly's sessions. The position became sufficiently serious in 1798 for the Assembly to declare that it caused "great detriment to the interests of this Colony" and to provide a fine of £50 currency for any person who refused to take his seat after being duly elected.[47]

"Regular and effectual attendance", as the Assembly itself put it, was another problem and the House soon found it necessary to provide that members who left Tobago to visit Britain for whatever reason should vacate their seats.[48] In May 1798 it went so far as to pass an Act regulating attendance. Yet in the very next month it failed on several occasions to achieve a quorum and in December 1799 proceeding to North America as well as to Europe was declared to be cause for a member to vacate his seat.[49]

The shortage of manpower attracted even more attention after the island was returned to France in 1803,[50] a number of eligible gentlemen having apparently left the island during the uncertainties of 1802-03, and great difficulty was experienced in achieving a quorum.[51] In December 1805 not more that nine of the sixteen members could be assembled, a bare quorum. When next the Assembly met, in March 1806, there was no quorum during the first week of the intended session, after which it was adjourned without doing business. In June 1806 there was again no quorum, this time during the first five scheduled days.[52]

In 1807 a new Act provided a fine of £16 10s. 0d. currency per day on members absent without "good or sufficient reason".[53] Such fines were in fact collected[54] but the quorum remained difficult to achieve.[55] In 1810 the governor at last reported that sessions were usually fully attended now,[56] but the difficulty returned and in 1814 a new standing order was adopted under which not more than four members might take a maximum of twelve months leave without vacating their seats.[57]

The timing, frequency and duration of sessions was another problem. Despite the presence of an occasional doctor, lawyer or clergyman, most members were planters. From January to July they were busy with the work of reaping cane, and making and shipping sugar and did not wish to leave their estates. This circumstance also produced a preference for a single, long annual session to compete all pending business rather than frequent shorter sessions with their inconvenient need to spend time in Scarborough.[58] The hectic session of the first half of 1794, with which the history of the new Assembly had begun, was an emergency matter brought about by the change in sovereignty and not to be lightly repeated. But the proper discharge of business really required more frequent meetings and in 1806 the Assembly passed an Act to provide that the legislature should meet at quarterly intervals.[59] The four quarterly sessions were fixed for January, April, July and October, but the governor of course retained the power to summon the legislature at any time in special session.[60]

It was not that councillors and assemblymen thought these bodies unimportant. Indeed seats therein were highly prized as "stepping stones to ... positions of privilege, power and profit in the colonial society" and indeed as tangible evidence of the possession of influence.[61] The coincidence of private and public business at those times of the year when sugar was being prepared for shipping was a very real problem. In 1814, for instance, the Houses met on 12 April as summoned but immediately requested an adjournment so that several members who were large planters could have time to oversee the loading of the fourteen large merchantmen which were being prepared to sail in convoy on 25 April. The Governor therefore granted an adjournment to 26 April.[62] Much the same thing had occurred in July 1807 when the legislature was prorogued from 20 July to 3 August to facilitate loading sugar to catch a convoy.[63]

It cannot be claimed however that the legislature was overburdened with business. Very few sessions lasted more than one week and it was rare for business to be held over from one session to the next, so that the houses were normally in session for a total of perhaps one month in each year. And in January 1812 and again in April 1813 the Council and Assembly actually met only to adjourn, for they found absolutely no business to do.⁶⁴ When they next met in April 1813 they did so for only a single day.⁶⁵ Special sessions were unusual, and normally lasted only a day or two.

On the other hand, the governorship of Sir William Young was punctuated with busily active sessions. The session of April/May 1807, immediately after he took office, considered no less than eight bills in a week and the October session was again a busy one as was its successor in January 1808. Matters then quietened down a bit, but November 1811 saw five new bills mooted and July 1812 eight. 1814-15 was again a busy period with many new bills and resolutions coming before both houses. But even these busy sessions did not last very many days. Legislators could hardly complain that they had too much work to do; but their lives were so organized that three of the four sessions were held at times when serious planters would wish to be close to the work which determined their immediate economic status.

The governor

When the governor had reason to think that new legislation was required he would address the legislature and ask it to consider the matter but he had no means of introducing any bill in the Assembly. It follows that to some extent the Assembly determined the nature and measure of its own business: though it could not easily avoid replying to the governor's addresses and messages, it did not have to undertake consideration of legislation unless it so wished. The only inescapable call on its attention was the annual finance bill.

Governors differed in the energy which they showed in urging the Assembly in this or that direction, but most were content to let matters lie unless they really needed an intervention from the legislature. Part of the secret of Sir William Young's success indeed was the fact that while he understood very well that the slave laws, for instance, were in need of amendment, he would not push the Assembly more than he had to. Thus the amount of work it did during his governorship varied greatly according to the needs of the hour and the concerns of the Assembly itself. His own manner was decidedly relaxed.

The atmosphere of Young's régime is strikingly set off by the flurry of activity which John Balfour as President of the Council introduced into official business when Young died in 1815. Suddenly the Privy Council which had met relatively seldom and, so far as the surviving minutes go, done little business under Young, began meeting frequently and creating extensive minutes, while Balfour began to lead the legislature in several contexts and generally produced a high profile. Balfour suggested to the legislature means of financing the building of the long desired Anglican church[66] and urged it to meet the coming of peace with the USA in 1815 by making representations to the imperial government about trade with America, to take two examples.[67] Perhaps the fact that Balfour was only President, temporarily in charge of the Government, led him to wish to make his mark as soon as possible, while Young was so well established that he could afford to relax. Young would certainly have left the colonists to provide their own church and altogether his less conspicuous manner stands in clear contrast.

It is possible to deduce that the Secretary of State saw nothing amiss with the relaxed style and indeed approved of it. Official correspondence between London and the colonies in these years was never abundant, but no despatches were addressed to Tobago between 20 February 1808 and 21 February 1813, a full five years, save for the disallowance of two Acts in 1809,[68] while during the interval the governor periodically assured him that all was well. Such long silence was an indication that London was happy about the way in which the Governor of Tobago was doing his job. If he had displeased either the colonists or his imperial masters silence could not have been maintained.

Committees of the legislature

The legislature commonly did much of its work through joint committees of both houses for certain kinds of business which faced it frequently. In the 1790s there were many different joint committees each charged with a specific task. Each public building for instance was the responsibility of a different committee. This method of doing business was found to be a source of much delay and inconvenience however, and in 1800 a single Joint Committee for Public Buildings and Repairs was established.[69] Thereafter there were standing joint committees, consisting of one or two or three members of the Council and two to five members of the Assembly for Public Accounts, Public Works and Correspondence; and sometimes ad hoc joint committees were created for current business so that in 1810 there were standing committees in existence for signals and for arranging the printing of the colony's laws.[70] Standing committees had some measure of executive ("discretionary") power within the limits of any instructions which the two houses might lay down.[71] This procedure was no doubt a useful means of minimizing the time which members of the Assembly, in particular, who did not sit on the standing committees would need to spend on public business.

Probably the busiest of the standing committees of the legislature was the Committee on Public Buildings which was charged generally with the maintenance of such buildings and from time to time with specific pieces of construction or maintenance[72] such as the repair of "the public aqueduct and cistern" in 1810.[73] If the legislature agreed that any specific job of maintenance was necessary the committee would seek tenders for the necessary repairs and then seek legislative approval before concluding a contract for the purpose.[74] However, the Joint Committee on Public Buildings might be bypassed or ignored, as in 1808 when the building purchased about 1796 for use as Government House, "Colony House", was sold for £1,800 currency,[75] after giving way to a new Government House at Mount William. The transaction was handled by the Assembly and Council directly. Perhaps this transaction was considered too large to be delegated, but no explanation appears for the appointment in 1814 of a separate committee to locate a site for a public cemetery.

The judicial system

In 1794, as a British administration for Tobago was being created, the Secretary of State had urged the colony to make careful provision for the administration of justice and in particular for the appointment of judges. He remarked that in other colonies the interests of the Crown had frequently suffered from the lack of proper courts.[76] Two courts were subsequently established in 1794, a Court of Common Pleas presided over by the Chief Justice and involving three Assistant Justices was to sit five times a year;[77] and a Court of Chancery presided over by a Chancellor, who was normally the governor himself, or by the Chief Justice who also officiated as Master in Chancery.[78] The first Chief Justice, John Balfour, a prominent planter who served from 1794 to 1799, had no legal training but some zeal for the office. His successors were all professional barristers. Below these two courts were the Justices of the Peace, in each parish and in Scarborough and Plymouth. In 1810 there were altogether thirty-four Justices, nine in Scarborough and from two to five in each parish.[79] With the exception of the Chief Justice nearly all the judicial officers were also planters, the only clear exception being the medical doctor George Cumine who was appointed Assistant Justice in 1804. All were men whose principal occupations lay elsewhere and all lacked legal training. As for the Justices of the Peace, many held office as councillors or were members of the Assembly. When Sir William Young assumed the governorship in 1807 he found that no new justices had been appointed for several years during which time several vacancies had arisen.[80] Young made a number of new appointments, but when he died in 1815 there was again a shortage of justices at least in the windward part of the island.[81]

NORTH FRONT OF GOVERNMENT HOUSE, MOUNT WILLIAM.
Drawing by Sir William Young
Reprinted from Sir William Young, "An essay on the commercial and political importance of the Island of Tobago . . ." (1812). Manuscript.

If such a legal apparatus seems excessive for so small a community we have only to notice Sir William Young's report in 1808 that there were then 120 actions listed for hearing in the superior courts. He explained that the defendants in such civil actions used the legal process to gain time, appealing from the Court of Common Pleas to the Court of Chancery seeking a stay in proceedings, and some would even go on to appeal to the "Lords in Council".[82] Tobago in 1810 had enough legal work to support four professional barristers, one of whom also worked as Attorney General, at such a level that none would contemplate judicial work.[83] One in 1807 was assessed for income tax purposes as earning £2,000 sterling a year from his practice, which the governor regarded as quite enough to induce some able young barrister to go out from London to replace him when he left the island.[84]

The public officials

The final element in the structure of public business in Tobago, the public officials, may be grouped into three categories according to the manner of their appointment. First, there the direct Crown appointments, the major offices of Governor, Chief Justice and Attorney General, the first two with very substantial salaries, and the last paid by fees, a post conferring prestige rather than material reward. The Governor's salary was fixed in 1794 at £2,000 currency, raised to £3,300 currency in 1800;[85] the Chief Justice received £500 sterling in 1796, raised to £1,000 in 1805. Secondly, there were three appointments made in Britain by King's Patent but discharged by deputies, commonly on behalf of absentees: the Island Secretary, who doubled as Clerk of the Council, Provost Marshall and Naval Officer. All three earned substantial fees, the Provost Marshall exceeding £1,400 sterling per annum, and the Secretary also received the modest salary of £300 sterling. The major part of the fees, however, was paid over by the deputy to his principal in return for the privilege of holding the job. The prestigious position of Secretary was nominally held by Lord Harvey from 1793 to 1797 and thereafter by Charles Grenville, but neither of these gentlemen ever came near the island.[86] Thirdly, there were a number of appointments made by the governor, notably the Island Treasurer, who sometimes operated by deputy, up to three Assistant Justices, the Rector of Scarborough, the Harbour Master (first appointed in 1803) the Adjutant of Militia and his personal secretary. He also appointed two Assistant Justices with the consent of the Council, the most valuable of these posts being those of Treasurer and Rector, worth £350 and £375 respectively. The Rector also earned fees.

There were also three appointments of importance made directly by government departments in Britain responsible for the equivalent services in the colony: the Collector and Comptroller of Customs, who both had access to very substantial fees, were appointed by the imperial Treasury and the Postmaster by the Postmaster General in London.[87] The list of officials was completed with half a dozen minor functionaries.

In a number of cases the same official would hold two or three offices, though the odium commonly attracted by the phrase "pluralism in office" is hardly relevant when one considers, for instance, the nature and extent of the duties of the Naval Officer, Ordinance Storekeeper and Powder Officer, all held by one man.[88] Even in wartime, all were essentially part time functions.

Pluralism, however, occasionally achieved spectacular proportions, which is hardly surprising in view of the small size of the white population. Perhaps it began with the fact that assemblymen and councillors were also Justices of the Peace while many public offices in so small a colony could not be expected to take up a man's full time. Certainly in 1808 Elphinstone Piggott was not only Chief Justice and Justice of the Peace, but also a member of Council, Treasurer, and Master and Examiner in Chancery.[89] But then he served a community of about 800 free persons.

The most striking feature of the structure of these official positions is the limited extent to which the Assembly exercised any direct influence over appointments. It seems indeed that the only appointments which the Assembly controlled were those of the Colonial Agent in London and its own clerk, and even the latter was at least in theory subject to the ratification of the governor.[90] This is a striking contrast to the wide powers of appointment exercised by the Assembly in so many other West Indian colonies by the end of the eighteenth century, which saw the Assembly of Barbados, for instance, appointing even the island's Treasurer. The low profile of the Tobago Assembly in these matters can only be explained by its relative youthfulness and the discontinuity which had marked its history under British and French sovereignty, coupled perhaps with its deliberate avoidance for much of this period of any confrontation with the governor or with the authority of the Secretary of State.[91]

The fact that public officials were so largely paid by fees rather than by salary seems to have given rise to some dissatisfaction with their activities. Governor Young believed that the better rewarded officials at least understated their earnings from fees. The Island Secretary and Provost Marshall, both of them deputies, were likely to find their principals demanding a larger share of their fees if these were accurately reported. Both acknowledged receiving over £1,000 sterling a year in fees but were commonly believed to be getting much more.[92] The same was true of the Collector of Customs and lesser customs officers also did very well, even the clerk admitting to £400. Fees were sometimes but not always fixed by legislation, and it is not surprising that in 1807 the Assembly asked the governor to require all public officers, but especially those in the customs, to provide a return of the scales of their fees.[93] In 1809 the House passed a bill to establish an approved docket of fees, but the Council held it up until it lapsed with the adjournment.[94] By 1815, however, fees were fixed by the Council.[95]

The Restoration of British Laws in 1794

One of the first tasks facing the new British administration was to clarify the status of the pre-existing laws of Tobago, both French and English. Governor Ricketts would have preferred to scrutinize and legislate upon each existing Act, and produce a comprehensive code of laws; but such an exercise was hardly practicable at first, and experience seems to have shown that it was not really necessary. Under pressure from a planter community driven by anxiety as to the future, he assented in April 1794 to two Acts passed in February "for reviving and putting in force certain Acts of former legislatures of this Island".[96] These were Acts passed by the old island legislature before 1783 and supposed by some to have expired on the cession to France.[97]

These proceedings stemmed from the belief, recited in the preamble to the Act, that the conquest of 1793 had likewise terminated the life of laws passed by former legislatures. This was probably a misplaced concept, and it has been argued forcefully that the colonists' "birthright" as Englishmen entitled them to return to the status of the earlier period of English rule and not be treated as a conquered people. It is also noteworthy that in 1803 no one suggested that recapture had once more nullified old legislation.[98] Among the Acts thus revived were the slave laws of 1768 and 1775 which provided the basis of the slave system, an Act to regulate the administration of the public finances, an Act establishing magistrates' courts, and an Act providing for the establishment of roads.[99] In the same month a Militia Act was passed as well as an Act for the proper maintenance of the public roads.[100] Also passed were a Trespass Act providing for the impounding of straying animals, a Liquor Licensing Act, an Act for the recovery of petty debts and an Act appointing John Petrie to be the island's Agent in Britain where he was already resident. By July 1794 after several months of "close attention to public business" President Robley believed that there was little urgent legislation left to be passed.[101]

The Public Finances

The public finances had formed one of the first subjects to be addressed by the new Assembly following the British reconquest. In April 1794 the Finance Act passed in the previous year under French sovereignty, which was considered to have lapsed with the change of sovereign, was revived as a means of sustaining the revenue.[102] In December came the first of the series of annual Finance Acts on which the British colonial administration relied for its general expenses.[103] Before that, however, the urgent problem of putting the island in a more effective state of defence against a possible French counterattack had led to the first of several measures designed to raise additional funds especially in aid of the war. From the outset the Assembly acknowledged an obligation to provide "respectable support" for the government as regards both normal finance and special wartime expenditure,[104] and in both contexts the business of the 1790s was smoothed by the first flash of enthusiasm for the newly restored British allegiance and the Assembly's desire to appear co-operative and pliant to a Secretary of State who might well be able eventually to determine whether or not Tobago remained British.

The funding of local defence

In May 1794 the need to raise funds in aid of the war and the parallel need to ensure an adequate supply of gunpowder in the island combined to produce a gunpowder tax or rather a tax in gunpowder. All vessels arriving from Britain, Ireland or Africa were required to pay one pound of gunpowder for every registered ton on entering the harbour. Only in cases of "evident necessity" could the governor allow payment in cash rather than in kind.[105] The proceeds were allocated, rather vaguely, for "public uses", but in 1795 the proceeds of any cash payments were specifically allocated in aid of the expenses occasioned by declarations of martial law.[106] The gunpowder duty was renewed from time to time to remain in force until the end of the war[107] and in 1803 sloops and schooners trading regularly with neighbouring British islands were also required to pay it, but only once each year.[108]

In the early stages of the war this law was no doubt a useful means of obtaining gunpowder, which was at first in short supply.[109] But as the years passed without further hostilities stocks rose to an embarrassing level. In 1800 half the levy was required to be paid in cash at 2s. 6d. per pound of gunpowder.[110] Stocks continued to rise, however, as high as 6,000 lb.[111] and in 1809 payment in cash rather than kind was encouraged in the case of neutral ships[112] while the sale of surplus gunpowder was authorized.¹¹³ From the point of view of the Tobago Assembly this tax had the special advantage of falling almost exclusively on persons resident elsewhere.

Indeed, the need for funds for the special purpose of improving the defence arrangements served to direct the attention of the legislature specifically to the large number of absentee planters. In the words of the Preamble of an Act passed in 1795 to raise money "for the protection and security of the island", in such a time of danger

> it becomes highly necessary for those who have acquired Property in the Colonies and who wish to preserve it to repair without loss of time to the Place where their Property and the Danger are to Coalesce with those already on the Spot and by their United Abilities, Influence and Exertions endeavour to Avert the impending Storm which threatens to Overwhelm the Whole West India Colonies.

In fact, a large proportion of Tobago's planters remained abroad at a time when the country was in "in Hourly Dread of foreign Attack or Internal Convulsions". Therefore, continued the Preamble:

> such migrations of so many Principal Proprietors not only in a very Great Degree lessen the General Security of the Colony, but also cause the Burden, fatigue and Expense of protection to fall more heavy on those who Remain in the Country, And . . . it is just and Equitable that such Proprietors as do not Contribute towards the tranquillity of the Colony by that Influence which their Presence would naturally have nor by their Personal Exertions towards the Security and Protection of the Island should Contribute thereto out of their Estates which are Protected by the Resident Proprietors.¹¹⁴

The legislature therefore, in looking to meet defence expenditure, sought to devise taxes which would fall specially on the absentees. In 1795 a poll tax of 8s. 3d. each on the slaves of absentee proprietors was imposed. Later in the year a further tax of 4s. on each slave was imposed, this time on all proprietors, to finance the Black Corps which it agreed to raise for local defence.¹¹⁵ These Acts were confirmed and the taxes collected, but once the obvious crisis of 1795 had passed the British Government took a strong line against any attempt to place special taxes on absentees. Indeed it is striking that an imperial government largely committed since the loss of its American colonies to a policy of non-interference in matters relating to colonial domestic taxation intervened on a number of occasions to prevent what it saw as discrimination against one group of colonists. Of course, the absentees had much influence in Britain and this the local legislature proved unable to subdue. On the other hand, the legislature hardly fought vigorously. In this as in other matters it was for a long time unwilling to challenge a government whose protection and indeed sovereignty it sought to win.

In 1805 Tobago tried to revive the 1795 Act imposing a special tax of 8s. 3d. on the slaves of absentee proprietors,[116] but this was duly disallowed.[117] A similar attempt by the Assembly in 1807 was obstructed by the Council.[118] The preamble to this bill recited a further reason for penalizing the absentees. Not only did they fail to shoulder their fair share of local burdens, but "the Public duties fall heavy on the few and much difficulty is thrown in the way of the Legislative Business of the Government for want of persons duly qualified to form the same".[119] It is clear that in singling out the absentees for special taxation the Assembly was motivated to some extent by resentment at the way in which they gained from the efforts of others, such as its own members. It was a resentment which was probably increasing as the number of absentees tended to rise and was perhaps informed by the Assembly's own difficulties in finding a quorum.

However, a special additional poll tax on all slaves, on the lines of that of 1795, was again imposed for security purposes in 1802, this time of 3s. a head, to pay for the suppression of the slave conspiracy the preceding Christmas and the consequent tightening of internal defences.[120] In 1805 the sum of £6,000 was voted to purchase and fit out a vessel to protect the colony's coasting trade, raised by imposing an additional tax of 7s. on each slave.[121] With these exceptions, all related to extraordinary circumstances, the cost of defending Tobago was provided as part of the government's normal expenditure in the annual finance Act.

General taxation, 1794 - 1805

So far as the general expenditure of the colony was concerned, some money was raised through Acts effective for periods of years, usually three at a time, which imposed charges as a means of achieving non-financial ends. The most obvious case is the Tippling Acts, which required licences to sell liquor or to keep taverns or public billiard tables. Such licenses cost £50 currency in 1797,[122] but the liquor license fee was raised to £200 in 1804.[123] The Tippling Acts, however, never produced much revenue. More important were the Deficiency Acts, introduced for the first time in 1797[124] and intended to sustain the white population. They provided for fines of £100 currency on plantation owners for every man short of their legal quota of white employees, reduced to £50 in 1804.[125] Evidence of the extent to which the employers met these quotas or the amount produced by the fines is sparse; but in 1807 the proceeds were estimated at £3,500 currency, in 1809 at £1,200.[126] However, since bounties on the importation of white immigrants in excess of the plantation's legal requirements were a first charge on these revenues, the sums which may have been used for general purposes are unknown.

More important to an understanding of the Assembly's attitude to taxation than the special defence taxes or the incidental proceeds of Acts representing social policy were the annual finance Acts which provided the government of the colony with its normal revenue. The first of the series of annual Acts "to raise a sum of money for discharging the public debts of the colony" was passed in December 1794.[127] The titles of these Acts varied slightly from time to time but they form what is really a single series of revenue or finance Acts providing for the raising of revenue and appropriating sums to specific purposes often in considerable detail. The Act of December 1794, in effect the Finance Act of 1795, sought to raise some £10,000 from duties on produce, a poll tax on slaves and license fees. The 4½ per cent export duty applied in many other British islands was not imposed in Tobago after 1793.[128]

For 1795 the produce duties were fixed at 1s. 2d. currency on every 100 lb. of sugar, 11s. on every puncheon of rum and 4s. on every 100 lb. of cotton, while the poll tax was settled at 15s. on each slave between the ages of 14 and 60 who was not "attached" to a sugar or cotton estate. In addition, tax at the rate of 5 per cent was charged on the earnings of all attached estate slaves employed as task gangs or otherwise hired out. License fees were fixed at £20 on each public billiard table or each rum shop. There was also an urban property tax of 2½ per cent of the rental value of all urban buildings. This range of taxes was well devised to draw revenue from both those resident on plantations and the urban population, since townspeople usually owned "unattached" slaves.

The Act of 1795, covering the year ending in October 1796 and passed at a time when defence preparations were being pressed, substantially raised nearly all these taxes.[129] The duties on produce were more than doubled, to 3s. on sugar, 24s. 6d. on rum and 13s. 9d. on cotton, while a new duty of 15s. 9d. per 110 gallons was imposed on molasses. The poll tax on "unattached" slaves was raised to 33s., the urban property tax to 5 per cent. The tax on the earnings of hired estate slaves remained at 5 per cent. At the same time penalties for failure to make the returns required for the assessment of taxes were increased from a simple fine of £100 to £100 for each three months' delay. These taxes were additional to the poll taxes on slaves imposed in aid of defence preparations and the cost of the Black Corps in the same year. Altogether these taxes constituted a considerable burden which had clearly been assumed by the colonists in the expectation that since much of the expenditure concerned was of a capital nature related to the needs of a new administration, or specifically to meet the needs of the war, it was destined to be temporary. A similar situation again prevailed when Britain recovered the island in 1803.

To some extent this expectation proved true. The war apart, the anticipated expenditure of 1795/6, a total of £40,297, included much work on Government House, which absorbed £3,984 and also on the courthouse and jail. The Black Corps alone cost £17,147 between its foundation in 1795 and the end of 1796.[130] All of this was extraordinary expenditure which did not recur, at least in the same measure, in 1796/7, a year which apparently opened with a credit balance in the Treasurer's hands. Accordingly the taxes approved for 1796/7 were much reduced. Produce taxes came down to 6d. on sugar, little more than 15 per cent of the previous year's level, while those on other products were reduced by about two-thirds as were the other taxes generally.

So drastic a reduction in the level of taxation was destined to prove an illusion however, and 1797 saw levels almost double, the tax on sugar rising by 200 per cent to 1s. 6d.[131] Rapid fluctuation of the rates of taxation, however, was to remain a general feature of life in Tobago as each finance Act sought to meet the actual and immediately anticipated liabilities of its time, rather than to achieve a settled pattern of income and expenditure. Indeed there was no attempt to provide systematically in advance of estimated expenditure. The legislature from time to time would authorize activities and once a year would seek to provide money to discharge accumulated liabilities and provide a small balance, as was indeed usual in other colonies. The periods for which taxation was approved were not constant and the dates on which taxes were payable varied, which also militated against constant levels. Public works were an extremely variable item, £1,324 in 1806, £9,831 in 1807, £3,249 in 1808. Extraordinary expenditure, like the £3,774 spent to purchase a building for the legislature in 1798, could drive the total budget to special heights. So could the slave conspiracy which added about £4,000 to the needs of 1802. In 1803, £3,657 was provided as a first instalment on the purchase, repair and furnishing of Government House at Mount William which cost £6,044 in all.

The largest sum covered in a single year during the period of the war was the £40,247 provided in 1796. This however included £17,147 for the Black Corps, which continued to constitute a special burden until it was disbanded in 1801, and like the £25,442 voted in 1803 and the £21,235 of 1807 was otherwise inflated by extraordinary expenses or special public works. Without such special expenses, the funds provided for the government varied from £10,998 in 1814 to £14,377 in 1802. Of these sums government salaries, including that of the governor himself, accounted for £7,780 in 1802[132] and £8,868 in 1814. Public works in a normal year were very modest, £1,018 and £539 respectively in 1802 and 1814.

To raise the money which it agreed to grant, the Assembly juggled the levels of the poll tax on "unattached" slaves and the taxes on the earnings of hired slaves and task gangs and those on produce and on urban property which we have already noticed. Taxes were commonly paid in two instalments, in May/June and August/September, but in 1795 three were allowed while in 1796, a year of very low taxes, a single payment was ordained. In 1798 the tax on slaves employed in task gangs or for hire was altered from a percentage of their earnings to the same flat rate poll tax as on "unattached" slaves.[133] The low point of taxation on produce appears to have been reached in 1801 with 3d. on every 100 lb. of sugar, 2s. 6d. on each puncheon of rum, 2s. on molasses, 1s. on coffee and 3d. on every 100 lb. of cotton. The poll tax on "unattached" slaves and on "attached" slaves working in task gangs or hired out, however, was fixed at 10s., owners of three slaves or fewer being exempt, and the property tax at 3 per cent.[134] This represents a considerable shift away from taxes on estate production and towards a greater burden on other forms of wealth or property, more especially on urban property; but the produce taxes were soon rising again while the others remained fairly steady.[135]

Nevertheless, the French interregnum of 1802-03 came at a time when the planters seemed to be using their control of the Assembly to shift the burden of taxation away from the estates and towards the population of the two towns. During the interregnum, Tobago carried on very much as had been the case during the preceding decade. No legislation was passed save money bills for official salaries and public works and a donation of £4,000 sterling to Mme du Sahuquet, widow of the first French governor,[136] who appears to have set out to conciliate the wealthier planters and apparently hoped to encourage new settlers by offering small grants of land.[137]

In 1803, with the British once more in control but following a period of some confusion and uncertainty and the departure of some of the white population, came a simple poll tax of 30s. on *all* slaves as the sole impost.[138] Considering that there can have been few free families of any economic consequence who did not own slaves, this was perhaps a less arbitrary form of taxation than it might appear; but we shall see that it was soon to be urged that the number of slaves on an estate or in a household was not a good index of the slaveowner's income or even of his wealth. The productivity of slaves could vary very widely.

Soon, however, the Assembly's trend towards shifting the burden of taxation in the direction of those outside the resident planter interest was to continue further and to produce major political and constitutional issues. In September 1804, for the first time since the conquest of 1793, the Council sought to amend a money bill when the Assembly tried to impose two new taxes, an income tax of 5 per cent on "attorneys, agents and factors" and a special poll tax of 8s. 3d. on slaves owned by absentees, in addition to the poll tax, fixed at 9s.

The concept of an income tax was a very old one but it had commonly been set aside as impractical because of the administrative difficulties which were anticipated. It was only in 1799 that the world's first effective income tax had been levied, in Britain as an avowedly temporary expedient to raise money in aid of the war. This had been troublesome to operate and had yielded less than expected, and had been discontinued when peace came in 1802. It had however been sufficiently successful for the government to reimpose it as soon as the war was resumed in 1803. The Tobago Assembly therefore was seeking to adopt a form of taxation which, whatever its theoretical advantages, had only recently been shown to be practicable in Britain itself, and that with difficulty.[139]

In part, the Council seems to have been disturbed by the mere novelty of the income tax. It is noteworthy that when the tax was first introduced in Britain, only five years earlier, it was attacked as inquisitorial and excessively onerous on the moneyed classes, and had been accepted essentially as the price of the war. In 1805 taxpayers in the British Empire were not yet used to the idea of having their incomes scrutinized and taxed. In Tobago the fact that, suspicion of novelty apart, only three occupation groups who did not pay taxes on estate slaves were singled out for the income tax, lawyers, doctors and merchants, for example, being ignored, gave the Council a strong ground on which to protest that "all taxes ought to be laid equally on every person according to the Quantity he possesses of the Public Stock or in proportion to the Revenue he receives in the Colony".[140] As for the absentees, among whom members of the Council were very likely to become numbered sooner or later, it was noticed that they would already pay the 9s. tax to be imposed on all slaves. The Council found it "oppressive" and "unjust" to subject one class of proprietors to what was in a sense double taxation "on account of their not residing in the Colony" and pointed out that absentees would have to pay income tax in Britain. When the Assembly failed to respond to representations from the Council, the latter amended the bill.[141]

Control of taxation, 1805 -1815: Council vs. Assembly

Throughout the British West Indian colonies it was already generally accepted that the Council had only limited standing in relation to money bills. While it could certainly reject them outright, at the cost of chaos in public business, in most islands the Council's power to amend such bills had in practice been lost in the middle of the eighteenth century.[142] In Tobago it is fair to regard the question as less than wholly clear. In its earlier incarnation the Council had failed in an attempt to amend the money bill of 1780 when the Assembly stood firm,[143] but a single precedent did not necessarily make constitutional law. Nevertheless, as recently as April 1804 the Council itself had observed that "all money matters... have been long regarded as being more immediately under the management and direction of [the Assembly]." Yet the Council certainly claimed the right to make representations related to finance.[144] The Assembly, however, was incensed by its representations and more so by its amendments. The Assembly refused to accept the amendments and finally in January 1805 the Council rejected the delayed Money Bill of 1804.[145]

This was the beginning of a prolonged argument between the Houses which went beyond the details of proposed taxes to include the powers of the Council in relation to taxation. It may be that the political crisis was the more acute, and more difficult to resolve because there was no governor in office. The President of the Council, administering the government, was naturally too closely identified with one of the combatants to be able to do much towards an amicable resolution of the problem. James Campbell was a man of long experience in public affairs and appears to have been an able and level-headed man and the same applies to John Balfour, who followed him after a brief tenure by Robert Mitchell; but both had been members of Council for very many years.

The immediate problem of determining the revenue for the year 1804-05 was resolved by dividing the Assembly's proposals into two bills. The controversial taxes were removed from the normal money bill which was left to provide only for a poll tax on all slaves, now fixed at 12s. 6d. instead of the 9s. first proposed, in an effort to make up for the loss of the taxes which were dropped; and was accordingly passed on 26 February 1805.[146] Meanwhile, the income tax was dropped and the tax on the slaves of absentees was made the subject of a separate bill which was provided with a suspending clause so that it would not come into operation until the imperial government approved it.[147] This bill was passed in the Council by a majority, probably by four votes to two, on 16 February 1805.[148] It was sent to the Secretary of State with a statement of protest from the two dissentients and eventually disallowed as an unfair discrimination against absentees.

This episode was the product of a growing desire in the Assembly to shift the burden of taxation combined with the fact that some members of Council could see themselves being personally affected to their own

own detriment, while a ground of principle in the form of the need for equitable taxation was readily available as the basis for a fight, a ground sufficiently strong to override any apprehension or uncertainty as to the precise position of the Council in relation to money bills. The fight was the more significant because, although relations between the two Houses of the legislature had been less cordial of late, it came after a long period of close co-operation between them during which the evidence, or rather the lack of anything to the contrary, suggests that politics in Tobago were a very tame affair over which the planting interest and the few whites outside it were commonly in agreement. What may be called the politics of sovereignty had ever since 1793 united them in a great effort to appear as models of good behaviour deserving of permanent incorporation into the British Empire.[149] The destruction of those hopes in 1802 had certainly produced disillusion and in 1804 the internal politics of Tobago had, despite the return of the British, become less dominated by the concern for sovereignty now that the best efforts of the white population had proved unavailing. It was as if the assemblymen, having seen their best efforts fail, threw discretion to the winds and allowed narrow instincts of more immediate importance to their own *amour propre* to thrust the longer term political calculations into the shadows.

In 1806 a slightly reduced poll tax of 12s. on all slaves was approved without trouble[150] and before the island's finances again became a major political issue Tobago had a new, and able governor who was able to bring a new mind to the problem. Sir William Young began his governorship in April 1807 with unusual advantages. Since his family had long held property in the island he was regarded as having a common interest with the planters who showed every sign of goodwill towards him. Young for his part started not only with goodwill but by making effort. He set out to read through his predecessor's correspondence and to consult with the assemblymen so as to brief himself on the island's problems and soon determined to go on a familiarization tour.[151]

In dealing with the Assembly he at once struck a sympathetic note. In his first address to the legislature he spoke of his own strong interest in the "loyal and important Colony" that was Tobago and indicated that since the estates were busy with the crop and the councillors and assemblymen anxious to get back to them, he would raise very little business. Indeed he observed that the colony had done its recent business so well as to "leave me on the part of Government rather to make acknowledgements than to suggest recommendations".[152] Throughout his governorship he dealt with the Assembly from a low-keyed position, never seeking to push too much business upon it, always operating as if what he wanted done was patently desirable in the colony's own interest.

From the outset the Assembly and Council responded with promises of co-operation. When the legislature decided to provide him with a salary, £3,300 currency a year for one year only rather than for the duration of his office, contrary to all recent precedent, Young declined to fight the issue. While recognizing that a matter of principle was involved, he wrote to Lord Castlereagh, "I would not lightly risk the vantage-ground I thus stood on [his favourable reception] by a scuffle for inferior interests, when I had great and important concerns in view, & to the Attainment of which my Station appeared most favourable".[153] The matter was simply not important enough to be worth undermining the legislature's otherwise co-operative spirit. Young was rewarded a year later when his salary was voted for the duration of his office with a single dissentient.[154] Relationships with the governor remained cordial through the next seven years, even on occasions when the two Houses crossed each other[155] and he might have been caught in the crossfire and isolated.

In August 1807 when the Assembly passed the money bill for 1807-08, conflict over the finances broke out again. In addition to the now usual poll tax on all slaves, set at 16s. 6d., this bill introduced a tax of 33s. on each Scarborough householder who owned more than one slave in respect of use of the public water supply. However, this provoked no outcry. Again conflict centred upon a proposal to introduce an income tax in addition to the more usual taxes. This time the Assembly was careful not to single out a few occupations and proposed a tax of 5 per cent on "all white and free people" concerned in "any employment, commerce, occupation or business" whose gross annual income exceeded £300 currency, or 2½ per cent if with a smaller annual income they paid property taxes amounting to £20 currency.[156] This definition was so interpreted as to exclude plantation owners, property owning not being seen as an "occupation".

In part the Council was again disturbed by the novel principle of the income tax and it was upset, too, by the fact that the text of the bill referred to it as a "poll tax" which clearly it was not. The bill was also open to sundry other criticisms regarding its drafting. The Council therefore asked that the income tax should be made the subject of a separate bill which could be more carefully drafted. The Assembly unanimously refused to accept any amendments and responded in a manner which the Council found "extremely disrespectful". The Council then withdrew from the fray and accepted the bill, a major confrontation being averted essentially by its own moderation and good sense.[157] Thus did income tax come to Tobago. While no evidence has been found of any intervention by the governor, Young's subsequent efforts to resolve political problems involving the Council and Assembly make it more than probable that he worked actively and effectively against a confrontation.

The Council had been careful to indicate that it did not dispute the Assembly's long standing right to propose money bills: it merely insisted on the right to propose amendments in respect of "manifest errors and omissions". In the end it gave way before the pressure of the obvious damage to the public credit and hardship to individual creditors which would have followed if there had been prolonged delay in providing money for public liabilities, especially so late in the year.[158] The governor gave his assent for the same reasons, though he agreed that the bill was very badly drafted.[159]

The two legislative bodies, however, remained at odds. When the Council sent a message to the Assembly in October 1807 protesting at the latter's handling of the recent issue the Assembly passed a motion "that no notice be taken of the said message the same being contrary to the privileges of this house" and ordered that the Council's message be not entered in its minutes.[160] It is clear that the Assembly felt that the Council had no constitutional right to amend a money bill or even to suggest alterations, and the impression grows that the Assembly's desire to exclude the Council from any say in the determination of the arrangements for raising revenue had become a more important issue than the difference of view over kinds of taxes. The Council for its part took the view that its members were as deeply interested in the welfare of the colony as the assemblymen and this entitled their views to consideration even on a money bill.

It is noteworthy that this was a strong, if small, Council. John Balfour was one of the earliest colonists, a former Chief Justice and President of the Council; while George Morrison, George Cumine and C.A. Franklyn were all men of long experience.[161] While constitutional and financial deadlock had been avoided and the difference of view over the introduction of an income tax had been narrowed the power of the Council in financial matters remained loosely defined even while it conceded a general primacy to the Assembly. It would not abandon the right to propose amendments and with new taxes being canvassed this could still prove to be a most difficult issue. In the light of the fact that the Assemblies in other colonies had very generally won the point in earlier decades, and of the precedent set in Tobago itself in 1780, the Tobago Assembly was not likely to yield. The Council for its part cannot have failed to recognize that if it succeeded in setting a precedent by forcing an amendment, its constitutional standing would be immensely strengthened. Much would therefore depend on how the Council reacted to future bills.

The Money Bill of 1808 was passed without undue difficulty, but not before the parties had rehearsed their positions on the constitutional point.[162] In the light of subsequent events it seems possible that the Council's determination may have been strengthened by the appearance now of some difference of view within the Assembly over the income tax, still the major specific bone of contention although the modest flat rate of 2½ per cent where incomes exceeded £200 currency was now proposed. In the Assembly's debate, William Brasnell had emerged as an articulate supporter of the superior merits of an additional poll tax over the income tax while arguing that the effect of the different forms of taxation was so much the result of individual circumstances that no pattern of taxation could please everybody.[163] This could hardly be gainsaid, and the members of the Council must have thought that they would find more sympathy now than in the previous year.

With an eye to the future the Council sent the Assembly when passing the 1808 bill a series of "observations" exploring different methods of raising revenue.[164] It argued that the poll tax, which hitherto it had preferred to any income tax, "falls very unequal on the Proprietors in this island" because the number of slaves on an estate was an index of invested capital rather than of income falling as it did exclusively on one class of persons, and a tax on capital was "manifestly unjust". Such a tax on capital was in no way related to ability to pay as judged by income from production, rent, salary or commercial or professional profit.[165] The Council now put the case for relying rather on taxes on produce as had been done before 1803, noted that produce taxes would be closer to the income tax in effect than the poll tax, and implied that they should therefore find favour with the Assembly. The practice of fixing the poll tax on attached and unattached slaves at the same level was also criticized on the ground that the income generated by unattached slaves was otherwise tapped by the income tax paid by their owners.[166]

The Council thus seemed to be shifting its position on taxation: opposition to the income tax was giving way to an objection to the poll tax on slaves, the very method of taxation it had previously preferred. It might almost seem that the Council was seeking some new subject of conflict now that the dispute over the income tax was receding. But there was of course much truth in the arguments now advanced against the poll tax and the new concern seems to be related to the appearance of John Robley at the Council Board at the end of 1807. On the matter of taxation, Robley had strong views which were certainly influenced by its potential effect on his own pocket as one of Tobago's larger land and slave owners. There is no evidence that he was much concerned with constitutional niceties.

The Assembly, still fixated about its power over money bills, and perhaps seeing the thin end of a constitutional wedge, deemed the Council's resolutions an unwarranted interference, but it appears to have given their content serious thought. The Money Bill of 1809 abandoned the income tax much as the Council would have wished and set the poll tax at two levels, 6s. on attached and 33s. on unattached slaves, whose owners were by and large those who had been relieved of the income tax.[167] It seemed as if the problem of patterns of taxation had been laid to rest.

The Assembly's touchiness about its status and powers had not, however. Passing the new bill, it simultaneously adopted a resolution refusing to accept any communication from the Council except it be in writing, closing the door to informal messages through its clerk. This does not seem to have been a complete innovation, but it represents a pitch of tension in the relations between Assembly and Council which was not laid to rest until this resolution was rescinded in January 1813.[168]

Meanwhile the Council was to return to the arguments in favour of taxes on produce and to challenge the Assembly's control of taxation with unprecedented vigour. It is fair to say that the initiative lay consistently with the Council a majority of which followed the lead of John Robley, while the Assembly remained very sensitive over what it saw as the Council's interference in financial matters. The Council insisted on putting forward proposals which were no doubt based on practical considerations and Robley's vigorous personality, but which consistently ignored the Assembly's view of the constitutional proprieties.

Robley's views are not fully articulated in the surviving records until in 1811 he recorded a protest in the Council against the money bill of that year,[169] but it is appropriate to set them out fully at this point. He argued that the poll tax was too indiscriminate in that it took no account of the actual and very variable value of the slaves on an estate or the amount of produce or of profit which it produced. Apart from being a tax on capital which did not consider levels of income, the poll tax affected only one form of capital while income other than that derived from the ownership of slaves was not taxed at all. This said Robley in 1811 "is contrary to that Justice and strict impartiality which ought to prevail and is manifestly injurious to the planting Interest of this Colony". He added that it was also "contrary to the practice of the most enlightened nations of Europe and contrary to those legitimate principles of taxation laid down by the ablest writers on political Economy [who] declare that the subjects of every estate ought to contribute towards the support of Government as nearly as possible in proportion to their respective abilities . . ."

Robley pointed out that the value of a gang of slaves depended on its demographic composition and noted that the proportion of ineffectives could vary from 15 per cent to 40 per cent of the total. The return on the capital represented by slaves he estimated as varying from below 1 per cent to 12 per cent, yet the poll tax was levied at a flat rate. Further, the productivity of a gang depended on the fertility of the particular piece of land it worked. Poor soil meant more slaves to the acre and so more tax as well as more capital investment without raising productivity. Moreover less productive estates were already likely to be the more heavily burdened by mortgages and other encumbrances. It is easy to accept his view that the poll tax on slaves did not operate fairly.

In support of his view that revenue would be more fairly raised by taxes on produce, Robley noted that this was not a new idea: it had once, in the 1790s, been required that every manager or proprietor make an annual return upon oath of the amount produced on his estate so that its taxability could be accurately ascertained.

Finally, Robley argued that the poll tax would also discourage the increase of the slave population which had in the past been officially encouraged and he noted that in 1797 the legislature had urged that bounties be paid on "surplus" slaves at an annual census of the estates. His own wish was to substitute for the poll tax small taxes on produce and on commercial and professional incomes and import duties on "luxuries", by which Young indicated that Robley meant "Articles of convenience & of subsistence". In Young's view such articles were in practice all of British origin so that to tax them would be contrary to imperial law;[170] but the introduction of import duties was never a serious issue.

In July 1810 the Assembly proposed in its next money bill to perpetuate the 1809 pattern of taxation with slightly different rates. The Council proposed amendments; the Assembly rejected them; and the Council stood its ground insisting that taxes on produce or income were preferable to the poll tax. The Council urged that the planting interest was already overburdened and in decline and deserved special assistance rather than special taxation.[171] In the absence of clear-cut constitutional provisions its majority ignored the conventions which in the Assembly's view had come to surround money bills.

So far as the Assembly was concerned, the constitutional dispute had now finally taken precedence over rival views on taxation. The Assembly refused to address the merit of its bill, merely responding that "they do not recognize the authority of [Council] . . . to alter or amend any Money Bill or to suggest to this House any mode of taxation whatsoever".[172] The Houses adjourned without a settlement and when they met again in special session in the following month the Assembly passed the same bill once more and the deadlock persisted in spite of an appeal from Governor Young that the legislature should avoid the trouble which would arise from damaging the public credit by withholding the supplies and preventing payment of government bills and salaries.[173] Young again adjourned the legislature. On both occasions the majority in a depleted Council was three votes to two, but the majority included the experienced President John Balfour as well as John Robley and William Hamilton with George Cumine and Attorney General George Glanville inclined to accept the Assembly's bill.[174] Both Balfour and Cumine were survivors of the earlier struggle over the income tax in 1807 but, significantly, Balfour was a large planter with interests similar to Robley's while Cumine was not; and Glanville was to gain a considerable reputation as a respected Attorney General. The division was largely based on the self interest of large planters and one may speculate that their estates showed low productivity in relation to their large slave populations.

The Assembly stood adamantly on its supposed privileges, but it sought to avert or at least minimize damage to the government's credit by authorizing the Treasurer to pay bills drawn by the governor out of the previous year's unspent balance and any additional sums he might receive despite the failure to vote the supplies.[175] The police were accorded first claim on this small resource.[176] This, however, did not prevent the governor, when he prorogued the legislature to October, from animadverting on "the disgraceful and dangerous condition in which this Island will be placed" by this further delay in providing the supplies.[177]

Sir William Young did not take sides publicly, but it is clear that he was in favour of the Assembly's bill. In fact his report to the Secretary of State laid the blame largely on John Robley, who was able to take advantage of the simultaneous absence from the colony of seven of the twelve members of the Council to attempt to shift the burden of taxation to the personal advantage of himself and his friends and it is noteworthy that the only dissentient vote in the sixteen member Assembly in August came from Robley's brother George. Young blamed Robley the more because it was always perfectly clear that the Assembly would never agree to the taxes which he wished to substitute for the poll tax. Obstructing the Money Bill therefore could not in the circumstances be a fruitful exercise. As Young put it "no other scheme of finance [had] been matured".[178] It is to be noted, however, that Young's relations with Robley, who held a very large mortgage on his estates, were not good. He was not an impartial judge of the latter's conduct, self-interested as that was on this occasion.[179]

During this second recess the governor set about preparing the ground for resolving the conflict. The obvious way to do this was to increase the number of councillors so that the three trouble makers would be outvoted. The governor of course had power to fill up to seven seats in the light of absences and could thus have forced the bill through in August when the Assembly passed it for the second time. At first Young had imagined that he could persuade at least one of the dissident councillors to change his vote, but the August session had shown that he could not.[180] Immediately after the prorogation therefore, very conscious that delay would further damage the financial stability of the colony, he appointed two members of the Assembly to be members of the Council: William Brasnell, the Speaker, and a planter described by Young in 1811 as being "our principal Merchant in general Trade",[181] and who, having played a leading part in the Assembly's assertion in 1807 that the Council had no status in relation to money bills seemed certain to support the current one;[182] and Archibald Napier, another substantial planter. The resultant vacancies in the Assembly were then filled by by-elections and early in September Young called a special session to consider a third Money Bill.

By this time there were no funds in the Treasury and Young opened the session with a long exhortation to both Houses on the importance of restoring the credit of the colony.[183] When the Assembly sent up a third bill it found Messrs. Robley, Hamilton and Balfour unrepentant, but the new Councillors provided a majority in favour of the Bill on 6 September.[184] This Act provided a poll tax of 14s. 6d. on attached slaves and 24s. 9d. on unattached slaves together with a tax of 33s. on all householders in Scarborough in respect of their use of the public water cistern,[185] which was exactly what had been proposed in July.

The story of the Money Bill of 1810 was however repeated in the following year despite the fact that it reduced the poll tax from 14s. 6d. to 9s. on attached slaves and from 24s. 9d. to 13s. 6d. on unattached slaves and was described by the governor as "this reduced and moderate Tax Bill". Once more Robley's brother was the only dissentient in the Assembly while he himself headed what Young described as a "Cabal of three" in the Council, where the absence of one important member in England enabled Robley to muster a majority in July 1811.[186] When the Assembly passed the Bill for the second time in August John Balfour, hitherto one of Robley's weightiest supporters, at last changed sides and the Council agreed to it.[187] By this time the government was wholly without resources[188] and Balfour was President of the Council; and while there is no evidence of his reasons for voting for a bill he had earlier so vigorously opposed, it is probable that they were related to the deterioration of the public credit. The repeated delays over money bills had produced a new reluctance on the part of tradesmen and others to tender for public contracts[189] and it would have been difficult for the President of the Council to continue to figure as a principal cause of such disruption of government business.

In the years that followed the Council did not again venture to obstruct the money bill, but the argument over the relative merits of poll and produce taxes persisted. George Robley was succeeded by Charles Wightman as the sole assemblyman to oppose the poll tax[190] and in the Council John Balfour, still President, recorded a protest against it in 1813,[191] but the bills of 1812-15 all passed without trouble though the tax on attached slaves moved from 9s. in 1811 to 7s. 6d. in 1812 and was back at 14s. in 1814.[192] So far as the constitutional powers of Council and Assembly were concerned, it is noteworthy that Governor Young never overtly supported the Assembly's view that the Council had no power to amend money bills, or even to make less formal proposals concerning taxation, though as the island's administrative head he would have everything to gain if such a position could have been sustained. One is forced to the conclusion that in this series of disputes with the Council between 1804 and 1811 the Assembly, whatever the merits of the specific issues involved, was seeking to establish a constitutional privilege rather than to vindicate an existing one. That the Assembly of Tobago had not yet established such a constitutional privilege beyond dispute is not surprising in the light of its recent origin (1768) and the interruption of its maturation during the twelve years after 1781.

In attempting to enhance its constitutional position, especially in relation to finance, the Tobago Assembly cannot but have been influenced by the example of the better established Assemblies of neighbouring colonies. Foremost among these is likely to have been the Assembly of Barbados, an island with which Tobago had close and constant contact and whose Council had long been deprived of the power to amend money bills. But the same was true of Antigua, St Kitts and Nevis; and a similar trend was evident in Grenada and St Vincent, with which Tobago also maintained close contact. In seeking to broaden its effective constitutional powers the Tobago Assembly was merely following a widespread and hallowed example. After its repeated successes between 1804 and 1811 it must have felt fairly confident that the Council would not challenge it again for some time, at least over finance.

Two special salaries

In the years between 1793 and 1815 there were two other financial issues which occupied the special attention of the legislature from time to time, both being settled without particular dispute, namely the salaries of the governor and Chief Justice. The governor's salary was quickly fixed in 1794 at £2,000 currency,[193] but there was some feeling among governors that this was inadequate and when Governor Master was appointed in 1800 he was accorded a salary of £3,300 currency.[194] In 1807 Sir William Young was allowed the same sum though there was on general grounds some reluctance to accept a commitment to maintain that level throughout his tenure of office, which was the usual procedure. That commitment was not in fact accepted until 1808.[195]

The salary of the Chief Justice, the other public officer with an unusually large salary, was also the subject of generally easy agreement. When in 1796 a number of legal problems arose which appeared to require decision by professional lawyers the legislature agreed to offer £500 sterling if a barrister of ten years' standing could be found for the post[196] and suggested that the imperial Treasury offer to top this up with another £500.[197] But the Secretary of State was satisfied with the untrained John Balfour who remained in office until 1799, to be succeeded by another non-barrister, Robert Paterson, so that the appointment of a professional lawyer did not become a practical issue until 1804 when Paterson died.[198] At that time the Council and Assembly easily agreed that Elphinstone Piggott, a former Attorney General then serving in St Vincent, should be offered £1,500 currency.[199] In 1805 the salary of the Chief Justice was raised to £2,000 currency.[200]

The control of expenditure

All public accounts were required to be audited by the legislature's Committee of Public Accounts from the first passage of a money bill in April 1794. Payments were at first authorized by the governor though the public moneys were kept by a Treasurer[201] but soon the Council came to be involved in the procedure. By 1795, once an item had been included in a money bill specifically acknowledging and providing for payment of an account presented to the government for goods or services rendered, payment fell to be made on a warrant from the governor to be signed before the Council, and his signature of such warrants was from time to time recorded in the minutes of the Council.[202]

It is clear that as time passed the Tobago legislature, like those in other British West Indian islands, sought to play a larger part in the disbursement of government moneys and to scrutinize public accounts more closely. In 1807 the Public Accounts Committee complained that the accounts presented to it were often excessively informal, sometimes being written on scraps of paper and frequently without proper certification that the work had been performed or the materials supplied, while contracts were sometimes awarded by persons having no proper authority. The two Houses agreed that in future they would insist on accounts being presented in proper form and being duly certified.[203] It was by now the practice that before the governor in Council could authorize a payment, the legislature had to agree that the service concerned had been properly performed and pass the bill for payment. In 1810 the two Houses agreed that no account for public works or materials should be passed unless proper performance was specifically certified following the award of a contract by public advertisement and tender.[204] It is clear, however, that contracts continued to be awarded without advertisement on occasion and this practice was the subject of a protest by several artisans in 1813.[205]

Yet the need for legislature approval of the account could sometimes lead to difficulty, as in the cases of James Cumming and James Torry, overseers engaged in the construction of a new road from King's Bay to Trois Rivieres Hill in 1811 whose bills for £39 and £25.10s.0d. respectively were accepted by the Assembly but held up by queries in Council.[206] Such queries were not unusual. Again, in 1814 John Nisbitt presented a bill for £401 for building bridges in Scarborough to find that the authority of the waywardens who hired him was disputed. The Assembly proposed to pay him only £250, the Council nothing, but three months later the whole claim was accepted with the rider that in future the authority of waywardens would not suffice in such cases.[207]

The payments which had to be authorized in Council, each of which had to be separately entered in legislative and executive records were infinitely variable in size and importance. At one extreme were trivial payments like the £1.16s.0d. paid to Delaford Estate in 1814, probably for providing slave labour for public purposes.[208] More orthodox bills identified in the records of the legislature include £180 paid to John Robley in 1808 for slave labour on a gun battery;[209] £85.8s.0d. to one Cleghorn, a mason, in 1813 for work on the roads;[210] and £42.19s.0d. to J.M. Collier & Co. for supplying provisions to a militia party in 1812.[211]

Relations with the Imperial Government

We have noted that the relationship between Council and Assembly after 1793 appears to have been uniformly harmonious until a difference of opinion over taxation developed following the recovery of Tobago by Britain in 1803. The relationship between the Assembly and the governor was also generally amicable. Here more particularly the special desire of the white population to cultivate the good opinion of the British government, represented of course by the governor, is of great importance.

It is fair to say that on its inception in 1794 the Assembly set out to do whatever the Secretary of State wished, and so to work easily with the governor. At least three members of the Council, John Balfour, Thomas Wilson and John Franklyn, believed at this period that actions which might be construed as interference with the Crown's prerogative or opposition to imperial wishes so soon after being rescued from the French were most impolitic.[212] The Assembly's co-operation with the governor and the Secretary of State was unruffled until 1797 when, as we shall see, Governor De Lancey trod on its toes.

Thus, as we have seen, money was willingly provided for defence and for administrative expenses, and addresses passing between the administration and the assembly sounded like the utterances of a mutual admiration society. The Secretary of State was suitably appreciative of the colony's co-operation and praised its "wisdom and liberality".[213]

The recruitment of black troops

The story of Britain's attempt to recruit black troops in the West Indies in the 1790s has been fully and clearly told by Roger Buckley. However, the episode forms an important part of the political history of Tobago and its details as they affect that island show that its attitude to the proposal was, initially at least, far from typical. Once more there appears a readiness, even a determination, to co-operate with imperial desires which was most unusual among British colonists and which was almost certainly related to the desire to ensure that, when peace would come to be negotiated, Tobago would remain British.

The factors which led Britain to adopt the novel policy of recruiting black troops may be summarized as an inadequate supply of white recruits combined with a belief that blacks enjoyed a measure of immunity from yellow fever which made them specially suitable for use in the Caribbean, where white troops died from it in thousands. The principle of employing black and coloured men, both slave and free, both in combatant and non-combatant roles in the British Army was well established by the end of the American War of Independence in 1783,[214] and with the start of the French war in 1793 regiments or corps of black "rangers"[215] under the jurisdiction of the local Assemblies were raised in several islands as they sought to improve their preparedness against attack. The rangers were usually slaves deemed to be sufficiently trustworthy to bear arms. Further, the army found need for corps of slave labourers to assist it on an unprecedented scale,[216] and instructions were sent out in September 1793 that the colonies should provide each garrison company with four labourers.[217]

In Tobago the question of raising black combatant troops appears to have been first raised in May 1795 when the governor proposed that a "Black Corps" should be raised for local defence, apparently without knowing what the imperial attitude would be.[218] The Council and Assembly agreed on 15 May to the creation of a corps of 150 men, with seven white officers, and an appropriate Act was passed in June[219] requiring all proprietors with between 50 and 150 slaves to provide one able bodied male for the purpose and one more for each additional 100 slaves. The proprietors were to be paid 12 per cent per annum of the value of the slaves so long as they continued to serve. The blacks were to be armed with muskets, bayonets and cutlasses and privates would also have felling axes. The headquarters of the corps were to be at Great Courland Point.[220] Apart from its obvious value as a defence measure, this step may reasonably be seen as an effort to raise Tobago's profile in imperial eyes, and the governor was careful to point out that the new corps would lessen the island's dependence on regular troops.[221]

Meanwhile, the imperial government had decided independently to raise a large force of blacks to be attached to the regular army. The making of this decision has been narrated in detail elsewhere.[222] Authority to raise two black regiments was sent to General Sir John Vaughan on 17 April 1795, and the number of regiments to be raised was soon increased to eight.

The general reaction to the new recruiting policy was strongly adverse among both local whites in the West Indies and absentee proprietors. Not only did the planters fear for the loyalty of black troops in the circumstances of 1795; they also saw in the proposal for black regulars, rather than mere rangers, an increase in the strength of imperial at the expense of colonial sovereignty, for the regulars would be an imperial force. Moreover, the mere size of the projected force, nearly 9,000 men, was enough to ensure strong colonial opposition. The force was to be raised from the slave population, any deficiency being made up by recruiting free coloureds, and the West Indian planters in general were strongly opposed to an expedient which they believed might suggest to the slaves a new weakness on the part of their masters and which would also lead to the eventual release into their society of thousands of blacks with military training.[223]

The First and Second West India Regiments were given substance by drafting into them the Black Carolina Corps, raised during the American War, and corps of rangers already raised in the conquered French islands which provided the majority of those enlisted[224] and in some British islands, notably St Vincent. Altogether several hundred men were thus provided. The Seventh West India Regiment enlisted 395 men at Barbados in December 1795, about which we shall read more shortly. But otherwise recruiting was a total failure.

There were several reasons for this. In the early months there were a number of delays in communication and some internal opposition to the scheme within the British army from senior officers involved in recruiting. But the fundamental factor was the opposition of the planter interest, for reasons which included the capital cost of providing slaves and potential loss of labour as well as the social and political implications of arming blacks on a large and regular scale.[225] It has been pointed out that there was some inconsistency in such opposition coming from people who had already agreed to the formation of corps of black rangers,[226] but such corps were a temporary expedient under local control, while the proposals for black regular regiments also raised a new problem of scale, and many planters felt that by providing the rangers they had already done their part.

In this context the reaction of the Tobago planters to the suggestion that they contribute recruits for the new black regiments is very significant. Portland's circular despatch of 18 April 1795 authorizing Vaughan to raise such troops reached Tobago late in June. The first reaction of the Council was favourable, while the Assembly promised to consider the matter and the governor envisaged no difficulty in meeting Vaughan's wishes.[227] The despatch had reached Tobago without details of how or on what terms the new regiments were to be raised, so that the governor was unable at first to put any precise proposition to the Assembly. Meanwhile news arrived that the Assemblies of some of the neighbouring islands had refused to provide recruits, and in August Governor Lindsay wrote that the mood of Tobago's planters had changed. He was convinced that in June a specific proposal would have been accepted, but he now anticipated strong opposition. The Tobago Assembly was not only affected by the attitude of its neighbours; it believed that in providing a corps of rangers of 150 men towards the island's own defence the planters of Tobago had already done their fair share towards the war effort.[228] It is noteworthy that for the first three or four months of their existence, precisely the period of uncertainty as to the raising of the new regiments, the rangers were being rationed at the expense of the public funds of Tobago[229] and the Assembly provided quarters for them.[230] When in mid-August the details arrived and Tobago was asked to provide 100 men for each of three Regiments, the Assembly refused.[231]

In taking this decision, however, the Tobago Council and Assembly in joint consultation were at pains to avoid conveying an impression of non co-operation, and vigorously protested "their attachment to the king and

and zeal for the general interests of the British Empire". They reminded the governor of their efforts in relation to the rangers and proclaimed themselves "ready and willing to co-operate with our sister colonies in every measure which may tend to our general safety and protection".[232] The governor believed that if other colonies agreed to provide black troops Tobago would change its position. For the present, however, assemblymen were driven by "the dread of the consequences of having a black garrison after the peace".[233]

The planters of Tobago were no less reluctant to contemplate a regular force of black troops in the West Indies than their fellows elsewhere, yet their response to the proposal, though negative, was distinctly muted. They were conscious of their island's status as a colony newly recaptured by Britain and of the risk of being returned to France, and wished to do nothing which might make the British government think ill of them. Therefore, in effect, they tried to temporize, and their governor sought to explain what was at stake for them. First of all, he claimed the slaves would be reluctant to enlist, and to compel them to do so, thereby abandoning their homes, families and "property" for overseas posts, would excite disaffection and worse among them. Moreover, the proposed quota of 400 men would constitute a capital loss of £32,000 to the colony and further deprive it of labour worth £8,000 a year, at a time when most Tobago estates were heavily in debt. Governor Lindsay believed that Tobago would more readily provide £32,000 than 400 men.[234]

The Assembly's attitude however was to be further tested. In October 1795 it learnt that the Quartermaster General, Colonel Knox, had been ordered to use his discretion as to the terms to be offered in raising "a considerable Corps of Negroes" to be collected at Barbados, to "act as Pioneers and perform other duties of Labour and Fatigue". It was proposed to hire the men required through a levy on each estate, and to compensate the proprietors for any who did not return. They were not to be confused with the proposed regular regiments of black troops and an assurance was given that they would not "form of themselves separate and distinct Garrisons" but would be used only in a support role.[235] By 30 October Council and Assembly had passed an Act authorizing the recruitment of such pioneers.[236] Such a corps was not of course the answer to the imperial demand for black troops, and there were many other colonies willing to make similar provision. Two years later a pioneer corps of 3,500 slaves was raised in the Leeward and Windward Islands.[237] But Tobago's contribution, described as being "picked men'",[238] was another earnest of her desire to co-operate.

An unknown number of these pioneer recruits left Tobago in December 1795. Part of the group was captured by the French but others reached

Barbados. Three months later the Quartermaster General suggested that the pioneers "might if circumstances should require it be armed and disciplined", and used as combatant troops; and the Council and Assembly of Tobago agreed that "in order to set a laudable example to the other islands and evince their loyalty and zeal" Tobago would not object to the arming of the pioneers she had provided.[239] As it appears that the 395 blacks enlisted in the Seventh West India Regiment at Barbados were recruited in Tobago in December 1795,[240] it seems that the attempt to convert pioneers into combatant troops was a success.

In October 1796, in view of the small success of the plan to recruit West India Regiments, Sir Ralph Abercromby was authorized to recruit by purchasing slaves at a price not exceeding £70 sterling a head, employing recruiting contractors.[241] Most of the island Assemblies set out to thwart this scheme and in the end it had small success, but again Tobago's response was exceptional.[242] In February 1797 the Assembly agreed to provide 160 blacks for the Seventh West India Regiment "on terms of purchase" and was prepared to provide more if they were needed.[243] The necessary Act was passed in August: 1 per cent of slaves, or 1 in 60 if the result was a fraction, were to be drafted and the appraised value paid for each, any excess over the £70 being paid by the colony.[244] Altogether the record of the Council and Assembly of Tobago in the matter of raising black troops is one of unusual co-operation in imperial plans at some cost to the planter community which they represented, partly in lost capital but more particularly in lost labour at a time when they were striving to increase the production of their estates. This is to say nothing of their fears for the long term consequences of creating large bodies of armed blacks.

It remains only to notice the later history of the Tobago Rangers. They soon came to be highly regarded, and in 1796 the Quartermaster General at Barbados conceived the idea that they might be drafted into the West India Regiment, as so many other local ranger corps eventually were.[245] But the rangers were sometimes employed in local construction works,[246] and the planters looked forward to their eventual return to the estates and were reluctant to see them leave the island. However, Abercromby revived this proposal in the following year when preparing to attack Puerto Rico and authorized to recruit by purchase. That was too much for the legislature, which had just agreed to provide 160 blacks for the Seventh West India Regiment, but they did agree that the Tobago Rangers might at their own option be employed with the British forces in the campaign then in progress, provided that they were returned to Tobago when it ended and that the proprietors were compensated for all men lost.[247] Abercromby accepted these conditions,[248] and the Rangers served in the attack on Puerto Rico.[249]

In July 1797 the Commander in Chief decided that as the several island garrisons were up to strength the Crown's responsibility for defence could be regarded as having been discharged, and the cost of rationing the ranger corps, which it had assumed during the defence crisis of 1795, could safely be thrown back on the colonies. The Tobago legislature responded by suggesting that the rangers should be allowed to return to their respective estates, which were anxious to have their labour, subject to recall in case of need, and to the men being assembled once every three months so as to keep them in training.[250] When the peace negotiations then in progress broke down, and the need for troops again became pressing the Rangers were reassembled in January 1798.[251] In May 1799, however, the legislature agreed that the behaviour of the rangers "has lately been so notoriously disorderly that the good of the public requires that they should be ordered to their respective plantations on furlough",[252] and the men were sent back to their estates in June.[253] No doubt four years of service, and participation in an overseas campaign, had had an effect on the thinking and behaviour of these slave soldiers which their owners did not approve and which military training was not enough to efface. The social consequences of military service for blacks, albeit on a temporary basis, were possibly already visible. In January 1800, the Act authorizing the raising of a corps of black troops was duly repealed. The state of the war presented a very different picture from the dangers of May 1795 when it had been passed and as the Ranger officers declared "there is no apparent probability their services will be again called for".[254]

In September 1801 Brigadier Hugh Lyle Carmichael, commanding the garrison, proposed to revive the black corps, conceiving of a body of 140 men "to be attached to the Troops in Garrison whose duties they would considerably ease". Carmichael had had long experience of black troops as commander of the Second West India Regiment and thought highly of them. He was particularly mindful of their superior resistance to tropical diseases at a time when the garrison was hard hit by them and generally small in numbers. But this time the Assembly would not co-operate and the Secretary of State did not support the brigadier.[255] The planters, of course, had never been really comfortable with the idea of black troops and while the Assembly might defer to the wishes of the Secretary of State it had no awe of the garrison commander.

Governor De Lancey

The smooth co-operation between the colony and imperial authority was not unbroken, however. Apart from the small differences of view already noticed, in the later part of 1797 the normally close relationship between the Assembly and the governor was disrupted. Becoming more confident and more conscious of its privileges, and perhaps observing its fellows in better established colonies, the Assembly began to assert itself in opposition to Governor De Lancey who seems to have had an unreal view of the deference due to his wishes. First, it refused to provide the governor with copies of its journals, which left him in ignorance of authoritative information concerning their business, on the specious ground that this would be a breach of their freedom of debate. Then they refused to meet the Governor and Council at Government House to complete the business of the session, with the result that he met them in their own chamber. When De Lancey indicated that this was an act of grace which they had no right to expect of him they sent an obdurate reply.[256]

The Assembly next attempted to force the governor to open the new session in a place selected by itself. He responded by refusing to open it in person and sending a written message instead, requesting the House to proceed to business.[257] This deterioration of relationships was at least partly due to a quarrel between De Lancey and the officers of the militia, some of whom were also members of the Assembly.[258] John Balfour, Chief Justice and the senior militia officer, on one occasion told the governor that the militia were not bound to obey him except in time of martial law,[259] and generally led an opposition faction, while De Lancey does not seem to have fully understood the complex nature of his powers as governor or the need to handle the Assembly with consistent delicacy.[260] When the Assembly took its case to the Secretary of State, he censured the governor in forthright terms. Portland wrote "On the face of the Proceedings . . . there is in your conduct, to say nothing more of it, a manifest departure from that prudence and propriety which are so absolutely essential to the Performance of the King's Service in the situation you hold". He urged De Lancey to take steps to restore the accustomed harmony between executive and legislature. Perhaps Portland had no right to expect such skills of De Lancey, and the episode savours more of personality clashes than of any serious issue.

The crisis passed with De Lancey, however, and fifteen months later, when Governor Master assumed office in 1800, governor and Assembly were again exchanging polite platitudes.[261] Soon afterwards another delicate phase of peace negotiations with France began and the Assembly once more was on its best behaviour, seeking to ensure that Britain would retain so model a colony. No other episode of open dispute between governor and assembly has been identified in the years down to 1815 while mutually complimentary addresses appear constantly.

The question of future allegiance

The most important political question in Tobago during this period was not the internal question of the government's finances, nor the question of black troops, but rather the matter of the island's future allegiance, which was of course outside its control. It was not just a question of sentiment, for the whole question of further white settlement and the development both of the production of export crops and of the much needed mercantile facilities depended on whether or not Tobago would remain British. The possibility that peace might bring the restoration of French rule was a nightmare for the white population. In October 1795 Prime Minister William Pitt began to aim at an early peace, and in March 1796 he began to make overtures accordingly.[262] There was much apprehension in Tobago and among its absentee community in England over the probable fate of the colony, and in November 1796, when formal peace talks began, a memorial was presented to Portland from the "Planters, Merchants and Others interested in the Island of Tobago" against its being returned to France.[263] The immediate problem was solved by the breakdown of negotiations on 19 December.[264] Meanwhile, Tobago would continue to do everything possible to ingratiate itself with the British Government. Indeed, writing in 1805, John Campbell, who became President of the Council on Robley's death and was then acting as governor, recalled that Tobago had done everything possible to show gratitude to Great Britain after 1793, and this had "induced easy hope" that the island would remain British. It is clear that the currying of imperial favour was quite deliberately done.[265] In January 1797 both Council and Assembly resolved that they would ratify any arrangements which the island's Agent in Britain might make with the British Government in order to ensure that it remained British.[266]

But 1797 was a year of disasters for Britain's European allies and soon Austria was so badly in need of peace that Britain was ready to give up even Tobago if that were necessary to buy her respite.[267] As it was, Austria made a separate peace in April 1797 and Britain became more reluctant to give up her various conquests.[268] The King himself had always wanted to retain Tobago since "it is settled wholly by British planters", and gave it priority over Britain's other West Indian conquests, and when General Abercromby visited in June, fresh from his conquest of neighbouring Trinidad, the occasion was seized for a vigorous protestation of affection for and loyalty to Britain.[269] Pressure for peace recovered force, and in June 1797 the British Government sent Lord Malmesbury to Lille to reopen negotiations.

As Malmesbury pursued his business Tobago again became increasingly anxious, and sought support from all quarters. As one planter-merchant member of the Assembly wrote from Tobago, "the late proposals made by Lord Malmesbury makes me & every Person who has Property here very uneasy as we never can think of Remaining in the Island if it ever becomes French again".[270] The planters were determined that they could not face another transfer to France: leaving Tobago would involve them in heavy loss[271] and they could not face the thought of a return to French rule. When General Cuyler succeeded Abercromby as Commander in Chief the Council and Assembly sent him an address of welcome, recalling their gratitude to him for their deliverance from French rule, and "the steady line of conduct" which Tobago had thereafter pursued.[272] The legislature then resolved to send him a piece of plate to the value of 100 guineas "as proof of remembrance".[273] And then Malmesbury's negotiations broke down on 17 September[274] and they were granted another, longer respite.

In 1800 unofficial soundings about peace came from a French envoy sent to London to discuss the exchange of prisoners,[275] and soon the same defensive process was again set in motion. In October 1800 Council and Assembly agreed to draw up a joint memorial to the King stating the case for Britain's retaining Tobago and imploring him to stand firm.[276] Meanwhile a slender hint of approbation went out from Portland, who wrote that Tobago's handling of its finances had been such as "to render the island truly respectable and to increase its weight and consequence in the scale of His Majesty's West India Possessions".[277] When the memorial arrived he replied that His Majesty would pay it "all possible attention".[278] The memorial made the obvious point that most of the Tobago planters were British subjects who had been induced to settle there by the assurances held out to them by the Royal Proclamation of 1764, which had offered them the full protection enjoyed by other British subjects. It recalled how, at the cost of considerable capital, "they boldly attacked the formidable forest . . . and with a courage perseverance and rapidity seldom equalled but never surpassed converted the desert land of Tobago into fruitful fields."[279] Then came the French conquest and, it was alleged, the value of their property had fallen by 25 or 30 per cent at once and more subsequently, so that the produce of their estates had barely sufficed to pay the interest on the mortgages with which they had been established.

However, since 1793 they had been happily restored to British rule and had gone to great lengths to co-operate with Britain, so that French retribution would be very probable if the island changed hands; many of the planters, if not all, would be obliged to leave the island, abandon their properties, and look to British generosity for some compensation. The memorialists claimed that as Tobago had become both more populous and more wealthy since 1793 it was now of considerable commercial importance to Britain, its produce paying over £200,000 a year in duties to the British Crown on goods imported to Britain, to say nothing of the value of its trade. It was responsible for the employment of about fifty British merchant ships.

The island also had great strategic importance since its windward position was such that, in enemy hands, it could be a most convenient base for a descent by sailing ships on Grenada, Trinidad or St Vincent. Being beyond the general reach of hurricanes it was a good place for a naval station. As Sir William Young wrote subsequently, "the Hurricane whirls round Tobago; but affects it not".[280] It was also well placed as a centre for trade with the mainland region around the River Orinoco.

Finally, it was argued that if Tobago was restored to France its planters' British creditors would have difficulty getting their money back from planters who had passed under French rule.

This memorial was a comprehensive statement of the case for Tobago's retention by Britain, though some of its points could have been elaborated. A year later, for instance, the Garrison Commander, Brigadier Carmichael, provided a fuller if somewhat exaggerated statement of the island's strategic importance in which he argued that if Tobago were left to the enemy the retention of Trinidad would be of little avail because people would be reluctant to develop an island so vulnerable to attack from its neighbour, and that Tobago's own terrain, with many commanding heights, made it easily defensible -- a good theory despite the failure of successive garrisons to put it to good use.[281] This memorial, and the whole process of striving to persuade the British Crown and Government that Tobago should remain British after 1793, more than nullifies Eric Williams' view, expressed with special reference to 1793 and 1802, that "the changes of flags did not bother the planters to any great extent; they became part of the routine of existence".[282]

We have seen that in principle both King and Cabinet supported the retention of Tobago, though the need to retain a free hand in any negotiations, and the fact that Napoleon was known to bargain hard, made it obviously unlikely that Britain would give any clear commitment. Both countries desired at least a breathing space after eight years of war. On 14 April 1801 Britain put forward proposals in which she aimed to retain Tobago, as well as Trinidad, Demerara, Berbice, Martinique and some other conquests outside the West Indies. At first Napoleon had held out against any cession of territory by France.[283] In September, he dug his heels in over Tobago and threatened to resume the war.[284] Under this pressure Britain agreed to give up all her conquests except Ceylon and Trinidad.

Tobago, however, was not entirely forgotten. In signing the preliminary treaty Britain relied on an oral understanding between the French negotiator, M. Otto, and the Prime Minister and Foreign Secretary, that when a definitive treaty came to be negotiated France would be willing to cede Tobago to cancel out the expenses Britain had incurred in maintaining French and Dutch prisoners.[285] With the British public in particular calling for peace, it was a treaty in the making of which haste and secrecy had played major roles, and the vagueness of the understanding about Tobago was to prove a major error on Britain's part.[286] At Amiens, where the negotiations took place, the French took their stand on the letter of the preliminary treaty and Otto's informal promises in London were dismissed as unauthorized and invalid.[287] Further, in a private preliminary interview with Cornwallis, Napoleon himself maintained that "he could be induced by no pecuniary consideration to give up the island of Tobago, which he looked upon as a dishonourable act; that if we wished for it because it was an English island he would exchange it for a French island, several of which were in our possession, or for any establishment or territory in India."[288] Cornwallis replied that he did not think his masters would agree to any such exchange.

As time passed the advantage swung to "the negotiator who was the more independent of his country's desire for peace".[289] The First Consul was now proving obdurate, and the French insisted on setting aside Otto's informal commitments.[290] On 2 January 1802 the British Prime Minister, Addington, wrote that the "only prudent course" was to fall back on the terms of the preliminary treaty.[291] Giving up Tobago was the necessary price of concluding a treaty at all, for as Napoleon wrote on 7 March with perhaps more confidence than he really felt, "if peace is not made immediately I do not fear war".[292] The Treaty of Amiens was finally signed on 25 March 1802 and Tobago went back to France, to the acute chagrin of King George III[293] who had only been persuaded to assent to the preliminary treaty by Otto's undertaking that a formula would be found for the cession of Tobago.[294]

In Tobago the planters had not generally put much faith in the possibility of amending the terms of the preliminary treaty. As soon as those terms were known some began to plan to remove from the island as much of their wealth as possible before the final treaty took effect. Within a few weeks, Joseph Robley's London-based nephew, John, was ready to despatch two merchant ships, which he happened to own, with cargoes of stores, and to take off a last consignment of sugar from the

Robley estates.[295] Joseph Robley, again in charge of the government, lamented that "the dutiful and loyal inhabitants of Tobago are once again devoted to destruction".[296] Others began planning to emigrate either to other colonies or back to Britain.[297]

In seeking to explain why Napoleon should have been so adamant over the fate of Tobago, the first point which springs to mind is the simple converse of the strategic arguments which the planters used in their memorial to the Crown. If Tobago was so located that in French hands it would be a threat to several British colonies, then its possession was likely to make as much sense to France as to Britain. Joseph Robley wrote when he heard of the preliminary terms that Tobago was "a point from which Trinidad may be easily invaded at any time in twelve hours", and again "certain it is . . . Great Britain can never retain Trinidad in the event of another War if Tobago be given up to France".[298] Neither Grenada nor St Vincent would be much safer.

Napoleon himself seems not to have contemplated for a moment that Tobago might be ceded, except for some other territory. Indeed he seems to have had a rather grandiose plan for sending the future Marshal Bernadotte to be Captain General of a territory including not only Guadeloupe, Martinique and St Lucia, but also Louisiana and perhaps a recovered St Domingue.[299] Since 1795 France had been pressing Spain to hand back Louisiana, ceded to her by France in 1763, and on 7 October 1800 an extraordinary secret bargain was concluded for the return of Louisiana in exchange for the cession of Tuscany to the son of the King of Spain. Napoleon had a vision of a revived French Empire in the Western Hemisphere which would include a recovered St Domingue as well as the other territories mentioned. In November 1801, taking advantage of the lull in fighting provided by the long negotiations, he despatched General Leclerc to recover control of St Domingue. In such an atmosphere he was not disposed to envisage the cession of Tobago, and only the renewal of war with Britain and the eventual disaster which befell his expedition to St Domingue later in the year caused the dream to be abandoned.

The colonists in Tobago, however, would have been much gratified to know that as soon as it was clear that peace would not endure, on 16 May 1803, the Secretary of State wrote a secret despatch to General Grinfield, the British Commander in Chief in the Eastern Caribbean, based in Barbados, with instructions that he should prepare for a renewal of the war with France by preparing to seize Martinique, St Lucia and Tobago, or such of them as his force was equal to, as soon as war should be resumed. Moreover,

From the amount of British property connected with the island of Tobago, the uniform attachment of the Inhabitants to His Majesty's Person, and the importance of its position, I am induced to recommend that the earliest steps should be taken for placing it under the King's Government; and the more so, as from the Accounts I have received of the State of the French Force upon the Island, there is no probability of any Serious Resistance.[300]

Clearly the representations so consistently made by the colonists since 1803 had been effective.

Grinfield, meanwhile, had himself reached the conclusion that Tobago should receive early attention on any renewal of war, as should St Lucia, and began to prepare his forces. On 17 June he received final orders and two days later his army embarked. Tobago was surrendered to his superior forces on 1 July.

The recapture of Tobago in 1803 was of course greeted by the almost exclusively British free population with relief and exultation, but for that very reason it brought a renewal of the campaign, so prominent in the 1790s, for the confirmation of British sovereignty as permanent. In September 1803 a "Humble Memorial" was presented to the King by the Council and Assembly which began by reciting their "Veneration and Attachment" to the British Constitution, then noted their indescribable "Despondency and Despair" at having been returned to "Foreign Dominion" in 1802, and ended with a stirring plea that "they may never again be made a Sacrifice and be compelled to submit to a Foreign Yoke".[301] Soon they were pointing out that the uncertainty as to the island's future was once more hindering its commerce since British merchants were reluctant to establish business there and no others were practicable.[302] In 1806 rumours of a possible attempt at peace negotiations prompted urgent representations to the Secretary of State both from John Balfour, acting governor,[303] and from the colony's London agent, John Robley supported by a group of Tobago's absentee proprietors.[304]

Subsequently protestations of loyalty to Britain and apprehension about a possible restoration to France continued to appear. In December 1813, with peace once more seemingly in sight, there came a full scale memorial from the legislature to the Secretary of State which recapitulated at length all the familiar arguments about the value of Tobago to Britain and the loyalty of "a Colony in all senses British" in pleading against any restoration to France.[305] In London a committee of planters, mortgagees and merchants with interests in Tobago sought an interview with Lord Bathurst to present a further memorial.[306] When a few months later peace was signed and the fate of Tobago once more put on the negotiating table, the colonists were in a state of the most acute anxiety. As the Assembly put it: "Having never understood, or been able to calculate, upon what principle this Island . . . has been upon any occasion separated from its ancient Government, we cannot measure the intention of that Government, even in the present crisis."[307] Governor Young, however, professed optimism, on what basis he did not say, and the uncertainty was lifted on 12 July when the terms of the peace arrived.[308] The two Houses appointed a joint committee to prepare an address of gratitude to the Prince Regent[309] and the legislature voted the sum of 500 guineas to the island's Agent, Sir Arthur Piggott, in recognition of his exertions in aid of Britain's retention of Tobago.[310]

At once preparations for a celebration were set on foot. The ensuing birthday of the Prince Regent, 12 August, was selected as a day of "Joy and Festival".[311] A joint committee proposed a "General Holliday for the Negroes", but the Assembly chose instead to hold a public dinner and that "a Ball be given to the Ladies of the Colony", and the Council consented.[312] A sum of £1,641 currency was provided for the celebration.[313]

While the years 1793 to 1815 were a period in which the Assembly, representing the views of the planters, was thus determinedly co-operative towards imperial authority, the principal issues on which it restrained its own wishes for the sake of such co-operation occurred before 1798, and after the restoration of 1802 the same measure of fervour is less often evident. It may be that the occasion arose less often, but it is possible to sense a change of atmosphere which was probably due to the Assembly's chagrin at being returned to French rule. In 1803 for instance, amid the rejoicing at the return of the British came a note of reproof hardly conceivable in the mid 1790s.

> The Inhabitants of Tobago never for a moment suffered themselves to imagine they should be again separated from the Blessings of the British Government. It is impossible therefore to describe to their August Sovereign the Despondency and Despair which took possession of every Individual when they learnt they were again abandoned by the Country which gave them Birth; turned over to the Government of their Ancient Oppressors, without the smallest Indemnification or any Stipulation made to ameliorate their lot . . .[314]

The general loyalty and devotion to Britain which the document expressed has already been noted, but the impression remains that the white inhabitants were less enthusiastically devoted after 1803 than before. Or perhaps they were merely tired and disillusioned after the great exertions of the previous decade.

Throughout the twenty-two years since 1793 when the Assembly, at one with the whole white population, had been concerned, often preoccupied, with the question of the island's political future, that issue had been one on which the Assembly had been in agreement with the Council and with successive governors. No governor would wish to see the colony over which he presided pass to a foreign power. If there was another issue on which governor and Assembly were similarly close together it must be the question of what steps should be taken to avert the shortages of food and other merchandise which were so common during these years principally because the normal flow of imported goods was interrupted by the war or because such goods were available only from sources prescribed by the imperial laws of trade. There was room here for conflict: Assemblies never considered that imperial laws of trade deserved respect if they caused a shortage of goods; governors, sworn to uphold those laws, differed in their judgement of the circumstances which might justify their dispensation, and were sometimes not on the Assembly's side. But even then the governor was able to fall back on the defence that he had no option. The attitudes of governors and assemblies to the commercial system will be considered in another chapter.

THE SLAVE SYSTEM

The Slave Law in the Later 18th Century

When Britain recaptured Tobago in 1793 the slaves were controlled under an Act passed in 1774-5 and confirmed by the Crown in 1776, "An Act for the Good Order and Government of Slaves..."[1] It was an Act typical of the slave laws of the British West Indian colonies at the time of its passing, predicated upon the racist assumptions which had come to dominate British West Indian society in the later eighteenth century. This is at once clear from its preamble, which declares that "the Slaves brought into this Island... are of a barbarous, wild and Savage Nature and such as Renders them wholly unfit to be Governed by the Laws of Great Britain ..." The preamble further demonstrates that the whole code, both the clauses aimed at controlling the slaves and those which sought to guarantee them a minimum livelihood, was directed at securing the prosperity of the white masters. The slave had no intrinsic rights, being essentially a piece of property, a chattel. The Act was passed

> for the preserving of Good Order and Government among them as may Restrain the Disorders and Disturbances to which they are naturally Prone and inclined and for keeping them under due Subordination and Subjection as well as for Granting them such allowances and Encouragements as may be fit and needfull for their Support, to the end that the Lives and Fortunes of His Majesty's Subjects in this Island may be Preserved and Secured and the Peace and Happiness of the Colony thereby established.

The principles upon which the British West Indian slave laws were based were of course developed long before Tobago came to be settled

The Slave System / 95

BETSY'S HOPE ESTATE, QUEENSVALE
Drawing by Sir William Young
Reprinted from Sir William Young, "An essay on the commercial and political importance of the island of Tobago . . ." (1812). Manuscript.

in the 1760s and the legislature there was able, when the time came, to adopt principles, and often specific clauses in its code, which had been worked out elsewhere. Tobago differed from its neighbours only in small details. Slaves were property, indeed real property, but they were also persons possessing the faculties of reasoning and will; and it was the need to regulate those areas of conduct in which this special kind of property asserted these faculties and acted unlike normal forms of property which really gave rise to the elaborate slave laws providing legal sanction, backed by force, for the institution of slavery. The greater part of the slave code aimed to ensure that the slaves, acting as persons, did not escape from their position as property. Because the problems with which the slave laws were designed to cope were the same in all the West Indian colonies the slave codes of the several islands were generally similar.

There was a heavy emphasis on police regulations, providing for the detection and punishment of efforts at slave rebellion and slave desertion and theft by slaves. Such activities were threats both to the property rights of the slave owners and to the public order of the island communities. By the later eighteenth century the police regulations had been supplemented by laws controlling the economic activities of the slaves which had threatened to make it possible for them to evade total subordination to their masters.[2]

The very first clause of the Tobago Act established the total legal subjugation of the slave. The magistrates, duly appointed, were empowered to punish with death, transportation or any other punishment they might choose any slave who struck or wounded any white person who "contrived" or "imagined" his death. The same penalty applied to slaves wounding another slave or setting fires to canes or buildings, attempting to run away from the island or inciting others to do so, or stealing property to the value of £6 currency, or plotting to wound or poison any horse, male or cattle. Likewise any slave who, having run away, remained absent for six weeks or for two months in twelve or who knowingly harboured a runaway would pay a similar penalty. The slave who did "personally insult, abuse, threaten or in any other manner contemptuously threat any white person" faced a public flogging at the discretion of any Justice of the Peace. Running away, which of course could potentially disrupt the whole system, provided one of the few points at which the slave law impinged on the white population: a white who harboured a runaway was to be fined £20 currency or serve one month in prison for a first offence, £100 or six months for a third.

No slave was permitted to carry or have the custody of any firearm unless in pursuit of a runaway under the direction of a white or free coloured person or when attending upon a white person, except with a pass from his master. The restriction on the carrying of cutlasses, knotted or pointed sticks or other offensive weapons was less stringent only in the sense that necessary plantation business was a lawful occasion. The penalty attached to these clauses was a public flogging. Any free person who gave or sold any firearm, cutlass or other offensive weapon to a slave was liable to be fined up to £50.

Any slave accused of any of the several crimes which could carry the death penalty could be committed to jail by any Justice of the Peace, subsequently to be tried by a court consisting of two justices and three freeholders of the district sitting as assessors. Such a court, known locally as a Jurors' Court would in practice necessarily consist entirely of slaveowners. The evidence of slaves was always admissible in court against another slave, but not against a white person. It is noteworthy that the court had an absolute discretion in the choice of any penalty it could conceive, subject only to the fact that the Act itself prohibited mutilation and torture. And except where a capital sentence was pronounced, there was no possibility of appeal or of any review of the proceedings by the executive authority of the island, for such courts usually kept no records.[3]

All slaves found outside their owner's plantation without a pass were deemed to be runaways and liable to apprehension by any person, including another slave. So elaborate was the effort to prevent successful running away that the law permitted any person to destroy any plantation which might remain deserted for more than six months lest it became a haven for fugitives, and the Justices were empowered to order the destruction of any food crops left on an abandoned estate. Every person having charge of slaves was required to make a quarterly return of all runaways.

The other side of the effort to prevent slaves from running away lay in an attempt to remove the more obvious incentives. All settled plantations were required to have one acre planted in provisions for every five slaves so that food shortage should not be used as an excuse for running away, or they would be fined £10 for every acre lacking. As time passed, though, this law became disused as emphasis was shifted to allowing the slaves to plant their own provision grounds. All slaves were to be provided with "good sufficient cloathing" once each year. It is noteworthy that the quantity of clothing required was not specified, nor was the amount of food to be allowed to slaves, though the law clearly implied that the master had a duty to feed and house them. These gaps in the law are indicative of the failure to see the slave as a human being except in so far as he became a potential criminal.

The law of 1776 provided certain controls over the punishment of slaves by the estate authorities. In the first place any one who "shall willingly or wickedly Kill a Slave" was deemed guilty of murder and thus incurred the mandatory death penalty upon conviction. Tobago was the first British island to treat killing a slave as murder in law[4] though no case has been found of any such conviction before 1813. Owners or renters of slaves however were explicitly permitted at their own discretion to put them in chains or to impose "a moderate whipping or some other moderate Correction suitable to the fault"; but torture, mutilation or punishment "with cruelty" was unlawful and punishable with fine or imprisonment. This law certainly opened the door to much extremely cruel treatment. Throughout the islands a flogging was often followed by the application to the lacerated parts of the victim of a mixture of salt, lime juice and pepper.[5]

Many clauses in the law were concerned with the concept of the slave as property and the accompanying notions that if he was damaged his master was entitled to compensation, while if he inflicted damage his master must pay compensation rather as if he were a marauding bull. When a slave was judicially executed his master was to be compensated from public funds, a sum not exceeding £50 to be assessed by the three freeholders who sat on the court. If one slave murdered another the compensation was to be divided between the two masters. Free persons harbouring runaways were to pay compensation to their owners at the rate of 15s. per day in addition to being fined. Stealing a slave and taking him away from the island was punishable by death.

In the light of past experience in other islands the sale of liquor to slaves was prohibited without the written permission of the master. "And whereas great mischief may arise from a number of negroes belonging to different plantations assembling together" slaves were not permitted to beat any drum or similar instrument or to blow horns or shells, or to gather in groups from different plantations "for that or any other bad purpose". The maintenance of such discipline was a matter for the estates, but the Slave Act provided for a fine of £10 on any master who permitted such behaviour. Experience elsewhere had shown that they might be used as cover for plots and other manifestations of unrest. The number of holidays to be allowed at Christmas was to be fixed by the Justices in October each year. The usual object of such a law was to standardize the holidays rather than to protect the slaves in their enjoyment of them.[6]

The economic activities of the slaves were also controlled by the law. Slave owners frequently hired out the services of their slaves to those who needed them but no master was permitted to allow his underemployed slaves to seek such employment for themselves. The master must always arrange the hiring, on pain of a £10 fine. The Act declared that the practice which had grown up in the early years of Tobago's settlement of slaves moving from place to place selling various kinds of goods "tends to the manifest prejudice of trade and to many other dangerous consequences" and provided that "no mulattoe, Indian or negroe whatsoever shall Hawke or Carry about to sell from Place to Place or shall sell in any Open Street or Market any Sort or Sorts of Goods Wares or Merchandizes or any Sort of Produce such as Rum, Sugar, Cotton, Ginger, Coffee, Cocoa or any other Product whatsoever". Offenders were to forfeit all the goods concerned and might also be flogged. An exception was made to permit masters of slaves to authorize in writing the sale of provisions, fruit, fresh milk, fish, poultry and other small stock. Here, as in the prohibition of self hire, was a clear recognition of the contradictions of the slave system. The law sought to prevent slaves from behaving in ways natural to any human being and objectionable only because they held a potential for placing the slave in competition with white men. Yet those same acts were permissible if required by the slave's master.

It is noteworthy that these economic regulations were much less stringent than those in force in the Leeward Islands where the only slaves who could take employment without the specific consent of their masters were the town porters and where there was an extensive network of laws designed to prevent slaves from profiting by stealing from their masters, especially by selling plantation goods or iron, copper or brass items stolen from the mills. Laws prevented the cultivation of plantation crops by slaves.[7]

The Slave Act of 1775 was among those laws re-enacted in 1794 when the Assembly began to function again following the return of British rule. In May of that year, however, a new law was passed to reinforce the control of the slave population in the light of the prevalence of French revolutionary propaganda in the region and a fear that "Ideas of Equality and Liberty totally subversive of all good Government" might be transmitted to the slaves of Tobago. This added the specific penalty of transportation to those normally available for slave convicts who by words or actions sought "to excite sedition, promote conspiracies or spread a spirit of revolt, mutiny or disobedience either against their respective owners or the Government, Magistrates or white Inhabitants of this Island".[8]

This law was allowed to lapse after the crisis which gave rise to it had subsided, but when in 1801 a conspiracy among the slaves again focused attention on the supposedly subversive activities of slaves introduced from neighbouring colonies, the penalty of transportation for offenders who were not executed was revived.[9] It remained in force until peace came in 1815.[10]

It will be seen that in Tobago as elsewhere the slave law was silent on a number of very significant matters. The master's power to punish his slaves was limited only by the prohibition of killing, mutilation and torture and was otherwise undefined save for the meaningless injunction against "cruelty".[11] Flogging was the most common punishment for the statutory offences and the plantations tended as a matter of convention and perhaps of convenience to echo this picture; but the stocks were probably widely used and the masters were unlikely to be very different from their colleagues in other islands who often sought to devise ingenious forms of punishment. The allowance of clothing was vague and that of food and shelter depended purely on convention. So did the medical care of ailing slaves, regulated in the Leeward Islands in 1798.[12] As a piece of property the slave was hardly thought to need serious protection against his master. He had no right to property of his own even, and as against strangers his only redress was through his master, who would claim damages for interference with his slave property. Nevertheless, while the slave law was clearly a masters' law, it has been noted that in Tobago it was not quite as careless of the slave's interests or as restrictive of his activities as in some other colonies.

The Campaign for Amelioration

Elsa Goveia has shown that at the end of the eighteenth century the whites of the Leeward Islands were not hostile to the amelioration of the slave laws. In fact they were well placed to relax their treatment of their slaves because the latter had been largely socialized into accepting their subjection. Most had known no other condition. In the Windward Islands, and certainly in Tobago, where the number of African-born slaves was larger, and significant numbers were still being imported, there would have been more reason for greater stringency, but we shall see that the planters in Tobago were quite prepared to contemplate amelioration. Even in the Leewards, however, there was a reluctance to disturb the relationship between masters and slaves, so that while the duties of the master towards the slave were increasingly recognized by custom there was great reluctance to convert these duties into rights which the slaves could enforce through an official guardian or protector.[13]

After 1793 Tobago was naturally caught up in the repercussions of the existing agitation in Britain against the slave trade, and the desire of the Tobago planters to cultivate the goodwill of the British government also appears to be closely involved in the consequential attempt which began in 1797 to ameliorate the slave laws. In February 1796 the latest proposal for the abolition of the slave trade was lost in the House of Commons by 74 votes to 70. This margin was so narrow as to prompt the West India interest in Britain to think that they had better take the initiative and make concessions which would satisfy the more moderate of the abolitionists without antagonizing the colonial assemblies too much.

Sir William Young, an absentee with wide interests in the Windward and Leeward Islands and the future Governor of Tobago, now put forward a new programme of action for the West Indians based on the belief that Wilberforce's campaign to abolish the slave trade would be likely to succeed eventually unless some alternative could be put forward which could satisfy the abolitionists' "ideas of humanity".[14] In conjunction with another West Indian proprietor, Charles Rose Ellis, he therefore proposed to the West Indian group in the House of Commons that the King should be requested by means of a Humble Address to instruct the governors:

> to recommend to the respective Councils and Assemblies . . . to adopt such Measures as shall appear to them best calculated to obviate the Causes which have hitherto impeded the natural Increase of the Negroes already in the islands, gradually to diminish the necessity of the Slave Trade, and ultimately to lead to its complete termination; and particularly with a view to the same effect, to employ such means as may conduce to the Moral & Religious Improvement of the Negroes, and to secure to them throughout all the West India Islands the certain immediate, and active protection of the Law . . . .[15]

This resolution was put to the House of Commons by Ellis on 6 April 1797 and approved.

As the colonial responses were formulated over the next two years or so, it became clear that planters and Assemblies generally had no intention of ending the slave trade or even of working to that end, though some islands made small gestures of amelioration. In 1797 the Assembly of Jamaica declared that it had no intention of countenancing the end of the slave trade,[16] and in 1800 a committee appointed by it took the view that everything possible had been done "to render the condition of the slaves . . . as favourable as is consistent with their reasonable services, and the safety of the white inhabitants".[17] In the Windward Islands, with their recent experience of revolts involving slaves in Grenada, St Vincent and Dominica, planter opinion was very hostile to the new proposals for amelioration, though Grenada passed an Act on the subject in 1797.[18] That Act most importantly provided for the appointment of inspectors or visitors to oversee the treatment of the slaves in relation to the law.[19] In practice these "guardians" did little, but the Act was a considerable gesture.[20]

The Leeward Islands, where Young himself tried hard to urge action, responded that they saw no hope of an early end to the slave trade and that efforts were constantly being made to promote the welfare of the slaves, but undertook to frame new laws for their comfort "from motives of humanity".[21] Two laws making the most fundamental changes in the slave codes were indeed passed in the Leeward Islands: the murder or wounding of a slave was declared to carry the same penalties as if the victim was a free person and, perhaps more important, a coroner's inquest was to be held on slaves who died suddenly.[22]

The resolution passed in Parliament duly reached Tobago in July 1797 and supporting letters came from the Duke of Portland and Sir William Young, who owned estates there.[23] Council and Assembly set up a joint committee to formulate a response. Young, writing to the President of the Council, put the case for positive action with much force:

> ... on every ground of past experience in Parliament from the first agitation of the question ... and from all speculations on the future that my mind can reach, it appears to me indispensably necessary to take some steps in our colonies by Legislative provisions, touching the position of Negroes in respect to Society to promote a natural increase of the population, & thus not only stop for the present but gradually supersede the very pretensions at a future period to a measure of direct abolition of the Slave Trade by the Mother Country, a measure which would blast the roof of all our Settlements of property – change the foundations of every bequest loan & security, turn every Mortgage into an annuity, on the lives of negroes, institute a general system of foreclosure and depreciating our estates preclude all immediate resources and ruin every interest. I hope this fatal & sure alternative will be precluded.[24]

It was to be some considerable time before Tobago produced the Act Young sought. The joint committee of Council and Assembly made little headway and Portland, disturbed by the lack of progress almost everywhere, circulated guidelines for ameliorative legislation in April 1798.[25] He suggested that pregnant women should be exempted from field labour for the last six or eight weeks of their time; rewards should be granted to mothers for rearing children; mothers of six children should be exempted from all hard labour as already provided in Grenada; slaves should be encouraged to marry, that is to pursue regular and recognized concubinage; and missionaries should be employed to provide religious instruction. To provide enforcement machinery, he recommended the Grenadian provision for the appointment of inspectors or visitors to superintend and enforce the regulations in favour of the slaves. Finally, slaves should be removed from an estate only with their own consent.[26] In Tobago a new committee finally reported in September 1798.[27]

Apart from a natural lack of enthusiasm for ameliorative measures, the delay was partly due to the fact that for most of 1797 the inhabitants were much preoccupied over the possibility that a negotiated peace with France might involve them in yet another, most unwelcome, change of sovereignty. This left little time for deliberations about amelioration.[28] When the excitement had subsided it seems probable that the legislature hoped that inaction would help the problem to disappear, until Portland began to prod. Then the planters' desire to cultivate the good opinion of the Secretary of State, the Crown, and the House of Commons came back into play. Moreover, it was not slavery, or even amelioration it itself, which was at issue, but rather a diversion to distract the abolitionists. There was every reason to make at least a pretence of effort.

Eric Williams has described the committee's report, with much exaggeration, as "a landmark in the history of all the slave colonies that ultimately formed a part of the British West Indies";[29] but fundamental to that verdict seems to be a mistaken belief that the Tobago legislature was taking an initiative rather than merely following certain other colonies in responding to a lead from Britain, or at least a failure to realize just how far the report's details followed the lead of others.[30]

All of Portland's principal suggestions were accepted, the joint committee recommending that mothers be awarded one dollar each Christmas for each living child born during the year, and that the master should provide a comfortable house for each female slave who married unless the husband already had one, plus a gift of livestock and superior clothing. Regarding supervision and enforcement, it advised the appointment not of inspectors but of two or three Guardians of the Rights of Negroes in each parish to receive complaints of ill-treatment from the slaves and to guard them against it, one of the most striking of the new recommendations.

The committee, however, did go on to make detailed suggestions of its own. Many were little more than codifications of existing widespread practice, like fixing the rations to be issued to slaves and providing that each should receive two outfits of clothes per year. Proper houses should be erected on each state, with wooden doors. Night work during crop should be restricted. The period during which young children were suckled, in practice up to two years or even longer, should be limited, and slave mothers should not be permitted to take young children into the fields. Rather, each estate should be required to provide a properly attended crèche.

The joint committee believed that absenteeism was a principal cause of the low rate of natural increase among the slave population since resident proprietors tended to take better care of their slaves. It therefore recommended a tax on absentee landlords to be used for the better care of the slaves. Suggesting that the legislature should try to make the health and fecundity of an estate's slaves the criterion of status rather than the quantity of sugar it produced, it proposed that the island Treasury should offer £10 for each additional slave each year to the man in charge of the slaves, and six prizes of £50 to £100 for the six estates showing the greatest natural increase each year. While in practice most slaves had adequate provision grounds and half a day each week to work them, it was recommended that this should be guaranteed to them by law.

Finally the committee proposed that the Guardians of the Rights of Negroes should have authority to summon both black and white witnesses, and either redress grievances or punish frivolous complaints. They should visit each estate in the parish every six months.

The presentation of this report, however, was not to give rise to an Amelioration Act. Under repeated pressure from Portland,[31] the draft of such a bill was not laid before the legislature until 25 March 1800.[32] Having demonstrated a willingness to conform to imperial wishes in principle and on paper, the planters of Tobago were really in no great hurry to ameliorate the condition of their slaves. In the 1790s, if Sir William Young and Governors Lindsay and Master believed that the slaves in Tobago were well and kindly treated by indulgent masters and fairly well contented in consequence,[33] there was also the view of the Royal Navy Captain who commented on the excessive use of the whip in the field, which he deemed "a very oppressive situation".[34] There is no real evidence that slave masters in Tobago practised special indulgence.

Moreover, despite the example of Grenada and the Leewards, Tobago soon learnt of Jamaica's cavalier response to the suggestion that her slave laws were in need of reform,[35] and by 1799 saw no good reason to make a gesture which seemed likely to be costly, at least in the short run, while others ignored the issue.

The Assembly now allowed the idea of amelioration to die of inaction. On 9 April 1800 it resolved

> that on account of the great importance of the report . . . for the amelioration of the state of the slaves, and from a consideration that there are a considerable number of the proprietors absent from the island, and residing in Great Britain who are highly interested in the subject of the report .. further discussion of the report be postponed until the sentiments of the Tobago proprietors resident in Great Britain be had thereupon.[36]

The Council concurred. Months passed while the Agent in London sought to collect the opinions of the absentee proprietors.[37] In vain did the Secretary of State and the Governor plead with the new session of the Assembly in October.[38] The bill was never revived.

The abortive bill of 1800 provided for the implementation of almost all the joint committee's recommendations. In some cases there were changes or additions of detail. A new dimension was added, however, where punishments were concerned. The bill set out to encourage the use of the pillory rather than flogging, said to beget a "contempt of punishment", and also provided for the erection of a public chain gang prison in Scarborough and a cage in the market place or nearby where slaves found drunk or disorderly could be confined. Flogging at the will of the master was limited to thirty lashes, though a court of two justices could order fifty lashes, whereas earlier laws had merely prohibited "cruel punishment". Recognizing that debarment from giving evidence against free persons deprived the slaves of "an equal distribution of justice", clause 7 provided that they should be competent to give evidence, which the judges should weigh appropriately in the light of the fact that slaves were thought generally ignorant of the meaning of an oath. No slave should be convicted of a capital crime without the evidence of at least one white of good character, or two slaves, or one slave supported by strong circumstantial evidence; and slaves accused of felony were to be tried by three justices and a jury of five persons who must possess at least eight slaves. The provision for slaves to give evidence was perhaps the most far-reaching innovation proposed by the Tobago Bill, at least in its potential effect. It was not entirely without precedent, but the Dominica Act of 1798 had admitted slave evidence against whites only in very specific types of cases for a limited time, and was aimed merely at stopping trading with runaway slaves.[39] Also of greatest importance, but again borrowed from the Leeward Islands[40] was the proposal to adopt the general principle that "if any Doubt or Difficulty shall hereafter raise concerning the construction of any Clause in this Act the same shall be construed favourably for the slaves".

This seemingly impressive bill then certainly contained innovations, but its ameliorative intent was declaredly limited: "... [it] is the Intent and Meaning of the Legislature to administer to the Comfort and Satisfaction of the Slaves as far as is compatible with the Tranquillity and Security of the Free People". Moreover, it was original in very little. What it added to the report of the joint committee was mostly taken from the ameliorative laws which other colonies had already passed. We have seen that certain significant clauses were borrowed from the Leeward Islands. Dominica in 1798 had limited flogging to thirty-nine lashes,[41] Tobago now fixed fifty. Only in relation to the law on slave evidence may Tobago be said to have been a potential pace setter in 1800. Significantly, the bill was never enacted, and one is tempted to ask whether, at that late date, its authors really intended it to be taken seriously. In Tobago, where the slave population was still being significantly augmented by importations from Africa[42] and a major slave conspiracy aimed at revolt was to be discovered at Christmas 1801, there was perhaps less concern with actual amelioration than with avoiding the displeasure of the Secretary of State. It is not surprising that the ensuing bill was shelved until it disappeared from view amid the restoration of sovereignty to France in 1802. On the other hand the planters in the legislature spent a great deal of time over this potentially far-reaching bill and if they were short of a positive desire to ameliorate the slave laws, it seems fair to say that they appear to have been less averse to the idea than their contemporaries in many other islands.

Conspiracy and Restiveness among the Slaves

Despite the fruitless efforts to reform the slave law in the years 1798 to 1800, the Act of 1776 remained without substantial amendment until 1802. Then the last minute discovery of elaborate plans for a slave revolt in December 1801 produced a tightening of the regulations. During December 1801 rumours were heard that disturbances would occur during the Christmas holidays, so that on 17 December the garrison commander gave instructions that the fort should be kept on alert over Christmas and suggested mounting a patrol in Scarborough.[43] Then on the evening of Tuesday 22 December a Mr Houston overheard a conversation among some of his slaves, probably at Calder Hall, which suggested that a revolt was planned, probably for Christmas night, and reported the incident to the President of the Council who was acting as governor. The four slaves concerned were arrested that evening and next morning three Justices of the Peace went to Houston's estate, took depositions, and ordered more arrests. It was from one of those arrested that the first clear information of a slave conspiracy was obtained. More arrests followed and steps were taken to warn all the white inhabitants. On Thursday 24 December the Council met and agreed that martial law should be declared and the Christmas holidays deferred. As those arrested were questioned more arrests followed and under martial law the militia were called out. By Christmas Eve the whites, many of whom had fled their homes, had begun to breathe more easily.

On Christmas morning preparations were made for an attack that night, as the questioning of suspects continued and arrests continued to mount. On Saturday 26 December a court was constituted under martial law to deal with those arrested. One alleged leader was hanged and another, a coloured militiaman, was shot under martial law. Five others were executed a few days later under civil authority and several received uncertain but lesser sentences. In all nearly 200 blacks and a small number of free coloureds had been arrested. The Council meanwhile determined to proceed only against the leaders, not wishing to have to cope with too many prisoners, and instructions were sent to commanders of districts to promise slaves who continued to work normally and gave what information they might have that there would be nothing to fear. Military activity slackened off after 28 December and martial law was lifted on 6 January 1802, by which time three companies of infantry had arrived from Barbados.

The details of the conspiracy cannot be known with absolute certainly, having to be pieced together largely from the evidence of the conspirators. But it seems that at least seven estates were involved – Bacolet, Belvedere, Cove, Friendship, Friendsfield, Hope and Mesopotamia – though allegations were made about another nine. In addition slaves belonging to fourteen individuals who were not estate owners, at least four town slaves from Scarborough and a few free coloureds had been concerned in the plot. The town slaves, however, do not seem to have been prominent.

The leaders had pretended that their planning and organization were aimed at the better working of their provision grounds, and their plotting had been facilitated by the fact that all the estates concerned lay within a radius of five or six miles and slaves were able to visit neighbouring estates. It is also likely that their planning was facilitated by the practice of allowing slave funerals to be marked by large night time gatherings. Belvedere, Mesopotamia and Bacolet had provided the principal leaders, most of whom were elite slaves, drivers or tradesmen. This was a fairly common feature of slave conspiracies and revolts elsewhere, despite the facts that masters almost always declined to believe that their trusted favoured slaves would do such things.

None of the principal leaders of this conspiracy put forward any very specific cause of complaint, so that their objective almost certainly was simply to escape from enslavement. Their aims, however, were quite specific: "the total extermination of the white and coloured people by a regular and systematic attack", according to a statement attributed to one of those arrested. It seems probable that this objective was directly related to the revolts in St Domingue, Grenada, and elsewhere since 1791. Grenada was specifically mentioned by one of the leaders, and others made similar comments.

The plan was to set fire to the canes, probably on three or four different estates, on Christmas night. This was to be the signal for an attack on the Scarborough barracks which were also to be burned, in the hope that this would attract the garrison from the fort which could then be attacked at its most vulnerable. The whites were to be set upon when they went to put out the fires. There were fairly elaborate plans for possible victory: Roger of Belvedere was to become governor and at least five colonels had been designated with sundry lesser officers.

It is possible that the abortive attempt in 1800 to ameliorate the slave laws may have helped to stimulate this conspiracy. It was a potentially very formidable plot despite the total lack of firearms, for it involved much of the most fully developed part of Tobago and the capital town. As one might expect, the aftermath saw a considerable tightening of security. The legislature at once set about framing regulations "for correcting the relaxed state of the police of this colony" and an Act to improve the policing of Scarborough and Plymouth together with another to amend the Slave Law were passed in March 1802. The conspiracy had brought out the fact that over the years doubts had arisen as to how far the Slave Act applied to slaves who were not employed on plantations and their masters and the first clause clarified the position: a slave was a slave wherever he might be employed, and the new amendment to the Slave Act specifically stated that the law applied in full to slaves resident in the urban or semi-urban areas of Scarborough, Plymouth, Milford, Hillsborough and Georgetown.[44] Here is certainly an echo of the fact that slaves in Scarborough had been involved in the recent conspiracy and we shall see that town slaves were often under less rigorous discipline than those on estates.

The second clause in effect prohibited the practice of obeah, specifically any pretence to supernatural powers to affect the health or lives of others or to promote rebellion, under pain of death or appropriate lesser punishment. The third declared that all slave funerals must take place before sunset, since the practice of holding them after dark had occasioned large gatherings of slaves from neighbouring estates at which there was commonly too much feasting, dancing and drinking which endangered the slaves' health and morals. In fact, the object was to prevent gatherings in the dark which were believed to have facilitated the planning of the recent conspiracy. The onus was put on the masters to control slave funerals. Further, lists of runaways were to be published either in the *Gazette* or on public notice boards as the reports were made to the Register Office.

The preoccupation with the need to guard against any recurrence of conspiracy among the slaves is further shown by the offer in the new Act of manumission at the public expense and a pension of £33 currency per annum to any slave who gave information leading to the defeat of any intended insurrection. Probably the same motive lay behind a new provision for the public flogging at the discretion of a single Justice of any slave who insulted, abused or treated contemptuously any free coloured person. This was a measure of protection and privilege previously reserved for whites and its extension to the free coloured of Tobago probably represents a desire to ensure solidarity among free people in the face of threats of slave revolt.

The disquiet about the conduct of the slave population following the thwarting of the conspiracy was no doubt also responsible for an Act in March 1802 for improving the policing of the towns of Scarborough and Plymouth.[45] It was asserted that the slaves tended to assemble "on the streets and bye places . . . to the great annoyance of the inhabitants" and to ride or drive animals carelessly and dangerously; but these were not new problems, nor were other aspects of order and cleanliness in the towns which had nothing to do with slaves but which now received some attention. The Act was first and foremost an attempt to tighten control of the slaves. Any free person, white or coloured, was empowered to apprehend any slave found in the street or in any empty lot between 8 p.m. and 5 a.m. without a pass and carry him off to jail. Next morning the offender could be flogged on the sworn evidence of his accuser alone. Any free person permitting an assembly of slaves on his premises was to be fined £10 and the assembly of slaves "on the streets and by places" on Sundays and holidays or on weekdays in the afternoon or evening "to the great annoyance of the inhabitants" was declared illegal. The constables were directed to disperse such assemblies and empowered to arrest those behaving in "an insolent, riotous or improper manner", who then faced flogging and imprisonment. Any slave riding or driving a horse or mule "at a greater pace than a moderate walk" could be taken before the justices by any free person and flogged and imprisoned. Young believed that there was an immediate improvement in the behaviour of the public on market day.[46] But in essence the measure represents a further tightening of the police regulations governing the conduct of the slaves, as events showed that they were still in a position to cause trouble.

Just as the slave conspiracy of 1801 had occurred immediately before Christmas, so a similar if less important plot emerged at Christmas 1805. Some days before Christmas a conversation was overheard among the black pioneers at Fort King George which led the commanding officer to suspect "a scheme to be in agitation by the Negroes to destroy the White Inhabitants of this Colony". He at once placed the pioneers in "close confinement" and informed President Mitchell.[47] The Privy Council agreed to the declaration of martial law and proceeded to examine several suspects.[48] A court consisting of two justices and three freeholders sitting with the Chief Justice was set up to try the alleged conspirators.[49]

Just what had been afoot was never discovered with certainty but if all the evidence is pieced together it seems that some of the pioneers had obtained poison with which they intended to poison the garrison's water supply so as to dispose of the troops while rebel slaves attacked the fort. A gap had been cut in the hedge around the fortifications through which the attack was to have been mounted on 24 December while a general insurrection began on several plantations. There is some evidence that the water actually was poisoned, "as all the Frogs and other insects in it died soon after", and about 10,000 gallons was let out. It was alleged that after the fort was attacked, "[t]heir next object was plundering the Country previously murdering the inhabitants".[50]

Martial law having been proclaimed, the militia cavalry and the coloured Scarborough company of militia were kept on duty for eight or nine days while the trials proceeded.[51] Four pioneers were brought to trial, and one, named Nero, was found guilty of inciting insurrection and hanged; but the witnesses gave such conflicting evidence and "prevaricated" so much that it was impossible to convict the others[52] despite the fact that two pioneers were promised their lives in return for their evidence.[53] However the garrison commander sent away to Barbados six pioneers who had come under suspicion and plans were made to remove them all.[54] These pioneers had been in Tobago since 1803 and thus had more than two years in which to fraternize with the local blacks.

That some pioneers were engaged in a plot to cause a revolt seems to be well established, but there is no evidence that it was widely supported; and while the pioneers alleged that the plantation slaves were involved, the Privy Council came to the conclusion that they were not. All the estate slaves who had been accused were later discharged[55] and it is inconceivable that this could have occurred if there was any shred of evidence against them.

The tightening of the slave laws in 1802 had helped to allay the fears of the white population for the time being, and the suspicion of a slave plot in 1805 seems to have produced no particular reaction in the absence of any hard evidence. It is clear that slaves were still sometimes able to behave in ways which demonstrated that they had a surprising freedom of action and the possibility of rebellion or disturbance was always there. When the imperial Act abolishing the Slave Trade was passed in March 1807, Sir William Young just taking over the governorship, asked the legislature to consider whether this was likely to unsettle the slaves sufficiently to raise a problem of internal security. He himself believed that the slaves had been unsettled by news of the Act, but that any attempt to revise the slave laws would excite them further.⁵⁶ The restrictions surrounding them were numerous and Young expressed the view that they should not be further augmented, except perhaps in Scarborough. He declared, "I shall ever favour the Negroes, where I can do it without endangering their Masters and therewith the sovereignty of this Island". But events soon pushed him rather in the opposite direction, at least so far as freedom of movement was concerned.⁵⁷

The abolition of the slave trade could not, of course, be concealed from the slaves, and it led them to speculate among themselves about further plans for the reform of slavery, some supposing that the new Act involved emancipation. In July Young reported rumours that many slaves were convinced that he had been empowered to introduce a scheme for allowing the slaves to work for themselves for three days each week. It is not clear how far this rumour was believed among the slaves, though the governor thought many accepted it; but clearly they were unsettled and uncertain of just what was going on. Young sought to avert further rumour by discouraging "Table Converzation on the Subject before the Negroe Servants", believing that trouble among the slaves was usually the product of the tales of the domestic slaves.⁵⁸

In August, however, large groups of slaves from Culloden estate went to Government House at Mount William with complaints against their master and Young thought they had some further undisclosed objective. In September sixty slaves from Sir William Bruce's estate went to Government House and, finding the Governor absent, stayed there for three days while they sent a deputation of eight to follow him to Queen's Bay, a journey of twenty-six miles as the road then went. Soon afterwards another group, from Studley Park, appeared at Government House.⁵⁹

All these groups listened to what the governor had to say "with apparent respect". But he showed them little sympathy, hoping to discourage further similar incidents. Of this he was hopeful: "I seem'd to have convinced them of the impropriety & disadvantage of coming in Gangs as if to enforce attention to their complaints by declaring that I would neither give ear or redress to any complaints however just if made by a deputation of more than two or three".⁶⁰

The problem, however, did not end there. On 27 October 1807, while the legislature was in session, "a large & riotous gang" from Joseph Robley's estate at Cove tried to pass through Scarborough on its way to Government House and forty-two slaves were arrested and jailed by the magistrates. This gang had quit work, "throwing down their Hoes together with the most opprobrious Language to their Manager & Overseers present", and in a manner described by the governor as "clearly preconcerted", left the estate. They were led by a slave called Rodney, who had been prominent in the 1801 conspiracy but had then been pardoned in return for turning state's evidence. Recalling these events four years later, Young asserted that many of the slaves involved in these expeditions had been armed with cutlasses. Rodney and four others described as ringleaders were put on trial and the others returned to their estate: they had committed no offence under the Slave Act since absence from the estate was a domestic offence rather than a crime unless the period of absence amounted to six weeks or a total of two months in twelve.[61]

The legislature was already inclined to view the uncertainties surrounding the abolition of the slave trade as a "crisis", and considered that "this novel & most dangerous practice of traversing the country in gangs" should be suppressed by law.[62] On the very day of the Scarborough fracas a member called Collier proposed a bill on the subject in the Assembly, which next day suspended its own procedural rules to allow it to be passed in a single day.[63] The Council was less precipitate[64] but a week later the colony had a new "Act to prevent more effectually Slaves absenting themselves from the Service of their Masters, Owners or Renters".[65] Any slave absent without leave or running away in a group of two or more "for any space of time whatever" was to be flogged or otherwise punished and ringleaders might be executed. The governor explained that the intention was not to deem every small group of slaves to be a "mutinous gang", but rather to direct the magistrates' attention to the investigation of why slaves were "traversing" the country so that cases of conspiracy or public mischief could be dealt with.[66] The Secretary of State approved.[67]

The visible disquiet among the slaves seems to have subsided after the new law was passed and it seems that no case was brought under it at the time. Young saw a case of cause and effect,[68] but it is entirely probable that the excitement following the slave trade Act was subsiding naturally as it was realized that it was not intended to change the existing regime on the estates and it became apparent that no dire consequences were likely in Tobago yet awhile.

The Policing of Scarborough and the Chain Gang

Before the issue of the movement of slaves in groups had come to a head, however, Young had concluded that the Scarborough Police Act needed revision. Every week the market occasioned an influx of "people of the lowest Order of Society" and he saw a danger that "without strong control extreme Licentiousness must be the result of such frequent concourse and of such description."[69] Proper policing of the market was, he thought, all-important in providing the population of any West Indian island with an example of good order and "a sense of duty and subordination". Unless "regularity and discipline were maintained, market day would become "a sink of contagion and mischief' affecting the morals and peace of the whole island. The Police Act he thought was not properly enforced and he urged that the arrangements be improved.[70] More specifically, "the Market & Grog Houses of our West India Towns are ever the places of evil Communications & Design & where any Negroe leaders of Mischief may Form or strengthen their Party". Police regulations were the answer.[71] In this context, the governor was not thinking only of the behaviour of the slaves. Policing was a more general problem; but the law affecting the slaves was of course part of it.

While the legislature was considering a new Police Act the question of internal security was rendered much more acute by the action of the slaves on Cove estate. The Police Act and the new Act restricting the movement of slaves passed the Assembly on the same day, 28 October 1807.[72]

In 1808 the legislature passed an Act for the establishment of a chain gang of slave convicts to work on repairing the streets of Scarborough or on other public works.[73] This Act sprang from a desire to utilize the labour of slaves who remained in jail for long periods without either being brought to trial or claimed by their masters as well as that of convict slaves. An overseer was appointed by the legislature at the substantial salary of £330 currency, assisted by a driver, and the operation was under the control of the way wardens. Every day except Sunday at 6 a.m. the jailer delivered to the overseer all slaves in the jail who were not on capital charges as well as any who might be sent by their masters to join the chain gang. They returned to jail at 5 p.m. The gang worked chained together from 6 a.m. to 9 a.m., from 9.30 a.m. to noon, and from 2 p.m. to 5 p.m.

The Justices were empowered to sentence slaves to the chain gang for any length of time they thought fit for any offence not amounting to a felony, and the governor was empowered to commute death sentences and other sentences imposed by the Jury Courts to work on the chain gang, rather than simply granting a full pardon. While a slave worked on the gang the Treasurer provided 1s. 6d. per day from public funds for his food. An amending Act was passed in January 1809 providing that no chain gang slave should speak to any other slave while at work on pain of a public flogging after one warning, and allowing chains and collars to be taken off at night.[74] The commitment of runaways to the chain gang was now limited to those still unclaimed fourteen days after their presence in the jail was advertised.

The Chain Gang Act was originally authorized for one year only but it was repeatedly prolonged at least until 1816.[75] In practice, slaves could be sent to the chain gang by their masters, for unlimited periods, without being accused of any crime much less brought to trial, while it was normal for slaves in jail awaiting trial to be worked on the chain. The governor seems not to have realized what was going on until 1813. When he did, he was disturbed particularly by the use of a formal public punishment on slaves not accused of any crime, seeing it as contrary to "a universal principle of justice". Young asked the legislature to amend the act to require the bringing of a charge before any slave could be worked on the chain.[76] The Assembly, however, appears to have disliked the proposal and only after fifteen months' debate during which the matter came before the Assembly on three separate occasions, was an amending Act finally passed in January 1815 but without any amendment on this point.[77]

The new Act merely empowered the Scarborough justices to enquire into the condition and treatment of the chain gang,[78] but its passing brought the whole system under an unprecedented measure of imperial scrutiny which resulted in its disallowance and the use of the chain gang lapsed. Growing controversy in Britain over a proposal that all slaves in the colonies should be registered had led the Secretary of State to look with new attention at measures affecting their treatment. It seems probable that the extension of the chain gang to include slaves not accused of crime was an inadvertence, if to many slaveowners a convenient one, resulting from the fact that the 1809 Act, while providing that consignment to the gang would be through the jail, had not specifically required that a charge should be formally brought. One of the Secretary of State's legal advisers when faced with the amending Act of 1815, took up a rather wider point: "the system of inflicting on persons committed for any offence the same punishment to which they would be condemned in case of conviction is not to be reconciled to the principles of English Law". Moreover, as the writer went on to point out, "the application of this principle to persons committed as runaway slaves is open to peculiar dangers because it may easily happen that a person really innocent may be unjustly suspected of that offence". This would be especially true of newly arrived free coloured persons, raising the hideous prospect of inflicting a slave punishment upon a free man who, having no owner to claim him, would spend the rest of his life working in chains.[79] The Privy Council agreed with this view, and the Act was disallowed.[80]

The available evidence of the working of the chain gang hardly shows more than that the slaves were worked in chains and that at least one received a sentence of as long as seven years on the chain before the governor pardoned him.[81] The comment of a Colonial Office lawyer in 1815 that working in irons on the public works in Tobago "appears to be extremely painful and severe" may well be true, but no evidence has been found on how slaves stood up to the chain gang.[82] Young, however, thought that the chain gang had been a useful instrument and preferable to too much flogging: "The Negroe's natural uneasiness under confinement and the shame of being exhibited with a Chain, as a public Spectacle to his fellow Negroes on Sundays, have shown the value of this Establishment, in the less occasion for, and use of the Whip on Plantations".[83]

Slave Occupations and Living Conditions

We have noticed that slaves performed a wide variety of tasks, from working in the fields, mills, boiling houses and distilleries through the domestic service to the work of skilled artisans and tradesmen. It was the field slaves who performed the most physically demanding work. In the 1790s, when sugar cultivation in Tobago was being expanded, they no doubt had sometimes to clear new or derelict land and prepare it for cultivation; but for the most part their work was confined to the ongoing cultivation of established fields. In the Windward islands the slaves were commonly divided into two or sometimes three field gangs according to their age and strength, and each was allocated tasks graded according to that strength. On the largest estates four gangs might be used, while on small estates however, with only a few dozen slaves, this differentiation of function can hardly have existed.

On the larger estates the first or "great" gang would prepare the soil with the hoe and bill, the plough being unknown in Tobago. Then the gang would plant the canes and manure them where manure was used, cut them in due course, and work in the mill during the crop season. Cane "holing", the digging of holes 4 or 5 feet square by 6 or 9 inches deep, in preparation for planting, was regarded as the heaviest work on the estate, each adult male slave being expected to dig sixty to one hundred holes in a day depending on the size of the hole and the quality of the soil. Only a proportion of the estate had to be holed each year, however, as where practicable the canes were allowed to "ratoon" for a second or third year instead of being replanted. Sometimes, if a three-year cycle were adopted, one of the three areas would be put in provisions instead of being left to ratoon, a practice which some thought would improve the productivity of the land for cane.[84] But in stiff, poorly drained soils it was often necessary to replant every year, and in any case new planting produced more sugar. In the West Indies generally, planters tended to replant as much as their labour force would permit.

Planting and manuring made lighter work than holing, though the latter was often specially detested, and in this the first gang might be assisted by the less robust second or "small" gang. During crop the first gang would cut the cane, tie it into bundles, trim off the tops for planting or as cattle fodder, perhaps assist the carters with moving it to the mill, and undertake a variety of jobs in the sugar factory. Not all of these were unskilled jobs such as carrying containers. Many field slaves worked as mill feeders, sugar boilers and fire men and in other skilled tasks when the need arose, but probably about two-thirds of the first gang would remain in the field. Very often a first gang canecutter would cut cane by day and then work in the mill at night until after 1800 night work was gradually given up, though on small estates cutting and grinding would often take place on alternate days.

Second or "small" gang slaves, mostly composed of teenagers, undertook a number of lighter tasks. They worked with hoes and bills, weeding, molding, "trashing" and "cleaning" the canes. The arduousness of these tasks again depended on the stiffness of the soil, but they were considerably lighter than holing. So was collecting trash for use as fuel. In the factory second gang slaves would often carry bagasse and sometimes they would be used to grow provisions.

The work of the third gang, made up of children, and not always differentiated from the second, was the lightest of all, consisting mostly of collecting grass for the livestock. It could also be used to supplement the second gang in the lighter of its tasks.

On estates producing cotton or coffee the slaves performed a smaller range of tasks and the work was less demanding, being widely similar to that of the second gang on a sugar estate. The gang system was generally not used. In Tobago such estates disappeared during the 1790s for all practical purposes. By 1800 small amounts of both were occasionally exported but no estate can have depended to any significant extent on either crop.

Apart from the cultivation and processing of crops all types of field labourers were employed in a variety of manual tasks out of crop, so that they were fully employed throughout the year. They collected stones for the masons, and dung for the next planting, built the estate fences, cut and collected wood for fuel and provided the basic labour for the construction and repair of estate buildings and the roads.

Hours of work could be very erratic, but sunrise to sunset with a minimum of about ten hours was the core of the system,[85] supplemented by sometimes very long overtime hours during crop. In the boiling houses the skilled boilers were often worked in three or four shifts of six to eight hours.[86] In the early nineteenth century, however, hours tended to grow shorter and the Tobago Assembly reported in 1816 that night work on the estates had been totally abandoned,[87] though how this came about remains mysterious.

The usual routine involved working from daybreak until about 9 a.m. when half an hour would be allowed for breakfast. At noon there would be a break of up to two hours for lunch, and a rest unless there was something specific which they were sent to do.[88]

Hours of work among urban slaves were much more chaotic than among the estate populations. The great majority were of course domestics who, as might be expected, worked long and undetermined hours, always at the beck and call of their masters and mistresses. Sailors and fishermen, too, worked very erratic hours at the behest of wind, tide and other facets of the weather. But most other urban slaves generally worked shorter hours than plantation slaves. There was no regular night work such as the estates had required during crop time until the early nineteenth century.

Slaves usually had Sundays to themselves, principally in order that they might use it to contribute to their own maintenance, through the cultivation of garden plots and the marketing of their produce. The law had originally provided that the estates should be responsible for cultivating provisions, but land for the purpose was amply available and the planters had early found it to their advantage to allow the slaves plots of land and time to cultivate it. The planters in Tobago were generally liberal with the allowance of provision grounds and in addition to Sunday it was the practice on large plantations to allow the slaves Thursdays off so that the whole slave family could work in the gardens.[89] The produce of these grounds was wholly at the slave's disposal, to eat or sell in the market as he wished.

At Christmas, the holidays allowed to the slaves were regulated by law in an effort to achieve uniformity between the various estates. The slaves were accustomed to three days' holiday and a special ration of beef and port to which very great importance was attached. The celebration, described by Governor Young as "a three days Saturnalia", involved large gatherings of slaves, somewhat to their masters' apprehension, together with much liquor and dancing to the music of "fiddles and tambourines", sometimes in the masters' halls.[90] Christmas was clearly a very special indulgence, of great value as a safety valve for slave frustrations. Some recognition of Christmas was common to all the slave colonies. Less common among them was Tobago's practice of allowing the slaves a little tobacco on occasion. As Young wrote in 1808, "every poor Negro Slave is begging each Master and each Master's friend for a leaf of tobacco. It is a craving equal to that of food and even more pressing".[91]

The feeding of the slaves followed a variable programme. Where their provision grounds were large enough they were expected to produce a surplus for market from the proceeds of which they would buy salt meat and fish where the master did not provide them. They grew plantains, yams, maize, cassava, sweet potatoes and fruit and vegetables, and raised pigs and poultry.[92] More commonly, where provision grounds were smaller, the master would provide the salt meat and fish; and sometimes the slave was fed entirely from the estate though this does not seem to have occurred often in Tobago.[93] Either way, we have noticed that the slaves' nutriment was not commensurate with their exertions when they worked in the field.

Urban slaves depended for their food on rations provided by their employers, since provision grounds were not readily accessible. In any case the domestics would not have time to cultivate gardens. Many urban slaveowners were poor however, and in times of drought and shortage and hence high prices urban slaves probably suffered more than rural, especially where cash was provided in lieu of food as was often the case with slaves being hired out.[94] In some islands urban slaves were sometimes given money to find their own board and lodging but there is no evidence that this happened in Tobago.

In Tobago, apart from the fact that fish and meat had always to be imported, there was in most years a period when the supply of local provisions failed and supplies of flour oatmeal, maize, beans, peas and other items had to be found from abroad in order to feed the slaves as well as other population groups. This period commonly lasted from August to January depending on the weather.[95]

In consequence, after 1807 the amount of land devoted to provision grounds in Tobago was increased, probably substantially, and shortages grew less common. There was ample land available and Governor Young sponsored an agricultural society which saw the extension of provision cultivation as one of its objectives.[96] The response was immediate.[97] By 1815 Tobago seems to have been nearly self-sufficient in provisions, at least in years when the rains were abundant.[98] But the supply could still be very badly affected by adverse weather, as it was in 1810[99], and complaints about a seasonal shortage of provisions were not infrequent.

The provision grounds also gave the slaves an opportunity to acquire in some measure a kind of economic independence. Especially if the plantation was in the southern part of Tobago, better populated and near to Scarborough and to a lesser extent Plymouth, they had an opportunity to earn cash by selling their surpluses and sometimes grass and firewood to the whites and free coloureds.[100] Every little thus earned enabled the slave to improve his standard of living. He might for instance buy special items of food or clothing of his own choice or a little tobacco and there was always the outside chance of saving enough to purchase his manumission.

Skilled slaves of course, and sometimes domestics in the towns, had much better opportunities to earn cash, than those working in the field, especially if they were hired out. Carpenters and coopers, by far the most numerous of the artisans, could earn significant sums, even two or three shillings a day, on hire to neighbouring estates or in the towns. And while the master took a proportion of the hired slaves' earnings the slaves themselves retained a part.[101] Similar opportunities were open to those with other skills, both on the estates and in the towns where transport workers, cartermen, boatmen, fishermen, even porters were often in great demand. Slave sailors were widely hired for the coasting trade. To some extent this compensated for the fact that town slaves were usually fed entirely by their masters and had no access to the opportunities which went with provision ground. These opportunities for economic advancement benefited both master and slave.

Domestics, the majority being women, were more numerous and less well paid than the skilled artisans or tradesmen, who were all men; but they had many opportunities for their normal rewards to be supplemented by perquisites, beginning with certain advantages in relation to food, clothing and housing derived from their presence in or around the master's household, where they were likely to do better than their fellows outside it. On the other hand the domestic slaves probably had less opportunity to earn cash: they usually had neither provision grounds nor so much opportunity for hire.[102]

The amount of clothing issued to slaves was usually minimal, the law again laying down no standard in the islands generally. Most slaves seem to have received two changes of clothing each year and a blanket less frequently, men receiving a jacket, shirt and trousers, women a jacket and petticoat or shift. All usually got hats or caps. But the durability of slave clothing was poor so that field slaves often worked half naked to save what they had for other occasions. Children often went naked, receiving little clothing if any at all.[103] Domestic slaves and others in close contact with their masters sometimes were given the latter's cast off clothes. Urban slaves were probably better clothed than rural on the whole, being closer to their owners. The fine clothes often worn on Sundays were purchased by the slaves themselves from their small cash earnings.[104]

The slaves were provided also with lodging which they were usually required to build themselves. In the Windward Islands the houses were usually built of wattle and daub and thatched with cane leaves with an earthen floor, though the elite slaves sometimes made themselves wooden houses, especially, it was reported, the carpenters and coopers. The cost of upkeep seems to have been borne by the plantation. Probably a typical slave house was about 25 feet long by 12 feet wide divided into three rooms.[105] Those on Franklyn's Estate c.1807 were built of wood, 26 feet x 14 feet, with two apartments and a covered porch or walkway, a kitchen and a storeroom. The roof was of shingles.[106]

But the quality of slave housing was likely to vary according to the size of the estate and the wealth of its owner. In both town and country slaves performing domestic functions usually lived within their master's premises or in huts or rooms within his yard. In town, even the artisans and labourers would live close by though often in separate yards. Even so, the propinquity of the master ensured that the standard of accommodation would not often fall below a certain minimum and would generally be reasonably comfortable.[107]

We have noted that slaveowners were concerned about the medical care of sick slaves, if only to preserve valuable property, and increasingly so after 1807. Large plantations had some arrangement for the provision of medical attention, including some sort of hospital and the services of a doctor who seems to have received an annual fee for each slave on the estate, put by Young in 1813 at 12s.[108] Each doctor commonly had contracts with a number of plantations which he visited regularly, sometimes indeed daily. On smaller estates the doctor might visit only when specially called.[109]

Despite the presence in Tobago of one doctor for every 1600 to 1700 slaves,[110] not a low ratio, medical attention was not of a high standard. European medical skills were poor, being based on false etiological theories concerning measures and humours, and the efforts of white doctors had little effect on the survival rate of their patients. The one real success of European medical science was the vaccination against smallpox, widely used with much success after 1800, so that there were no cases in Tobago in 1819-21. Indeed there was something in the frequent comment that on the whole slave "doctors" were more successful than white. These worked to some extent under the supervision of white doctors but they also used their own herbal remedies.[111] Obeah men and women also were skilled in the use of herbs and made a useful contribution to combating disease,[112] though they often operated in opposition to the white doctors. The slaves for their part were commonly reluctant to accept the ministrations of white doctors and preferred the herbalists and obeah men.[113]

Field slaves were under constant supervision during their working hours from drivers and overseers. Skilled slaves, however, were generally subject to a more relaxed authority and were seldom under the same continuous scrutiny. Indeed their occupations sometimes took them beyond the range of supervision for hours on end as in the case of fishermen, watchmen, or stockkeepers.

However, the fact that domestic slaves lived in constant contact with their masters or mistresses, in strong contrast to the remoteness which surrounded the field slave and to a lesser extent the skilled artisan, meant not only opportunities for perquisites but also fairly constant supervision, especially if the owner had a wife or was herself a woman. Again, most urban slaves worked under the direct supervision of their owners without the intervention of drivers or overseers, and the small size of many urban slave holdings meant that supervision was often very close.[114] But there was also a group of urban slaves who enjoyed a striking degree of freedom either because they followed occupations like transport work or because they were allowed to arrange their own board and lodging or to hire themselves out. In the event, complaints about the behaviour of town slaves were not unknown, in spite of the existence of a town jail to supplement the disciplinary authority of the slaveowner.[115]

Plantation slaves were almost wholly isolated from the rest of the community. They could meet with the free people of colour in the Sunday market, but this was a limited opportunity made more circumscribed by the fact that the two groups usually met there as competitors. Otherwise the free coloured were mostly concentrated in the towns where the field slaves were hardly ever seen. Slaves living on neighbouring estates were more accessible, but even these were at least in theory kept at a distance by the pass laws which restricted the slaves to their own plantations,[116] though in practice mixing between neighbouring plantations was not uncommon even without the special event that was a funeral or feast. Contact with the whites was perhaps the most limited of all, since very few lived on the plantations and these had little direct contact with the field hands except on the smallest estates.

There were, however, occasions when the slaves had some freedom of movement and of social contact. In Tobago they were allowed to attend slave funerals on other estates within reach and such ceremonies could attract as many as 900 slaves from within a radius of up to ten miles. Those involved would walk back to their homes to be ready for work next morning.[117]

SLAVE HOUSE IN TOBAGO
Drawing by Sir William Young
Reprinted from Sir William Young, "Memoranda respecting estates of Sir William Young, Bart. in the West Indies with plans, etc . . ." (1804). Manuscript.

The Treatment of the Slaves

It is difficult to provide a picture of the treatment of the slaves in Tobago during this period, for the evidence is extremely thin. In the first place, however, the law on the killing of slaves in Tobago was relatively advanced. From the outset in 1768 this had been regarded as murder, though of course the likelihood that the planter-dominated courts would convict a white person on such a charge is another matter. In the one case which has come to light, however, a conviction was secured. In 1813, admittedly at a time when the treatment of slaves generally was known to be attracting attention in Britain, Young reported the conviction of Catherine Traynor, a white servant, for the murder of the slave Anne. The case is untypical in that the murderer was of such low status and in that sexual jealousy was the principal motive.[118]

Traynor was employed by Dr Rourke "in every Household Drudgery that a Slave could be made to do" and lived with Anne "as a sister".[119] She shot Anne with Rourke's pistol when she learnt that the latter had called the constable to arrest her, seeing a deliberate attempt to displace her as his sleeping partner.[120] The evidence was clear and she was convicted by a jury of twelve after a charge from Chief Justice Piggott which had stressed that a slave had the same right to be protected against being killed as had a free colonist "without distinctions of Colour or Condition". In this respect at least Tobago had more respect for the rights of the slaves than many of its neighbours. Young praised the jury despite being embarrassed by its recommendation of mercy. Ultimately he granted a reprieve on the ground that this was a case of "female jealousy" not involving "malice aforethought" or "personal ill-will" and bearing in mind that Traynor was in very bad health. He was also influenced by the fact that Traynor was not a slaveowner and he thought it unlikely that the outcome would influence the conduct of masters towards slaves.[121]

The case of Catherine Traynor apart, the principal evidence bearing directly on the treatment of the slaves in Tobago before the slave registration returns began in 1819 to indicate the demographic facts, lies in the writings of Sir William Young. On the one hand it may be suggested that Young, as a plantation owner and governor of the colony, had a vested interest in presenting the colony and its planters in the best possible light. On the other, he had a reputation as a supporter of the amelioration of slavery dating back at least to 1797, and it is clear that he wished also to see the slave laws, such as they were, fairly enforced. On the one hand, he complained to the legislature that the law requiring a regular quarterly return of all runaways and absentees was much ignored although that information was needed "for the detection and apprehension of Vagrant Slaves" and to prevent the formation of gangs of runaways.[122] On the other hand he was a strong critic of unfair or unjust punishment and later of the legal procedures surrounding the trial of slaves.

Soon after Young became governor in 1807, on the initiative of Assemblyman Lyons, a bill was passed "for the better protection of slaves from being wantonly beaten and ill-treated by white or free persons of colour".[123] The object was to protect slaves from being beaten or ill-treated by persons other than their masters, by providing a legal process which would get round the difficulty of finding free people as witnesses to testify against the accused. The Act provided that in any case of that kind if the admissible evidence were insufficient for conviction the accused should be compulsorily examined on oath. The penalty for thus ill-treating a slave was to be a fine of £10 or three months imprisonment.[124] The compulsory examination of an accused person under oath was of course contrary to the whole principle of the English criminal law, and in due course the Act was disallowed.[125] The episode is important, however, as showing that the Tobago House of Assembly was rather ahead of its time in relation to the measure of protection which the law might give to the slave, and as demonstrating the governor's own willingness to innovate in seeking to ensure that the slaves were fairly treated. Young believed that "so invincible is the Objection of our Colonists to the testimony of slaves where a White Person is concerned", and so great the difficulty of convicting a white person of ill-treating a slave without such evidence, that the peculiar procedure proposed was a lesser evil than continuing to leave such offences unpunished.[126]

Writing in 1811, Young expressed the view that those slaves who worked on plantations were generally well treated: they were adequately fed and cared for when sick and in return were required to do "moderate labour"; It is noteworthy that night work during crop was by this time fading away.

The extremely high mortality rate among the slaves and the general correlation of mortality with patterns of work would seem to destroy Young's view of the labour régime in Tobago as "moderate". It has been estimated that in Tobago in 1807 with a total which Young put at 17,254 slaves, there was one slave to every two acres in cultivation and that this was a lower ratio than in the other Windward Islands and much lower than the one to one ratio often thought normative indicating that the slaves in Tobago must have been, relatively speaking, rigorously worked.[127] This was the more so because sugar, the most exacting of all crops where labour was concerned, was the only significant one.

Young was clear, however, that in practice the slaves were relatively well treated on the larger estates, meaning those employing about 300 slaves. Small estates, and he had in mind those with about sixty slaves or less, were so burdened by overhead expenses necessary to the working of any estate that they were much less profitable, perhaps less than half as profitable as one with 300 slaves, and would in consequence be forced to exploit their labour force much more rigorously. "The little Planter, poor and often distressed for articles of personal Comfort, which Habits of Life have rendered indispensable to him, to procure a fund for these, will at times overwork his Negroes".[128] The importunities of mortgagees were another form of pressure which led small planters to work their slaves more rigorously than the owners of larger properties. However in 1811 only nine of the eighty-nine plantations in Tobago employed less than seventy-five slaves.[129]

Young claimed that the harder life which slaves on small estates faced was reflected in a higher death rate and a higher rate of natural decrease in the slave population. The number of estates and the mortality rate in terms of the number of slaves employed is shown in Table 4.1.[130]

TABLE 4.1 SLAVE MORTALITY AND BIRTH RATES IN TOBAGO, 1819-1821

Number of slaves	Under 50	51-100	101-200	201-300	301-400	Over 400
Number of estates in 1811	1	19	39	20	4	2
Registered births in 1819-21	19.4%	14.1%	21.3%	23.2%	19.1%	18.6%
Registered deaths in 1819-21	33.5%	52.0%	50.5%	47.6%	43.7%	32.7%

Barry Higman's calculations for the years 1819-21 bear out Young's view of the relationship between mortality and estate size so far as they go. Slave mortality was highest on plantations with 50-100 slaves, and lowest on the largest ones. The rate was 52 per cent against 32.7 per cent, but the latter figure applies only to a handful of properties.[131] Moreover, mortality rates are not necessarily an index of how well the slaves were treated outside the context of their work but they do tend to reflect conditions of work. Young conceded the need for regulations to correct "over-thrift" and overwork on the estates, but did not see how this could work in practice.[132] It is clear that Young's view of working conditions was very much too sanguine.

Granted the greater rigour of the owners of small plantations and his obvious blind spot when looking at work practices, Young had not heard of any "wanton cruelty" towards the plantation slaves, and he thought that he must have heard of it if it did take place.[133] To put his views in perspective we must separate the work régime from the planters' treatment of their slaves in their non-working hours and in relation to their social life and to the question of punishment. He had faith in the effectiveness of the master's self interest in not damaging his labourers. So far as legal process was concerned it is perhaps significant that only one instance has been found of a master being compensated for the execution of a slave, a fact which would normally be recorded in the minutes of the Assembly.[134]

Young believed that the abolition of the slave trade in 1807 had set off a trend towards improvement in the care of the slaves "since they cannot now be replaced",[135] a view which modern scholarship generally supports. He thought, however, that where numbers fell significantly in the absence of new supplies the remaining slaves might be driven to work harder, a view supported by recent analysis of the situation in Jamaica,[136] and that there were other respects in which abolition perhaps brought new difficulties to the slaves. As numbers dwindled small estates tended to be abandoned, as occurred to at least two in Tobago, and the resultant transfer of slaves to those which remained sometimes involved the separation of families. Yet it is noteworthy that the early Methodist missionary Jonathan Raynar reported in 1818 that the treatment of slaves in Tobago was usually above average and "cases of cruelty were comparatively rare".[137]

On the whole, then, the evidence seems to suggest that while the rigours of plantation slavery were inescapable and the labour régime more rigorous than in many other islands, and excessive use of the whip did draw adverse comment in the 1790s, by the early 1800s the slaves on the estates in Tobago were relatively fortunate by the standards of that system if they survived the ravages of their work. Within that context the following account by Sir William Young written in 1811 is worthy of note:

> the Slaves on the Plantations show a Cheerfulness and an easiness of service which note a contented and Orderly People. Many of them, considered as the lowest class in the community, and looking to the class of common Labourers in the freest Country, are comparatively rich. Every householder supplies his family with pigs, poultry, corn fruits, & vegetables by purchase from the Negroes coming to Market . . .
>
> I may be told that I am not describing Slaves, but an *happy Peasantry*; be it so.[138]

Young thought that such behaviour on the part of the slaves could only point to generally good treatment. But he agreed that there were problems, notably the naturally decreasing population which has already been considered. In another version of the same report Young noted:

> ... their Masters ... sleep in the Planter Mansion without Boll or Bar, within the Circle of their Negroe Village: Gentlemen & Ladies from dinner or supper parties ride home, at all hours of the night, across a wild Country through Thickets, or by solitary Passes, without the least Apprehension of any Negro whom they meet, there has not been a single Instance of Robbery or Violence by a Negro committed on a white Person travelling the Public or private Roads, in the nearly five years of my Government, & be it remembered that every Negro has a Cutlass in his Hut.[139]

Almost the only adverse comment to be found in Young's general view of the slaves in Tobago observed that theft was very common among them. It is noteworthy that except for the two conspiracies which we have noticed, the slaves in Tobago were consistently reported to be "quiet and orderly" during these years.[140] On the other hand, the fact that these conspiracies occurred further indicates that Young's view of the situation was again too optimistic. Further evidence is the fact that slaves regularly ran away, and while it is impossible to say how often they did so, it seems that even in so small an island as Tobago gangs of runaway slaves were not unknown.[141]

Young did believe, however, that ill treatment, cruelty and unjust and excessive punishment were to be found in good measure among the town slaves, "the narrower trading or household circles of unattached slaves", especially among slaves owned by "lower white or Coloured people" who owned up to about ten slaves. To put it at its lowest, the owner of a few town slaves was not restrained, as the master of a plantation gang was, by the possibility of setting off a revolt. These were the slaves who suffered from the shortcomings of the protective laws, and he noted an occasional robbery of a store in Scarborough by slaves.[142] Higman notes the presence in many West Indian towns of stocks and cages in addition to jails for the confinement of town slaves though there was no cage in Scarborough down to at least 1800.[143] It was, after all, a small town, without the refinements of Bridgetown or Basseterre.

The generally law-abiding character of Tobago's slaves is not of course evidence of contentment or good treatment. It may mean merely that the penalties of transgression were sufficiently horrific to be an adequate deterrent. But it remains unlikely that someone with Young's known inclination to see the slaves justly treated would either be ignorant of or seek to conceal visibly inhumane treatment as this was understood under the slave system. Young was in many contexts perfectly willing to criticize Tobago's planters.

At the same time the failure of surviving official records to mention any incident of brutality against a slave by his or her master or mistress cannot mean that such occurrences did not take place. Rather it suggests that none took place which struck contemporaries as worthy of special notice. If the lack of evidence of brutal treatment supports Governor Young's generally sanguine view of the situation, it also suggests that much harsh treatment was regarded as routine. Indeed it was inseparable from the nature of plantation slavery, the more especially in a monocultural sugar colony. Alternatively if such treatment was unusual enough to be noticed, any attempt to take action on it was known to be useless and Young's own views on the question of slave evidence, reviewed below, suggest that this was sometimes the case. It is also significant that as the years passed the slave code grew steadily tighter as every incident involving slaves which showed them as less than quiescent in the face of authority brought further restrictions upon their already very limited freedom of action or further penalties for breaking regulations. This was always done in aid of the security of the slaveowners in their wealth and property not to mention life, always the paramount consideration.

The notion that the slave was less than human may well have had something to do with the casual attitude of some slaveholders to the treatment of their slaves. Many whites appeared to believe that discomfort meant less to blacks than it did to themselves. Even when the slave was accepted as human his inferiority was widely regarded as self-evident. As one Tobago observer noted, the slave was "a poor depressed part of the human species".[144] This view must have helped many to allow maltreatment to pass unnoticed.

What little protection the law offered to the slave was largely vitiated in practice by the difficulty he faced in taking legal action to enforce it. In the first four years of Young's governorship, for instance, no free person, white or otherwise, was ever convicted of any breach of the protective laws[145] and he wrote in 1811 that "Circumstances in the Administration of whatever Law, render it a dead letter".[146] Young was referring chiefly to the fact that the evidence of a slave was not admissible against a free man. This meant that slaves were in practice without redress against a cruel master: even if some free person were present to witness his cruelties, none would give evidence against a fellow free person on behalf of a slave, while a slave accused in court by white testimony could scarcely hope to be able to rebut it. On small plantations the resident master might well be the only free person. The non-plantation slaves too often had regular contact with only a single free person, their master or mistress. As Young put it, "In the back yard of the Jobber of a small Gang for hire; in the Workshop or out buildings of each Artisan or petty Tradesman, and within every House, the greatest Cruelties on a Slave may be exercised, without a Possibility of Conviction". Young saw this situation, which was of course not confined to Tobago, as a radical defect in the administration of justice throughout the West Indies. As he wrote: ". . . in whatever case the wrongs done to a Slave are under Consideration . . . Justice cannot in truth be administered, controlled as it is by a Law of Evidence, which covers the most guilty European with Impunity".[147]

In theory adequate protection for the slave might have been provided by an elaborate and efficient system of police backed by a magistracy outside the control of the planters and their Assemblies. In practice this was quite impracticable in the conditions of the time.[148] Young's solution to the problem was to admit slave evidence before the courts, at least in some circumstances.[149] This view he admitted to have been derived from his conversations with the Chief Justice, Elphinstone Piggott, whom he regarded as an outstandingly learned, wise and just judge.[150] It was not an original idea, though only a very few individuals could have been found to support it. In Dominica slave evidence had been admitted in 1798 against whites accused of harbouring runaways, or of selling or giving them weapons or food, though this was less the product of any spectacular regard for the rights of the slave than a response to a special fear of "evil-minded white persons" who assisted runaways, a very dangerous practice which endangered the stability of the island's society and was thought to justify very special measures.[151]

Once more Tobago seems to have been a place where some enlightened opinion existed as regards the slave law, both governor and Chief Justice being supporters of a reform which, while urgently necessary in the interests of justice, was generally anathema to the slaveowning classes in the West Indies.

Young adopted this view fully conscious that throughout the West Indies the planters would reject it. The fact is that even the abolitionists were afraid that to give the slaves the right to testify against whites seemed likely to make them conscious of the question of civil rights and so to undermine their acceptance of slavery.[152] More specifically they were convinced that vindictive slaves would give false evidence and argued that they had "no sense of religion" and "no feeling of the moral obligation of an oath", the two observations being of course interconnected. But Young argued that "Truth is by God implanted in the Heart & Mind of Man, however uninstructed" and that in fact a primitive people had a higher regard for truth than the more highly civilized. If slave evidence was inherently unreliable it was equally so whether the accused be slave or free. Young drew a distinction between the "competency" of a witness and "credibility" of evidence and saw the slave as entirely "competent": his credibility was to be determined in the light of the other evidence in any given case. The governor was convinced that it was only a matter of time before slave evidence was admitted as competent, and at least in "instances of known and good Negro character" as credible if corroborated.[153]

In many British West Indian colonies the manumission of slaves was regulated by law by the late eighteenth century. To some extent these were protective provisions which sought to avoid the manumission of old, diseased and disabled slaves who were unable to provide for themselves and who would pose a humanitarian as well as a security problem if allowed to wander around and/or to beg. Manumissions intended to enable the masters concerned to escape the poll taxes on slaves were another obvious problem providing another argument for regulation and again security was involved. Altogether the restrictions on manumission owed more to a concern for public order than to any desire to protect the slaves.[154]

In Tobago, however, it seems that no law on the subject existed until 1814. We do not know the rate of manumission before 1808, by which date there were 253 free persons of colour in Tobago; but between 1808 and 1813 it was generally steady averaging about thirty-six or thirty-eight a year, two-thirds of them women.[155] In 1810 a Mr Lyons proposed a bill to regulate manumissions in the Assembly, but this made no progress.[156] There is evidence to suggest, however, that increasing numbers of slaves were being manumitted without proper provision being made for their support. Usually they were old and/or indigent and became a nuisance to the public. Some of them seem to have been slaves from other islands who were manumitted in Tobago, possibly to escape the restrictions in their own islands. In 1814, however, the Tobago legislature passed an Act to compel persons manumitting slaves in that island to provide for their support. Under this law no manumission was to be valid unless £100 currency was paid to the Public Treasurer on the slave's behalf and all manumissions were to be recorded at the office of the Island Secretary. In return the Treasurer was to pay the slave £8 a year during his or her lifetime, but this benefit did not apply to slaves from other islands. After this the rate of manumission fell to about twelve each year.[157]

Mixed blood slaves, since they were usually skilled and privileged, had the best opportunities for gaining manumission. First, their occupations brought larger cash rewards than were available to the unskilled slaves in the fields; and, secondly, their blood relationship to the whites provided some chance of gratuitous manumission by a white father. Indeed there is evidence that in other islands a white man who did not free his slave children would be regarded with disfavour by his fellows, at least if he was a man of any consequence, and the position in Tobago was hardly different.[158]

In Tobago, as throughout the West Indies, the whole society and economy were utterly dependent upon slavery. More than 90 per cent of slaves in Tobago in 1815 were working on sugar estates, the remainder being employed in the two towns. Certainly the professional and managerial posts were held by whites, and whites and free coloured shared the skilled trades with the elite slaves, but the whole edifice depended on the wealth generated by the sugar estates. Moreover, almost every white or free coloured family acquired at least one domestic slave and the wealthier planters might have fifteen or more in the household. In 1811 Tobago had 1,464 domestic servants to cater for a population of 583 whites and 350 free coloureds according to one calculation, and Governor Young thought this figure likely to be too low. Moreover, the possession of a number of slaves was recognized to be a means of rising in the social and economic scale for the lesser whites and the free coloureds, for apart from the status which ownership of slaves conferred, the hiring out of a wide range of slaves was an important source of income. It was perfectly possible to make a respectable livelihood entirely from the hire of slaves.[159] In 1807 an estimated 462 slaves were working in hired gangs, most of them apparently on plantations.[160] But some town residents kept gangs of twenty to forty slaves to hire out[161] and in 1811 there were some 400 town slaves who were commonly hired out to estates.[162]

Slaves were also used to reinforce the slave system itself and to defend the islands against invasion as well as revolt. Slaves were used to supplement the white and free coloured militia especially in the manning of the coastal batteries.[163] In 1812 when a soldier from the garrison murdered an officer and took to the bush, the two militia officers sent to track him down were authorized to requisition the services of "such number of stout able [negro] men as they may judge proper", especially those who worked as huntsmen, and did in fact employ about thirty slaves.[164]

Slaves, therefore, sometimes willingly supported their masters even against their own kind. We have seen that the mixed blood elite slaves came to share the view of the free coloured that the black race was inferior to the white and to seek to emulate the ways of the latter while deliberately submerging much that was of African origin. Similarly as the decades passed the black slaves themselves derived from their whole environment the lesson that their race was inferior to the white even though they moved much more slowly away from their African origins.

In the end the slaves were successfully subordinated so thoroughly because the whites succeeded in persuading many of them that their race was inherently inferior to the white. The myth of Negro inferiority became a pillar of the slave society and was self-perpetuating because it so precisely fitted the actual facts of the black slaves' existence. Thus the white colonists were able to subjugate many times their number of slaves: in Tobago some 500 to 800 whites supported by 300 or 400 coloureds dominated 17,000 or 18,000 slaves.[165] Their success of course owes something to the fact that they were backed by the armed imperial power of Britain; but the social conditioning of the slaves was of fundamental importance.

THE ECONOMY

Land Grants

The economic development of Tobago began only in 1764 when the British government, having just acquired formal sovereignty over the island, began to sell land on terms calculated to promote its utilization and penalize the holders of grants which were left idle. The development of sugar plantations and the small scale production of cotton, coffee and indigo, on the basis of slave labour, was quickly put in hand. This pattern continued under French rule after 1781 and by 1793 Tobago was producing over 5000 tons of sugar annually, a not insignificant amount, and had also made an impact on the British market for raw cotton.

When Tobago returned to British rule in 1793 it was not long before the London based absentee proprietors began to think vaguely in terms of new development in the island's economy. They soon urged that the governor should be empowered to make grants of Crown land. They wished both to enlarge their own holdings and to attract new settlers for the further opening up of the island.[1] Soon the governor was being asked to make specific grants of Crown land to various colonists, both town lots and agricultural land,[2] and in 1795 Governor Lindsay himself proposed to try to attract small settlers with such grants[3] and asked the Secretary of State for a grant to himself of all the lands remaining ungranted and unallocated, which he described as "among the mountains and . . . of little or no real value".[4] The British government however adhered rigidly to an Order in Council of March 1790 prohibiting any further grants of Crown land in the Colonies.[5] Yet grants of occupancy were possible and from 1796 were made from time to time. Three agricultural sites and seventeen town lots in Plymouth are known to have been granted in occupancy between 1796 and 1800.[6]

In 1800 however, John Duncan, who held the lifetime occupancy of a lot in Plymouth, petitioned for it to be converted into a grant in fee simple since he had built a substantial house and offices on it.[7] There were several other colonists with similar claims. In reply the Secretary of State now decided that since the Proclamation of 1764, which had conditioned the original settlement of Tobago, had envisaged the creation of a town in each parish and provided for one to be laid out, unallocated town lots laid out at that time might again be granted in fee simple. Other lands should remain available only for grants of occupancy. It was hardly reasonable to expect people to undertake new development on the basis merely of lifetime occupancy only,[8] so attention was now focused on the towns.

Within a year nineteen grants in Milford and four in Plymouth had been approved. By 1811 a further six lots at least had been granted in Plymouth, one in Milford and eight in Scarborough[9] in addition to a number of grants in occupancy, both urban and rural. Indeed Plymouth and Scarborough became the centre of a new effort at development in Tobago. The absence of significant new agricultural grants is not surprising since, apart from the reluctance to develop holdings of any size on the basis of rights of occupancy, only the evidence suggests that the grants originally made in the 1760s and 1770s were not yet fully utilized and there was no real demand for more.

On the basis of the demand for and allocation of new lands, therefore, one would not expect that Tobago after 1793 was the scene of any substantial economic development beyond the better exploitation of the existing estates and a slow and gradual rise in urban activity.

The Change of Commercial System in 1793

However, the exchange of French masters for British in 1793 naturally meant a complete transformation of the island's commercial position. After being subject to the French *Exclusif* system for twelve years and compelled to trade only with French ports or those of France's allies, even if the goods obtained there frequently originated in Britain,[10] Tobago was suddenly required to conform to the British Navigation Laws and so to send her produce in the very different direction of Britain and her colonies. Trade with Britain's colonies in North America became free of restriction and trade with Europe was transformed in that all sugar was required to be exported to British ports. The trade of the whole of the British West Indies was subject to vagaries imposed by war, and once the initial adjustment of routes was made Tobago was hardly different from the other colonies. The same was of course true not only of sugar but also of the import trade in British manufactures, brought in ships seeking to take off sugar. There were periodic shortages of food and of all sorts of manufactured goods. In 1812, for instance, it was necessary to send to Barbados for paint and brushes with which to redecorate Government House.[11]

The principal developments of the period 1793 to 1815 were the expansion of sugar production on lands already in private ownership and the associated decline of cotton in the 1790s, followed by the contraction of sugar, and after 1807 a distinct increase in local food production. The expansion of sugar production was already in progress under the French and its acceleration was the result of the market opportunity provided by the extinction of the export trade of St Domingue after 1791. It resulted in an increase in exports of sugar from about 5,300 tons (8,154 hogsheads or hhds.) in 1794 to a peak of 8,890 tons (13,677 hhds.) in 1799, after which they declined somewhat[12] as British colonial sugar experienced the natural consequences of overproduction and forced production for a market which finally became alarmed at the size of its stockpiles and the high level of prices. Markets for British colonial sugar were also diversified somewhat as the protected one in Britain became overstocked and more emphasis was placed on re-exports to Europe. A pronounced boom brought about by speculative development of sugar cultivation when shortage occurred in the 1790s, even though much of its terrain was not really suited to large scale exploitation of sugar, to be followed by a serious decline after 1799 which hardened after 1807, merely made Tobago typical of its time.[13] British rather than French sovereignty was hardly an important factor in the decision of sugar planters to exploit a seller's market, though it may have made both slaves and capital rather easier to find since in these matters Britain was better provided than France.

The Sugar Industry

Tobago entered the nineteenth century as a very thorough example of a monocrop economy, sugar being the only crop to which any significant effort was now devoted. After the sugar boom ended in 1799 in consequence of overspeculation, overproduction and glut, production declined fairly sharply. While the available statistics are not wholly reliable, Young suggests that sugar production fell from 13,677 hhds. (8,890 tons) in 1799 to 10,276 hhds. (6,679 tons) in 1800, that it then recovered somewhat but suddenly fell again to 8,121 hhds. (5,279 tons) in 1803. Another recovery followed and then production steadied at rather over 12,000 hhds. (7,800 tons), until another, irregular, decline began in 1808. The production of rum followed much the same course, though its ratio to that of sugar was less than constant. See Table 5.1.[14]

TABLE 5.1 EXPORTS FROM TOBAGO, 1794-1815

Year	Sugar (hhds)	Molasses (puncheons)	Rum (puncheons)	Cotton (bales)
1794	8 317	91	4 598	1 515
1795	6 071	301	4 368	1 090
1796	7 446	42	5 693	1 327
1797	7 658	4	4 893	245
1798	9 792	-	7 415	83
1799	13 677	151	7 669	23
1800	10 276	1 383	6 429	30
1801	11 411	662	7 686	103
1802	13 300	585	7 864	81
1803	8 121	95	3 435	88
1804	11 044	381	6 390	64
1805	13 215	620	8 621	118
1806	12 580	655	8 192	97
1807	10 440	686	9 000	93
1808	10 775	206	7 934	68
1809	11 151	73	7 663	114
1810	10 221	35	1 018	-
1811	8 194	59	6 814	-
1812	11 100	22	8 423	-
1813	10 004	4	7 760	-
1814	9 444	-	6 765	-
1815 [to 5 Oct]	9 758	70	6 867	-

While Tobago's production thus showed only slow long term decline after 1799, the island was far from prosperous. Selling prices in Britain, where nearly all Tobago's sugar was sold, were very low by 1807, the best muscovado selling for only 32s. to 38s. per cwt. compared with a high of 87s. before the crash of 1799. In 1807 too it was estimated that one-third of the property in Tobago was mortgaged to merchants in Britain and the net returns of the colony were less than the total of the planters' obligations.[15] In 1809 Governor Young reported that despite efforts at economy the debts of the estates were on the whole still increasing while their resources were diminishing and the difficulties of the planters' were "extreme".[16] While in 1805 there were ninety-six estates in production, sixty of them owned by absentees, by 1810 there were only eighty-nine.[17] He estimated the total income of the "proprietary class" at only £52,000, or 1½ per cent on invested capital, which was much below their annual outlay. This situation he believed to be stifling development of the island's considerable potential.[18] In 1811 the colonists asserted in a petition to the Prince Regent, that they were being forced to sell their sugar at a loss for the most part. Low prices, the high cost of provisions and lumber, and the fact that the British government exacted a duty of £20 sterling on each hogshead of muscovado sugar were seen as the principal causes of their extreme distress.[19] Another factor was certainly the rising price and growing shortage of slaves. Only exceptionally fine sugar, they said, now brought any profit at all. The petitioners did not address the question of why their production costs were not lower. However, in these circumstances it was only natural that production was tending to fall slowly. Young remarked: "I believe the condition of the Sugar Planters to be distressful in the extreme, & to be approaching to a Crisis of Utter Ruin, and finally an Abandonment of all Colonial Interest; if means of relief & Prevention are not timely devised & taken".[20]

This gloomy picture might seem to contrast with J.R. Ward's estimate that the average annual profit of sugar estates in the so-called "ceded islands," which include Tobago, in the period 1799-1819, while significantly lower than in the preceding seven years, was yet 10 per cent.[21] Tobago, however, was in all probability the least prosperous of these islands; and the estimate in any case, while much adjusted to allow for various probabilities, is based on a chance collection of only seven plantations, none of them in Tobago, in the absence of more abundant records.

In 1812, however, the price of sugar began to rise and the planters took heart. Young said the higher prices "give life and spur to their Industry" as the crop proceeded.[22] The coming of peace in 1814 brought further optimism.[23]

The cultivation of the cane has already been described in indicating the work pattern of the plantation slaves. Obviously the crop was largely dependent on the type of soil on which the estate was located and was extremely vulnerable to the weather. If the processes of planting and reaping went well the attention of the planter would turn to the mill in his effort to achieve a successful output.

The sugar mills were powered by wind or water and occasionally by mules, though animals were sometimes in short supply. Since many plantations did not have a reliable water supply easily available in the appropriate place, windmills were generally the most common form of power in the Windward Islands as a whole. Windmills, however, posed certain problems. In high wind they had to be stopped and the sails feathered to avoid damage, while canes already cut proceeded to spoil.

Even in good weather the speed of the windmill had to be controlled as if it turned too fast it was liable to be damaged. Altogether, when windmills were employed it was difficult to integrate the speed of the grinding process with that of cutting the canes, so that canes were sometimes wasted, and grinding was sometimes not completed before the time came to begin preparing the land and planting the next crop. In 1788 Stephen Hooker of Bristol invented a windmill which was faster and could endure heavier wind, while employing fewer slaves, than those then in use; but little attention was paid to it. It has been suggested that the possibility of improved efficiency was subordinated to the desire to keep the slaves fully occupied as a means of maximizing the use of the investment they represented and also of ensuring their subordination,[24] but on the whole the evidence does not indicate that the performance of the mill was an especial problem. More important in all probability was what happened to the juice which the mill expelled.

After the cane was ground the juice flowed along a canal called the "mill bed" into a "receiver" holding between 300 and 500 gallons whence it passed into the boiling house, where it was drawn into a clarifier or "copper". Here lime carbonate was added before the juice was boiled in five or six different coppers each smaller than its predecessor. How much lime to add depended on the quality of the juice and could be a source of serious misjudgement. From the smallest copper, the "teach", the sugar was sent through a spout to the cooler as it approached granulation. Judging the right moment thus to "strike" the sugar was a highly skilled business performed by the head boiler who was usually a slave. This was a fundamental matter, where misjudgement could ruin an otherwise excellent crop by producing poor quality sugar.

Sugar was thus a notoriously unstable crop. Not for nothing has Douglas Hall written of the "incalculability" of sugar planting in the eighteenth century[25]. The problems of obtaining adequate finance and labour and of marketing the crop, the ease with which burdensome long term debt could be contracted, and the vagaries of weather and metropolitan taxation are well known and in no way peculiar to Tobago.

Tobago does, however, provide an excellent illustration of the intricacies and tentacles of plantation finance and the peculiar difficulties which could and did arise. The law of property in relation to mortgages was such that when an estate was sold or foreclosed on, or when its proprietor died, the new owner could in practice refuse to honour the debts contracted by the old, who was under no obligation to provide for it himself, until any mortgage was liquidated. This frequently created difficulties for employees or suppliers to whom money might be due, since pre-existing mortgages could take many years to liquidate. This situation sometimes meant that merchants would refuse to supply a heavily mortgaged estate for fear that foreclosure might deprive them of payment, and this in turn could possibly lead to the slaves being deprived of foodstuffs such as beef, pork, salt fish or corn which had to be purchased outside the estate. Foreclosure or collapse might thus be unfairly precipitated.

When James Campbell died in 1805 the mortgagee of his many large estates, valued at £100,000 sterling, had a first claim on his assets. This he proceeded to enforce, refusing to consider the claims of the estates' staff for outstanding salaries, or those of tradesmen who had supplied them with staves, until his mortgage was first satisfied. Such a settlement might have taken years; but some of the claimants sued and in 1808 Governor Young as Master in Chancery followed an English precedent provided by Lord Chief Justice Lord Eldon in allowing priority to claimants without whose services the estates would have had to cease functioning and so became valueless. The mortgagees, Ruckers of London, appealed, but the Privy Council confirmed Young's judgement and in December 1811 the legislature sought to ensure that this course would be followed in future with "an Act for more effectually securing the payment of certain debts controlled for the use and benefit of the Estates and Plantations in this Island . . ."[26] This Act provided that a new owner should be liable for any debts in respect of estate stores or supplies or staff salaries provided during the year preceding the change of ownership, and such debts were declared to be a first lien with priority over all other debts, thus removing one potential source of difficulty from the path of an estate which ran heavily into debt.[27]

By the end of the eighteenth century it was a very common experience for an estate which had become over-indebted to find that the servicing of its mortgage grew insupportably burdensome. When added to the other general difficulties then facing sugar planters this could lead to disaster. In Tobago soon after 1800 the number of estates began to fall as the less securely placed ones sometimes were forced to go out of business.

At a general level, then, the war rendered sugar planting an even more uncertain business than usual. Shortages of plantation supplies, and of food for the slaves, and in consequence high prices, which could ruin a planter's calculations and perhaps break him, were frequent and unpredictable in their timing. Critical shortages of shipping occurred from time to time and could destroy the value of a planter's crop. All of this without reckoning the occurrence of actual warfare and in addition to the normal hazards of the enterprise.

The impact of wartime hazards can also be illustrated at an individual level, for instance by the story of Thomas Ruddack, a merchant in

Scarborough and owner of the newly settled Adelphi estate in the parish of St George not far from Scarborough. Ruddack wrote shortly after the change in Tobago's allegiance in 1793 that, while much indebted, he had remitted "very large sums" (to France) in the previous year and had high hopes of the future though the change in the local commercial scene and shortage of shipping had made 1793 a disappointing year.[28] In March 1794 he still expected to make much money from the crop then in progress and so reduce his considerable debts.[29] But he then experienced great difficulty in finding shipping for his crop, which he eventually despatched, reluctantly, to Liverpool, Bristol and Glasgow though his merchant factor was in London.[30] The price of sugar then fell suddenly, so that the crop realized less than had been hoped and Ruddack was unable to clear his debt. He began to contemplate selling out, but without much hope of finding a buyer.[31]

In 1795 the crop was short and the convoy left Tobago earlier than expected so that there was not time to make the most of what crop there was and Ruddack's hopes were dashed on two fronts.[32] In 1796 he sold his merchant business[33] and in 1797 he at last had a good year, shipping 128 hogsheads and 30 tierces of sugar, about one third more than he had anticipated when planting his crop.[34] Thomas Ruddack may well not have been the most organized of planters, but without the special wartime problems of volume and timing of shipping, which the high prices of the 1790s did not fully counteract, he would certainly have done less badly.

A state of war was also in itself a direct danger to the security of property and so to economic stability. The changes of sovereignty in Tobago in 1793 and 1803 brought real hazards to the property of colonists who were British by birth but French in formal allegiance, and therefore legally in the position of enemies of Britain for the short period between the outbreak of war and the capture of the island by Britain. Enemy property was of course liable to seizure and estate produce being carried to Europe by ship, and the ships themselves, were especially vulnerable. In 1793 cargoes and ships owned by British born subjects had been secured to their owners and exempt from being made prizes of war by British forces,[35] while General Cuyler's Proclamation immediately after the capitulation had recognized the British born colonists, who included all the resident estate owners, as British subjects. They had suffered no loss on account of their short-lived status as enemy subjects.

In 1803, however, although similar immunities were granted,[36] the dangers attached to owning property while formally an enemy citizen were sharply demonstrated. Soon after hostilities broke out at least one ship carrying cargo from Tobago was seized by the British and it at once became clear that even if it was not forfeited the procedures involved would be costly to the owners.³⁷ Then on 21 June, before news of the outbreak of war had reached Tobago, the British frigate *Venus* cut out four French merchant ships from Little Courland Bay and took them to Grenada as prizes of war. As luck would have it one of the four, the *Phoenix* was owned by no less a colonist than Joseph Robley and two of the others were chartered to him. All four were laden or loading with sugar and rum destined for France and Robley put his loss at nearly £40,000.³⁸

Robley wrote to both military and naval authorities and then to the Secretary of State seeking restoration of his vessels and cargoes. His nephew John, in London, interceded on his behalf.³⁹ But it appeared that the exemption from capture of the property of British born subjects resident in the island only took effect when the British attack began. Robley recited the tale of his services to the colony since his arrival there in 1768 and complained that he was "almost the only person belonging to Tobago" who appeared not to be covered by the indemnity to local property owners of British descent.⁴⁰ The "Planters, Merchants, Mortgagees and Others interested the Island of Tobago resident in Great Britain" petitioned the King in Council on his behalf.⁴¹ But the Secretary of State did not intervene and the Court of Admiralty found that the vessels were lawful prize as being the property of French subjects.⁴² This was of course a unique episode but it yet serves to illustrate the hazards of war.

Abolition of the Slave Trade and its Repercussions

One vital aspect of the complex instruments of sugar production was of course the slave trade, on which the Tobago plantations at the end of the eighteenth century were still largely dependent for their labour force. Tobago had been a sugar colony for only thirty-odd years and its slave population was as yet far from self-sustaining. Since 1787 however the slave trade had been increasingly attacked in Britain on humanitarian grounds.

Although Tobago was largely insulated from the crescendo of the British agitation against the slave trade in 1791-3, the agitators of course kept their cause alive if less than hopeful and soon the Tobago planters were watching the question as closely as any. In 1796 the two Houses of the legislature presented a joint address to Henry Dundas praising his efforts to damp down the agitation. This suggested that but for Dundas the House of Commons might well have abolished the slave trade on 16 March 1796. He was, said the address, a great comfort to "friends of order, subordination and tranquillity",[43] and the island's Agent in London, John Petrie, urged him to "persevere in your endeavour to protect liberty and oppose the wild schemes of visionary reformers".[44]

For some years after 1796 the political climate in Britain was such that while the amelioration of slavery might still muster much support, the notion of abolishing the slave trade did not have to be taken seriously. However in 1799 the British agitators against the slave trade began to turn from a full blooded attack, which appeared to have no immediate future, to smaller measures by which they sought to halt the supply of slaves by British slave traders from particular areas of the African coast or to particular colonies like the newly captured Trinidad and the Dutch colonies in Guiana, where development was just beginning and more slaves were badly needed. When in 1804 a new burst of agitation began it centred on the supply of slaves to these same colonies.

It could be argued on two important grounds that supplying slaves to these colonies was contrary to Britain's national interest. First, such colonies might be restored when peace arrived, as Tobago had been in 1802, and the development which new slaves made possible would then be to Britain's disadvantage as the restored colonies would become rivals of her own. Secondly, it was becoming clear that increasing the supply of British sugar itself was unwelcome, since the British market was now overstocked and an abundant supply of foreign sugar together with the difficulties produced by the war was making it difficult to find markets for re-exports. Even if captured colonies were retained, increasing the supply of sugar to Britain by pouring slaves into newly developed areas might bring down prices to the British consumer, but low returns would endanger the status of Britain's tropical empire. And the planters of the old colonies were beginning once more to see a threat in the development of new ones. Under pressure from Wilberforce, Pitt prohibited the supply of slaves to the newly captured colonies by Order in Council on 15 August 1805, which came into force in 1806.[45]

In deference to the interests of the owners of existing estates the prohibition was not absolute. The importation of slaves to work on lands not already under cultivation was absolutely prohibited, but to keep up existing estates which needed to replace slaves lost or to make up shortages already existing, importations were permitted up to 3 per cent of the slave population each year, by special licence from the governor.[46]

The evidence suggests that only one shipload of slaves reached Tobago after the 1805 Order became effective, 168 slaves arriving directly from Africa in 1807 with the appropriate license,[47] and no case is known of any attempt there to evade the restrictions on their importation,[48] though illegal importation occurred in some other colonies.

In Britain the abolitionists pressed forward with their demand for the total abolition of the slave trade. In May 1806 Parliament passed the Foreign Slave Trade Bill replacing the Order in Council of 1805 and prohibiting the supply of slaves by British slave traders to all foreign colonies. The argument employed was similar to that which achieved the Order in Council in the previous year: as Lord Grenville put it, "it was a clear and obvious policy that we should not give advantages to our enemies, it was surely equally clear that we should not supply their colonies with slaves, whereby affording them additional means of cultivation, contributing to increase the produce of the islands, and thus enabling them to meet us in the market upon equal terms of competition, or perhaps to undersell us".[49] In passing the new Act, Parliament was moved essentially by considerations of national interest and not by the humanitarian arguments of the abolitionists but a major step had been taken towards the abolition of the trade by thus reducing its scale to little more than a quarter of its earlier level.[50]

The abolitionists were now much encouraged and proceeded to redouble their efforts for the total abolition of the trade. Parliament passed the Act for the Abolition of the Slave Trade in March 1807, to take effect from 1 May.[51]

Tobago viewed these events with dismay. In January 1807 the Assembly had asked that its Agent seek leave to have the Island's case against abolition presented from the bar of the House of Lords, and generally to do everything possible to prevent it. The House argued that abolition would be contrary to the original contract between the colonists and the British government under which the island had been first settled in the 1760s and to the terms of the 1803 capitulation.[52] This view lies in the fact that in 1763 it had been assumed that the plantations would be worked by slaves to be imported from Africa, and in 1803 the sanctity of existing laws had been guaranteed. Neither fact could insulate Tobago from the use of the imperial power to achieve reform, and in any case the future of the slave trade was surely a matter for Britain to decide in so far as British traders were involved.

In May 1806 the President of the Council, Robert Mitchell, administering the government, persuaded a special session of the legislature to send a memorial to the King pointing out "the great hardship this Infant Colony will suffer" if the slave trade were to cease, asserting that it would lead to their "inevitable ruin". It was not just a question of the supply of labour. The probable effect of treating Tobago as a captured colony and depriving it of supplies from Africa would be

> the removal of most, if not all, the Artificers, Tradesmen, Overseers and White Servants in the Colony; and most certainly will deter all those who might otherwise be disposed to resort to it in the future. The [artificers] . . . will retire to the Islands where they can supply themselves with negroes, to be trained up in their trades, to assist them in their labor. The profit to be derived from their own personal exertions in these Climates is not worth their exercise when their wonted means and advantages are entirely destroyed. The [overseers and white servants etc.] . . . have been accustomed, from the little savings they might accumulate, to profit by the purchase of negroes to assist them and their families, when their own efforts might be blunted by age or sickness. By Your Majesty's Order in Council these means are wholly taken from them all in Tobago".[53]

Thus did the Assembly see Tobago being soon deprived of its free population, as those unable to purchase new slaves to assist their economic and social advancement moved to the older islands which could still draw slaves from Africa. The Order in Council allowed new importations, even from sources outside Africa, only to meet the needs of the plantations, and planters were a small proportion of the white population. As the two Houses emphasized, "The Salvation of Your Majesty's Colonies depends upon the white population".[54] They argued that Tobago should not be treated like the Dutch colonies in Guiana but as if it were substantively British.

It is true that Tobago's position in 1806 was substantially the same as that of Grenada, St Vincent and Dominica, islands which had been ceded to Britain like itself in 1763 and where development had begun late. The difference lay merely in the uncertainty over Tobago's political future and the fact that the experience of 1802 had demonstrated that the British origins of its population were not an adequate protection against being returned to France. The threat that inability to purchase new slaves would lead many whites to emigrate, and so cause the economy to run down, was a very real one, and it is impossible not to sympathize with the colonists. When it became clear in 1807 that even the trade by British slavers to the old British colonies was doomed, President Balfour told the Secretary of State that he considered it fortunate that it was not himself but Young who would have to deal with the "certain Ruin" which he anticipated and added dramatically, "The only Consolation that remains . . . in my opinion, is such as may be used after a Hurricane or any severe public or domestic Calamity, that Time or Death will bring Relief".[55] In imperial eyes this uncertainty would clearly be enough to render the stocking up of Tobago with slaves, an as yet undesirable project. But the planters in Tobago had another perspective.

Sir William Young, as Member of Parliament, had looked on this bill as a "boon" to the British West Indies, since it stood to raise the price of slaves to foreign sugar producers.[56] As Governor of Tobago, however, he later reported that the Act had dampened the spirit and confidence of the colonists and undermined their credit in Britain because it accentuated the doubts about the island's future which were already making it difficult to secure capital. This distrust of the future also prompted mortgagees to foreclose. Some mortgages contained clauses requiring the maintenance on the estate of a specified number of slaves. Such clauses would now become unenforceable and many mortgagees must be expected to withdraw their money. Young feared a snowball effect, with mortgagees competing to withdraw or foreclose, which might ruin many planters.[57] There was also much protesting of bills of exchange and many court actions for debt.

This atmosphere combined with falling prices for sugar to reduce the volume of business as planters had little to spend and small shops in Scarborough came under pressure. Many of those who could afford it now sought to leave Tobago to live in Britain[58] so that the process of depopulation which the legislature had anticipated was actually in motion. The number of men in the militia fell from 350 to 270 in six years as people left the island.[59] Young thought that two-thirds of the "respectable Proprietors of Estates" had risen from the ranks of the overseers or had fathers who had been overseers, rising in the socio-economic scale by gradually acquiring a number of slaves and exploiting their labour until there were enough to start a plantation or money to buy one, and by 1811 many who had hoped to follow that path had been led by the abolition of the slave trade to abandon Tobago and return to Britain. These included men with a sound education in "Writing and Accounts" and a few with a "scholastic Education". Such people would be replaced by "An inferior Description of Persons, less intelligent, less accomplished & less interested in the Safety & Welfare of the Colony, where they can have nothing their own." This, thought Young, was the most damaging consequence of abolition for the planters.[60] Another was a gradual fall in the slave population which declined fairly steadily if gradually from 17,252 in 1807 to 16,076 in 1815,[61] causing a rise in the value of an able bodied field slave from £65 - £70 in 1807 to £105 by 1811.[62] The failure of the slave population to sustain itself had always meant that continuous expenditure on new slaves inflated production costs. Now that new slaves could no longer be obtained and the planters were beginning to take greater care of those they possessed, the slave system became increasingly expensive in the Eastern Caribbean generally, putting great strain on an already burdened economy.[63]

Lesser Crops

While sugar production was incomparably the most important economic activity in Tobago, the existence of lesser crops, including a certain amount of food, has already been indicated. All except food crops were in decline by the later 1790s and showed little sign of recovery. The decline of cotton production after 1793 was a natural corollary to the boom in sugar. Between 1789 and 1792 Joseph Robley's estate had become famous as the producer of perhaps the finest raw cotton in the world and between 1792 and 1797 he supplied his product, known as Robley's Bourbon, to R. Runcorn & Co., Cotton Spinners of Manchester, who produced from it extremely fine cotton yarn which sold at premium prices for the manufacture of muslin. But as the demand for and price of sugar rose after 1791 Robley began to convert his estate to that crop. Simultaneously cotton prices began to fall and in 1792 there were "considerable tracts" of abandoned cotton along the Windward road between Queen's Bay and Scarborough. [64]

Few people now attempted to buy Robley's very fine product and after 1797 he apparently ceased to grow it in quantity.[65] It was a natural response to the fact that by 1796 one acre of moderate land planted in Bourbon canes was said to produce £70 sterling worth of cane, nearly double the cost of the land, in a single year.[66] In 1794 Tobago exported 454,500 lb. of cotton, but by 1800 the crop had almost disappeared. In the following decade exports averaged less than 30,000 lb. a year.[67] The production of the small scale crop indigo appears to have almost ceased by 1793 and soon afterwards vanished.[68] Tobago also exported a small quantity of coffee and occasional amounts of lime juice, a kind of rum punch called "shrub", tortoiseshell, arrowroot, fustic, hardwood, and an item described as "sweetmeat".[69]

The changeover from the French to the English economic system, together with wartime privation, might in theory have stimulated the cultivation of provisions to substitute for imports from the United States of America which were severely restricted by the British navigation laws. We shall see that this restriction was largely set aside in practice and little new effort was devoted to growing food crops until the restrictions on trade with the United States were again enforced to some extent after 1805. Tobago had always sought to provide a substantial measure of the food consumed by the slaves from local production, even to the point of a clause in the Slave Law which laid down how much land an estate should devote to provisions. When this law became disused because planters preferred to allow the slaves to cultivate individual gardens, an arrangement which held advantages for the slaves themselves, it was never intended to rely wholly on imported food. After 1793, moreover, American food had in practice been fairly easily and regularly available and there was no incentive to develop local food production. There came to be a period each year, after the crop and before the provision harvest, when local food was commonly short.

When Sir William Young arrived to assume office as governor in 1807 he was of course very familiar with the history and problems of the island and within a few months he proposed the formation of an agricultural society in an effort to develop its resources more fully. Indeed he believed that Tobago was capable of being made self-sufficient if it were properly exploited. He pointed out that only a little more than half of the 57,408 acres held by the settlers of Tobago was actively occupied and that much once productive land had been allowed to revert to bush, crops of cotton and coffee had deteriorated and indigo had vanished. Young believed the soil was very rich and as regards sugar he suggested experiments with the new Bourbon cane, with manuring and with economies in the manufacturing process and labour saving devices. Otherwise he called for experiments with cattle rearing and he stressed the importance of growing food for the slaves locally. He even thought it worth considering whether both land and labour should perhaps be diverted from sugar to cattle and food, especially maize, root crops and plantains, in an effort to reduce Tobago's dangerous dependence on imported articles. Young believed that pigs might be reared and bacon produced locally with success, while local woods could be exploited for dyes, furniture and guns.[70]

In August 1807 Young, touring the windward district, observed that his exhortations for the cultivation of more provisions which had been emphasized by a falling off in the provision trade with the United States following the Non-Importation Act of 1806,[71] had been widely heeded. He did not say whether plantation land or slave gardens, or both, were involved; but there had been a great expansion in the planting of maize and roots, he thought, by 200 per cent, in May to June and when the harvest came in September maize fell in price from three dollars to one dollar per bushel.[72] In November an Agricultural Society was in fact formed at a meeting held at Government House (Mount William) attended by thirty-four persons including most of the more important planters. Young was chosen as patron. John Balfour was elected president and George Morison, another member of the island Council, vice president. Subcommittees were set up for each of the eastern, central and western districts, to meet monthly, and a general meeting was to be held every six months. A centre for the deposit of seeds and samples was set up at Government House.[73]

Secretary of State Lord Castlereagh welcomed the Society in principle but was nervous lest it became an instrument for political pressure and warned Young against the possibility that it might be "perverted to the possible furtherance of a party or Cabal, if any should at any time rise in the Island".[74] He urged the governor to restrict discussion at its meetings strictly to agricultural matters. Young took the point and promised that the Society's business would be simply that of communicating information about agricultural experiments and the distribution of seeds and he would not allow open debate at meetings.[75] Castlereagh need not have worried. No evidence has been found of the Society's activities, but though Young claimed in 1811 that its activity had given rise to similar societies in other islands,[76] it seems unlikely that it could have been a significant success and it had ceased to exist by 1815.[77]

Some long term response was forthcoming, though, to the governor's plan to grow more provisions. Apart from the initial enthusiasm evident in 1807, Young reported in the following year that the supply of maize and yam was such that the new American trade embargo had caused no serious hardship to the slaves though the European population still hankered after flour.[78] In 1809 a long drought produced a temporary shortage of provisions,[79] but in 1811 and again in 1812 and 1815 large areas were reported to be planted in provisions.[80] The principal factor in the supply of provisions to the slaves seems by this time to have become the weather rather than the inflow of imports. A very good harvest in 1815 not only eliminated shortage but brought prices down by perhaps 50 per cent as against the previous year.[81] But there was still a tendency to shortage of provisions between June and the beginning of the local provision crop in October, and during this period Tobago was still largely dependent on imported provisions, especially in the event of a drought in mid year.[82]

The influence of Young and his Agricultural Society may also be seen in the growing use of local woods for building containers after 1807. The American embargo caused a very serious shortage of staves which in 1808 was made up locally,[83] and in 1813 one planter applied for a grant of land in occupancy in the interior specifically for the purpose of cutting staves.[84] Local staves however could be obtained only with great labour and much inconvenience.[85] Tobago's woods were deemed unsuitable for "the tight cooperage of rum" and likely to affect its flavour, so that planters lacking imported staves tended to make little.[86] In fact planters often had to interrupt sugar production for lack of containers.[87] In 1815 it was asserted by both Houses of the legislature that many buildings had been pulled down to make heading for hogsheads yet some planters had still been forced to stop making sugar for lack of packaging.[88]

Much of the provision crop was of course produced by estates or by individual slaves for their own use, but a good deal of local produce was sold either in the Sunday market or by slave or free coloured hucksters. Indeed, it has been noticed that free coloured hucksters, most often women, have been credited with conducting a very large proportion of the island's internal trade.

Internal Marketing

In 1798 the people of Scarborough petitioned the governor to take steps to control the town's market.[89] A month later the legislature passed an Act "to establish regular markets in the Towns of Scarborough and Plymouth". This Act authorized the appointment of Clerks of the Markets who would have power to confine in the public cages any disorderly persons committed by the justices, and provided for the proper regulation of weights and measures.[90]

Closely allied to the control of the markets was the question of the policing of the town. Before the passing of the Scarborough Police Act of 1807 this appears to have been very lax,[91] but nothing was done about it, though the question of public order in the towns and their market places was recognized to require attention.

Recalling after four years the conditions in the Scarborough market early in 1807, Sir William Young claimed that slaves who came there to sell had been frequently "defrauded in weight and measure", or forced to sell at unreasonably low prices if not simply robbed of their goods by "miscreant white people" or by the free coloured. Not being able to give evidence against free people, the slaves could get little redress and accumulated instead a fund of grievances. The result, according to Young, was that every Sunday Scarborough became "a scene of squabble and riot" and after sunset there would be "outcries of complaint and menace" from the country slaves who, encountering difficulty in obtaining payment for their goods, would then get drunk at the rumshops and return to their plantations in "a Spirit of ill-humour and revolt". Feelings were further inflamed by the fact that numerous incidents of violence might end with slaves being punished.[92]

Those aspects of the Scarborough Police Act of 1807 which concern the control of slaves generally have been dealt with elsewhere, but the Act was also concerned to provide for the general policing of the towns and to regulate the operation of their markets. Though its object was avowedly "the preservation of good order and decorum among the lower Classes of Society" who might sell in the markets, the problem was not simply a matter of the irritation and indiscipline among the vendors described above, whether they were slave or free. The root of the matter was the behaviour of purchasers rather than vendors.

Every Sunday a constable was now to be stationed at each market to keep order generally and to see that the Act was enforced. Meat, fish and turtle were not to be sold in either town elsewhere than in the market and, there, ten minutes' notice of the commencement of sale was to be given by sounding a bell. In the market, sheds were to be provided for the sale of these articles. The purchase of meat, fish, poultry or provisions with intent to resell was not permitted either in the market or on the road thither. Vendors were expected to sell their own produce.

Slaves attempting to sell sugar, rum, coffee, molasses, cane or slave clothing in the markets without written permission from the master were to be committed to jail. These were all items of plantation produce and it was supposed that if their sale were permitted the slaves would steal their masters' goods in order to sell them. A penalty of £10 currency was provided for selling short weight or measure; otherwise a breach of the Act was penalized by fines of up to £50 and in the case of slaves by flogging.[93]

The governor thought that this Act at once produced better order on market days and provided greater safety for those involved in market transactions.[94] Subsequently the Clerk of the Market was given authority to settle disputes about sales and payments from which the slaves could appeal to the justices. Reviewing the functioning of the markets in 1811, Young thought that slaves using it were now generally satisfied with their dealings and the discontents identified in 1807 had generally disappeared.[95]

Despite the close control of the Sunday markets, however, the evangelical missionaries took grave exception to the whole system. It affronted their conception of the proper purpose and use of the Sabbath. In 1809 the LMS missionary Purkis described the Sunday market in Tobago as "the most prolific source of evil to every class of people". It brought "thousands" of slaves to Scarborough who after selling their goods "crowd the shops and stores to buy necessaries to carry home". The missionaries objected to the fact that this situation put everyone under pressure to buy and sell on a Sunday when trading was at its best. Moreover, since most slaves went away from their estates on a Sunday the managers and overseers also seized the opportunity to go to town, for pleasure if not for business.

According to Purkis, "the employments of the evening are truly shocking to the ears of anyone that is concerned for the honour of God. [In] every direction around the house we hear organs, violins, humstrums, dancing by the slaves, and roars of laughter and prophane songs by the white and free people and this frequently even in the house of a magistrate [sic]".[96] He summed up: "The Sabbath is made completely a 'devil's holiday'," which was one way of reacting to the fact that the market made Sunday not only an occasion of widespread commerce, but also a festive day.

The idea of eliminating the practice of selling on the sabbath would never be very far from missionary thoughts, but this could only have been done if the plantations were to sacrifice one of their working days for a market day and the whole purpose and nature of the slave plantation system made that unthinkable.

The Act of 1807 dealt overwhelmingly with the control of the market and the question of general policing appeared chiefly in the provisions for enforcing the laws concerning trading. It provided for the appointment of a town jailer who was to be present at the courthouse in Scarborough every day and be available at night to receive persons convicted or committed to jail. Two justices were to sit in Scarborough every Monday and Friday with a constable in attendance, less frequently in Plymouth. Plymouth had no jail, but in 1810 stocks were provided in the marketplace. It should be noted that the appointment of constables does not imply the existence of regular police; they were part-time officers paid by the day.

A year later the governor commented on the outstanding success of this enforcement machinery.[97] The Act, originally effective for one year, was continued unhesitatingly and made perpetual in 1810.[98] In 1813 Young thought the justices of Scarborough were doing their duty well, though their powers were not adequate for the effective control of the slaves in the town after dark. "Frays of Negroes" in the streets at night were still sufficiently common for the inhabitants to have established a voluntary system of night time patrols in order to keep the peace.[99]

The 1807 Act also sought to deal with the problem of animals wandering in the streets, an old hazard to passers-by often due no doubt to the negligence of the town slaves, but for that their masters were formally responsible. Sometimes the animals may have strayed from estates just outside the town. The Act provided a penalty of £50, half of it to any informer, for permitting horses, mules, donkeys or cattle to wander loose in Scarborough or Plymouth; and anyone who encountered any pigs or goats in the street was allowed to kill them and to appropriate the carcass after waiting for two hours.[100] The nuisance was not ended however and in 1815 authority was given to kill any pigs straying in the streets or on the lands of the towns.[101]

The markets apart, the sale of liquor was the subject of separate and specific legislation. It had been controlled in Tobago since the first period of British occupation, and the Tippling Act indeed had been one of those revived in 1794. But liquor remained quite freely available and the inclination of the garrison troops towards it attracted unfavourable attention.[102] In 1797 a new Tippling Act was passed following a petition from one Joseph Macay and other whites whose businesses were allegedly being injured by competition from free coloured liquor sellers.[103] This provided that licenses for the sale of wine, beer and spirits were to be granted by at least three justices, one of whom had to be a member of the Council. They were only to be granted to persons who could find two freeholders to stand as sureties, and cost £12. 10s. 0d. currency per quarter. The sale of liquor to slaves was totally prohibited and it could only be sold to soldiers and sailors on an order from an officer.[104]

It was the continuing sale of rum to soldiers, sailors and slaves which prompted the passing of a new Act in 1804. This provided that not more than four liquor licenses should be granted in Scarborough and one in Plymouth at any one time and raised the license fee to £50 per quarter. The Act also sought to streamline the procedures for obtaining convictions, empowering the justices to examine under oath any licensee suspected of breaking the law.[105]

The penalty for selling liquor without a license was however the very large fine of £330 currency without the option of imprisonment. This was counter-productive since so heavy a fine could not in practice be recovered from persons who had no property on which to levy distraint and such persons could often break the law more or less with impunity. The illegal sale of liquor by unlicensed persons was not therefore eliminated until in 1810 an alternative penalty of three months imprisonment was provided.[106] Thereafter we hear no more of illegal liquor sales.

It is not clear how far the peace and order of Scarborough generally or the market in particular were affected by the two substantial fires which occurred in 1812-13. On 9 May 1812 there was a large fire in which Thomas Blakely suffered losses estimated at £2,000 currency, seven others lost property valued at a total of £1,750 and the Assembly agreed to grant a total of £2,500 currency in compensation to the victims.[107] Another fire occurred on 16 July 1813 but the extent of the damage cannot be determined.[108] On both occasions the garrison played an important part in fighting the fire and was rewarded by a lavish distribution of liquor.

The Supply of Coin and Bills of Exchange

Economic activity in Tobago, as in the other West Indian islands at this period, was impeded by a constant shortage of coins of convenient denominations. Like all the British West Indian colonies, Tobago depended upon coin brought in from abroad while the usual tendency was for it to flow outward to Britain and, via the North American traders, to the foreign islands. Only base coin was likely to remain long in Tobago since traders were anxious to take away good examples. With a free population of only about 700 persons the volume of internal trade was small and, notwithstanding the involvement of the slaves, could only recirculate the small volume of coin which was retained. The only significant source of good coin was the pay of the garrison, which found its way to the "hucksters and grog shops". Some gold and silver did issue from the Customs House and other public offices, mostly concerned with naval or military affairs,[109] and a little gold was attracted by the relatively high local price (90s. per ounce in 1808 against the Bank of England's 80s.). The gold was used in the trade with the Spanish Main.[110]

The coins in normal circulation were a heterogeneous mixture of European items at the best of times, including gold johannes and half johannes and doubloons, moidares and pistoles, and Spanish silver dollars, copper estampees and "black dogs". The bit, worth 9d. in local currency, normally related to sterling at a rate of about 2:1, was in practice a unit of value since such coins were hardly seen. The value of these coins was frequently suspect, as while it was accepted that normal wear would not affect their value, many of those in circulation showed abnormal wear and not a few were clipped, both kinds being described as "base". The difficulty of using coin as the basis of commercial business was further enhanced by the presence of counterfeit coins.

In 1798 the number of false coins circulating in the islands was large enough to prompt the British Government to issue a circular warning to all its governors.[111] Later in the same year the governors were instructed to issue a proclamation warning against the prevalence of underweight coins and urging people to weigh those they used as a check on their value.[112] In Tobago the Council appointed a committee to study the problem,[113] the amount of base copper coin in circulation, much of which was so obvious as to be impossible to use, being a pronounced hindrance to small purchases.[114] The committee estimated that 75 per cent of the 8,000 johannes in circulation were underweight.[115] In August an Act was passed requiring all estampees and black dogs to be "stamped" as genuine and of satisfactory weight or withdrawn from circulation at the colony's expense[116] and fixing their value, but this was disallowed in April 1799 for reasons which are not clear.[117]

One solution to the problem of underweight silver or, less commonly, gold coin which was canvassed from time to time, was to fix a standard value according to weight and pass light coin by weight. In Tobago, however, this idea was widely resisted, for while it would stop the deplorable practice of mutilating or clipping coin it would cause loss to those caught with light coin, and the amount of such coin in the island was a large proportion of the whole. This fear of loss not only prevented action to correct the situation, it had in 1798 almost wholly stopped the circulation of silver.[118] The difficulty of fixing a satisfactory value for weight, bearing in mind the fact that coin would move to the islands where it was most valuable and would thus desert Tobago if too low a figure was fixed there, was another impediment to such a reform.[119]

Despite the opposition of a majority in the Council however, in October 1798 Governor De Lancey issued a proclamation establishing value for weight for a variety of foreign coins on a scale only slightly more generous than that used in Britain and indicating that light coin should pass pro rata. The value of the gold johannes was fixed at 72s. sterling for 18 dw. 8 gr. and of the Spanish silver dollar at 4s. 6d. for 17 dw. 6 gr.[120]

By 1806, however, the circulation of counterfeit copper coin, some of it deliberately introduced into the colony by unscrupulous traders, was again causing serious concern,[121] as it did at intervals thereafter since laws prohibiting the importation of base coin remained less than effective in the face of the profits to be gained.[122] Secretary of State Castlereagh thought Tobago's coinage in "the most deplorable state" but could see no immediate remedy.[123]

In practice the estampee was now, and remained for several years, the only market coin in use, worth 2¼d. currency or 1⅛ d. sterling, which was said to be equivalent to twelve times its intrinsic value. The other commonly recognized coins were the black dog, worth about 1½d. currency or ¾d. sterling; the cut dollar, with a circular piece 4½d. sterling in value cut from its centre so as to keep the coin in the island, worth 4s. 1½d. sterling or 8s. 3d. currency; and the full or round dollar worth 4s. 6d. sterling or 9s. currency. Gold johannes and doubloons passed by weight at 9s. currency or 4s. 6d. sterling per dwt, a slight increase on the 1798 values.[124]

Subsequently the persistent shortage of coin persisted and became such that goods were normally sold with a one-third discount for cash and rum was very commonly used as a substitute medium of exchange. The fact that in Tobago the estates produced two puncheons of rum to three hogsheads of sugar, against a regional average put by Bryan Edwards at 1:3, made this expedient easier to accept. In 1808 a gallon of rum was passed as 3s. currency in puncheons of 120 gallons plus £2 for the container, or £20 currency (£10 sterling) per puncheon. In 1813, with the local currency rising against sterling, rum was current at 2s. sterling per gallon.[125] Merchants selling for rum would usually agree to future delivery, commonly in April, with the price being inflated by up to 50 per cent to cover interest during the waiting period and other risks. Young said that this was the most usual means of paying for provisions supplied by local merchants.[126]

Most planters sooner or later found themselves paying in "rum to be delivered" and subsequently it became extremely difficult to escape from a perpetual cycle of committing the produce of the following crop and paying 30-50 per cent for the credit. Most American cargoes were paid for thus. There were actually two methods of paying for imports in rum. *Rum at Cash Price* represented an agreed price per gallon and the seller priced his goods to include interest until the rum was sold. *Rum Price* carried no indication of the cash price on either side but was a straight barter arrangement which represented a speculation on the part of the American merchant who would later sell off the rum for what he could get.[127] Physicians, managers and overseers often received their salaries in rum. Shop bills were sometimes "priced in rum" and Young reported that it was sometimes preferred to "an assured bill of exchange".[128] Import duties, which had to be paid in cash, were sometimes the occasion for a grace period of up to six months.[129] Irish beef however posed problems as the Irish would not take rum and the sugar was usually committed to Britain. Planters therefore had to pay in bills, and if they could not, the beef was liable to be taken elsewhere.[130]

Good bills of exchange on Britain were also scarce, since Tobago's credit was poor. Reputable bills of exchange were normally passed at about "200%" (£200 currency to £100 sterling). Bills on the Imperial Treasury or Board of Ordinance would usually be rather higher up to 225 per cent.[131] In 1808 bills of "sure acceptance" fetched £212 and government bills £215 to £225.[132]

Subsequently the value of gold and silver in Britain began to rise and the London value of the silver dollar mounted from 4s. 6d. sterling to 5s. 6d. so that exporting a dollar from Tobago to London brought a profit of 22½ per cent. The result was an accelerated movement of the already scarce gold and silver coin out of the islands and into Britain. Governors therefore began to raise the local values of gold and silver coins, notably the dollar, and the Tobago Assembly, recognizing a matter beyond their competence but within the governor's prerogative, followed his lead.[133] Young was concerned to avoid a competition for coin between the various British islands and urged a uniform policy to be directed from London.[134] But none was forthcoming and gold and silver coin almost disappeared. Shortage of coin caused the price of £100 sterling bills to fall to £180 currency by 1813,[135] which in effect increased the imperial government's expenditure, especially on the garrison, apart from the inconvenience and difficulty caused to purchasers. The imperial authorities however could see no remedy other than an eventual increase in trade.[136]

By 1812 gold was priced 5s. an ounce higher in Tobago than in Barbados, equivalent to 3d. in the dollar,[137] and by 1814 both gold and silver coin were valued higher in other islands. They were accordingly even more than usually scarce in Tobago so that it was "extremely difficult to procure sufficient for the current purposes of life".[138] Pressed by both Houses of the legislature to raise the value of foreign gold and silver coin as had been done in other colonies similarly placed, Young issued a proclamation in May 1814 setting the value of gold at 10s. currency per pennyweight and that of the Spanish silver dollar at 14 bits or 10s. 6d. currency or 5s. 3d. sterling instead of 9s. currency or 4s. 6d. sterling, while the locally "cut" dollar was fixed at 13 bits or 9s. 9d. currency, and the piece cut from the dollar at 2 bits or 1s. 6d. currency. This proclamation was to be in force for one year,[139] but seems to have been prolonged.[140] Young did not in fact expect this step to have much effect[141] and it is not clear just how much it achieved.

External and Internal Communications

The supply of coin was, of course, an important link between the internal economy of Tobago and the external trade which was its source. That external trade had always to proceed in a context in which knowledge of events abroad arrived weeks if not months after the event. Governors had to deal with Assemblies, as managers had to conduct the business of their absentee principals, in circumstances which left them isolated from news from Britain for long periods. As soon as the British recaptured Tobago in 1793 its British oriented planters sought a regular mail service to and from Britain,[142] lacking under French rule, apart from the needs of the colonial administration for regular external communication. A regular service was arranged by the British Post Office in 1794. This was conducted via Barbados, to which the mail packets sailed from Britain, and was quite often delayed there, apart from those occasions when the loss of the mail boat by enemy action in wartime caused a total break. In September 1794 President Robley complained to Secretary of State Dundas "The delay of the Tobago Mail at Barbados is a very great grievance to the Colony, not only to individuals, but also to the Public Service."[143] He asked that mail should be arranged twice instead of once a month, as was the case with the better established British colonies. This was eventually achieved in December 1794 when three mail boats were put into service among the islands.[144]

Barbados, however, remained the distribution centre from which mail boats were sent around the islands and the problem of delay there persisted. Sometimes the difficulty was the loss of a boat, but more often it was a simple matter of delay.[145] The two factors together could mean that mail, when not completely lost, could take more than three months,[146] and there were times during the war when several packets were lost to enemy action in a short time. Apart from the delay occasioned to official communications, the planters found their arrangements for exporting produce and importing supplies seriously disrupted and the merchants even more so. In 1801 the legislature became seriously disturbed about this[147] and in 1803 the postmaster at Barbados was reprimanded by the General Post Office in London for the delay to General Grinfield's mail.[148] Two months' worth of mail which reached Barbados in three separate boats arrived in Tobago simultaneously in March 1809[149] and this was not a unique occurrence.[150] In the later stages of the war however greater regularity was achieved, mail normally taking between five and six weeks and seldom more than eight without specific mishap.[151]

Communication with North America was much less difficult than with Britain, and less vulnerable to the effect of warfare. But the war produced blockades, embargoes and restrictions which interfered with the normal movement of shipping so that even in relation to America the latest news was always eagerly awaited and delays of several weeks were not uncommon.

While external communications were thus vital to Tobago's development as a source of tropical crops on the basis of plantation slavery, its economic life was also conditioned by the pattern of internal communications. One of the old laws revived when the restored British constitution began to function in 1794 empowered proprietors of estates to establish access roads to market, harbour and church, but no effective machinery existed for their maintenance. An Act for this purpose was passed shortly afterwards,[152] but the results were inadequate and after an abortive attempt at further legislation a few months later[153] a new and comprehensive Road Act was passed in November 1795.[154] This Act identified seven roads whose maintenance was to be a public responsibility: the coast road running all round the island; roads across the island from Rockley Bay to Courland Bay, Scarborough to Courland Bay, Scarborough to King Peter's Bay and Barbados Bay to Castara Bay; and subsidiary roads from Plymouth through Les Coteaux to the road to King Peter's Bay and from Scarborough to Fort King George. Together these would provide a network of roads giving reasonable access to the leeward part of the island, though the western area would have only the coast road.

Subsequently new roads were constructed on occasion, like that built in 1811 from King's Bay to Trois Rivieres Hill.[155] Between three and five way wardens were appointed for each parish and for Scarborough, charged with overseeing the maintenance of relevant sections of road and empowered to requisition slave labour and animal transport for the purpose from the adjacent estates, and to impress overseers to supervise the work. They were also empowered to take materials from any adjoining field which was neither cultivated nor fenced. If any public road was reported impassable the way wardens were required to take action within twenty-four hours on pain of a fine of £33. They were also authorized to undertake improvements in their discretion as well as simple maintenance, to widen roads up to 30 feet and to brush the shoulders to a width of 60 feet, subject to the right of the estate affected by any proposed improvement to appeal to a jury of seven freeholders.

Estates which possessed fences along the side of a public road were obliged to cut them back to a maximum height of 4 feet twice each year, throwing the cuttings away from the road, because high fences produced so much shade as to create mud in wet weather. If the estate failed in this duty the way wardens were empowered to do what was necessary and bill the estate at the rate of 10s. for each day's labour. Since cattle, horses and mules allowed to graze on the roads were both dangerous to passers-by and liable to break up the road if it was wet, animals found thus were liable to be impounded except where the road passed through an estate pasture. The proceeds of fines imposed for non-compliance with this Act were to be applied to road maintenance. However no estate could be obliged to provide more than 150 days' labour a year for every 100 slaves except as a credit against the next year's liability, unless the road was positively impassable.

The fact that the roads were seen as important and their maintenance as a considerable responsibility is illustrated by the presence of several prominent planters, including councillors and assemblymen, among the way wardens. The important power to requisition slave labour was not one which was likely to be conceded to lesser colonists, though any resident of the parish was eligible for appointment. The initial corps of way wardens was named in the Act but subsequently they were appointed annually by the justices.

The Act also provided a scale of compensation to be paid when labour was requisitioned: 4s. 6d. per day for a slave, 3s. for cattle, 3s. 6d. for a mule, 10s. to 16s. for a cart, 5s. for a driver. If a road was relocated compensation for damage to any plantation was to be assessed by four planters, two being nominated by the proprietor concerned and two by the wardens. There was a practical limit however to the amount of slave labour which could be obtained for the roads by levy on the estates and it was occasionally necessary for the legislature to allocate public funds to pay for additional labour.[156]

No evidence has been found as to the working of this Act, except that in 1803 it was thought necessary to provide for a fine of £50 currency on any way warden who neglected to discharge the duties which it imposed on him. Certainly wet weather could wreak havoc with the roads even to the extent of wholly interrupting communication between Scarborough and even the nearby leeward districts, not to mention the more remote areas to windward.[157]

The limited success of the Act is further attested by the fact that a new Road Act was passed in December 1805 to replace that of 1795 but it has not been possible to trace its text, which is missing from extant collections of the Tobago Acts. It is clear however that the new Act sought to make the cost of road maintenance a colony-wide rather than a parochial responsibility, so that parishes with a large population and thus with comparatively good roads would contribute towards the maintenance of the roads in sparsely populated parishes with small reserves of slave labour. An argument occurred in the Council however over how best to achieve this, Charles Wightman protesting in vain that it could be most equitably done by paying for the labour needed to maintain the roads from the colonial revenues rather than by broadening the way wardens' power to requisition labour. It also seems that disputes had arisen over the amount of labour requisitioned in particular cases since the justices were now given power to determine them.[158] This Act applied not only to roads as had its predecessor, but also to the streets in Scarborough and Plymouth.[159]

Subsequently, the legislature was frequently concerned with the state of the roads. A further Road Act was passed in 1811.[160] Thus if Tobago's roads were not always in good order it was not because the government did not recognize their importance but rather a matter of persuading its substantial citizens to recognize their responsibilities. The fact that several parishes were sparsely populated and so unequal to the task of providing their own roads naturally complicated the problem.

The provision of adequate bridges requiring specific resources which the way wardens could not provide, was also a matter of constant concern though little action. In 1798 the Assembly set up a committee to undertake the repair of the bridge at the western entrance to Scarborough, which provided access from both Courland and Sandy Point, while planning to import bricks and building lime from Britain for a more permanent structure.[161] In 1806 the legislature resolved to build a masonry bridge over Cooks River, "at the corner of the Court House" in Scarborough, to facilitate communication between the bay and both the Upper Town and Concordia[162] but as late as 1815 this project had not yet been implemented.[163] Bridging the road at Bacolet Bottom was mooted in

1808,[164] in 1810 a bridge on the road to Mount William was approved, and in 1813 the Houses agreed that a bridge should be built over the Bacolet River on condition that Bacolet estate paid half the cost of £650 currency,[165] but no evidence has been found that these projects, all of which required public money, were actually completed.

Another problem of communication which affected commercial activity in Tobago in common with the whole complex of politics and especially law enforcement was the simple matter of printing. In 1793 one George Burnet apparently operated a printing press there but it does not appear to have been much used: while he printed official documents upon it on occasion, the colony's laws and the minutes of the legislature exist only in manuscript and there seems to have been no newspaper. In 1796 Burnet disappears from view and for more than two years there was no printing press in the island. Then in October 1798 David MacDonald was granted a twenty-year monopoly of printing and in 1799 he was publishing a *Gazette* in which official notices appeared from time to time together with commercial advertisements. However, only two items printed in Tobago are known to survive from this period, a single copy of an "Act to establish and regulate a small coinage" passed in 1798 and one of an issue of the *Gazette* dated in 1801.[166] Official documents continued to be produced in manuscript. Soon after 1801 there was again no printer in the island.

In view of the limited amount of printing being done, laws were commonly publicized by posting handwritten copies or notices in public places, which meant that many people must have remained in ignorance of them for long periods. The courts normally had only handwritten copies of the laws to consult and information had commonly to be spread by word of month. Merchants had no regular means of announcing the arrival of new cargoes and planters had to await personal messages from their agents before learning of prospective sailing dates.

This was a source of concern both to the executive and to the legislature and in 1806 the Assembly resolved that any printer who would establish himself in Tobago would receive its "liberal support". It seems to have been anticipated that the St Vincent printer, one Johnson, might have been induced to transfer his business or open another in Tobago.[167] Whether the Assembly's resolution was a factor must remain uncertain, but in August 1807 Governor Young reported that "a printer is just set up here" and for the first time the annual Money Bill was printed.[168] A few weeks later the *Tobago Gazette* was restarted.[169] Not only did this ease enormously the task of informing the population about official business and decisions; it was a great help to the merchants who at once started filling its columns with advertisements for all sorts of goods as and when they arrived in the colony. The *Gazette* also carried despatches about international affairs culled from British or American newspapers.

The Import Trade

Economic life in Tobago was thus complicated by infrastructural difficulties including problems of communication, the circulation of money and the exchange of goods. Another vital concern was the supply of foodstuffs and of building and packaging materials. The accustomed importation of provisions and lumber from North America in return for rum and molasses, was disrupted by the return to British sovereignty. In 1788 an Act of Parliament had confirmed that the former British colonies now comprising the United States of America would be allowed to export their produce to the British West Indies only in British ships while British West Indian goods exported thither were to be subject to export duties. These were not terms which the Americans could easily accept and the effect was to prevent the restoration of the use of American provisions to anything like prewar levels. Since British opposition to trade with the United States was in 1793 still generally vigorous while the French islands traded with them, and indeed many Tobago planters had had contracts with American suppliers during the French period, a significant change of pattern was to be expected.[170]

When war broke out in 1793 however the British restrictions on trade with the United States broke down because foodstuffs and plantation supplies became short and prices rose very high when French privateers captured a number of British vessels.[171] A week after the capture of the island General Cuyler, acting no doubt under the pressure of his newly appointed Council, granted permission for the importation of American produce into the ports of Scarborough and Great Courland Bay for a period of twelve months. As there was an acute shortage of cash, Cuyler also gave permission for the export of rum to the USA in payment for the articles imported.[172] These dispensations, which have been overlooked by Lowell Ragatz,[173] enabled the commerce in provisions and rum to continue subject to the exigencies of wartime. They enabled life to continue in normal channels, but did not prevent a growing shortage of provisions. Although the number of ships arriving from the USA is impressive, twenty-six in the first six months for instance, they were usually small vessels of limited capacity, averaging only just over 100 tons.[174] It was to become necessary to allow further relaxation of the normal regulations and to extend the special indulgence for much longer than twelve months. During 1793 provisions remained generally in short supply, and there was no prospect of obtaining much from Britain, so that prices continued to rise.

The Spanish Main and the free port

Meanwhile the Tobago planters sought to make arrangements for importing supplies from the widest possible range of sources despite the fact that a British colony would normally be restricted to trade with Britain and her colonies. The Tobago absentee interest in London at once began to argue that the island should have a free port as part of the existing system of free ports in the British West Indies which had been used since 1766 to encourage trade with the Spanish and French colonies under special restrictions.[175] In March 1794 Council and Assembly made the same request, in order to promote commerce generally and so the expansion of production.[176] The fact that sailing vessels could run from Tobago to the Orinoco and back easily and "without a tack", while good cattle could be obtained there, made the prospect of such a trade additionally attractive and the proposal was reiterated at intervals. Eventually in April 1796 an Imperial Act was passed (36 George III c.55) making Scarborough a free port "on the same footing and with the same privileges" as the other British West Indian free ports.[177] Tobago was, however, never of any consequence within the free port system.[178]

In 1798 President Robley proposed that Tobago should be allowed to trade with the Spanish colonies, notwithstanding hostilities with Spain, by means of a system of special licenses,[179] as Trinidad and Jamaica had been in 1797 and Grenada a few months before.[180] At first the British Government were not impressed;[181] but the request was repeated, Britain was keen on access to the Orinoco from which her statesman expected much,[182] and in March 1800 the Duke of Portland agreed. The Spanish vessels involved were to have not more than one deck, they were to carry licenses and trade only between specified ports, each license being valid only for a single voyage to be performed within a stated time.[183] By proclamation on 3 June 1800 the governor enumerated the commodities permissible as imports:[184] wool, cotton wool, indigo, cochineal, drugs, cocoa, tobacco, logwood, fustic, dyewoods, hides, skins, tallow, furs, tortoise shells, hardwood timber, cabinet woods, horses, asses, mules, cattle, provided they were the produce of the Spanish colonies; and coin, bullion and precious stones coming from those colonies. Such goods might be re-exported but exports were otherwise limited to rum produced in any British island, goods lawfully imported (meaning essentially British manufactures) but not masts, yards, bowsprits, pitch tar, turpentine, other naval or military stores, or tobacco. It does not seem however that Tobago gained very much from the concession of this typically one-sided arrangement, the nature of which demonstrated that it was intended to benefit Britain by boosting her imports of scarce raw materials and exports of manufactures while offering Tobago little more than a boost to an as yet non-existent entrepôt trade and the chance of acquiring a little coin and livestock. Its success depended largely on Tobago's ability to provide British manufactures in exchange for Spanish colonial produce and the island seldom had surpluses of such goods. But certainly a small trade did develop in livestock and timber and cotton, hides, indigo and dyewoods also figured.[185]

The return of the French in 1802 naturally terminated Tobago's free port trade and when the British came back a year later free port status was not at once specifically reactivated, although the privileges which Tobago had enjoyed before the return of the French were generally restored. Without free port status the trade did not revive "owing to a belief amongst the Spaniards that under the present circumstances the Spanish Vessels which frequent Tobago would be liable to Seizure but more particularly in the event of hostilitys commencing between the Two Powers".[186] That this fear was well founded is shown by an incident which occurred in 1805 when the Spanish schooner *Nuestra del Carmen* arrived with mules. While the Collector of Customs and the President of the Council, acting as governor, wished to admit the vessel and allow the mules to be sold, the garrison commander tried to seize it.[187] The Secretary of State ruled that the ship's entry was proper, but the fact is that general orders had been given for the detention of Spanish vessels and property and the naval and military officers did not always appreciate that this was not intended to affect the free port trade.[188] There is evidence that the suspension of the trade after 1802 did cause hardship.[189] Even though it was not large, the Spaniards were the primary suppliers of mules which were essential to the estates.

In 1804 John Robley, who at this time was residing in England, took up the question of the restoration of free port status.[190] There seems to have been some apprehension among ministers that this might provide "an opportunity for the illicit introduction of foreign merchandise" since restrictions surrounding the free port system had been shown over the years to be difficult to enforce. But Robley argued that if trade could not be conducted with the Spanish colonies supplies would have to be obtained from the United States of America and in 1805 an Act was passed reestablishing the free port, war or no war, on the same terms as set out in 1800.[191] Subsequently the trade with the Spanish colonies was revived, three vessels arriving in 1806 and eight in 1807 as against one in 1805.[192]

The principal items imported were mules, of which some hundreds arrived each year, as well as cattle, pigs, rice and some tobacco. Most ships took only coin in exchange, but some accepted British manufactures re-exported by Tobago merchants or rum.[193] After Spain joined England in the war in 1807 the special provisions of the Free Port Act were amplified in practice under more general laws of trade in wartime. The range of goods which could be traded and of vessels which could be employed was broadened.[194] But trade with the Spanish was adversely affected by the war from time to time and later by the rebellions in Spanish America.

Throughout this period, however, the expansion of the free port trade was hampered by the shortage of merchant houses with active contacts in Britain which could supply British manufactures, one of the consequences of the uncertainty as to Tobago's future. The Spanish colonies remained Tobago's principal source of mules, and every ship arriving in these years seems to have brought some. Most also brought hides and some also brought horses and indigo. Mules sold in Tobago for between £16 and £25 sterling and brought good profits to the Spanish.[195] The United States, however, was a much more important supplier of cattle and horses, at least in the years after 1805 and also supplied a few mules on occasion. Small numbers of these animals were also obtained from other British West Indian islands.[196]

The lumber and provision trade

In 1794 it became necessary to extend the dispensation which General Cuyler had issued in 1793 allowing the importation of goods from the USA in the face of continuing shortages and steadily rising prices. Governor Ricketts was now very specific. Instead of Cuyler's very general dispensation, the governor's proclamation granted exemption from the Navigation Acts for the admission from the USA in American ships of provisions of all kinds, lamp oil, and all articles which could be lawfully imported in British ships, and for the export of rum and molasses in American ships, for a period of four months.[197]

This effort at ensuring the arrival of adequate supplies was perhaps even less successful than Cuyler's, for in March 1794 the United States had laid an embargo on trading by American ships with the British West Indies in retaliation for British seizures of neutral and in particular American shipping carrying French colonial produce or supplies destined for the French islands. This was lifted three months later as America and Britain began to negotiate,[198] but no American ships called at Tobago for several months[199] and the shortages accordingly became worse. In prolonging the dispensation for a further six months in August 1794, President Robley extended its application to "all States in Amity with Great Britain".[200]

In the circumstances the Secretary of State had no option but to approve these emergency measures[201] and indeed 1794 had seen strong representations for such trade relaxations on behalf of all Britain's West Indian colonies.[202] When Britain and the USA signed the Jay Treaty in November it seemed that relief was in sight, but America's refusal to ratify the West Indian clauses of the treaty made with Britain, which prohibited American ships from taking British West Indian produce to foreign destinations either directly or as re-exports, left this trade to continue on the basis of special dispensations. In February 1795 and again in August the governor granted another six months' extension of the emergency relaxation.[203] The British government accepted the necessity and indeed in 1796 Britain formally relaxed the general restrictions to allow the colonies to import American provisions in return for rum and molasses though sugar was still in theory to be sent only to Britain.[204]

These successive dispensations, common to most West Indian colonies and always renewed while the war continued,[205] enabled enough American provisions to reach the island to sustain life, but not to end shortages.[206] As the war dragged on, despite the fact that the prohibition of imports from the United States remained suspended, American goods were continuously scarce in Tobago, sometimes acutely so. Ships arrived in significant numbers year by year as Table 5.2 shows[207] but the quantities they brought were small in relation to a population of about 16,000 distributed among over 100 estates. And long periods sometimes passed during which no supplies were received.

TABLE 5.2   SHIPS REACHING TOBAGO FROM THE UNITED STATES, 1794-1801

Years	1794	1795	1796	1797	1798	1799	1800	1801
Ships	43	42	56	40	50	39	70	54
Tons	4,842	4,210	5,574	4,002	6,427	5,113	8,042	5,641

It is instructive that in 1800 a minor crisis occurred when a British ship arrived with salt provisions and the Collector of Customs sought to take action on the ground that she was technically in breach of the Navigation Laws.[208] After a petition against any such action by a number of "respectable inhabitants" the crisis was ended by amending the law.[209] The price of flour had now risen to the unprecedented level of $30 (about £6. 15s. sterling) per barrel, while rice and salt fish were also particularly expensive. Normal pressures had been enhanced by a poor crop of local provisions in 1800 through "dry weather and destructive vermin",[210] and the failure of supplies from Europe had intensified the competition between West Indian islands for American goods. Wild fluctuations in prices took place as stocks rose and then disappeared to rise again eventually. In 1801-02 flour ranged from £3. 6s. 0d. to £8. 5s.0d. per barrel, butter from £13. 4s. 0d. to £4. 8s. 0d. per firkin and back to £13. 4s. 0d.[211]

Throughout this period fish was the only item imported from British North America (which we may conveniently if anachronistically term Canada) in any quantity. Lumber and staves, both indispensable for successful sugar production, arrived in Tobago from Canada only in trivial quantities even during the war with the United States in 1812-15.[212] The British government's view that the West Indies should obtain the goods they needed from Canada was always wishful thinking: British North America had no such large surpluses.

It should be noted however that the Tobago planters, like others in the British islands, had other motives besides ensuring a regular supply of provisions at reasonable prices for seeking to keep open their trade with the USA. Molasses and rum were subject to duties in Britain, where their consumption was tending to fall, and brought much better profits when sold to Americans. Moreover, as their production of sugar was expanded in line with that of the other sugar colonies following the revolt in St Domingue production of rum as a by-product also rose. The USA was the best possible market for it.[213]

While the dispensation to American ships was intended to apply only to provisions, oil, livestock and lumber, it seems clear that other American goods were sometimes landed throughout the British islands. In Tobago specifically for instance, in December 1797, the Council advised that a petition from two American captains to be allowed to land a quantity of brandy, gin, sherry, Madeira wine, soap and candles should be granted as the articles were in short supply.[214] All were non-essential and prohibited goods. In March 1804 the Council persuaded the governor to allow the landing of another very similar cargo on the same grounds.[215] Several other examples could be cited, including tobacco and ale, until the Secretary of State on the advice of the Privy Council Committee for Trade and Plantations directed that only provisions and lumber should be admitted after 1806.[216]

The Peace of Amiens brought to an end the justification for the special exemptions and licenses by which the British West Indies had been able to ignore the normal laws of trade and conduct commerce with almost all comers, especially with the USA, on the ground of the exigencies of wartime. The licenses were not at once discontinued, but soon after the Peace British shipping and mercantile interests pressed for the general revival of the old restrictions in aid of their own business. These proceedings were at the time irrelevant to Tobago, then back in French hands, but its recapture by Britain and the theoretical return of British law was immediately followed in July 1803 by a proclamation allowing the importation of salt provisions and lamp oil from the USA in American or other neutral ships for a six-month period.[217] Such concessions were repeated on one basis or another until the war ended. This was 1793-1802 all over again.

The large share of the British West Indian trade which thus fell to the Americans quickly attracted the further attention of British shipowners, merchants and manufacturers, who called for the rigid enforcement of the laws which sought to restrict British colonial trade to British subjects. Representatives of the West India interest argued that open trade was essential to the economic success of the colonies but the Committee for Trade and Plantations recommended that the laws of trade be enforced.[218]

Thus in September 1804 the governors were warned not to open their ports to American goods other than lumber and provisions except in cases of "real and very great necessity" and to report fully the circumstances of all such cases.[219] And in January 1805 came the further instruction that even in such extreme circumstances only lumber and provisions were to be admitted from the USA in American ships, and that the terms of any permission should be rigidly administered.[220] The white population of Tobago, as in most of the other colonies, then put great pressure on the governor to keep the port open and so it remained. In 1804 what appears to have been a record quantity of American shipping, fifty-seven ships totalling 6,461 tons, had entered Tobago.[221] But the Americans were now said to be alarmed at the new possibility of their ships being seized and for a while few cargoes arrived. In April 1805 there was no beef, butter, maize or peas in the island and no American flour; and butter and peas were still unobtainable in August[222] though the records show that by the end of the year eighty ships totalling 8,711 tons had arrived from the United States. In 1806 what beef and pork came to hand from Ireland was too expensive for many of the planters being twice the price of the American product and sometimes more.[223] Canadian supplies too, when available, were very expensive. Shortages and high prices occurred whenever the supply of American goods was obstructed and sometimes even when it was not. Both the supply of goods and the level of prices over many years suggest that American trade was indispensable not only to Tobago but to the British West Indies as a whole.[224] Neither Ireland nor Canada nor Britain herself could provide adequate quantities of food or lumber for the estates.

In Tobago, where the opening of the ports to a fair range of American goods after 1803, and the occasional licensing of cargoes of yet other goods, did not succeed in keeping the colony supplied, there were other factors besides the simple shortage of goods from non-American sources which hindered the flow of legitimate imports. Tobago's future was still so uncertain, a restoration of French rule being still regarded as a distinct possibility, that few would invest money in commercial enterprise there. As President Campbell put it: "From the particular circumstances of this Colony it is not to be expected that mercantile houses will be established here for the mere purpose of importing into the Island Provisions from Ireland . . . The circumstances of the Island deter the adventurous Mercantile men. If they were to form establishments, they could not count upon their permanency, and they will prefer other Colonies".[225]

Without mercantile houses to organize imports from British sources, only the Americans would bring goods to Tobago, situated so far to the south as it was, on their own initiative. There was no merchant in Tobago, for instance, who imported Irish goods routinely and without special consignment, as happened in most other British islands.[226] And Irish vessels normally avoided Tobago because all the latter's produce was earmarked for merchants in Britain and there was no acceptable means of paying them. The planters were accustomed to paying the Americans in rum which the Irish would not accept. Moreover, if they paid the latter in bills or in sugar, their unsaleable rum would be a dead loss which they could not support. In practice, however, Tobago's planters almost never needed to find a means of paying for significant quantities of Irish provisions. They almost never appeared.

British merchants dealing with Tobago usually had continental rather than Irish connections, as did Messrs Ruckers, as a result of the period of French rule after 1783 when Tobago had to pay bills through France. This was unlike other islands, whose British connections had links with Ireland which were used to send out Irish provisions.[227] It was also important that Tobago was further to the south, and therefore less readily accessible to shipping from either America or Europe, than any other Caribbean colony except the rather differently circumstanced Trinidad. It was not to be assumed that trade restrictions which worked elsewhere would work equally well in Tobago, where special steps to attract shipping might well prove necessary. The available evidence suggests very strongly that without American supplies Tobago could not hope to escape periodic shortages and their accompanying high prices, even when local food production rose significantly after 1808. But those British interests which sought to enhance their position through the exclusion of all American goods from British colonies, as well as those specifically concerned with the export trade of the British North American colonies, continued to press their case and the colonial relaxation of the restrictions which the British mercantile system postulated was the focus of constant pressure. The outcome was that the actual restrictions which government sought to impose were constantly changing in detail as the imperial authorities sought to balance imperial interests and colonial necessities in a practicable policy.

By the end of 1805 the British Government had adopted the position that while necessity might require the importation of provisions and lumber from the United States, the West Indian colonies should be encouraged to buy from Canada or from Ireland whenever possible. This in practice meant holding American competition at bay in favour of Canadian fish and Irish butter, beef and pork.

The imperial Parliament now passed an Act authorizing the issue of Orders in Council while the war lasted, allowing the import and export of enumerated goods in neutral ships in the British West Indian colonies. This Act, which provided formal powers to relax the instructions previously issued to the governors to limit their discretionary power to lumber and provisions, formed the basis of a series of regulatory Orders issued over the next ten years. In March 1806 the imperial government decided that the British Treasury should pay a bounty of 2s. sterling per quintal on Canadian salt fish imported into the islands, for one year from 1 June 1806. Colonies which agreed to repay the bounties to the British Treasury and to offer a bounty of 1s. after the imperial offer expired were allowed to import fish from the USA as well. Meanwhile gubernatorial permission to import American provisions and lumber should exclude beef, pork and butter.[228]

Thus a fiscal preference could be offered to Canadian fish which recognized that it was impracticable to prohibit the American article altogether, at least for the time being; and American provisions and lumber would be openly accepted. This was a realistic stance. The development of the Canadian fishing industry was a legitimate imperial objective and some subsidy from imperial funds, at least while the scheme was set on foot, was more than justified by the importance of not interrupting the supply of fish to the West Indian colonies. Salt fish was an item of special importance, being almost the only source of protein in the slaves' diet except for special issues of salt beef or pork at Christmas. The mixture of salt fish with their provisions and plantains was, as Young put it "a habit of life which it would be irksome to their feelings, and might be prejudicial to their health, suddenly to forego".[229] When the imperial advances for bounty ceased in 1807 the Tobago Assembly, like several others, agreed to continue it from its own resources so as to retain access to this vital item, American fish.[230] But the success of the effort to build trade with British North America would also require the development of a market there for the rum which Tobago would use for the majority of payments and was the principal freight she could provide for the return journey.

The imperial view of Tobago's problem owed much to a refusal to conceive that a colony should be treated in accordance with its peculiar needs rather than with a generalized imperial policy. The Governor of Barbados had said that provisions could be obtained from British sources and Grenada, Antigua, Montserrat and Nevis managed without the Americans, and it was in the view of the committee for Trade and Plantation "of essential importance that the same Rule should be observed as nearly as possible in His Majesty's several Islands in the West Indies, as well from a Principle of Justice and Equity, as to avoid Dissatisfaction in those least favoured". The Committee further thought that if any special indulgence was after all to be offered to Tobago it should be a purely temporary measure. It was inclined to think that Tobago's pleas over American provisions were not really justified[231] and that the difficulty would be removed if only the planters would arrange larger importations from Britain. But it recognized the necessity of allowing the governors to permit importation in their discretion and on their own responsibility *in extremis*.[232] The British position was formalized with two Orders in Council made on 17 September and 1 October 1806. The first authorized the governors, under the Act of 1805 "to permit, for a limited time, the importation in any ships belonging to the subjects of any state in amity with His Majesty of staves and lumber and any kind of provision (beef, pork and butter excepted) being the produce of the country to which such ships shall belong; and also to permit the exportation, in such ships, of Rum, Molasses and other articles".[233] The second Order added to the list of permissible imports horses, mules, asses, cattle, sheep, hogs, poultry and all other livestock.[234] Both Orders came into force in Tobago on 31 March 1807.[235]

Until that date, however, beef and pork continued to be imported from the United States by virtue of a dispensing proclamation which was the last vestige of the old wartime laxity.[236] As for fish, the bounty achieved very little, four ships being paid a total of £303. 18s. 0d. sterling during the twelve months of its operation.[237] Indeed no vessel arrived from British North America for a period of about eleven months in 1806-07[238] Canadian exporters were hampered by rising freight and insurance rates and by enemy privateers, apart from the lower prices of their American competitors.[239] Moreover the effect of the Orders in Council was to exclude from British West Indian ports all American beef, pork and butter and to prevent the Americans from being paid in sugar. Their response was to try and insist on being paid in cash or bills of exchange, which were often not available, and widespread shortages ensued while Tobago's planters found great difficulty in disposing of their rum.[240] Later experience clearly demonstrated that even with the bounty which was paid on fish from 1 June 1806 Canada could not possibly supply all that Tobago needed. At no time did the number of ships entering Tobago thence exceed ten in any one year (ten entered in 1814, totalling 1,110 tons) and over the period 1804-15 it averaged only five per year.[241] Yet the problem was shortage of goods rather than of ships. The quantities of goods imported into Tobago during the three years 1805-1807 from the four sources of supply are set out in Table 5.3.[242]

TABLE 5.3 QUANTITIES OF GOODS IMPORTED INTO TOBAGO, 1805-1807

	USA	BNA	BWI	UK
Flour (barrels)	10,068	220	2,368	591
Corn (bushels)	26,937	-	1,029	-
Peas (bushels)	3,715	-	365	213
Rice (tierces)	1,350	-	582	-
Butter (firkins)	1,277	102	127	193
Beef and Pork (barrels)	4,235	304	594	522
Dried Fish (qtls.)	4,458	2,392	2,062	46
Pickled Fish (cwt)	10,120	8,254	-	-
Lumber (000 board ft.)	5,949	27	7	-
Staves and Heading (thousands)	2,779	5	63	-
Shooks (pkts. of 50)	32,363	-	-	-
Hoops (thousands)	90	3	-	-
Shingles (thousands)	4,895	21	59	-

Even after Britain went to war with the United States the position hardly changed as regards lumber of which indirect imports in the period 1 January 1812 to 3 May 1815 are set out in Table 5.4.[243]

TABLE 5.4 QUANTITIES OF LUMBER IMPORTED FROM THE USA AND BNA, (1 JANUARY 1812 - 3 MAY 1815)

	Lumber (000 board feet)	Shingles (000)	Staves (000)
USA	72,256	5,196	2,562
BNA	88	30	2

Apart from Canada's inadequate efforts to supply fish to the British West Indies generally and Tobago in particular, the latter's overwhelming dependence on the United States for every other item of food and lumber is self-evident. If lumber was in a class by itself, grain for instance was subject to a wartime prohibition of export in Britain[244] and was hardly available from Canada, while re-exports from other islands were necessarily limited by their own local needs. If ships from British North America arrived infrequently, from the USA they were irregular and inadequate. Tobago remained unable to attract American traders in adequate numbers even when the governor was prepared to admit their cargoes.

In August 1807 Tobago faced a "Crisis of Actual & extreme Scarcity of Provisions", and the governor saw no hope of receiving any significant supplies for at least four months. It was reported "that not a Single Barrel of Flour or Bushel of Corn was in any Store for Sale throughout the Island"[245] and a census revealed that the shops together had stocks of only seventy-four barrels of pork and eighty-four barrels of beef, while six of the nine merchants who responded had no stocks at all.[246] Prices meanwhile had risen sharply, beef from 66s. to 91s. 6d. per barrel and pork from 82s. 6d. to 149s.[247]

The members of the Council joined with others to petition the governor to relax the restrictions to allow entry to American provisions by any means for six months. Caught between the facts of the situation and his instructions, Young temporized; but meanwhile reports suggested that the risk of war between Britain and the USA was increasing. This increased the pressure on the governor, for it suggested that the wise thing to do was to stock up on American provisions before war intervened, especially since the ensuing crop could hardly be shipped without American lumber to package it. Some flour might perhaps be found from Britain and the local provision crop, which would feed the slaves for several months, was only six weeks off; but without American lumber the crop would be lost.[248] Nothing could be had from neighbouring islands without cash or credit which the planters did not have at the time.[249] American beef and pork were supposed to be absolutely excluded in all circumstances but no doubt the governor was conscious that American ships were known to sail off to alternative destinations if a governor refused to let them land beef and pork.[250] Young therefore issued licenses for the admission of certain American vessels, notably in order to obtain the vitally important salt meat for the slaves' Christmas. But he did this reluctantly and sparingly.[251] In October 1807 a crisis was avoided through the arrival of a number of ships bringing flour, lumber and fish both from the USA and from New Brunswick.[252]

The situation indeed was generally worsened by the American Embargo Act of December 1807 detaining vessels which sought to sail for British ports, save only for those carrying staves with which to package the rum they sought.[253] In 1807 the number of American ships entering Tobago fell from seventy-one to fifty-six, and in 1808 the figure was down to eleven, trading under special American licenses.[254] This experience of serious crisis and the expectation of worse followed by sudden relief through the unforeseeable arrival of ships with provisions was to become typical of the years that followed.

By 1808, therefore, a pattern had emerged which ought in theory to have provided Tobago with adequate supplies in the long run even if they arrived irregularly. Orders in Council had admitted pretty well all items except for beef, pork and butter. Even fish was accepted though subject to fiscal discrimination. In practice, however, the colonies had to contend with the American embargo and goods continued to arrive in a haphazard fashion and to be subject to shortages. In the three months, July to September 1808, no ship arrived from Britain and only 39 barrels of beef and pork, and 181 barrels of flour arrived from other sources. These items were almost unobtainable in October[255] and were in short supply for Christmas.[256]

Then on 23 January 1809 a convoy arrived from Britain with ten merchantmen and "the inhabitants now have every comfort and convenience" except that flour was still unobtainable except for the garrison's own stocks.[257] American supplies were "extravagantly dear" in March 1809 because the embargo was proving effective but arrived suddenly and in abundance in May and June,[258] eleven ships appearing in one week as the Americans learnt of the intention to impose new duties on the neutral trade. About thirty ships arrived in the month of July.[259] Young reported that "the Colony has started in a few days from actual Want to a very glut of Market". Prices for staves and lumber fell by one third, for fish, flour and rice by one half, though the three chronically troublesome items, butter, beef and pork, remained scarce and expensive.[260] About two months' supply of the permitted provisions and much more of the nonperishable lumber were accumulated. Cattle and horses were also landed from the United States at this time[261] and as the Americans learnt how to evade their own restrictions, supplies became more easily available.[262] American vessels cleared for Spanish American ports, landed at British ports, then returned with forged Spanish clearances, and continued to play a most important part in supplying Tobago. The fact that there was an old Indian town near Crown Point called La Guira facilitated this kind of subterfuge, and in February 1810 there were no less than five American vessels in Scarborough bearing clearances for La Guira.[263] Between November 1810 and January 1811 there was another influx as the Americans relaxed their restrictions and in February 1811 Young reported nine to twelve months' stocks of lumber and staves.[264] Such fluctuations persisted in the months that followed until war stopped the trade in 1812.[265]

The USA apart, supplies of many kinds arrived from the neighbouring West Indian islands and fish of course from Canada, but Britain provided only a very little flour, beef, pork and butter. Yet pork, beef and butter could still be lawfully imported only from British sources and remained very scarce, so that American cargoes of these items were still admitted by governor's license from time to time, especially in the later part of the year when it was thought desirable to lay in stocks for the slaves' Christmas.[266] The bounty on Canadian fish greatly increased its sale in the British islands generally in 1806-07.[267] Then in 1808 the island Assemblies assumed direct responsibility for the bounties. The supply, if still unsatisfactory, had clearly improved. In April 1809 a new pattern was set for dealing with the problem of fish which was eventually to lead to a new method of regulating the trade in provisions and lumber as well. Instead of offering a bounty on Canadian fish, duties were established on foreign fish at a minimum rate of 1s. sterling per quintal of cod. This Order also set out on a new path for encouraging the importation of Canadian produce and the British shipping industry generally by establishing a tonnage duty of 5s. sterling per ton on all neutral vessels bringing imports of fish, lumber or provisions. It came into effect on 1 November 1809.[268] Its operation was conditional on the colonial Assemblies establishing the required duties, but the dropping of the bounty which they had been required to finance was a substantial bait and Tobago quickly passed the necessary legislation.[269] The money to be raised by these duties was appropriated in aid of government expenditure.[270] Under this new regime British colonial fish became generally less plentiful in the islands as importers sought fish from the United States and paid the duty.[271]

Imports of fish were thus the subject of a special campaign ultimately resulting in a change of policy. Then trade with the USA in other goods was brought within the ambit of special duties designed to protect British and British colonial merchants and shipowners. On 7 February 1810 a new Order in Council required that duties be imposed on a full range of goods from neutral sources as a necessary condition of their continued importation, with effect from 1 December 1810.[272] This policy had been adopted in Jamaica some months earlier and the governors were instructed that if their Assemblies did likewise they should use their licensing and dispensing powers to admit such goods from neutral, in practice largely American sources. Only beef, pork and butter were, as always, to be excepted.[273] The Tobago Assembly, like those in most other colonies, reluctantly imposed the new duties as the price of the continued admission of American supplies.[274] The effect of such duties however was certainly to raise prices and thus the production costs of a sugar industry already tending to decline.

The scale of duties imposed by the Tobago legislature was as follows, in Tobago currency.[275]

> fish 5s. per quintal or 6s. per barrel
> flour 9s. per barrel
> bread and biscuit 4s. 6d. per barrel
> cornmeal and other non-wheat meal, 4s. 6d. per barrel
> peas, beans, maize 1s. 1½d. per barrel
> rice 4s. 6d. per 100 lb.
> Boston chip shingles, under 12" 4s. 6d. per 1,000
> Other shingles 9s. per 1,000
> Red oak staves 27s. per 1,000 (really 1,200)
> White oak staves 20s. 3d. per 1,000 (really 1,200)
> White or yellow pine lumber 13s. 6d. per 1,000 ft
> Pitch pine lumber 20s. 3d. per 1,000 ft
> Other timber 20s. 3d. per 1,000 ft
> Wood hoops 6s. 9d. per 1,000
> Livestock 10% ad valorem

These rates were determined by a committee of the legislature working on the basis of those already adopted in Jamaica. As was the case with the earlier fish and tonnage duties, the proceeds of these new charges were appropriated in aid of government expenditure. It was in 1810, too, that the American trade in particular was provided with a new facility through the opening of Courland Bay, in effect the town of Plymouth, as a port of entry.

In March 1807 John Balfour acting as governor, had pointed out to the Council the impediment to commerce resulting from the fact that Scarborough was the only authorized port of entry where a customs establishment existed. Scarborough was admirably placed to trade with South America, and perhaps adequate for trade with Britain, but vessels coming from the north often found that they could reach it only by sailing against both wind and current. Thus many North American vessels chose to miss Tobago altogether.[276] Courland however, on the north coast, was easily reached from the north and would attract American vessels more easily, whether directly or from other islands. It was also in its own right an altogether better harbour than Scarborough, and was adequately protected by its own fort and garrison.[277] The Council agreed that Courland too should be declared a port of entry, and the Committee for Trade and Plantations agreed to recommend the setting up of a Custom House at Courland in October 1807.[278] It was not however until 1810 that the British Treasury acted. Courland was then declared a port of entry and a Collector appointed there, considerably increasing the chances of a casual call by passing ships carrying American goods.[279]

The problem of fish, however, would not go away. British merchants connected with the Canadian fishing industry pressed for the total prohibition of foreign fish. These merchants argued that unless the protection was increased the British North American fishing trade would have to be abandoned while only the total exclusion of foreign fish would really assure them of the British West Indian market, without which that trade could not hope to develop so as to bring down its high prices and perhaps develop new markets.[280] The evidence submitted by the merchants was drawn overwhelmingly from Jamaica with a little from the Windward and Leeward Islands; no reference was made to Tobago. But the Committee of the Privy Council for Trade and Plantations saw the colonies still as a single unit and decided that the importation of fish from the United States should stop altogether unless it could be demonstrated that this would cause "serious inconveniences" in the islands.[281]

From Tobago Sir William Young's response was extremely tame. He was "impressed with the strongest Prepossession in favour of the Appropriation to national Adventurers, & exclusively, of the entire Trade for Fish".[282] However in 1809, under the system of discriminatory duties, British North America had supplied only about two-thirds of the fish reaching Tobago and in 1810 one-half,[283] so he accepted the case for better protection. British colonial fish was about 4s. per quintal more expensive, but it was better cured and lasted better while the slaves thought it had more "substance", and so preferred it.[284] He suggested that if the merchants of New Brunswick and Newfoundland could be induced to accept the rum and molasses which was all Tobago could offer in exchange it might be possible to enforce a ban on American fish if it were introduced gradually.

Young had hardly suggested that the British colonies could not in fact satisfy the market, and it does not seem that other West Indian governors did much better. Feeling that no case had been made, the imperial authorities decided to terminate the importation of foreign fish on 1 July 1812, giving nine months' notice.[285] A new Order in Council of 26 October 1812 excluded fish as well as beef, pork and butter from the governors' authority to license vessels to import specified American goods if specified duties were charged.[286]

Meanwhile Britain's relationship with the United States of America was becoming increasingly strained. In March 1811 a new Non-Importation Act prohibited the entry of British goods into the USA.[287] Britain responded in July 1812 with an Act permitting the re-export to the USA in foreign ships of sugar and coffee imported into Bermuda in British ships and the importation into British West Indian colonies in British ships of provisions and lumber imported into Bermuda from the USA in foreign ships in return.[288] This was a measure designed to enable trade between the USA and the British West Indies to continue, using Bermuda as a staging post, but there is no evidence that this benefited Tobago in particular and the stratagem did not in any case produce much result.

Britain, however, persisted in searching American vessels at sea for goods which she had declared to be contraband and this eventually led to war. American privateers operating around Halifax disrupted the trade in British colonial fish while British warships blockaded United States ports and seized a number of ships at sea. But meanwhile a contraband trade in American goods passing through Canada began to develop[289] and on 10 June 1813 an Order in Council authorized governors to issue licenses for trade with any American port which was not under blockade, despite the hostilities. By these means limited quantities of American goods continued to reach the British islands, including Tobago, though no United States vessels were formally entered between July 1812 and the beginning of 1815.[290] The virtual stoppage of the American trade after 1812 was countered to some extent by devoting more land and slave labour to growing provisions though this meant a smaller sugar crop.[291] Some provisions and some lumber were obtained from other islands, notably from the free port in Grenada in 1813, which were very probably of American origin.[292]

When peace was concluded with the USA, however, the general authority of the governors to admit American vessels was withdrawn as from 16 April 1815.[293] With the coming of peace therefore the American trade at once became strictly clandestine once more. But it could not cease, for the alternative sources of supply were never remotely adequate. It may seem strange that American goods were thus more easily admitted when Britain was at war with the United States than during peacetime, but war was considered to justify strange practices and, in the event, few American cargoes were admitted after it broke out.

The fact that the governor's duty to determine when to allow normally prohibited cargoes to land was far from easy and sometimes very difficult is well illustrated by two incidents with which Balfour had to deal in 1815. Naturally views were coloured by the desire of the colonists to have not just adequate supplies but large stocks at low prices, but the governor was sometimes the subject of special pleading if not deliberate misrepresentation and it was quite common for him to receive contradictory advice. In March 1815 a petition from Samuel Dellaway, master of the schooner *Favourite*, to land a cargo of American provisions and lumber was supported by a number of merchants and planters who alleged shortage, but opposed by William Lang who claimed to have more than 30,000 feet of lumber in stock. Lang was supported by Mr Reilley, agent for a Barbados merchant, who stated that he was expecting several cargoes shortly. Lang and Reilley were summoned before the Council where Reilley admitted that he did not know what goods he expected and did not really expect anything for another three weeks. The Council sought further information about the needs of the estates and finally agreed to advise the governor to allow Dellaway to land his cargo. The decision may well have turned on the argument that the lumber was needed to enable the slave quarters to be repaired before the rains set in.[294] It may seem in retrospect, as it seemed to Balfour, to be eminently reasonable, but the Privy Council disapproved.[295]

In May 1815, after the news of peace with the United States had reached Tobago, Horace Stocking, commanding the American brig *Independence*, arrived with a large cargo of horses, cattle, corn, flour, tobacco, lard, potatoes, rice, onions, cheese, hams, hoops, staves and puncheons. When he arrived the Order in Council under which these items had previously been admitted had been terminated as from 16 April 1815 in consequence of the coming of peace. Stocking however had sailed from New London on 7 April before the Order had been annulled and without knowing of it. He asked permission to land his cargo and was supported by several of the inhabitants including five members of Council. Councillor William Brasnell, agent for supplying the garrison with fish and beef, reported complaints that the available beef was of poor quality and the garrison commander was anxious to buy Stocking's cattle. On the other hand the same William Lang urged that he had on hand supplies of flour, ham and cheese, imported from Europe, for which he could find no sale even at low prices. He urged that the cancellation of the Order in Council showed clearly that apart from his personal interest in the case, Britain intended that cargoes like Stocking's should not be admitted. Thomas Blakeley and one Watkinson urged that they had tobacco in stock with which Stocking's would be in competition and tobacco was not one of the items which had previously been admitted. The Council summoned the principal deponents on both sides, seeking details of their stocks and prices. George Wightman told members that with one exception the estates for which he was responsible were short of provisions and the local ground provision crop would not be ready until October in consequence of unusually dry weather. Other witnesses too anticipated a shortage of provisions. Wightman was also running short of staves, as was John Anderson. But conditions were obviously not the same in all parts of the island: shortage and the fear of it were largely confined to the Windward district. The Council was faced with a difficult decision, but finally agreed that except for the tobacco the cargo should be admitted.[296]

With the end of the war the problem of shortage, paradoxically, reared its head again with new vigour. Without the war the British government adopted the view that there was no longer any justification of admitting foreign cargoes contrary to the normal laws of trade. The colonists however had anticipated that with the coming of peace the American trade would be revived and had not sought to order provisions in anticipation of the usual shortage in the later part of the year, no doubt an extraordinary piece of optimism or wishful thinking which invited nemesis, while an unusually severe dry season had ensured a very late harvest of local food crops. Finally the resumption of war in Europe when Napoleon escaped from Elba ensured that supplies from Britain, which the theory of the laws of trade postulated, would not be forthcoming in larger quantities.[297] By May 1815, while a shortage of provisions was anticipated, lumber and staves were unobtainable.[298] There was an enormous need for American lumber, five years of normal imports thought President Balfour, to fill a long accumulated need during which buildings had been allowed to deteriorate very badly.[299] Prices rose so high that speculators from other islands began to bring their stocks to Tobago and some estates interrupted the crop for lack of containers.[300]

In May President Balfour summoned the Council in special session to consider allegations of shortage and it advised him to open the port to cargoes brought by British vessels from neutral islands for three months, as an emergency measure.[301] Balfour did just that and within a month had permitted entry to two ships from neutral islands, and to two from the United States by special dispensation.[302] The legislature sent a supporting memorial to the Secretary of State claiming that a shortage of food for the slaves and of packaging had made it necessary to admit foreign cargoes[303] and the three-month period was extended.[304]

The Privy Council, however, was wholly unsympathetic and Balfour received a letter of censure. He was instructed to admit no more cargoes contrary to the general laws of trade,[305] so that even a cargo of English supplies brought from the USA could not be admitted.[306]

The position of the British government was simply one of general and accustomed principle "as the Produce of His Majesty's Colonies is effectively protected in the Home Market against Foreign Competition, it is not unreasonable to expect that a Preference should be shown in the Colonies to the Use of British Ships and the Consumption of British Produce".[307] It was still adamant that to grant Tobago the indulgence which it desired would be unfair to the other West Indian colonies,[308] despite the Council's talk of the "Horrors of Famine".[309]

It was, moreover, the view of the Privy Council Committee that the standing objective of building up the commerce of the West Indies with

British North America would never be achieved if trade with the United States was allowed to continue. Furthermore, the Committee for Trade and Plantations had two telling points which suggested that the colony's arguments were less than objective: the interruption of the United States trade by the war of 1812, albeit alleviated by a certain amount of indirect or disguised commerce, had not in fact crippled the colony[310] and "the long existence of War has hitherto prevented the question from having a fair Trial". Certainly the attempt to sustain Tobago without American supplies had never been made in peacetime since Canadian trade had become a serious factor. The Privy Council agreed that rigid adherence to the laws of trade might well cause "temporary inconvenience and pressure". However, the committee members felt "a strong conviction that it is temporary pressure only which is to be apprehended."[311] They recalled that more ground provisions were being grown in Tobago while the quantity of supplies available from British North America had increased. Moreover exports of grain from Britain were now free of restriction and the West Indies would get more from this source. From the imperial point of view there was certainly a case against the North American trade, and though without it Tobago would certainly suffer shortage, collapse was unlikely.

By July, when the imperial response reached Tobago, there was no beef, pork or butter in the island and none was expected from Europe until December.[312] In the event food was obtained for the slaves at Martinique, from which no less than twenty ships arrived in three months, this at high prices allowing a spectacular profit to the merchants there. Lumber, staves and shingles however were still in short supply. Their bulk and high cost meant that they were seldom the subject of speculation[313] and British North America could supply none for more than a year.[314] One shipment of lumber brought from Martinique was sold at a profit of about 800 per cent to the French.[315] At this rate the planters sometimes took to re-importing the casks in which they exported their produce. But they survived, albeit at some cost in inconvenience and the loss of potential profit.

The Problem of Economic Development

Between 1793 and 1815 therefore the economic development of Tobago, at first very promising, made little or no overall progress. A sugar crop about 20 per cent larger than at the start of the period hardly did more than make up for the effective disappearance of cotton and coffee as regards the value of the island's products and the development of its land. A major factor in this disappointing result was the long uncertainty over the island's political future, especially after 1802 when its return to French sovereignty served to enhance the apprehension that such a thing could happen again when eventually the war should finally end. British merchants were understandably reluctant to invest capital and effort in expanding commercial connections with, or sugar production in, an island exposed to such risk and Americans or French were both unwelcome and uninterested in a British colony. In this context it is instructive that while Tobago languished, Trinidad after 1802 attracted notable attention from metropolitan capital, so that between 1802 and 1809 the number of sugar estates rose from 193 to 248, steam engines began to appear and sugar exports almost doubled.[316] Certainly the development potential of Trinidad was greater than that of Tobago, but its settled future allegiance gave it a special advantage over the latter in the eyes of British capital despite doubts about its form of government. Moreover, the political uncertainties in Tobago were augmented after 1807 by the general doubt about the probable effect of being unable to import new slaves. Tobago therefore had to make its way essentially on its own resources and the planters already engaged there had little capital at their disposal and needed all their energies to avoid losing money on their disadvantaged estates.

Their difficulties were considerably enhanced by production costs made higher than they need have been by the imperial restrictions on the importation of food and lumber in a situation where local production of such items was strictly limited. Certainly more might have been done to grow food for the slaves at the expense of a reduced production of sugar, but the effective displacement of the imported supplies was hardly practicable, nor indeed was it envisaged. The imperial view that Tobago like the other West Indian colonies, should adhere strictly to the increasingly obsolete mercantilist restrictions was an important factor in the island's overall economic stagnation.

At the same time there was some change for the better in internal economic conditions. The roads, primitive as they were, appear to have been better and more numerous in 1815 than in 1793. Local commerce in foodstuffs was better ordered as a result of new facilities for and rules about markets. Some effort was made to improve the chaos in the system of circulated coin. More attention was paid to the production of food crops even if these were limited to basic foods and still not adequate. And by 1815 the resident planters had, through twenty-two years of war, acquired a greater identification with Tobago though still wholly dependent on an external political authority for that determination of political allegiance without which they could not expect a more hopeful future. Wartime conditions had been responsible for many of their economic difficulties; but the war was now over, and if only the island remained British it seemed that a new era might open.

THE CHRISTIAN CHURCHES

The Anglicans

The formal spiritual life of Christians in Tobago, like that of the other British islands in the area, fell within the jurisdiction of the Bishop of London who was empowered to license clergymen to preach. The appointment of clergy to posts within the Established Church of England, financed from government funds, was however the prerogative of the governor and was commonly used as a means of preferring a protégé either of the governor himself or of his connections in Britain. Throughout this period Tobago was provided with a single Anglican clergyman, holding the position of rector and resident in Scarborough.[1] The Assembly provided him with a salary and house allowance, together usually worth about £750 a year, and he also received a further £200 a year as garrison chaplain as well as fees for conducting baptisms, marriages and funerals.[2] It was altogether a substantial remuneration, though complaints were sometimes heard that it was not enough to attract keen and competent men of "respectability".[3]

This single clergyman was responsible for all of the seven Anglican parishes in the island, though in practice his attention seldom strayed far beyond Scarborough. The sparseness of the Anglican population in these circumstances made it difficult to assemble a congregation outside Scarborough.[4] Moreover, in terms of parishioners rather than land area Tobago could scarcely expect more than one clergyman from a church which considered that it was responsible for ministering only to whites and perhaps coloureds but certainly not to slaves. And that was the view of the Church of England throughout this period.[5]

In 1793 when Tobago changed hands Scarborough already had a rector, Revd John Matthews, as a relic of the old English connection and a consequence of the English antecedents of its population.[6] Probably in ignorance of this and even before he arrived to assume office Governor Lindsay offered "the Living of this Island" to Revd Anthony Thomas, a protégé of Secretary of State Dundas who was "discontented with his situation" in Grenada. Lindsay's avowed object in making this choice was essentially to please Dundas.[7] But Thomas did not move to Tobago until 1795 and in 1799 the position was again vacant. However, Revd Thomas Fancourt arrived in November, sent out from Britain by the Bishop of London on the recommendation of the absentee planters in England.[8] Fancourt however left Tobago in April 1800 after a stay of only five months[9] and was replaced by Revd James Pons who was appointed by Governor Masters.[10] In 1803 however the post was again vacant[11] and Tobago seems to have remained without a clergyman until 1806. Revd William Terrill was appointed in 1804[12] but he took two years to arrive, only to die in December 1807. Terrill's short stay was clearly very successful and he was described by Sir William Young on his death as "an Example of Decent & Moral Observance, which checked every loose or profane propensity in Conversation, . . . his Conversation was courted, his Congregation was crowded"[13] and again as "That most excellent & exemplary Man".[14]

Young sought to have the Bishop of London send out a replacement for Terrill,[15] but when none was forthcoming he appointed Revd Richard Weekes of Barbados, who had applied for the job, in September 1808.[16]

Tobago's ecclesiastical establishment was however destined to remain unstable as Weekes died within the year[17] and there was more than a year's interval before his successor arrived from England because the governor was anxious to find a good man.[18] This was Revd Charles Newton, a friend of Secretary of State Windham, appointed by Governor Young.[19] Newton reached Tobago early in 1810.[20] Two years later, however, he was being accused in Council of so neglecting his duties that the mere holding of routine religious services was irregular even in Scarborough itself, not to mention the more remote districts.[21] In 1815 Newton resigned on the ground of ill health without having mended his ways and this time a new rector was found without delay: Revd William Wilson, who had once been to Tobago, was selected by President Balfour, acting as governor.[22]

If Tobago was sometimes left without any clergymen of the Established Church for months on end, and indeed for nearly three years in 1803-06 it is hardly surprising that throughout this period there was no church building and services were held in the courthouse, which had been equipped with a pulpit.[23] At the opening of the very first Assembly in February 1794 Governor Ricketts had pointed out the need to set aside a place for public worship,[24] but the necessary resources were not easily found. Some of the responsibility for this lies with the uncertain political future of the colony and the related economic stagnation. Specific proposals for building a church were put forward in 1809 and 1811[25] but not until 1814 did the legislature set up a joint committee of the two Houses to select a site and produce proposals for financing a church.[26] The construction of a building in upper Scarborough was finally authorized in 1816.[27]

Thus the work of the Church of England, even among the white population, was done in spasms and was in itself commonly unsatisfactory. Of the several clergymen who served in Tobago during this period only Terrill seems to have excited admiration so far as the sparse records available suggest, and his stay was extremely short. As for the smaller coloured population, while several of them attended Anglican services, especially women,[28] the fact that in the Church of England "a [white] pew is never allowed to be defiled by a quadroon, however rich",[29] must have severely limited its impact. Indeed, Anglican clergy in the West Indies generally tended to ignore the coloureds.[30] As for the slaves, Charles Newton certainly and no doubt other rectors would baptize slave children who came within his reach (that is in Scarborough)[31] but the Established Church mostly ignored the slave population, as it did throughout the West Indies, and they were not allowed to receive the sacraments.[32]

It is therefore easily understood that at the end of the eighteenth century the British West Indian Islands provided a potentially rewarding field for nonconformist missions which aimed to work principally among the free coloured and slave populations, and there might even have been significant opportunity among the whites in a small island short of clergy.

The Moravians

The Moravian Church, or the United Brethren, had first established a mission in Tobago in 1789 when the island was under French rule.[33] It had been largely prompted by an initiative from John Hamilton, a planter who, like some others, believed that through Moravian work in other islands "many had been brought to knowledge of the gospel but by obedience to its divine precepts, have become more contented and happy in their situation and more faithful to their masters".[34] Christianization

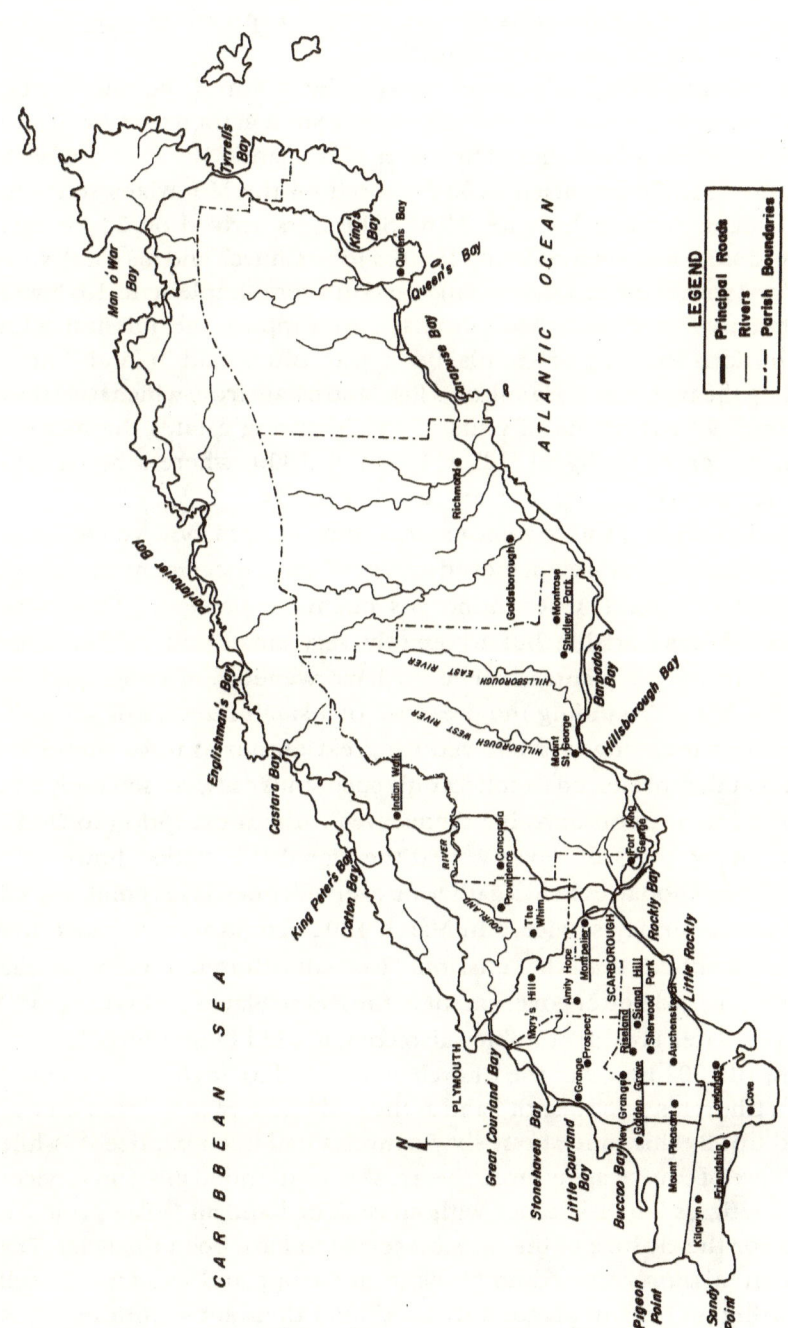

FIG. 6.1 ESTATES VISITED BY MISSIONARIES, 1798-1813
Names of plantations where missionaries resided or were specially active are underlined

was expected to make them more "faithful labourers",[35] though the principal aim of the missionaries was always to spread the gospel as a means of saving the souls of the heathen.

The mission collapsed, however, with the death of the missionary, James Montgomery, in 1790. But efforts were soon in train to revive it and in 1798 when Hamilton offered five acres of land and £300 to re-establish it and his brother promised £100 for a school the Moravians sent out Charles Schirmer and his wife.[36] The Schirmers arrived on 23 January 1799 and were followed on 2 July 1800 by John Church and his wife[37] who then lived with them in a single house and in a very simple style. No fewer than twenty-five estates had promised to support the mission with contributions totalling £643. 10s. 0d. a year, often paid in kind.[38] After spending the first year at Hamilton's Riseland estate from which base they undertook a programme of visits to neighbouring estates the mission moved its centre to Signal Hill in February 1800, where a house was converted for use as a church and meeting centre.

Initially curiosity was to some extent a drawing card, but even so, large congregations were rarely achieved except when management instructed the slaves to attend, when hundreds might be present.[39] Otherwise attendance was variable but frequently very small and by 1801 the enthusiasm of the planters seems to have waned and congregations declined, notwithstanding the presence of a small number of whites.[40] The missionaries however showed no great enthusiasm for numbers, saying that they preferred to collect only such souls as "were sincerely and earnestly intent upon devoting themselves without exception to God". Significant numbers of slaves visited the Signal Hill station however,[41] where the missionaries held a gathering every Wednesday evening as well as the usual Sunday service.[42] In March 1801 Hamilton and four other planters testified that the mission "has contributed greatly to the enlightening and better government of the Negro Slaves in this Colony"[43] and a year later President Robley also commended their efforts.[44]

In April 1802 however the Churches returned to England on account of John Church's poor health[45] and at the end of the year the mission was wound up. By this time about sixty converts had been baptized[46] while there were of course many more "hearers" who attended mission services and sometimes lent assistance without seeking baptism.[47] The principal reason for the closure of the mission seems to have been financial. The Moravian mission received no funds from Europe and was entirely self supporting and many planters discontinued their subscriptions when Hamilton died in December 1800[48] and two of his principal supporters returned to Britain shortly afterwards.[49] But the transfer of Tobago to

France by the Treaty of Amiens and the probability that this would obstruct nonconformist work certainly influenced the decision.[50]

The success of the Moravians had been decidedly varied. They started well with strong support from a small number of estates in the general vicinity of Scarborough and some large attendances, when subsequently they lost some of their early support and congregations thinned, the mission diaries nevertheless report new interest on some estates and some fairly well attended meetings. At the end of 1801 Church wrote in the diary: "A year in which faith and patience, as well as fortitude have been well exercised";[51] but even during this year new support was sometimes encountered[52] and several good congregations turned out during 1802.[53] While several of their early well wishers failed to produce much tangible help, they did not encounter much positive opposition from the planters such as later generations of missionaries were to face in many West Indian islands.

The departure of the Moravians at the end of 1802 left the Church of England as once more the only representative of organized religion in Tobago. Then in 1807 John Robley, who had supported their work, having failed to interest them in returning in the then existing circumstances, asked the London Missionary Society (LMS) to send out a missionary to instruct his slaves and offered to subscribe £50 a year.[54] Like John Hamilton in 1798, Robley thought that a missionary might mould the slaves to the planter's advantage, and he warned from the outset that he wanted "a man who would conduct himself with propriety and not preach liberty to the Negroes".[55] Robley having agreed to provide financial support, Roger Elliot, a lay missionary, arrived in Tobago on 11 April 1808. He established a mission to the slaves from a base on Robley's estate at Golden Grove and was soon also working on six others as well as among the free coloureds in Scarborough and later in Plymouth. Elliot left Golden Grove at the end of 1808,[56] by which time he had visited ten different estates, going as far as Queen's Bay, and several times attracted more than 100 hearers. In Scarborough he had attracted as many as forty whites and another forty coloureds at a time when there was no Anglican clergyman in the island.[57] A second LMS missionary, Isaac Purkis, arrived on 26 January 1809.

The London Missionary Society

The LMS had been formed in 1795 as an interdenominational organization of Baptists, Presbyterians, Congregationalists, Independents and other nonconformist sects, but it soon came to be dominated by the Congregationalists. It emphasized freedom of conscience for the individual and freedom of governmental style for the church while concentrating on the propagation of the gospel. Its missionaries were usually people of the lower middle classes, godliness and biblical knowledge being better qualifications then intellectual calibre. Their education was often limited, especially in the West Indies, where it was thought that scholarship would be wasted on the slaves.[58]

When Elliot began his work, however, he found only limited support from the planters few of whom seem to have shared John Robley's view that the mission would help the slaveowners. In some contrast to the Moravian experience in 1799, the majority were at best indifferent, some positively hostile. Perhaps the news of missionary activity in other islands had generated some suspicion. Certainly, the Assembly refused to help Elliot.[59] Managers limited the frequency with which slaves could attend mission functions.[60]

On top of these difficulties the LMS mission was soon sabotaged by a quarrel between Elliot and Purkis which was finally disposed of only when the Society recalled Purkis in 1810. The episode however illustrates very strikingly the fact that nineteenth century missionaries were not all cast in the same mould, even as regards their attitude to the job and to their followers. It is possible to regard Elliot as orthodox -- puritanical, hardworking, a zealous evangelical, submissive to the authority of his mission in England -- and to see the less idealistic, even self-seeking Purkis as a maverick.[61]

Elliot criticized Purkis for being self-indulgent and wasteful of money and time, while Purkis thought his fondness for overwork and a simple life rather foolish.[62] Elliot kept himself aloof from the people like most missionaries of his time, so that he was often afflicted by extreme loneliness. Purkis went too far in the other direction. He found the "lack of all Christian society very difficult to bear" and lost respect of the whites for himself and his mission by socializing too much with coloured people.[63] This was a genuine problem for any missionary. They had to keep some distance between themselves and their congregations in order to maintain respect for their teaching in a society where the slaves easily thought familiarity contemptible, but too much distance could produce intolerable loneliness. Social contact with coloureds was dangerous to the missionaries' social standing and few whites were inclined to be friendly.[64] Purkis's conduct enabled Elliot to complain that "he is paying his addresses to a coloured young woman who makes no pretensions to religion. She is fond of balls and pursues with eagerness the pleasures and vanities of the world . . . He is with her every night till a very late hour . . ."

Elliot thought such activities "inconsistent with the Gospel".[65] He also accused Purkis of condoning drunkenness and dancing, the pet hates of missionaries everywhere, and thought him disrespectful to the Society's directors because he replied critically to their letters. And the quarrel extended to personal matters.[66] Ultimately Purkis was recalled in 1810 because of Elliot's complaints against him, but the quarrel undermined the mission and attendances dropped sharply.[67] By 1811 much support had drifted away. Unlike the Moravians, the LMS mission was almost wholly supported from England and few whites were found among the congregations.[68] In 1811 Elliot took to concentrating on about four estates only and the LMS directors began to think that it was not worth the effort. They decided in 1812 to close it on financial grounds. Elliot left Tobago in 1813[69] leaving behind him a new church building in Scarborough paid for by local contributions collected over the past two years.[70]

Missionary Attitudes to the Slaves

The Moravians never had any doubt that their business was to work among the slaves, though they did pick up a handful of white followers. Elliot and Purkis however saw their purpose in different ways. Elliot, like his Moravian predecessors, aimed primarily at the slaves though he also worked with the coloureds and whites.[71] He tended to see a correlation between heathenism, which was his quarry, and blackness of skin. He thought that blacks were intellectually inferior to whites and was in consequence extremely paternalistic towards them. Purkis on the other hand found distinctions of colour intolerable, assailed the Anglican church for sustaining them and attacked his own congregation's practice of segregated seating with the result that a few whites did begin to sit among the coloureds in Scarborough.[72] He appreciated as Elliot did not that the language barrier and the effects of slavery itself were largely responsible for the seeming ignorance, even stupidity of the slaves. At the same time, in view of the language problem he preferred not to attempt to work with the slaves since he could not properly reach them and sought rather to concentrate on the whites and coloureds, whom he thought just as "heathen" as the slaves. He also preferred to work in town rather than on the estates where managers could easily frustrate the mission.[73]

Most fundamentally, Elliot and Purkis also differed in their approaches to slavery. The Moravians saw it essentially as a fact of life which they did not question and worked within that context. Elliot disapproved of it, complained that the estates restricted his access to the slaves and that when he did preach to them their responses were inhibited by the atmosphere of the plantation and the presence of white managerial staff.[74] Yet, rather like the Moravians, he never dreamt of challenging the system even in its details.

> I am persuaded that it is neither my business nor in my power to deliver them from the bondage of men. I have always considered it my duty, to endeavour thro' divine assistance to direct the poor Negroes how they may be delivered from the bondage of sin and satan and to teach them the pure principles of christianity which will not only lead to sobriety, industry, and fidelity, but make them loyal subjects, obedient servants and children, loving husbands and wives, of which principles they are quite destitute. I not only endeavour to avoid every expression which might be misunderstood in this respect, but always endeavour to endear them to each other, and particularly their employers, in fact all who have authority over them.[75]

In all of this Elliot was carefully following the instructions of the LMS which took the view that its missionaries "should abstain from all observations on the subject of slavery either in public or in private". This was the typical missionary attitude at this time, though things would change in the later 1820s.

Purkis on the other hand denounced slavery in the most forthright fashion: "... the accursed system of West Indian slavery was deviz'd in hell by a full assembly of devils and is put in execution and supported only by the agents of Mammon & of Beelzebub; every kind of sin is interwoven with the System with so much ingenuity that its origin can be ascribed to nothing but the subtilty of fallen angels".[76] In writing to the directors he vigorously attacked the planters, managers and overseers for not aiding, indeed for obstructing the mission's work among the slaves.[77] Such language, had it been used publicly in Tobago, would of course have endangered the mission which had been invited by people who sought to strengthen the system and would be tolerated only so long as it accepted that system.

Missionary Techniques

The first approach of the missionaries to the slaves was to preach about the sufferings and death of Christ.[78] They defined sin, the cause of those sufferings, and urged their hearers to repent.[79] Elliot however did not think sermons of the first importance.[80] He quickly decided that the slaves were so ignorant that his best procedure was communication by rote of a simple catechism at the level of "Who is Jesus Christ?" or "Who made the world?"[81] In time he developed a formula the first part of which was thus to "catechise" his slave congregation. Then he would "ask them and suffer them to ask questions, and talk with them in a familiar manner". He thought the slaves liked this method and that it was "a good way to give instruction". Finally he would "give them an address for 15 or 20 minutes".[82] His short sermons often centred upon incidents of sickness and death which, as one writer has put it struck his hearers where they were vulnerable.[83] He laid stress on the theme of salvation through faith in Christ.[84] Elliot judged his success among the slaves partly by the extent to which they could repeat the answers to the questions he posed, partly by the public display of emotion.[85]

Purkis used methods which were certainly most unusual at the time. He seldom "catechised" the slaves and did not think much of the repetition of memorized answers; neither did he attach much importance to displays of emotion. He recognized a language barrier, for even when the slaves learnt English African grammatical structures and the lexicon of other European languages tended to creep into their speech so that in fact they spoke not English but a Creole, he yet refused to "talk down" to the slaves in what he thought to be "broken English". Purkis thus tended to rely on sermons, often lengthy rather intellectual ones little suited to a slave congregation but in keeping with his preference for work among urban coloureds and even whites, whom he did not hesitate to warn about the judgement of God.[86] The evidence suggests that only the Moravians paid any noticeable attention to teaching the scriptures and they did not begin to do so until nearly two years after the start of the mission.[87]

The missions found, naturally enough, that it was difficult to arrange regular meetings with the slaves, especially during crop, because masters grudged the loss of working time.[88] For similar reasons services on estates tended to be short. Like the Moravian missionaries, Elliot held prayer meetings on weekdays. He also held Sunday School classes, rewarding those who learned their catechism successfully.[89] Purkis seldom did these things, preferring to hold singing sessions which he found were better attended but which Elliot frowned on because the singing tended to be rowdy and to develop African-derived features like rhythm and even dancing.[90] All the missionaries paid much attention to visiting their followers and even "hearers", and the Moravians frequently visited the slaves in their huts. The Moravians especially spent much time in conversation with individual slaves[91] both in order to keep in touch with the people and monitor their habits generally and as a means of trying to ensure that the sick achieved a state of grace in case they should die. Nor was the visiting technique confined to the slaves. Purkis believed that it was largely by visiting their homes that he had built up his free coloured congregation to nearly 100 persons.[92] Elliot also wished to teach the slaves to read but found that the planters were generally afraid that this would lead to subversion and John Robley in particular was determined not to allow it.[93]

Elliot adhered rigidly to the orthodox church rules about marriage, as did the Moravians, while Purkis made sufficient concession to the facts of life in a slave society in which the marriage of slaves was in effect nearly impossible and until 1837 only Anglican clergy could conduct marriages among free people,[94] to be ready to condone a state of faithful concubinage. In any case the most that the missionaries could do was to conduct non-legal religious ceremonies of marriage for their slave followers. There were other respects too in which Elliot thought Purkis much too ready to compromise with African or African-related Creole habits, while Purkis in turn thought him "narrow minded and impractical".[95] If Elliot's determination to downgrade African culture and to change their whole way of life was typical of the nineteenth century missionary, Purkis' greater sympathy deserves notice.

While conversion was the missionaries' principal aim, they were in no hurry to baptize large numbers and criticized the Anglican clergy for a casual attitude to this ceremony, claiming that the latter often baptized people, including slaves, who merely wanted to call themselves Christian for material reasons. The missionaries wanted to be sure that they baptized only true believers and not merely people who professed faith in Christ.[96] Faced with candidates for baptism they took the view that the first thing to look for was "true repentance on account of sin".[97] After repentance, faith in Christ was the prime necessity.[98] The Moravians went further: "unless they duly attend to their meeting for further instruction, & we trace in them a real concern for their salvation, we cannot think of baptising them: for otherwise, instead of having a living Congn. of Jesus, we shall have a baptized heathenish Congn. which will be worse than having none".[99] Careful questioning therefore preceded a decision to baptize and candidates were often rejected, sometimes repeatedly.[100] Even after these precautions the Moravians found that "in too many instances the Negroes rest upon the act of baptism, & thus when they have attained to that, seem pretty well satisfied".[101] Schirmer and his colleagues were looking for a much more meaningful commitment. They concluded that on the whole the slaves had too little concern for their souls.[102] The LMS missionaries were only a little less exacting.

But it was one thing to set rigid standards, another to determine the criteria to be applied in judging conversion. The Moravians would examine candidates for baptism carefully and sometimes repeatedly, while Elliot required them to answer questions about the meaning of Christ's death[103] and even so backsliders emerged in a matter of months. It was not long before the slaves became seized of the things the missionaries looked for in a convert and they sometimes deceived them deliberately. Baptism and acceptance into the Church could confer status and even indirect material benefits on a free coloured and more especially on a slave, being a kind of passport to the ranks of favoured slaves where the master was not hostile to the mission.[104] They marked out those concerned as having taken a major step towards the culture of the slavemasters. Evidence of rote learning, often emphasized by the missions, was no evidence of understanding or real acceptance of Christian teaching. And the missionaries' tendency to insist that those who refused to turn to Christ would burn in hell must have intimidated many whose understanding of Christianity was imperfect. And the Christian concern for monopoly, which meant that converts had to abandon a great many of the habits and ideas on which their lives had been built, made the chance of backsliding very great indeed.[105]

In Tobago as elsewhere the Moravians monitored the private lines of their converts carefully. They tried to speak individually with those they baptized at least once each month[106] and did not hesitate to suspend or to expel backsliders. They were particularly careful to insist on sobriety and monogamy and faithfulness within sexual unions. In this connection a mulatto slave, Rachel, of Riseland, was suspended from the meeting of the baptized in February 1801 "until we found she was truly convinced of having sinned and turned again unto the Lord with sincere repentance".[107] Rachel was readmitted four months later when the missionaries were convinced of her repentance.[108] Thomas, of Lowlands was expelled after several warnings, also in February 1801, "his conduct being no other than that of a heathen".[109] Susanna, also of Riseland, not only left her husband for another man but deceived the missionaries by persuading them to baptize her while "living in adultery". It was decided to tell her that "she had by such conduct forfeited her privileges as a baptized negroe; and until she truly repented we could not look upon her in any other light than a heathen".[110] When Susanna subsequently "sought to justify herself" she was told that "her immoral conduct . . . had brought reproach upon her as a baptized Negroe, & likewise in the cause of our Saviour". But the hope of readmission was still held out if she should repent[111] and the Moravians generally were very concerned to bring their "strayed sheep" back into the fold being more conscious than some others that too harsh a discipline might deprive Christ of potential followers.[112] The records of the LMS mission do not reveal how they dealt with cases of relapse, but they certainly encountered them.

The difficulty of the missionaries' task may be further illustrated by noticing that their concept of sin, the related notions of repentance and salvation, the idea of individual rather than collective worth and responsibility, of morality as a matter of thought and "being" rather than of conduct, the notion of Satan as an evil deity to be fought rather than placated, were all very strange to traditional African thinking. Baptism however could be related to certain African water god cults and so the slaves could respond to the practice more easily than to its implications.[113]

The Impact of the Missions

The arrival of both Moravians and LMS missionaries caused considerable interest at first, followed within a couple of years by a measure of disappointment on one hand and a small degree of solid success on the other. Even in the early stages of the work of the LMS however the evidence suggests that only about 25 per cent of the estate population, often less, attended missionary services unless the management applied pressure.[114] As the novelty wore off congregations tended to contract. It seems probable that some slaves, and even perhaps some of the free coloureds, had anticipated material gain, possibly an improvement in their conditions of life and work, from the advent of these new white men who took an unprecedented interest in them, and became disillusioned when things did not work out that way. Such a pattern was not uncommon in missionary enterprise in the West Indies.[115] But the missionaries did win lasting if small groups of converts, more especially, it appears, among the Creole rather than the African born slaves. They set on foot something which others were to take up again in subsequent years.

The effect of the missions on the slaves within this period was obviously limited, but very varied. Too much catechizing, rote learning and paternalist indoctrination, to which Elliot for instance was clearly inclined, could inhibit their development and enhance in some of them the tendency to passive obedience and an acceptance of inferiority. Thus the overall effect of the missions, certainly made some contribution to sustaining and stabilizing the slave society in Tobago. This was not a direct aim of the missionaries, but they recognized, with the partial exception of Purkis, that the survival of their work and of the opportunity to save souls and spread the gospel depended on at least the acquiescence of the planters. It should be noted however that one writer believes that Purkis' preference for avoiding work among the slaves was the result of his reluctance to work within the constraints of the system. But very few missionaries in the West Indies thus refused to compromise.[116] It was not that this involved the deliberate suppression of a feeling that slavery was either unchristian or otherwise intolerable; rather did they simply set the question on one side as hardly relevant. Both missions were established on the initiative of slave owners who hoped that they would reinforce the slave system; both depended, the Moravians wholly, on financial support from the slaveowners without which they could not exist for long; their whole effort must be seen in this context. The missions therefore could not preach liberty to the slaves even had they wanted to. They preached the virtues of obedience to lawful authority and peaceful and non-violent behaviour, apart from seeking to save souls through conversion and the spreading of the gospel. This had the effect of reinforcing the status quo; but Christian missions could hardly have avoided preaching thus and the contradiction between the message of Christ and the facts of slavery would eventually undermine the fabric of that same status quo since the missionaries sought to convince them that their lives and souls were valuable in the sight of God. This stood to enhance their sense of self-respect and in the long run, however strongly missionaries stressed obedience to lawful authority and non-violence, that in turn was likely to lead some to resent increasingly the limitations of their existence in the sight of man.

It is difficult to judge how much and what impact the missionaries had on the personal behaviour of those who listened to their preaching and teaching. Within months of his arrival in Tobago Elliot was convinced that he was producing noticeable results. In October 1808 he wrote that the slaves at Studley Park " are much more moral than they were " in that the accustomed complaints of stealing from each other were no longer heard. He saw this as evidence that the gospel was succeeding where the whip had failed.[117] Purkis, however, was more skeptical and some months later thought that "very little good has been done".[118] It is obvious however that the missionaries would be unlikely to be good judges of the impact of their work and almost no comment has been found from other sources. Clearly they did have some impact.

Before he left the island in 1813 Elliot wrote again of the slaves at Studley Park: "I think there appears a concern for the soul, a desire to profit by the preaching, when persons embrace every opportunity of hearing the gospel, after they have been hard at work from 5 o'clock in the morning till 7 or 8 (& sometimes later) at night . . ."[119] Beyond doubt, some slaves were deeply interested in what he had to say, even if the idea that the slaves sometimes understood the notion of concern for the soul is speculation. And the extent of the missions' success is not to be judged by numbers of converts. As for the pattern of that impact, we have noted Elliot's suggestion that theft became less common at Studley Park. Later he ascribed to the effect of the mission the fact that at the same estate Christmas 1811 passed, unprecedentedly, without disorder or drunkenness. The reformation of sexual behaviour was clearly a major feature.

Many who could not begin to qualify for baptism found their thinking and their behaviour affected in some measure by the things the missionaries said. Clearly the gospel message could comfort those in distress, and that in itself was a powerful drawing card, especially to the unfortunate. On the other hand many slaves understood very well that the missionaries were propagating the religion of the slavemaster and the conflict between slavery and the gospel the missionaries preached was self evident.[120] That alone was a powerful obstacle to missionary success. So was the fact that most missionaries saw the whole culture and lifestyle of Africa as being almost as much the enemy as Satan. Different slaves reacted to this combination of pressures in very different ways.

THE ORGANIZATION OF DEFENCE

The Garrison

The ease with which Britain had captured Tobago in 1793 underlined the need to improve its defences, and as the war lengthened it became obviously necessary to place the island firmly on a war footing. The misfortunes which befell British forces in some other islands in 1794-95 drove the point home, though it seems that an attempt at a reconquest by the French was regarded as less likely than a destructive raid, perhaps involving the liberation of the slaves once the French had abolished slavery in their own colonies in 1794.[1] When Spain entered the war in 1796 and until its capture in 1797 there was always the further possibility of "Picaroon skating over from Trinidad".[2] In 1795 particularly Tobago's Agent in London made urgent representations for better provision against external attack,[3] and the white inhabitants returned to this theme from time to time.

Several efforts were made to make Tobago more easily defendable, none of them very successful. A garrison of regular British troops was of course stationed there after 1793, and sustained throughout the war, and British reinforcements and replacements arrived from time to time; while in common with the other British islands of the Eastern Caribbean Tobago depended for naval defence on the British squadron based at English Harbour in Antigua. But like other British islands it was expected to contribute towards its own defence by providing money and labour to

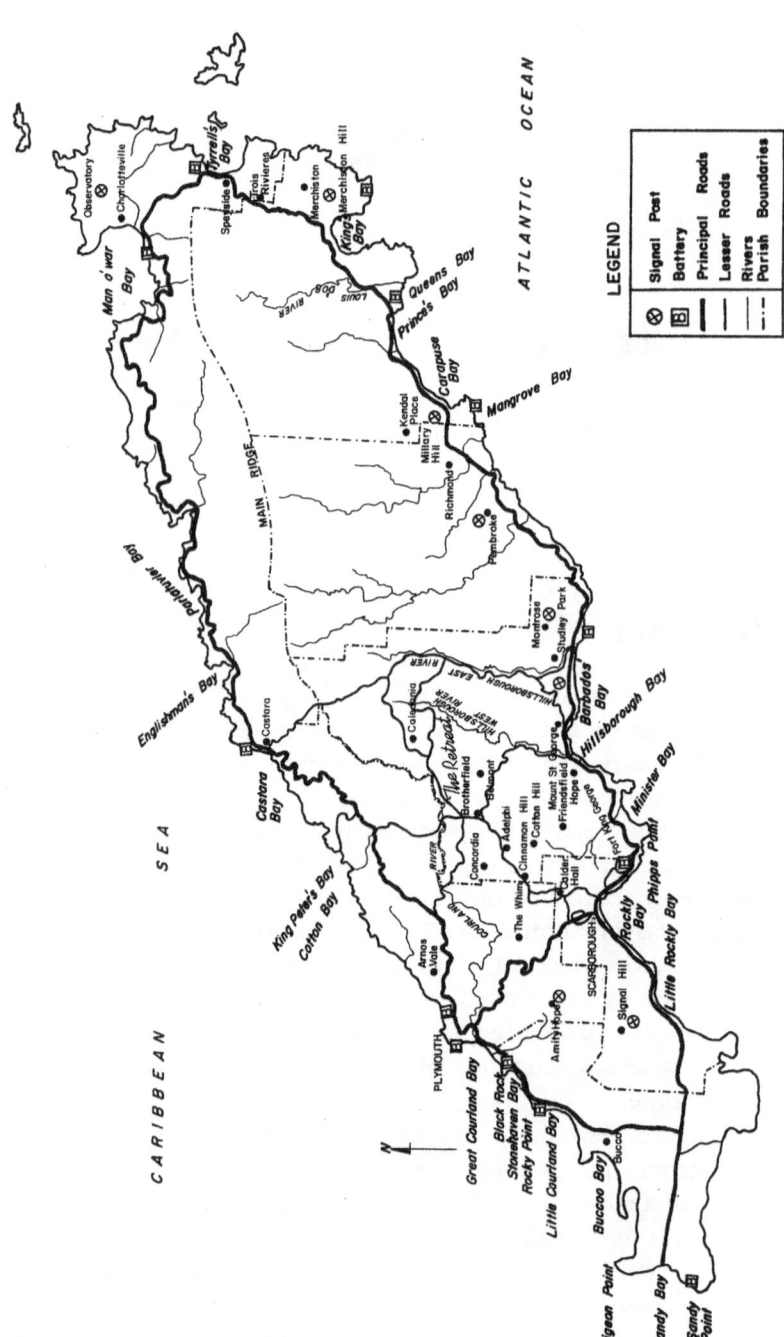

FIG. 7.1 COMMUNICATIONS AND FORTIFICATIONS CIRCA 1800

maintain the fortifications and quarters, and sometimes rations for the troops, and to maintain a militia force.[4] Local contribution was all the more important because in the 1790s up to half of the imperial garrison might be unfit at any given time, though the rate of sickness subsequently improved.

The size of the garrison varied considerably during the war. After the conquest in 1793 men were moved from Tobago to fight elsewhere and disease also took a noteworthy toll, so that by September 1795 numbers were down to 130 of whom only forty were fully fit.[5] But this was obviously an unacceptably weak force and several appeals were made to the Commander-in-Chief for a larger garrison. A year later the garrison had been augmented to about 600. Thereafter numbers rose to a peak of about 950 early in 1798, falling back to a norm of roughly 600 in the middle of 1799. This was the normal level for some years thereafter, except for the build up of troops when the island was recaptured in 1803.[6]

The recapture of the island by the British in 1803 merely underlined its vulnerability, which ought by then to have been sufficiently clear to British as well as French. As the Secretary of State wrote to General Grinfield, the British Commander-in-Chief in the Eastern Caribbean, when in anticipation of a renewal of the war he gave orders to prepare to attempt Tobago's reconquest, it was a very obvious target "from the amount of British property connected with the island, the uniform attachment of the Inhabitants to His Majesty's Person, and the importance of its position . . . and the more so, as from the Accounts I have received of the State of the French Force upon the Island, there is no probability of any Serious Resistance".[7]

When war broke out Grinfield quickly invested Tobago with 3,100 men on 30 June 1803. The French commander, General César Berthier, surrendered with 228 men without attempting resistance.[8]

The two British conquests of Tobago were ample evidence that a not very well equipped fort and a garrison of just over 200 men were quite inadequate to resist a substantial invading force. It is noteworthy that the British commonly deployed about 600 men after 1803. Even so, it was fortunate for the British that they were never required to resist an invasion. Indeed, as the French were effectively forced out of the Caribbean and even the Atlantic after the Battle of Trafalgar in 1805 and the threat of invasion subsided, the British garrison was reduced substantially. By 1807 a level of 300 to 380 men had become normal. From time to time plans were put forward for a larger garrison, but with many areas of risk making similar demands these generally went unheeded.[9] The basis of the garrison usually consisted of British troops, but European mercenaries and some Hanoverians were sometimes stationed there and some scores were usually drawn from the black West India Regiments though the governor, Sir William Young, was inclined to distrust these.[10] So were the colonists, though in 1795-7 they had for political reasons cooperated in the raising of the force.[11]

In the later 1790s the health of the garrison began to improve. Whereas up to 40 per cent had been unfit at any one time, the proportion began to fall in 1797 and by 1800 a figure of 5 per cent was not uncommon.[12] Subsequently the rate remained generally low. The reasons for this improvement are not clear, but they probably have something to do with a fall in the prevalence of malaria and yellow fever related to the draining of the Bacolet swamp, close to Fort King George, in 1803 and the attendant clearing of bush in that area.[13] It was well recognized that the disease was associated in some way with swampy areas. To some extent, too, the improved health of the garrison may have been related to an increasing use of black troops from the West India Regiments whose superior resistance to the prevailing diseases is well attested, but it has not been possible to identify in detail the extent to which such troops were in fact employed.

Forts and Batteries

Apart from the provision of a garrison of professional troops, wider preparations for meeting a possible enemy attack were of course undertaken. In December 1794, as British forces were being driven out of Guadeloupe, the militia officers drew up a contingency plan in case of a French invasion, based on the concept of a retreat into the interior[14] into which they sent at least two reconnoitring expeditions.[15] Governor Lindsay subsequently supported this notion, conceiving of all the inhabitants "fighting at the same time every inch of ground and harassing [the enemy] continually". Lindsay conceived that "destruction is the object of the French and debauching the Negroes the means they take to attack" so that if the slaves were moved out of the reach of any invading force "they may make as much destruction as they please among the canes &c., nature and industry will soon repair any such damage". On the other hand, if the French made contact with the slaves they could easily persuade them to join the republican cause, "and then the Colony is ruined".[16] A general movement into the interior in the event of an invasion was an obvious stratagem, though the notion that the enemy sought only to destroy and not to capture had become distinctly outdated. New contingency plans were prepared from time to time, and in 1802 Brigadier Hugh Lyle Carmichael had the rather different idea of appointing three different rallying points, Amity Hope, Rockly Bay and Phipps Point, all within a few miles of the fort at Scarborough. He also conceived of the possibility of a long stand at Cotton Hill, again not far from Fort King George.[17] But it does not appear that serious preparation of any of these plans was ever undertaken, though in 1795 the Council did appoint a committee to organize the storing of provisions at Courland River Estate and a joint committee of the two Houses was charged with arranging the opening of roads into the interior (from Courland River Estate to the Retreat and thence through Caledonia to Castara via the Main Ridge).[18]

The maintenance of the fortifications around the coasts of Tobago was a chronic problem which was never laid to rest. Despite repeated repairs the forts and batteries never seemed to be in good order when an attack was apprehended. Perhaps the simplest example of the problem is the routine need to keep the surroundings of Fort King George free of bush. Not only would high bush provide an admirable means of concealment for any enemy, it was also believed to threaten the health of the garrison by harbouring the carriers of disease; so the object was to keep the vicinity clear for a distance of about 100 yards. Yet the procedure for clearing the bush was excessively cumbersome. In accordance with a principle formally clarified by the Secretary of State when the war began and accepted by all the colonial legislatures, slave labour for the construction and maintenance of fortifications was provided by the House of Assembly at the colony's expense.[19] Normally clearing the vicinity of Fort King George involved about thirty slaves for two weeks, once a year.[20] The Assembly usually made no fuss about this, cheerfully accepting the cost involved; yet the operation was never undertaken until the garrison commander or garrison surgeon specifically requested it, and then the legislature would appoint a joint committee of both houses to advertise for the necessary labour.[21] This was certainly the normal method of getting public works done, but some attempt might have been made to establish a routine which could have avoided the waiting period of several weeks that was in the event inevitable. Moreover a single clearing exercise each year could not have been remotely adequate. In practice the surroundings of the fort were overgrown for significant periods each year.

Bush apart, the proper maintenance of Fort King George was the most obvious of the steps Tobago could take for its own defence. Yet keeping the fort in good repair was also a matter of *ad hoc* response to representations from its commander and not of any regular maintenance routine. Again the colony was usually willing to provide slaves to perform the work when asked. Yet the condition of the fort was a frequent subject of complaint. In 1794 plans for improving the fort were put in hand, partly at imperial expense but with the colony providing labour and some

FORT KING GEORGE VIEWED FROM THE NORTH
Drawing by Sir William Young
Reprinted from Sir William Young, "An essay on the commercial and political importance of the island of Tobago..."

money. Earth and lumber appear to have been important, if not the principal materials.[22] In July 1797, after several months of repair work, Sir Ralph Abercromby reported that it was still "very little capable of defence" and badly in need of extensive repairs.[23] By May 1799 newly repaired defences were awaiting the arrival of guns from Barbados and a road from Scarborough to the battery had been built. In 1801 the unusually large demand for 2,427 days' slave labour was approved by the Assembly.[24] Yet in July 1802 when the war was over for the moment the Officer Commanding the troops wrote "The Fort . . . is perfectly assailable by Coup de Main",[25] though this need not be a reflection on the condition of the defences then in place.

The fort was in reasonable condition when the French surrendered it in 1803, and large additional works were quickly put in hand. By the end of the year the governor described it as in a "respectable" state.[26] Yet fifteen months later it had deteriorated so far that the legislature agreed to provide 900 man-days of slave labour to put it in order. By August 1807 however it was again in need of attention[27] and by April 1808 some of its seventeen cannon were unsafe to fire.[28] Nothing seems to have been done however and a year later when a French fleet was believed to pose a threat it was necessary for Governor Young to take emergency measures to cover certain gaps in the fort's defences before the Assembly could be summoned, and therefore at some financial risk to himself since he might have been held personally responsible for the expense. This pre-emption of the Assembly's privileges prompted the House to announce that if it happened again members would refuse to provide the money.[29]

The condition of Fort King George was thus repeatedly before the authorities. Yet when war broke out with the United States of America in 1812 it was again necessary to take urgent steps to put it in readiness.[30] The precise nature of the repairs which were so often necessary never appears in the available documents but it seems likely that the deterioration under tropical conditions of crude earthworks and bare woodwork which included the gun carriages, played an important part.

The coastal batteries at the "out bays" were in even worse case. Apart from Fort James at Great Courland Bay, which had three 18-pounders and one larger gun in 1808, there were batteries manned by the militia assisted by slaves at Scarborough, Barbados Bay, Mangrove Bay, Queen's Bay, King's Bay, Tyrell's Bay (Speyside), Man o'War Bay, Castara, Arnos Vale, Black Rock, Little Courland Bay, and Sandy Bay. This last was the largest, with four guns, while the others all had one, or two or three.[31] These batteries were in a sense even more important than Fort King George, since the bays were constantly threatened by privateers which would never contemplate going near the fort.

There is little evidence about the condition of the batteries in the 1790s but in 1799 several of them were in need of repair.[32] After the French capitulated in 1803 most were in good order,[33] though they were not very effective against the privateers then in evidence and one ship was burnt by the enemy in Mangrove Bay despite the presence of a battery there.[34] In November the Assembly agreed that 1,200 days' labour should be provided to improve them where necessary.[35] Subsequently however they deteriorated in the usual fashion until in October 1807 the military authorities suddenly woke up to the fact that perhaps 800 days' labour was needed on the batteries at Great Courland, which the Assembly was hard pressed to provide.[36] Others were also in need of attention.

In 1812, however, as war with the United States approached, the batteries were again found to be in poor condition: "defenceless and unserviceable", said the Assembly in a resolution.[37] This time the surviving records indicate the nature of the major problems: the battery platforms, apparently not always of masonry but sometimes of timber, and the gun carriages also of timber, tended to rot; and the magazines were in bad condition. That so vital an element in the system of defence as the magazines should have to be the subject of a special resolution of the assembly to advertise for tenders is a graphic illustration of the shortcomings of the system.[38] When war actually broke out the batteries were still not ready and Tobago was much alarmed. American ships were well acquainted with its coastline and with the vulnerability of the bays to privateers. So a hasty attempt was once more made to put the batteries in order.[39] Only a year later however, with war still in progress, Mangrove Bay, Queen's Bay and Man o'War Bay batteries each contained one useless gun and other repair work was needed.[40]

The outbreak of war with the USA in fact frightened the planters as nothing had done since the threat that Tobago might be handed back to France in the late 1790s.[41] Having summoned the two Houses of the legislature to consider what measures should be taken for the defence of the island, Governor Young referred to "this new and to us most dangerous enemy", warned of the probable appearance of American privateers, and pointed out: "An American landing may be identified with and mistaken for a subject of Great Britain and this should be the more attended to as many of the old traders from the United States are acquainted with every bay and inlet to the interior of the island".[42] The legislature immediately petitioned the governor to ask the commander of the naval station to provide a warship to protect Tobago and to request the enlargement of the garrison. They also protested that the cost of repairing the forts and batteries was totally beyond the colony's resources.[43]

In general the Assembly gave no trouble over providing funds for the maintenance of the local defences despite the lack of any regular system for doing this. Just as slave labour for defence works was provided *ad hoc*, so money for defence was usually provided by passing special money bills as occasion demanded.[44] No case has been found in which the legislature refused to provide what was needed before this 1812 episode, though there was sometimes a lack of enthusiasm.

It was to be expected that any attempt to keep the batteries and forts in really effective condition would produce complaints about cost. Yet these were not forthcoming. In the period before the Peace of 1802 the Assembly had been reluctant to displease the British Government because it wanted to ensure that Britain would retain Tobago when peace came to be signed. Willingness to meet British wishes over expenditure was one aspect of this.[45] When the island was returned to France and then recaptured however the colonists became much more straightforward in their dealings with Britain. Certainly they were aggrieved at being handed back to France; possibly they now despaired of being able to influence Britain since their late efforts had been unavailing. At any rate the determined cooperation of the 1790s was now far less in evidence. Yet little appears to have been said about defence costs. The obvious inference is that the financial demands of defence were in fact not great, at least after 1805, no doubt because the threat of invasion was regarded as trivial in the period between Trafalgar and the war with the USA. It is not too much to say that after 1805 defence works in fact were commonly neglected except when unusual danger seemed to threaten, and reluctance to pay for them began to grow.

The Militia

The usual means of local defence in the British colonies, apart from the coastal batteries, was the militia. In April 1794 a temporary Militia Act was passed as part of the revival of old legislation which had lapsed under the French[46] and a permanent Act followed in 1795. A militia was needed at least as much as a protection against slave revolt as it was to combat an invasion and, as Secretary of State Dundas put it, "there should not be the remotest possibility of the Island being ever without such a System of Internal Defence".[47] This Act lapsed with the return of the French in 1802 and was replaced by a new one in November 1803 after the British recaptured Tobago. Subsequently the Militia Acts were amended or replaced from time to time.

The Militia Act of 1795 required that all free males, white or coloured, between the ages of 15 and 60 who were British subjects must enlist in the militia. Only a small handful of officials and servicemen were ever exempted. The force consisted of an infantry regiment commanded by a colonel assisted by a lieutenant colonel and a major and comprising eight companies, one for each parish and one for Scarborough, each under a captain and a lieutenant; together with a corps of artillery commanded by a colonel, a lieutenant colonel and a major and comprising sundry captains and gunners. The adjutant of militia was paid a salary of £100, later £200 currency, which made him almost a full-time officer.

The militia were required to exercise once each month at the appropriate company parade ground or artillery battery, for three hours, absentees being liable to fines. Free coloureds were assigned to the artillery wherever practicable and militia infantry could be assigned to guard the batteries on the basis of one free coloured to each white and not more than three of each to every battery. Specially selected slaves were called on to assist the artillery men with the batteries, but not more than four to each gun.[48]

The obligation to serve in the militia was however qualified by the provision that "one proper and discreet white person" must always be left on each plantation, though if there was only one such person he was required to turn out on parade every second month. Usually militiamen carried muskets and their officers swords, though after 1804 the men were required to have a firelock and bayonet.[49] All were required to transport their arms and ammunition personally at all times so as to ensure that slaves did not lay hands on them. Militia officers were always owners of real property, including slaves, or of rent-derived income of at least £100 per annum, or former army officers. They were empowered to commandeer slaves, horses, mules, cattle and carriages from the estates to mount or transport guns, up to a limit of 5 per cent of the slaves or one-third of the animals or carriages, though such levies had to be paid for at a daily rate of 4s. 6d. per slave or 6s. per horse.[50] It is noteworthy that a horse was worth more than a slave: certainly there were far fewer horses around.

On the declaration of martial law, proclaimed by the firing of guns from the fort and batteries, all militiamen were required to report to their parade grounds or batteries with their arms and thirty-six cartridges. The governor was also empowered, with the consent of the Council, to embody part of the militia without declaring general martial law for purposes of internal or external security, though in 1803 it was provided that no militiaman thus called out was to be on duty for more than fourteen days.[51] Selected estates were required to hold themselves in readiness to furnish mounted white messengers at any time to carry news of any alarm to the next post. The Militia Act also empowered the governor to conscript any merchant seaman who happened to be in the island's harbours during any period of martial law to serve in the local forts and batteries at night.[52]

In addition to the militia, the governor in May 1795 proposed that a "Black Corps" drawn from the slave population should be raised for local defence. The principle of employing black and coloured men, both slave and free, in the British Army was well established by the end of the War of American Independence and after the outbreak of war in 1793 a number of colonies had raised corps of black "rangers" as part of their preparations against attack. The legislature therefore agreed to the formation of a corps of 150 men with white officers, thus lessening their dependence on the imperial garrison. Apart from giving up the services of so many slaves, the colony also provided quarters for the rangers and rationed them for some months before the army took over this responsibility.[53] This corps proved a very useful body and in 1797 Sir Ralph Abercromby requested and was granted the loan of it for his attack on Puerto Rico. On its return however it was deemed to be surplus to the military requirements of the island so that responsibility for rationing them was thrown back on the colony.[54] Thus in 1799 the men were dispersed to their estates, there being "no apparent probability their services will again be called for", and in 1800 the corps was formally disbanded.[55]

In August 1796 when Tobago was alarmed at the possibility of an attack from Cayenne, Thomas McKnaight petitioned the Council for permission to raise a troop of light horse to assist in the defence of the island.[56] Council agreed, militia horse being known to have proven useful during the recent rising in Grenada,[57] and in September 1796 the troop was formed, consisting of three officers and twenty troopers.[58] Each man had to provide his own horse and weapons: short carbine and bayonet, pistols and sword. Subsequently the Troop of Horse was formally incorporated into the militia.

The Militia Act of 1795 was intended to last for the duration of the then existing war and so it lapsed in the middle of 1802. When the island was recaptured in the following year however steps were at once taken to revive the militia the more promptly because of the intense activity of enemy privateers which suggested that attempts at pillage were likely. The matter was attended with some difficulty because members of the legislature were reluctant to take positive steps for defence in case the island should once again be returned to France. If that happened the French might not be kind towards those who helped prepare to resist them.[59] Nevertheless, a new Militia Act was passed in November 1803.

This Act differed from its predecessor in a number of ways which reflected the preoccupations of its time. It was entitled "An Act for establishing a Militia for the sole purpose of Defence against Internal Insurrection and repelling the Attacks of Maurauders". The new emphasis on defence against internal unrest was reflected in the Assembly's proceedings as well as in the first clause of the preamble, which referred specifically to "keeping up a due subordination of the slaves". Here was a direct reflection of continuing concern with the situation created by the dangerous slave conspiracy of December 1801.[60]

The new Act altered the organization of the militia in one significant respect: the eight companies were grouped into two battalions, each with a lieutenant colonel and a major. The Leeward Battalion comprised the companies of St Andrew, Scarborough, St Patrick and St David and was required to parade at Cinnamon Hill once each year, while the Windward Battalion comprised the companies of St George, St Mary, St Paul and St John and was required to parade annually at Queen's Bay. The officers' powers to requisition labour and purchase materials for repairing the batteries were widened somewhat, and in several small respects the 1803 Act was decidedly more specific than that of 1795.[61] The whole Act suggests that there was some feeling that the earlier one had not been altogether satisfactory in ensuring that an efficient militia was available when required; and this suspicion is supported by the fact that the condition of the batteries had been often poor.

This Act, however, was validated only for a single year and a new Militia Act in November 1804[62] created a ninth company comprising the free coloured men of Scarborough. The island's free coloured men mostly resided in Scarborough and it was thought convenient, and no doubt desirable, to collect them into a single, in effect segregated company of about sixty men, under white officers.[63] An important new provision required the whole militia to be ready for "actual service" during the Christmas holidays and again one sees a relic of the slave conspiracy: the purpose was said to be to prevent "disorderly or riotous meetings of negroes". In 1806, following another alarm over the possibility of a rising among the slaves, an amending Act made it mandatory to call out at least half of each company over the Christmas holidays, which were defined to end on 2 January. This provision was repealed in 1814 as no longer necessary.[64]

In 1810, militia service was demanded of *all* free males between 16 and 60 years regardless of nationality. The three sections of the militia, foot artillery and horse, were now all brought under the command of the colonel; and the nine companies were grouped into Leeward and Windward divisions each of which comprehended the relevant detachments of artillery. The Horse were attached to the leeward division, being based on Scarborough. A surgeon was appointed to each division.[65] When the war ended in 1815 and the Militia Act lapsed three months later, legislation was passed to continue it in peacetime.[66]

The Use of Martial Law

Apart from providing for the organization of a militia the Militia Acts also attempted to lay down rules for the declaration of martial law, when militiamen could be required to muster. The power to declare martial law was vested in the governor by his Instructions, which formed the basis of the colonial constitution, but in doing so he was required to act on the advice of the Council.[67]

These provisions, derived from the Royal Prerogative, were however qualified by local legislation. The Act of 1795 provided that in case of an actual attack, invasion or insurrection martial law would automatically come into force for the duration of such emergency, and the governor had only to order the firing of the alarm signal. However if the emergency were occasioned only by threat or rumour the governor was still required to obtain the consent of the Council before martial law could be declared; and if the threat did not materialize within forty-eight hours martial law would automatically cease unless the Council renewed its consent. But with such consent martial law could be prolonged for innumerable periods of forty-eight hours.[68]

In part, these regulations were intended to bridle the power of the governor, who might otherwise be able to use martial law in an arbitrary fashion. The members of the militia, however, and this usually included all the planters and Assemblymen, had a very clear interest in ensuring that martial law was sparingly used, since while it prevailed they were all kept under arms and unable to attend to their normal business. This was always liable to lead to financial loss.

In April 1795, however, Tobago appeared to face a threat of attack which led Governor Lindsay to feel that he needed wider powers to declare martial law if adequate preparations were to be quickly made,[69] and the Assembly passed an Act empowering the governor for a period of two months to declare martial law without consulting the Council "when and as often as he shall think proper for the purpose of putting the Colony into a state of defence", on the sole condition that the legislature and the courts should function normally unless actual conflict began.[70] This Act was later continued in force for periods of two or three months at a time until August 1796.[71] Without it the Council would have had to assemble every forty-eight hours to prolong martial law unless an attack actually occurred.

The Militia Act of 1803 showed in a number of details a trend towards narrowing the scope of the governor's own powers under martial law. This trend towards greater precision and to limiting the governor's control of martial law was in keeping with a general pattern evident in all the West Indian colonies since the 1760s. That trend had reached its zenith in Jamaica in 1778 when the Assembly tried to gain control of the declaration of martial law for itself, ultimately with partial success.[72] The Tobago Assembly never went that far, nor did it try to define how great a threat would justify martial law as occurred in some other islands. But it clearly was anxious about the governor's powers in the matter and now that the pressure of the 1790s to appear as a co-operative colony in British eyes had abated somewhat,[73] it sought to control them.

The trend continued when the Act of 1804 declared that martial law should be automatic only in case of "insurrection" and declarable with the advice of council, like partial embodiment of the militia, only in case of "intended insurrection".[74] There is no reference at all in the Act to external danger, but there was a saving clause at the end of it to the effect that it was not intended to infringe the powers granted to the Commander-in-Chief under the Royal Instructions. Those Instructions specifically authorized him, with the consent of the Council, to declare martial law in case of "invasion" or "war".

The point was thereby covered, but it must be very doubtful whether this was intentional; for when next the governor faced an apprehended invasion many members of the Council took the view that there was no power to invoke martial law. The alarm began on 24 February 1805 with the receipt in Tobago of the information that a large fleet had arrived in Martinique carrying troops. Evading the British blockade of French ports, Admiral Missiessy had escaped from Rochefort on New Year's Day 1805.[75] The garrison commander requested that the militia be called out and arrangements made to requisition labour and draught animals to carry ammunition and supplies to the military posts.

For the government to provide what was asked required a declaration of martial law and President Campbell, with the Militia Act clearly in mind as well as his Instructions, was doubtful of his power to declare it though apparently he believed he ought to do so. The majority of the Council believed that martial law could be lawfully declared only in case of "insurrection".[76] When the Royal Instructions were considered the view was expressed that the relevant clause was intended only to prevent the governor from acting without the consent of Council and not to confer a positive power not envisaged in the Militia Act.[77] It is clear that many persons in the colony wished to keep the governor's power over martial law within narrow confines.[78]

The situation was saved for the moment because the Assembly happened to be in session and agreed to provide the necessary labour without recourse to martial law. But the Assembly might not have been sitting and in any case its procedures were slow: three weeks later nothing positive had yet been done.[79] It was left to the Secretary of State to point out to Campbell when the matter came to his attention that the Act expressly preserved the powers vested in the governor under the Royal Instructions and that while these were subject to the consent of Council they did include "time of invasion, war or other times when by law [martial law] may be executed". The governor was however advised to clarify the issue by amending the Militia Act.[80]

In June 1805 there was another alarm when a fleet, which later proved to be Nelson's, engaged in his celebrated pursuit of the French Admiral Villeneuve, was sighted off Castara. This time a hastily summoned Council agreed to a declaration of martial law though the Secretary of State's opinion on the February episode was not yet known.[81] In December 1805 there was yet another alarm and again the Council readily agreed to martial law; but this was a case of threatened insurrection.[82]

Nothing was done, however, to alter the law. Even the subsequent Act of 1810 referred only to cases of "insurrection", when martial law was automatic: otherwise it was the Royal Instructions which prevailed[83] and the Assembly was able to continue pretending that the law left the governor less discretion that in fact it did.

The Militia in Action

On a number of other occasions the militia was called out, in whole or in part. In 1795 Governor Lindsay took advantage of the special discretion granted him by the Assembly in relation to martial law to invoke it merely in order to facilitate the improvement of the defences.[84] In August 1796 President Campbell did much the same thing, with the Council's consent, though he was prompted by the news that a French fleet was gathering at Cayenne and was believed to intend an attack on Tobago.[85] In 1798 President Robley and the Council declared martial law on the approach of a fleet which a few hours later turned out to be American.[86] The slave conspiracy at Christmas 1801 provided yet another occasion for the declaration of martial law and in May 1804, when there were reports that the French planned an attempt to cut out vessels at anchor in the bays, parties of militia were sent "to do duty at the Batteries" with the aid of one sailor drafted from each vessel in harbour.[87] Except for the two threats of slave revolt in 1801 and 1805 all these occasions had to do with the possibility of attack by the French. No such attack ever materialized, but if the local authorities seem to have been very quick to take fright, it has to be remembered that it could take more time to get the militia together than for a fleet to reach land after being sighted. It was better to err on the side of preparedness.

When the militia was called out the officers sometimes squabbled among themselves. Moreover they were often members either of the Council or of the Assembly and were not always willing to obey without question the orders of a governor who might be no more than President of the Council, and so merely their senior colleague.[88] Further, they were commonly jealous of their position vis-à-vis the garrison officers. During periods of military law the militia were usually placed under the command of the garrison commander, an arrangement which they commonly disliked. Indeed the Militia Act of 1810 specifically provided that the militia should obey only its own officers, an invitation to confusion which was fortunately nullified by the sagacity of Sir William Young: he appointed himself colonel of the militia while he also held the position of Commander-in-Chief.[89]

In the light of these tensions it is not surprising that the embodiment of the militia, and more generally the declaration of martial law, was sometimes attended by a measure of confusion. One incident in particular deserves mention. On the night of 26/27 October 1801 a completely false alarm occurred when the Signal Hill station gave the alarm signal in circumstances which were never fully elucidated and the story gained ground that seven enemy ships had arrived at Great Courland Bay. Since the governor was out of town, martial law could not be proclaimed formally, and when the militia was called out it refused to obey the military command in the absence of martial law; while the militia colonel, Robert Paterson, who was also Speaker of the Assembly, engaged in a public quarrel with the Brigadier, Hugh Lyle Carmichael, in front of the assembled militiamen.[90]

Apart from the petty jealousies of its officers, the rank and file of the militia were certainly a motley crowd, including as they did pretty well every free adult male. Neither the regular monthly parades nor the annual period of duty at Christmas time seem to have been scrupulously observed. Attendance at the monthly musters frequently occupied the attention of the legislature and in 1806 it was thought necessary to increase the fine imposed on absentees by 200 per cent, to £5 for the rank and file and £10 for officers.[91] Even this did not produce regular attendance. In 1810 officers were empowered to require weekly drills of the "many" who did not know platoon exercises.⁹² The efficiency of the force had it been called to serious action can only be suspect.

On the other hand, the garrison commander reported in 1802 that those who had been called out for duty with the slave conspiracy had shown zeal and willingness⁹³ and in 1808 when there was a special effort at firing practice Governor Young thought that the men acquitted themselves well and showed much "esprit de corps and pride in military attainment".⁹⁴ There were other occasions too on which the militia received praise. Though it never saw action save for the arrest of some slave conspirators, in practice it did do what was required of it so far as the scanty available evidence goes. Certainly the militiamen acted under the powerful spur of the knowledge that a successful invasion or revolt might well spell total disaster and they seem to have been generally willing to serve if less than conscientious about routine fatigues. The free population seems to have borne with fortitude and even good humour the disruption of routine that the embodiment of the militia invariably brought.⁹⁵

The popular spirit is further illustrated by the fact that in February 1805, when the first of that year's three alarms occurred, a number of the white inhabitants of lesser status (none were proprietors) volunteered to serve under the garrison commander in aid of the defence effort without waiting for the militia to be embodied under martial law. In this way a special Volunteer Corps was formed, consisting of about eighty men in two companies under the Collector of Customs, Mr W. Arnold, who held the rank of major. These men did valuable service not only in February but also in June 1805. After the arrival of Nelson's fleet in the following week dispelled the prevailing fears the Corps was disbanded amid much praise for its work.⁹⁶

In April 1794 when the militia was first being organized its strength was put at 150, so clearly many men had not yet joined it.⁹⁷ This was gradually corrected however. By June 1807 there were 409 militia, of whom forty-two were artillery men and twenty-three cavalry.⁹⁸ By 1810 there were 436 including thirty-seven artillery and thirty-one cavalry.⁹⁹ These figures tally closely with those for the free adult male population, white and coloured.

Military Communications

The preparations for a possible defence of Tobago repeatedly exposed the problem of communication within the island. We have seen that under the Militia Acts certain plantations were required to hold themselves in readiness to provide messengers to convey information to their neighbours about any declaration of martial law. Before that could become pertinent, however, arrangements were necessary to inform the authorities about the approach of danger. Normally a signal post at Amity Hope was used as the necessary intermediary in conveying information between the fort at Courland, where approaching fleets were usually first identified, and Fort King George. The signal post was not always in proper order.[100] But at least in theory messages between the forts could be conveyed quickly and easily. A post at Signal Hill was sometimes also used in conveying information to Fort King George. In time of anticipated danger messengers were stationed at each signal post.[101]

Communication with the outbays and their batteries however was a different matter. Not until 1812 was serious consideration given to the establishment of signal posts at other critical sites. At that time a Committee of Council agreed that signal posts were desirable at Observatory Hill, Merchiston, Kendal, Pembroke, Montrose, Mount St George and Signal Hill; but the problem of cost, estimated at £3,519 currency, prevented further progress[102] and the war ended without change in the system of messengers moving on horseback along the windward coast.

Naval Defence in Coastal Waters

Fortifications and militia apart, there was also another direction in which strong local defence could become necessary. While the responsibility for defence by sea generally lay with the British navy this was not always able to cope successfully with local attacks by small enemy craft which sought to attack the trade and harbours of the colonies, usually in the role of privateers. Though Martinique was quickly taken by the British in 1794, French privateers had an excellent base at Guadeloupe which Britain did not finally capture until 1810, and until 1808 they were also able to use the Spanish West Indian ports.[103] In this connection the idea of stationing a ship permanently at Tobago appeared early in the war and in 1796 a warship was detailed to watch the island for a while.[104] Then in 1799 the Secretary of State proposed to the several governors in the West Indies that small boats, ships' boats or coasting craft, should be fitted with a gun or carronade and used for inshore patrols[105] in the vicinity of the island harbours. Such boats were expected to be specially useful against small privateers. It was, however, not until the second phase of the war began in 1803, and Tobago was again recaptured by the British, that the activity of the privateers became a really serious problem. It is to be noted that the French had recovered Martinique at the recent Peace and so now possessed an additional base.

As soon as the war was resumed Commodore Hood wrote from Barbados to the several governors proposing that each island should provide one or two "Fencible Gun Boats" for the defence of its ports and bays, carrying one officer, a crew of perhaps five and twenty-four to thirty oars, and armed with a one-pounder in the bow. These gunboats would not be expected to leave their home islands without the governor's consent. Tobago was thought able to provide two.[106] The idea that local resources might be used to provide a ship was not entirely new, the Tobago Assembly having in 1794 proposed to hire one to maintain contact with British forces in the area,[107] and having in the following year declined an invitation from the Commander-in-Chief to provide a ship for war service on the ground of its limited resources.[108]

By the time this proposal was put to the Tobago legislature in October 1803[109] the need for better inshore defence was acute. A few days earlier Governor Macdonald had reported: "The island is for some time past in a perfect state of Blockade; from the number of the Enemy's Privateers hovering constantly round it, Trading vessels have very little chance of escaping them".[110] Tobago's coastal shipping had indeed suffered badly in the preceding months and the island had no British warship to hand, while the commodore's force was too small to permit of a constant presence. In a single week in early October, with at least two and possibly as many as four privateers constantly prowling the area, two sloops had been captured within sight of Tobago and a ship loading sugar in Mangrove Bay was boarded and burnt by a privateer, losing 300 hogsheads of sugar. In consequence the loading of sugar had come to a standstill with twelve ships waiting in Rockly Bay; and and the few droghers which had evaded capture had refused to continue ferrying sugar from the outbays[111] despite the fact that drogherage charges had risen as high as £4. 18s. 0d. currency (about 44s. sterling) per hogshead.[112]

Yet despite pressure from the governor, the legislature took the view that Tobago had not the means to provide a gunboat at that time.[113] Events, however, were to force its hand. In November a mail boat was captured by a French privateer while on its way from Barbados.[114] The same thing happened to the second December mail-boat,[115] at a time when the island was "completely invested by the Enemy's Privateers" and no vessel anchored in any of the outbays was considered safe. The shore batteries around the island had several times engaged the enemy but were commonly ineffective. Privateers had cut out three ships from their anchorages and captured a sloop off King's Bay.[116]

The danger remained chronic in the ensuing months.[117] Some planters found it impossible to ship all their sugar because of the blockade maintained by the privateers and the fact that they had captured most of the coasting droghers.[118] In these circumstances the planters began to grumble at the invisibility of the navy: ". . . the Cruizers are fonder of Blockading Martinique & Guadeloupe where there is a prospect of making Prizes, than of protecting the Property of their Countrymen . . ."[119] Thus the Council and Assembly gradually faced up to the need to spend more money and finally in September 1804 they agreed to purchase a vessel to carry fifty or sixty men and twelve guns, a much more formidable weapon than Hood had originally proposed.[120]

Further delay occurred because the two Houses could not agree on how to raise the money[121] but in February 1805 the sum of £6,000 currency was at last provided by means of a special tax of 7s. on each slave in the island.[122] A vessel was then identified, equipped at Barbados and Trinidad, and pronounced ready for service on 21 April 1805. The navy agreed to crew and maintain it.[123]

It has not been possible to trace the career of Tobago's warship however, except to establish that it was short. The ship was captured by the French towards the end of 1806 and it is perhaps some tribute to its potential and its achievement that soon after this happened the privateers reappeared and again began to do "considerable damage". It would be too much to expect that Tobago could easily replace a £6,000 vessel, and so the legislature's response was to ask the commander on the naval station to provide naval protection.[124] The situation does not seem to have improved much, however, and, possibly the effective elimination of their navy at Trafalgar in 1805, led the French to put even more effort into privateering. In June 1807 the prevalence of privateers led to the reorganization of the militia artillery which had responsibility for the batteries at the outbays, while Admiral Cochrane now sent HMS *Attentive* of fourteen guns to protect Tobago's coasts.[125] Yet in December 1807 as many as seventy privateers were believed to be operating from Guadeloupe alone and Governor Young reported ". . . our seas indeed swarm with those Marauders".[126]

However the enhanced naval protection may have been partly responsible for the fact that no significant complaints about enemy privateers have been found for the period from early 1808 until after the United States of America entered the war in 1812. The capture by Britain of Martinique in 1809 and Guadeloupe, St Martin and St Eustatius in 1810, all celebrated as privateering centres, also helped, as did the new alliance between Britain and Spain which prevented the use of Spanish bases by French privateers. With the whole of the eastern Caribbean in British hands there was now no base from which privateers could operate against the British colonies.[127] No doubt, too, the decline in French naval power after Trafalgar enabled Britain to strengthen her fleets in the

Caribbean, so that when war broke out with the United States Young was instructed to apply to the Admiral for protection in any case of serious threat.[128]

War with America however did bring a recrudescence of the privateering threat. The Americans could operate privateers from their home bases without needing centres in the Caribbean itself, and it was alleged in 1812 that they were allowed to dispose of their cargoes, and then no doubt to obtain supplies, in Puerto Rico. Spain denied this, and sent out instructions that it should not be permitted, but the possibility remains.[129] By the beginning of 1813 American privateers were around in large numbers and their presence had led to an increase in freight rates.[130] Yet Tobago was very far away from the Americans' bases and the middle months of the year were generally quiet.[131] Subsequently incidents multiplied and by 1814 the privateers, often in Tobago's vicinity, had been known to enter Sandy Bay, and had generally "induced a vigilance".[132]

Transatlantic Convoys

Privateers apart, the crossing of the Atlantic was always attended by some measure of hazard from enemy warships, though again the Battle of Trafalgar in 1805 served to minimize this. Thereafter few French warships were ever loose in the Atlantic. The risk of capture affected not only the owners of the ships and their cargoes, which were very likely insured; in the case of ships sailing from the West Indies, the revenue of Great Britain was also at risk for it was expected to reap substantial import duties. To combat these dangers Britain sought to provide naval escorts for her merchant ships both within the Caribbean and across the Atlantic. Indeed from the outset of the war, merchantmen were instructed not to sail the ocean without such convoy[133] and this instruction was reinforced by law when the Convoy Act was passed in 1798 in an effort to curb serious losses of shipping. This Act even required merchant ships to pay for the services of the escort. Subsequently there was no serious criticism of the convoy system during this war.[134]

Captains, however, were often tempted to ignore the law so as to save time and beat competitors to a market which might easily be glutted by the simultaneous arrival of several ships. Some who left the West Indies with a convoy would try to leave it once they were in the English Channel.[135] And while it was true that insurance rates were usually lower on voyages made with a convoy and this could enhance the rate of profit, waiting for a convoy or sailing a roundabout route in order to stay with it could cause costly delays. Convoys themselves were inevitably slow, being compelled to keep to the pace of the slowest member. Moreover, as we shall see, the sailing dates of convoys could be very uncertain. So masters were sometimes tempted to take their chances and after the law was tightened up in 1798, so that evasion of convoy was likely to be penalized, they sometimes sought to persuade the governor to grant them permission to sail without convoy.[136] But it does not seem that this stratagem ever succeeded in Tobago.

In 1812, however, with the Atlantic usually free of the enemy, the Admiralty agreed to a request from merchants trading with the West Indies to grant licenses for ships to sail outward and home without convoy, subject to the power of the admiral or the governor to revoke the license if it appeared from local information "that a Vessel sailing without Convoy would be exposed to a probable danger of Capture by the Enemy". In such a case steps would be taken to provide a convoy as soon as possible.[137]

Convoys moved in each direction four times a year, their timing dictated theoretically by the crop cycle. Those from England were normally timed to arrive in Tobago, usually via Barbados, in January/February, April/May, June/July and October. Their timing had reference to the need to take out plantation supplies which would be needed during crop. The return convoys to Britain were supposed to sail from Tobago in April, June, July and October, coinciding with the bulk and the tail end of the crop.[138] Sometimes however these general schedules proved very unreliable. Apart from the normal uncertainties to which sailing ships were liable, the navy took the view that its warships should not be detailed for convoy duty until the area was generally clear of the enemy so far as practicable. When times were not peaceful sailing dates were therefore always tentative. In June 1806 Admiral Cochrane, hearing that six French ships of the line had arrived at Martinique, postponed the anticipated convoy indefinitely - until they should leave the area or his fleet should be reinforced.

Such an episode could thoroughly dislocate the plans of planters and merchants as well as ships' captains, and could cause much financial loss. Waiting captains simply found, not for the first time, that an expected convoy mysteriously failed to turn up. Cochrane's decision to postpone the convoy was taken at the last minute and the news reached Tobago late.[139]

The size and organization of these convoys varied according to the circumstances. Outward convoys from Europe would normally assemble at a suitable British port,[140] and called first at Barbados, the most convenient landfall, before moving on to the other islands. Convoys to Europe would sometimes start at one point, perhaps Demerara in the south, and move around gathering ships as they went.[141] Sometimes merchantmen would sail, possibly under escort, from different islands to a point of rendezvous.[142] Usually the move out into the Atlantic began at Barbados, whence the merchantmen were escorted to European waters, sometimes by just a single warship.[143] When a lightly protected convoy approached the English Channel it was likely to be met by naval units based in Britain and escorted into port.[144]

Man o'War Bay

Throughout the war the significant bases in Tobago remained at Scarborough (Fort King George) and Courland Bay. However the French presence in Tobago in 1802-03 served to highlight the great potential of Man o'War Bay as a naval base. The French had planned to create a base there in the 1780s and General Berthier was now instructed to survey the bay with a view to fortifying it and building a road to connect it with Scarborough. The intention had been that if the survey proved satisfactory the French naval headquarters in the area would be moved from Martinique to Tobago and protected by a garrison of 1,200 men. Any such arrangement would have been a grave threat to the British position for Man o'War Bay was an unusually large anchorage[145] which could accommodate up to twenty ships of the line as well as a number of smaller vessels, and was unusually well provided with wood and water. Being to windward of most of the islands in the Eastern Caribbean, it could command, as Sir Thomas Picton put it, every part of the West Indies except Barbados, and sometimes Barbados too. It was particularly crucial to the defence of Grenada, St Vincent and Trinidad.[146]

Some argued, however, that Man o'War Bay was very exposed to attack, and though the British were impressed when they heard of the French plan nothing was done about it beyond the establishment of a battery of militia artillery, manned whenever there were ships in the harbour.[147] Then in 1810 three British warships were sent to the bay, there to sit out the hurricane season the governor said.[148] While there they spent some weeks taking soundings and a brigadier of Royal Engineers spent several days examining the site and its environs.[149] British warships began to call there for wood and water,[150] and Sir William Young came to treat Man o'War Bay as the navy's preserve.[151] However, it was never developed as a major base.

Precautions against Subversive Activity

The fact that Tobago was at war, and with revolutionary France at that, led to the enactment of some pretty rigorous wartime legislation aimed at possible foreign residents. The first of several Acts "to regulate the conduct of persons resorting to this Island" came in August 1794. This was at a time when the slaves in St Domingue had been freed by the French revolutionary government and British troops were fighting against people inspired by revolutionary doctrines in Martinique, Guadeloupe and St Lucia as well as in St Domingue. Common belief was that the French would try to infiltrate agents into the British islands and the preamble suggested that existing uncommon circumstances threatened the colony with "dangers of the most dreadful kind". All persons arriving in the colony were required to report to the governor, or in his absence to a member of the Council. Anyone not thus reporting, and anyone suspected of treason or of seditious practices or of plotting to disturb the peace, could be apprehended on a warrant from any member of the Council and detained during the governor's pleasure.[152] The Act amounted to a provision for arbitrary imprisonment without trial and was initially to be in force for three months, but it was renewed in 1795.[153]

The small French population which the British found when they recaptured the island, put at forty-six whites and seventy-five free coloureds in 1794, had almost entirely disappeared by the middle of 1795 through a combination of emigration and deportation of those who refused to take the Oaths of Allegiance and Fidelity to the British Crown.[154] Yet another Act, similar to that of 1794, was passed in 1803, when once again the British inhabitants feared the possibly subversive activity which might follow a change in the island's sovereignty. The lieutenant governor told the Assembly that "persons of all descriptions are daily arriving in the Colony upon whom there is no restraint or of whose characters and possessions there is no opportunity of being informed, and it is very manifest from such a custom there may creep in such as may become highly dangerous to the safety and tranquility of the Island".[155] This Act was to last for six months.[156]

In 1811 another such Act was passed, this time more elaborate and aimed particularly at the free coloured. It resulted from reports that "schemes of Revolution throughout the West Indies" were being instigated by emissaries from Haiti, and of an actual incident in Martinique which had caused an informal alert in the British islands.[157] Apart from reiterating the provisions of the earlier Acts, any two Justices of the Peace were empowered to summon any free coloured person, even if he were already resident in the island, who had no visible trade or occupation, and detain him indefinitely if he did not explain himself to their satisfaction. Further, the masters of vessels bringing passengers to the island were required to report their names to the port authorities.[158] This Act was to be in force for one year, but it was then prolonged until peace should be concluded.[159]

When peace came, however, the legislature sought to make the Act perpetual,[160] and the Secretary of State demurred. His legal officers pointed out that the powers of detention which it conferred were unknown to English law and had been established in time of emergency due to war. They should not be made permanent without some explanation of the need for such an extraordinary step.[161] President Balfour was called on to explain.[162] He replied that Napoleon's escape from Elba, followed by a report that Martinique and Guadeloupe would declare for him, had prompted the legislation.[163] It was an unconvincing reply, which did not explain the attempt to make the Act perpetual rather than extend it, and it does not appear to have been confirmed. There is no evidence that this legislation was ever invoked during any of the three periods when it prevailed. No foreigners arrived in Tobago between 1811 and 1815.[164] The Act is however evidence of the ease with which a xenophobic hysteria could take hold even in the absence of any real threat.

Overview

Thus Tobago's attempt to provide for the possibility of enemy attack during the Revolutionary and Napoleonic Wars involved three interrelated lines of action. The first was the maintenance of a set of fortifications around the coast from which efforts could be made to repel seaborne attack whether by regular forces or by privateers. These fortifications included the vital Fort King George above Scarborough, a lesser fort at Plymouth on Great Courland Bay and a number of small batteries in bays around the coast from which it was customary to load sugar either onto ocean going vessels or onto coasting droghers for transportation to the major ports. These bays were likely objects of privateering raids and some offered facilities for landing an invading army. Secondly, there was the maintenance of a militia force involving nearly all free adult males which could be used to protect and man the small batteries, leaving the forts to the regular garrison, as well as for normal infantry duties in support of the garrison troops. The militia were also vitally important as a protection against slave revolt, when they were almost certain to be the first line of defence. In third place came attempts to provide a token naval defence against raiders from the sea which could deal with the enemy before he came within range of the shore batteries. This was an unusual measure, adopted only in time of grave apprehension.

In all the above respects Tobago's efforts to provide local defence were in no sense unusual. They merely paralleled what was being done in other British colonies. Likewise the imperial contribution to the island's defence was merely part of a wider general system: a garrison of imperial troops and the acceptance by the British navy of responsibility for dealing with the possible approach of enemy ships. That system meant, broadly, that while responsibility for defence beyond local shores was an imperial matter, once the enemy came within range of shore-based batteries or landed troops, dealing with him became a matter for co-operation between imperial and local forces and authorities. In this context Tobago was perhaps fortunate: until the threat of invasion subsided after 1805 the island was allowed a relatively large imperial garrison in comparison with other islands of comparable size. No doubt what was largely responsible for this was its status as a new conquest of such strategic importance that an attempt at reconquest was not unlikely. In one sense, however, the local contribution was crucial: it was local action which determined the condition of the defence works without which the imperial troops could hardly withstand attack. The condition of those works was always problematical and never good for more than short periods of time. For this the imperial authorities must be held partly responsible, for if the Assembly failed to organize a regular and self-sustaining system of maintenance the evidence suggests that the garrison officers commonly acquiesced in poor maintenance until an alarm occurred.

The probability of successful resistance to an invasion must always have been remote unless the invading force was small. If Cuyler's attack in 1793 with a mere 500 men might have been thwarted by a garrison of reasonable size, Grinfield's 3,000 troops in 1803 were hardly likely to be denied by any garrison which Tobago was likely to achieve, even including her militia force, so long as the surrender of the fort protecting the capital town was equivalent to the capitulation of the island. Troops were simply too precious for every island to hope for a garrison strong enough to repel an attack by a large force which could roam around the Caribbean and select a target. An invasion in strength therefore could only have been withstood by some sort of withdrawal to the interior such as was talked about in the 1790s. But there is no evidence that such a possibility received more than theoretical attention, and certainly no attempt was made to prepare a strong point to which a defending army might withdraw so as to mount a long defensive campaign.

It is noteworthy that in those islands which managed to mount prolonged resistance to the British forces during this period the key to that resistance was not the formal French defences but the activity of guerrilla type forces inspired by French revolutionary ardour, usually insurgent slaves and free coloureds. This was the case not only in St Domingue but also in Grenada, St Lucia and Guadeloupe. In Tobago the population never contained a large French-oriented element and after 1795 it hardly existed. Revolutionary doctrines made hardly any impact.

The second object of defence preparations was of course to guard against slave revolt. In this context Tobago's provisions were not seriously tested during this period, but the fate of slave revolt in the Caribbean generally suggests that the militia and the garrison troops together were a perfectly adequate protection. Slave rebels might do damage, but were unlikely to prevail for long. In the context of the international situation during this period, however, it was defence against attack by the French, and later the Americans, which mattered. At that level the matter received repeated, but hardly continuous, attention from the Tobago Assembly. In the event this relative neglect brought no nemesis in its train. But that was essentially good fortune. The imperial authorities, in the context of their vastly extended military and naval commitment, did relatively well by Tobago – rather better in fact than the possibly impermanent nature of their concern with Tobago might lead one to expect.

CONCLUSION

In 1793 Britain recovered by force of arms a colony which had been ruled by the French for twelve years. During that time the population of Tobago had risen slightly but its economy had been unsettled and was probably in overall decline while sugar replaced cotton as the dominant crop. There had been no significant influx of French colonists, so that the white population remained very largely British, and the island's exports, though channelled through France, had mostly ended up in Britain. The French had indeed contemplated a policy of gallicization, but it had made little headway, though the old British constitution had been replaced by one of French pattern which allowed for less political power to the colonists.

The British conquest therefore brought restoration rather than disruption and the prompt re-erection of a typical eighteenth century British colonial constitution was seen by the white inhabitants as symbolizing their anticipation of a more congenial future. Having recovered the political liberties they had lost, they hoped that the restored British connection would provide access to means of new economic development with the emphasis on sugar production.

For a British-oriented population whose hopes of economic advancement had been disappointed under French rule, the first priority was to ensure that the restored political allegiance to Britain, itself a fortuitous product of a war brought about by concerns centred very far away, should be made permanent. With that end in view, they fervently protested their undying loyalty to the British Crown and for the next decade set out to provide a model of good behaviour so that that Crown should come to see its own advantage in making the political connection permanent. Such a step, however, was to be determined by considerations of grand policy at the imperial level rather than by the relationship between the colonists and their liege lord or his government; so that it was finally brought about only in 1815, after a year-long trauma in 1802-03 during which the inhabitants of Tobago were forced to see themselves French once more. When British sovereignty was finally restored in 1815 their celebrations were real and sincere, though their satisfaction with the conduct and policy of the British government and the exemplary pattern of their behaviour in political matters had been somewhat tarnished over the years.

Meanwhile the political system re-established in 1793 had not stood still. A House of Assembly at first preoccupied with its own image as an obedient instrument of the Crown gradually recovered the nerve and daring for which the Assemblies in the British Empire had become celebrated. By 1797 it was indulging in a quarrel with the governor which hardly had substantial cause beyond personality. By 1804 the Assembly was asserting the same sole control over money bills which its fellows in older colonies had long established, and was indulging in faction fights among members, to the discomfiture of an anxious governor. Gone were the days when nothing seemed to matter except earning the approval of the imperial government. Perhaps the passage of time had brought a certain disillusion to that project. Certainly members of the Assembly had come to deal more lightly with the uncertain future of their island and to take the view that other aspects of life must receive attention while the gods and imperial power juggled with their fate.

During this period both the white and the free coloured population of Tobago increased slightly, but neither group ever exceeded a few hundreds. The whites were rather the larger of the two but included few women or children, while among the free coloureds there were, as was to be expected, substantially more women than men. Both groups followed a wide range of occupations, though free coloureds were not found in public office or in the professions, where the presence of as many as ten or eleven doctors and four lawyers is striking. Only two free coloured planters have been recorded, while the solitary schoolteacher was white as was the only tavernkeeper noticed. Whites seem to have predominated in all the skilled trades save carpentry and perhaps leatherwork, but it should be remembered that among male adults whites outnumbered free coloureds by four or five to one. There was also the garrison which varied from 300 to 950 men, being more usually about 600.

The slave population rose slowly from a figure of 14,190 in 1790 to a peak of 18,153 in 1807 as the production of sugar was expanded, before falling back after the abolition of the slave trade to 16,080 in 1813.

Throughout the period the slave population appears to have recorded substantially more deaths than births in common with that of most West Indian colonies. Slaves were to be found in the usual wide range of skilled occupations as well as in the fields and sugar mills or boiling houses. Indeed the slave population in this period was a very varied group. Almost certainly more than 50 per cent were African-born in 1793, normal in a relatively new colony, but by 1815 this figure had fallen to about 40 per cent. Many of those born in Africa had by this time been "creolized" in some degree, often quite largely, and the culture mix presented by the slave population was clearly very complex.

The available evidence on the treatment of the slaves in Tobago during this period is inconclusive, but appears to suggest that it was at least not unusually harsh and perhaps rather better than average in the context of time and region. The proposed new slave law of 1798-1800, though it never reached the statute book, was in some respects very advanced. While most of its provisions were taken from ameliorative laws already passed in other colonies, the provision that slaves should be competent to give evidence against free persons, though limited by an injunction to judges to weigh carefully witnesses' understanding of the meaning of an oath, had very far-reaching potential for the easing of their lot and was in part original. Governor Young returned to this proposal in 1811 with the support of Chief Justice Piggott; and though it was not then pursued and the planters were implacably opposed to it, the re-iteration of the proposal confirmed Tobago's position as an island where some very enlightened views on the slave law could be found.

Meanwhile, the economic development of Tobago, to which the colonists had looked forward ever since the return of the British in 1793, made little overall progress. By 1799 sugar production was up by 60 per cent, largely a function of the general sugar boom of the decade, but when the bubble then burst, the level fell back among a series of fluctuations so that the figures for 1814-15 showed an overall rise of less than 20 per cent. The effective abandonment not only of cotton but also of coffee cultivation, which left the island literally with a single crop, pretty well counterbalanced this limited expansion of sugar production. Moreover, in the absence of the special boom conditions of the 1790s, the long uncertainty over whether Tobago would ultimately be British or French, enhanced by the interregnum of 1802-03, made British merchants reluctant to invest capital there, either in commerce or in agriculture; and as long as Britain held the island, capitalists of other nationalities would hardly pay it much attention. Meanwhile the existing planters, with a declining labour force, were hard put to avoid a slow contraction of their existing cultivation, which left much good agricultural land idle.

Their difficulties were significantly augmented by the obstacles which imperial policy placed in the way of the importation from the United States of the food and lumber which were essential to the successful working of the estates. For a decade after 1793 the restrictions on such trade were largely inoperative, being set aside on grounds of wartime emergency; but even so there were periodic shortages, for Tobago was remote from the main centres of the North American trade. And after 1805 the more or less effective enforcement of a changing but always substantial policy of restriction significantly enhanced the planters' production costs by inflating the prices of imported supplies. By 1815 the long desired development had still largely eluded them.

In 1793 there was in Tobago a single clergyman, the Anglican rector, though for a brief period in 1789-90 there had also been a Moravian missionary. The Anglican Church did not consider that it had any particular responsibility for ministering to slaves, so that a single clergyman was all that could be expected in terms of the population. Even that was not always forthcoming and on at least four occasions there was a substantial interval, one of them lasting two years, between the departure of one and the arrival of his successor. The work of the established Church therefore was done irregularly and the quality of its clergy does not appear to have been high.

The more importance therefore attaches to the presence of a new Moravian mission involving two missionaries during the years 1799-1802, and a mission of the London Missionary Society between 1808 and 1813. Both missions were ultimately closed for financial reasons.

The Moravians worked chiefly among the slaves, while one of the two LMS men aimed primarily at the slaves, the other at the whites and coloureds, thinking the language problem enough reason to ignore the slaves. Both missions were greeted with much interest at first, much less after the novelty wore off. Both achieved some solid success, including a small number of converts. How far they succeeded in altering the behaviour of their adherents is impossible to say, but they did have some impact. However, the work of the missions hardly extended beyond the southwestern third of the island and by 1815 a majority of the slaves in Tobago must have been untouched by Christianity.

Until the defeat of the French fleet at Trafalgar in 1805 invasion was always a threat to be borne in mind, and the possibility was kept very much alive by the scares of 1796, 1798, 1801 and 1805 (twice). There was also the repeated threat of privateering raids on the island's coast. Consequently repeated efforts were made to improve and maintain the island's defences, two forts and several coastal batteries. The size of the garrison fluctuated according to current estimates of the scale of the danger and constant attention was given to the militia. In 1804, at the height of a particularly dangerous onslaught by French privateers, came the decision of the Tobago Assembly to provide a gunboat to patrol coastal waters, a significant step though the boat was lost two years later. The threat posed by the privateers dwindled after 1808 and with the fear of invasion receding the defence establishment was able to relax until the Americans took up such activity during the War of 1812-14.

In between scares however, and apart from the fact that the protracted warfare between Britain and France, left Tobago in a state of long enduring political uncertainty which had adverse repercussions on the development of its economy and sometimes on its overseas trade, life in Tobago was largely unaffected by the long war. Indeed the first phase of hostilities, from 1793 to 1802, probably made the operations of the planters easier and cheaper by providing a reason for permitting the largely free importation of supplies from the United States. Otherwise war certainly made the export of produce uncertain and dangerous, increasing the risk of financial loss, and leading to rises in the prices of imports which increased the planters' costs, while the market price of their crops did not always rise to compensate. But the routine of life on the plantations or in the towns was noticeably affected only during short periods when the militia was embodied in response to specific threats and free men were thus removed from their accustomed occupations. Certainly there were occasions when lack of suitable lumber hampered the estates' operations or shortages of certain items of food interrupted normal feeding habits; but such shortages usually resulted from commercial restrictions which the war did not itself create.

In 1815, with the war over and its future political allegiance at last settled, Tobago was finally free to set out on the developmental path the colonists would have wished to follow in 1793. The circumstances, however, were now very different. The slave trade had been abolished while the price of sugar was now much lower than it had been in the boom years 1793-99 and was due soon to settle further. And in so far as British West Indian sugar was still good business the new colonies of Trinidad, Demerara, Essequibo and Berbice had advantages of scale and richness of soil which Tobago could not match. Twenty-two years' delay had done the older colony lasting damage.

NOTES

CHAPTER ONE
1. J.C. Nardin, *La mise en valeur de l'isle de Tabago (1763-1783)* (Paris: Mouton and Co., 1969), 65-72, 80-87. R. Pares, *War and Trade in the West Indies, 1739-1763* (London: Cass, 1963), 198; 202; 214.
2. H.I. Woodcock, *History of Tobago* (Port of Spain: Columbus Publishers Ltd., rep. n.d.), 57-58.
3. J.C. Nardin, "Tobago, Antilles Françaises (1781-1793)", in *Annales des Antilles* (Fort de France: Société d'histoire de la Martinique, n.d.), 32-33.
4. Woodcock, op. cit., 59.
5. Ibid., 38-39.
6. Ibid., 39.
7. Ibid., 33-34.
8. Ibid., 51.
9. Ibid., 52-55.
10. Nardin, "Antilles Françaises", 55.
11. Ibid., 55-56.
12. Ibid., 56.
13. Ibid., 37.
14. Ibid., 56-57. See also F.L. Nussbaum (ed.), *Documents Relating to the Claims of the Tobago Creditors, 1792* (Commission de recherche et de publication des documents relatifs à la vie économique de la Révolution).
15. Nardin, "Antilles Françaises", 57.
16. Ibid, 58, Nussbaum, op. cit., 447.
17. Nussbaum, op. cit., 460; 468.
18. Nardin, "Antilles Françaises", 64-65.
19. Ibid., 67.
20. Ibid., 68-69.
21. Ibid., p. 69.
22. C.O. 318/12, Dundas to Cuyler, 10 February 1793, Secret.
23. C.O. 318/12, Cuyler to Dundas, 18 April 1793.
24. C.O. 318/12, Disembarkation Return, enc. in Cuyler to Dundas, 18 April 1793.
25. C.O. 318/12, Laroque Montell to General Rochambean, 15 April 1793, enc. in Cuyler to Dundas, 18 April 1793.
26. M. Duffy, *Soldiers, Sugar and Sea Power: The British Expeditions to the West Indies and the War against Revolutionary France* (Oxford: Clarendon Press, 1987), 34.
27. C.O. 318/12, Cuyler to Dundas, 18 April 1793. Duffy gives a rather different account of this action, suggesting that Cuyler's main column was repulsed by the French while the flanking advance guard took them by surprise from the rear. Duffy, 35.
28. C.O. 318/12, Returns enc. in Cuyler to Dundas, 18 April 1793. The British return puts the French losses at a total of fifteen. The figures cited

29. C.O. 318/21, S/S to Grinfield, 16 May 1803, Most Secret.
30. C.O. 318/22, Grinfield to Hobart, 7 June 1803, no. 75.
31. C.O. 318/21, Grinfield to Hobart, 9 June 1803, no. 76.
32. C.O. 318/21, Grinfield to Hobart, 31 May 1803.
33. C.O. 318/22, Grinfield to Hobart, 10 June 1803.
34. C.O. 318/22, Grinfield to Hobart, 20, 22 June 1803.
35. C.O. 318/22, Grinfield to Hobart, 24 June 1803, nos. 87, 89.
36. C.O. 318/22, Grinfield to Hobart, 1 July 1803, no. 91, and enc.
37. C.O. 318/22, Articles of Capitulation, enc. in Grinfield to Hobart, 1 July 1803, no. 91.
38. C.O. 285/9, Johnston to Hobart, 25 July 1803, no. 1.
39. C.O. 318/22, Grinfield to Hobart, 1 July 1803, no. 92, Private.

CHAPTER TWO

1. Cited in E.E. Williams, *History of the People of Trinidad and Tobago* (Port of Spain: P.N.M. Publishing Co. Ltd., 1962), 61.
2. C.O. 285/3, Minutes of Council, 18 November 1794.
3. B. Marshall, "Slave Society and Economy in the British Windward Islands, 1763-1823" (Ph.D. thesis, UWI, 1972), 516-17.
4. Sir John Fortescue, *History of the British Army* (London: Macmillan, 1899-1930), Vol. 4, Part II: 135.

above are taken from the French commandant's report.

5. R.N. Buckley, *Slaves in Red Coats: the British West India Regiments, 1795-1815* (New Haven: Yale University Press, 1979), 9.
6. C.O. 285/2, Three Petitions to the Prime Minister from persons departed from Tobago in 1793.
7. C.O. 285/3, Robley to Portland, 30 January 1795. Robley suggests that seventeen of the twenty remaining French refused the Oaths, but we have seen that the militia commanders reported the existence of twenty-four Frenchmen.
8. C.O. 285/3, Robley to Portland, 30 January 1795.
9. C.O. 285/3, Minutes of Council, 9, 17 March 1795.
10. C.O. 285/3, Robley to Portland, 21 March 1795, no. 15.
11. C.O. 285/3, Lindsay to Portland, 18 April 1795.
12. C.O. 285/3, Minutes of Council, 6 April 1795.
13. C.O. 285/3, Minutes of Council, 6 April 1795.
14. C.O. 285/3, Lindsay to King, 21 April 1795, Private.
15. C.O. 285/3, Portland to Lindsay, 23 July 1795, no. 2.
16. C.O. 285/4, Minutes of Council, 29 October 1795.
17. C.O. 285/3, Lindsay to Portland, 2 October 1795, no. 15.
18. C.O. 285/10, f. 34, Campbell to Camden, 15 March 1805, Private. The name is unclear in the manuscript. Campbell does not indicate when Deugues left the island, if he

ever did.
19. C.O. 285/20, French Ambassador to Bathurst, 6 March 1815; Balfour to Bathurst, 3 May 1815. The French Ambassador claimed in 1815 that De Monteron had been a proprietor in the parish of St George but President Campbell had earlier described Deugues as the sole Frenchman ever to own an estate in Tobago.
20. C.O. 285/9, Macdonald to Grinfield, 11 October 1803, and enc.
21. J.R. Ward, "The Profitability of Sugar Planting in the British West Indies, 1650-1834," *Economic History Review*, Vol. 31, no. 2 (1978): 205-07; 213.
22. C.O. 285/21, Balfour to Bathurst, 12 April 1816, no. 6.
23. C.O. 285/20, f. 39, Memorial from Council and Assembly to Bathurst, 15 July 1815.
24. C.O. 285/3, Minutes of Council, 18 November 1794. C.O. 285/13, f. 64, Statistical Returns for 1808 (corrected arithmetic). B.L., Stowe MSS, 923, f. 44, *Tobago Almanack, 1810*, ed. Sir William Young. C.O. 285/18, f. 27, Return on Matters of Enquiry ..., 1 October 1911.
25. C.O. 285/18, f. 111, Statistical Returns, 1813.
26. B. L., Stowe MSS, 923, f. 41, *Tobago Almanack, 1810*, ed. Sir W. Young.
27. One such white "servant" was Catherine Traynor, who was housekeeper to a Scarborough doctor at $12 per month when in 1813 she murdered a female slave to whom her employer had paid too much attention. C.O. 285/18, f. 102, Young to Bathurst, 31 October 1813.
28. C.O. 285/11, f. 14, Memorial enc. in Mitchell to Windham, 26 May 1806.
29. C.O. 285/16, f. 127-8, Return on Matters of Enquiry ..., 1 October 1811.
30. B.W. Higman, *Slave Populations of the British Caribbean, 1807-1834* (Baltimore and London: Johns Hopkins University Press, 1984), 112.
31. C.O. 287/2, f. 141, Act No. 29, 11 August 1797.
32. C.O. 287/3, f. 96, Act No. 46, 7 November 1804.
33. C.O. 287/3, f. 237, Act No. 66, 18 October 1808.
34. C.O. 285/3, f. 320, Lindsay to Portland, 5 September 1795, no. 13.
35. C.O. 319/6, Précis of Secretary of State's Corres., West Indies, 1795-1801.
36. B.L., Stowe MSS, 921, Abstract of Trade and Navigation in the British West Indies compiled by Sir William Young.
37. C.O. 319/6, Précis of Secretary of State's Corres., West Indies, 1795-1801.
38. P. Curtin, *Death by Migration: Europe's Encounter with the Tropical World in the Nineteenth Century* (Cambridge: Cambridge University Press, 1989), 2; K.F. Kiple, *The Caribbean Slave: A Biological History* (Cambridge:

39. Kiple, op. cit., 171; Curtin, op. cit., 25.
40. Curtin, op. cit., 29.
41. R.B. Sheridan, *Doctors and Slaves, A Medical and Demographic History of Slavery in the British West Indies, 1680-1834* (Cambridge: Cambridge University Press, 1985), 17.
42. Curtin, op. cit., 6, 44.
43. Ibid., 43.
44. Kiple, op. cit., 164.
45. Sheridan, op. cit., 13; 25.
46. Curtin, op. cit., 33.
47. Kiple, op. cit., 161-3; Sheridan, op. cit., 9-11.
48. Kiple, op. cit., 172.
49. Sheridan, op. cit., 14.
50. Ibid., 25-27, 41.
51. National Library of Scotland, MS. 3972, f. 5, Macdonald to Grinfield, 5 November 1803.
52. N.L.S., MS. 3972, f. 18, Macdonald to Moncrieff, 12 February 1804.
53. Ibid.
54. N.L.S., MS. 3972, f. 13, Macdonald to Prevost, 23 Dec. 1803.
N.L.S., MS. 3972, f. 21, Macdonald to Moncrieff, 16 March 1804.
55. C.O. 319/9, Myers to Camden, 29 July 1804, Private.
C.O. 285/12, ff. 13, 116, Young to Windham, 25 April 1807;
Young to Castlereagh, 16 November 1807.
56. Compiled from B.L., Stowe MSS, 923, f. 37, Sir William Young (ed.), *Tobago Almanack, 1810*. C.O. 285/16, f. 4, Enc. in Young to Liverpool, 1 February 1811. Figures scattered through Young's despatches in C.O. 285/16-19.
57. Kiple, op. cit., 171.
58. C.O. 285/11, f. 4, Enc. in Balfour to Windham, 16 October 1806, no. 13.
59. C.O. 286/4, f. 13, Portland to Robley, 15 September 1794, no. 2.
60. C.O. 285/3, f. 135, Minutes of Council, 15 April 1794.
61. N.L.S., MS. 3947, f. 6, D. Macdonald to David Macdonald, 7 March 1804.
62. N.L.S., MS. 3972, f. 20, Macdonald to Moncrieff, 5 March 1804.
63. School of Oriental and African Studies, LMS, Folder 4, Jacket A, Elliot to LMS, 28 March 1811.
64. B.L., Add. MS. 37888, f. 165, Young to Windham, 27 July 1809.
65. C.O. 285/13, f. 94, Enc. in Young to Castlereagh, 27 April 1808.
66. Higman, op. cit., 433.
67. Ibid., 691.
68. C.O. 285/18, f. 26, Return on Matters of Enquiry, ... 1 October 1811.
69. Higman, op. cit., 77, 223.
70. C.O. 285/16, ff. 104-105, Return on Matters of Enquiry ..., 1 October 1811.
71. C.O. 285/13, f. 64, Statistical Returns for 1808.
72. C.O. 285/16, ff. 104-105, Return on Matters of Enquiry ..., 1 October 1811.
73. Marshall, op. cit., 374.
74. C.O. 285/18, f. 28, Return on

Matters of Enquiry ..., 1 October 1811.
75. Ibid.
76. Ibid.
77. 1810 : B.L., Stowe MSS. 923, f. 44, *Tobago Almanack 1810*, ed. Sir William Young. 1811 : C.O. 285/16, f. 105, Return on Matters of Enquiry... 1 October 1811. Slightly different figures in C.O. 285/18.
78. Marshall, op. cit., 283.
79. C.O. 285/16, f. 106, Return on Matters of Enquiry ... 1 October 1811. Also another, slightly different, version at C.O. 285/18, f. 29. See also the comment of the LMS missionary Purkis in 1809: "whilst european proprietors and tradesmen have nothing but land and produce they [the free coloured] have generally hard Cash". S.O.A.S., LMS, Folder 2, Jacket C, Purkis to Bogue, 1 November 1809.
80. C.O. 287/3, f. 237, Act No. 66, 18 October 1808, C1. 3. For a discussion of the Deficiency Acts see below.
81. Marshall, op. cit., 370.
82. C.O. 285/3, Minutes of Council, 9 April 1794. C.O. 287/2, f. 94, Act No. 47, 1804.
83. C.O. 285/14, f. 55, Young to Castlereagh, 10 September 1809.
84. C.O. 285/14, f. 55, Young to Castlereagh, 10 September 1809.
85. C.O. 325/10, f. 161, Young to Castlereagh, 20 September 1809.
86. See Marshall, op. cit., 416. Also E.V. Goveia, *Slave Society in the British Leeward Islands at the End of the Eighteenth Century* (New Haven: Yale University Press, 1965), 223; 246.
87. Higman, op. cit., 108.
88. S.O.A.S.-LMS, Folder 2, Jacket C, Purkis to Bogue, 1 November 1809.
89. C.O. 287/3, f. 237, Act No. 66, 18 October 1808, Cl. 3.
90. A. C. Ince, "Protestant Missionary Activity in Five South Caribbean Islands during Slavery, 1765-1826" (D.Phil. thesis, University of Oxford, 1985), 218.
91. Ibid., 237-38.
92. C.O. 287/3, f. 19, Act No. 38a, 2 March 1802.
93. C.O. 285/4, M.H.A., 8 August 1797.
94. N.L.S., MS. 3946, f. 206, Macdonald to Council and Assembly.
95. C.O. 285/24, Robinson to Goulbourn, 6 April 1819, cited in Marshall, op. cit., 370.
96. S.O.A.S.-LMS, Folder 2, Jacket C, Purkis to Bogue, 1 November 1809.
97. Ince, op. cit., 238.
98. Cited in Williams, *Trinidad and Tobago*, 61.
99. C.O. 285/5, Report of the [Tobago] Committee of both Houses ..., Enc. in Agent Petrie to Portland, 4 March 1799.
100. Deerr, *History of Sugar* (London: Chapman & Hall, 1949-50), Vol. 1: 202.
101. J.R. Ward, *British West Indian Slavery, 1750-1834: The*

Process of Amelioration (Oxford: Clarendon Press, 1988), 45.
102. C.O. 285/5, Report of the [Tobago] Committee of both Houses ..., Enc. in Agent Petrie to Portland, 4 March 1799. Higman, op. cit., 428. C.O. 285/13, f.65, Enc. in Young to Castlereagh, 27 April 1808. It is not clear how far the 323 slaves received in 1797 are included in the 1533 received between 1 July 1795 and 1 July 1797.
103. 1804 from C.O. 285/13, f. 65, Enc. in Young to Castlereagh, 27 April 1808. 1806 from C.O. 285/21, f. 39, Enc. in Campbell to Bathurst, 28 October 1816. 1807-1813 from Statistical Returns in C.O. 285/18, f. 111. Slightly different figures, usually higher by a few hundreds, may be found in other sources, including Young's Return for 1811. Those given here are from Young's last revision of his work, in 1813.
104. Higman, op. cit., 417, gives the following figures:

1807	1808	1809
18,845	18,560	18,280
1810	1811	1812
18,000	17,720	17,440
1813	1814	1815
17,155	16,875	16,595

105. C.O. 285/16, ff. 112, Return on a Matter of Enquiry ..., 1 October 1811.
106. Higman, op. cit., 116.
107. C.O. 285/16, f. 110, Statistical Returns. Higman, op. cit., 116.
108. Higman, op. cit., 89-90.
109. Ibid., 104.
110. C.O. 285/16, ff. 107-10, Return on Matters of Enquiry..., 1 October 1811.
111. Higman, op. cit., 107.
112. C.O. 285/16, f. 110, Statistical Returns. Bernard Marshall's ascription of these figures to the five years 1807-1811 appears to be a misreading of the MS. See Marshall, op. cit., 246-47.
113. Higman, op. cit., 309.
114. Ibid., 319.
115. Ibid., 31.
116. Ibid., 374.
117. Ibid., 136-41.
118. C.O. 285/18, f. 45, Return on Matters of Enquiry ..., 1 October 1811.
119. C.O. 285/18, f. 46, Return on Matters of Enquiry ..., 1 October 1811.
120. Ibid.
121. Ibid.
122. C.O. 285/18, f. 40, Return on Matters of Enquiry ..., 1 October 1811.
123. Marshall, op. cit., 245.
124. C.O. 285/16, f. 117, Return on Matters of Enquiry ..., 1 October 1811.
125. Higman, op. cit., 335.
126. Marshall, op. cit., 243-4.
127. Higman, op. cit., 317-20.
128. Ibid., 324-8.
129. Ibid., 336.
130. Ibid., 374.
131. Ibid., 375.
132. Ibid., 337.
133. Ibid., 329.
134. T.P.L., M.P.C., 8 May 1815, Deposition of George Cumine.

135. Higman, op. cit., 215.
136. Ibid., 339-40.
137. C.O. 285/18, ff. 37-8, Return on Matters of Enquiry ..., 1 October 1811.
138. Ibid.
139. Ibid. There are some problems with Young's arithmetic in calculating the totals.
140. In 1807 Governor Young had calculated that among the 17346 slaves then counted there were 1464 domestics, 527 carpenters, 527 coopers, 59 masons, 41 smiths, 90 fishermen and 30 tailors and saddlers (not mentioned separately in 1811). These figures suggest that while the number of domestics, carpenters and coopers declined, masons and smiths multiplied, but the figures are not sufficiently reliable to support this conclusion. B.L., Add. MS. 37888, f. 167, Returns of Negro Population in Tobago, 1807, by Sir William Young.
141. Higman, op. cit., 232-34.
142. Ibid., 235.
143. Ibid., 173-78.
144. Ibid., 232.
145. Ibid., 173.
146. B.L., Add. MS. 37888, f. 167-8, Young to Windham, February 1810. Similar versions of these remarks are to be found in Young's two "Returns on Matters of Enquiry" written in 1811 and 1813 respectively.
147. Higman, op. cit.,126-27. P. Curtin, *The Atlantic Slave Trade* (Madison: University of Wisconsin Press, 1969), 150. H.S. Klein, *The Middle Passage* (Princeton: Princeton University Press), 149.
148. Higman, op. cit., 128-33.
149. M.J. Herskovits, *The Myth of the Negro Past*, 2nd ed. (Boston: Beacon Press, 1958), chap. III.
150. Higman, op. cit., 365.
151. Ibid., 366-8.
152. Ibid., 370.
153. Ibid., 371.
154. G. Parrinder, "The African Spiritual Universe", in *Afro-Caribbean Religions,* edited by B. Gates (London: Ward Lock, 1980), 17-25.
155. *Methodist Magazine*, 1822 Vol. 45: 543-45, cited in Marshall, 407.
156. E. Brathwaite, *The Development of Creole Society in Jamaica, 1770-1820* (Oxford: Clarendon Press, 1971), 218-20.
157. Marshall, op. cit., 408-11.
158. *Methodist Magazine*, 1822 Vol. 45: 543-45. Extract from Mr. Smedley's Journal. Cited in Marshall, op. cit., 405.
159. T.P.L., M.P.C., 9 November 1815.
160. Ibid.
161. Marshall, op. cit., 411-13.
162. T.P.L., M.P.C., 9 November 1815.
163. Marshall, op. cit., 413-14. For references to dancing to fiddle in Tobago see T.P.L., M.P.C., 9 November 1815.
164. Marshall,op. cit., 415.
165. Marshall, op. cit., 383; Goveia, op. cit., 317.
166. Ince, op. cit., 194.
167. Higman, op. cit., 147, 154.
168. Marshall, op. cit., 382-85;

Goveia, op. cit., 232-33.
169. Higman, op. cit., 20.
170. Ibid.
171. Ibid., 458. Higman gives a figure of 38.9 per cent for 1819.

CHAPTER THREE
1. C.O. 318/12, Cuyler to Dundas, 19 April 1793, Private.
2. C.O. 285/3, Minutes of Council, 6 January-3 April 1794, passim.
3. C.O. 319/4, Instructions to Governor Ricketts, 14 September 1793.
4. C.O. 285/3, Ricketts to Dundas, 8 March 1794.
5. T.P.L., M.P.C., 7 June 1805, et. seq.
6. C.O. 285/3, Ricketts to Dundas, 8 March 1784.
7. C.O. 285/3, Robley to Portland, 26 December 1794.
8. C.O. 285/5, De Lancey to Portland, 24 April 1798, no. 9.
9. C.O. 319/4, Instructions to Governor Ricketts, 14 September 1793.
10. C.O. 288/5, M.P.C., 2 November 1801.
11. C.O. 288/6, M.P.C., 3 July 1803, 16 July 1804.
12. C.O. 288/6, M.P.C., 4 May 1804.
13. C.O. 285/15, f. 31, Young to Liverpool, 20 August 1810.
14. C.O. 285/15, f. 22, Young to Liverpool, 30 June 1810.
15. T.P.L., M.P.C., 9 April 1811.
16. C.O. 285/16, f. 26, Young to Liverpool, 21 June 1811.
17. Ibid.
18. C.O. 285/16, f. 37, Young to Liverpool, 17 July 1811.
19. C.O. 285/19, f. 30, Young to Bathurst, 21 May 1814.
20. C.O. 285/4, Campbell to Portland, 15 November 1796, no. 12.
21. C.O. 285/3, Robley to Portland, 11 April 1795, no. 17.
22. C.O. 285/4, Campbell to Portland, 7 September 1796, no. 9.
23. C.O. 285/4, Campbell to Portland, 2 June 1796, no. 2.
24. C.O. 285/5, De Lancey to Portland, 24 April 1798, no. 9.
25. C.O. 285/9, f. 53, Campbell to Camden, 27 August 1804, no. 3.
26. C.O. 285/10, f. 42, Campbell to Camden, 22 April 1805, no. 7.
27. C.O. 285/10, f. 52, Camden to Campbell, 6 July 1805, no. 3.
28. C.O. 288/6, M.P.C., 10 December 1806.
29. C.O. 285/10, f. 66, Campbell to Camden, 1 September 1805, no. 25.
30. C.O. 288/6, M.P.C., 14 June 1806.
31. Ibid.
32. C.O. 285/8, Robley to Hobart, 2 October 1802.
33. C.O. 285/12, f. 159, John Robley to Castlereagh, 15 October 1807.
34. C.O. 285/12, ff. 111, 121, Castlereagh to Young, 23 October 1807, no. 3; Young to Castlereagh, 28 November 1807.
35. T.P.L., M.P.C., 26 October 1808.
36. C.O. 285/4, Lindsay to Portland, 1 February 1796, no. 22; 28 May 1795, no. 6.

37. C.O. 285/3, Lindsay to King, 10 May 1795, Private; Lindsay to Portland, 28 May 1795, no. 6.
38. C.O. 285/5, Robley to Portland, 11 October 1798.
39. C.O. 285/6, Portland to Master, 11 July 1800, no. 2.
40. C.O. 285/5, Minutes of Assembly, 12 November 1798.
41. C.O. 285/6, M.H.A., 6 February 1800.
42. In August 1796, when on his way to Boston to recover his health, after being suspended by Governor Lindsay, Robley was captured by a French privateer and taken to Guadeloupe. Although several of his fellow passengers were then exchanged Victor Hugues at first refused to exchange Robley, perhaps because of his prominence in public affairs under French rule before 1793, and he remained a prisoner for about three months during which he alleged that he received "very harsh treatment". Eventually Tobago's Agent in London, John Petrie, asked the Secretary of State to intervene, with what effect we do not know. Robley was eventually released and returned to Tobago. C.O. 285/4, Petrie to Portland, 19 November 1796; Robley to Portland, 20 October 1798. Robley left a fortune estimated at £200,000, most of it to his nephew John Robley. C.O. 285/19, Young to Bathurst, 31 October 1814, Separate.
43. C.O. 286/4, f. 66, Hobart to Robley, 23 October 1802, no. 8.
44. C.O. 287/2, f. 15, Ordinance for regulating the Elections for the General Assembly of Tobago ..., 13 January 1794, no. 1.
45. C.O. 288/7, f. 239, M.H.A., 12 July 1810.
46. T.P.L., M.H.A., 9 April 1811.
47. C.O. 287/3, f. 4, Act No. 33, 28 May 1798.
48. Ibid.
49. C.O. 285/6, Minutes of Assembly, 4 December 1799.
50. C.O. 285/9, f. 53, Campbell to Camden, 27 August 1804, no. 3.
51. C.O. 288/6, f. 164, M.H.A., 6, 13, 19, 20 December 1805.
52. C.O. 288/6, ff. 168, 182, M.H.A., 4, 11 March, 15 May, 25 June 1806.
53. C.O. 287/3, f. 149, Act No. 56a, 4 May 1807.
54. C.O. 288/7, ff. 157-162, M.H.A., 26 April, 3 June, 12 July 1808.
55. C.O. 285/15, f. 32, Young to Liverpool, 20 August 1810.
56. C.O. 288/8, f. 165, M.H.A., 12 April 1815.
57. C.O. 285/5, M.H.A., 8 May 1798. C.O. 288/5, M.H.A., 18 August 1801; M.L.C., 28 August 1801. See also C.O. 285/3, f. 116. Address to Council and Assembly from President Robley.
58. C.O. 288/6, M.L.C., 5 August 1806.
59. C.O. 288/7, ff. 162-3, 194-96, M.H.A., 13-18 July 1808; 11-27 July 1809.
60. C.O. 287/3, f. 123, Act No. 51a, 6 August 1806.

61. Marshall, op. cit., 197-98.
62. C.O. 285/19, f. 116, Young to Bathurst, 24 April 1814, Private.
63. C.O. 285/12, f. 44, Young to Castlereagh, 23 July 1807.
64. C.O. 288/8, f. 129, M.H.A., 4 January 1812. T.P.L., M.L.C., 14 January 1812.
65. T.P.L., M.L.C., 14 April 1812. T.P.L., M.H.A., 13 April 1813.
66. C.O. 288/8, f. 165, M.H.A., 11 April 1815.
67. C.O. 288/8, f. 86, M.L.C., 14 March 1815.
68. C.O. 286/5, ff. 121-9. The Colonial Office Entry Book shows no other entries.
69. C.O. 285/6, Minutes of Council, 6, 7, January 1800.
70. B.L., Stowe 923, f. 18, *Tobago Almanack, 1810*, edited by Sir William Young.
71. C.O. 288/6, f. 198, M.H.A., 15 October 1806.
72. C.O. 288/6, f. 205, M.H.A., 12, 15 December 1806. C.O. 288/8, f. 66, M.L.C., 14 October 1814.
73. C.O. 288/7, f. 226, M.H.A., 16 April 1810.
74. C.O. 288/8, f. 171, M.H.A., 11, 13 October 1815. T.P.L., M.L.C., 16 July 1812.
75. C.O. 288/7, f. 30, M.L.C., 13 October 1808.
76. C.O. 286/4, ff. 12, 14, Portland to Robley, 7 August, 18 November 1794, nos. 1, 3.
77. Woodcock, *History of Tobago*, 72.
78. B.L., Stowe MSS. 923, f. 18, *Tobago Almanack, 1810*, edited by Sir William Young.
79. Ibid., f. 20.
80. C.O. 285/12, f. 45, Young to Castlereagh, 23 July 1807.
81. T.P.L., M.P.C., 12 October 1815.
82. C.O. 285/13, f. 48, Young to Castlereagh, 25 April 1808.
83. B.L., Stowe MSS. 923, f. 18, *Tobago Almanack, 1810*, edited by Sir William Young.
84. C.O. 285/12, f. 123, Young to Castlereagh, 28 November 1807. C.O. 285/13, f. 31, Young to Castlereagh, 2 March 1808.
85. C.O. 287/2, f. 41, Act No. 9, 17 August 1794. C.O. 287/3, f. 9, Act No. 35, 8 February 1800.
86. C.O. 286/4, f. 33, Portland to De Lancey, 13 May 1797.
87. C.O. 325/10, f. 163, Enc. in Young to Castlereagh, 20 September 1809.
88. Ibid.
89. Marshall, "Slave Society and Economy in the British Windward Islands, 1763-1823" (Ph.D. thesis, UWI, 1972), 197-98.
90. C.O. 325/10, f. 163, Enc. in Young to Castlereagh, 20 September 1809.
91. See below.
92. C.O. 285/14, f. 31, Young to Castlereagh, 29 August 1809 and enc.
93. C.O. 288/6, f. 138, M.L.C., 2 May 1807.
94. C.O. 288/7, M.L.C., 15 January, 14 April, 29 July 1809.
95. T.P.L., M.P.C., 14 March 1815.
96. C.O. 287/2, ff. 21, 26, Acts Nos. 2, 4 of 20, 22 February 1794.
97. C.O. 285/3, Ricketts to

98. Dundas, 28 April 1794.
99. H.I. Woodcock, op. cit., 69-72.
100. C.O. 285/3, f. 45, Schedule of ... Acts revived by an Act ... to revive and put in force certain Acts of former Legislatures of this Island.
100. C.O. 285/3, Minutes of Council, 28 March, 2, 3, 9 April 1794.
101. C.O. 285/3, f. 116, Address to Council and Assembly from President Robley.
102. C.O. 287/2, f. 29, Act No. 5, 15 April 1794.
103. C.O. 287/2, f. 48, Act No. 13, 24 December 1794.
104. C.O. 285/3, ff. 25-6, Address of House of Assembly to Governor Ricketts, 13 February 1794.
105. C.O. 287/2, f. 38, Act No. 8, 19 May 1794.
106. C.O. 287/2, f. 86, Act No. 18, 12 May 1795.
107. C.O. 287/4, f. 78, Act No. 100, 17 July 1815.
108. C.O. 287/3, f. 76, Act No. 43, 15 November 1803.
109. C.O. 288/6, f. 205, M.H.A., 15 December 1806.
110. C.O. 287/3, f. 143, Act No. 53, 16 December 1806.
111. T.P.L., M.H.A., 9 April 1811.
112. C.O. 287/3, f. 276, Act No. 71, 31 July 1809.
113. C.O. 287/4, f. 78, Act No. 100, 17 July 1815.
114. C.O. 287/2, f. 99, Act No. 21, 20 June 1795.
115. C.O. 287/2, f. 109, Act No. 24, 17 August 1795. The Black Corps is discussed below.
116. C.O. 285/10, f. 40, Campbell to Camden, 11 April 1805, no. 16.
117. C.O. 285/11, f. 11, Windham to Mitchell, 17 July 1806.
118. C.O. 288/6, f. 147, M.L.C., 6 August 1807.
119. C.O. 287/3, f. 113, Act No. 49, 17 February 1805.
120. C.O. 287/3, f. 36, Act No. 41a, 3 March 1802.
121. C.O. 287/3, f. 109, Act No. 48, 16 February 1805.
122. C.O. 287/2, f. 148, Act No. 31, 5 September 1797.
123. C.O. 287/3, f. 82, Act No. 45, 5 November 1804.
124. C.O. 287/2, f. 141, Act No. 29, 11 August 1797. In the 1770s taxpayers had been offered a tax credit for every white servant over 14 years old and for each member of their own families. Nardin, *La mise en valeur* (Paris: Mouton and Co., 1969), 200; 203.
125. C.O. 287/3, f. 86, Act No. 46, 7 November 1804.
126. C.O. 285/14, Enc. in Young to Castlereagh, 10 September 1809.
127. C.O. 287/2, f. 48, Act No. 13, 24 December 1794.
128. C.O. 285/4, Portland to Campbell, 7 October 1796, no. 4.
129. C.O. 287/2, f. 104, Act No. 23, 17 August 1795.
130. C.O. 287/2, f. 119, Act No. 26, 28 July 1796.
131. Ibid.
132. The governor's salary of £3,300 currency must be added to the £4,490 required for other public officers. C.O. 287/3, f. 39, Act No. 42a, 26 June 1802.
133. C.O. 287/3, f. 1, Act No. 32, 16 May 1798.

134. C.O. 287/3, f. 11, Act No. 37, 29 August 1801.
135. C.O. 287/3, f. 39, Act No. 42a, 26 June 1802.
136. C.O. 285/18, f. 88, Young to Bathurst, 29 September 1813. C.O. 285/19, f. 52, Young to Bathurst, 31 October 1814, Separate.
It may be noted in passing that in 1814 Mme de Sahuquet complained that she had seen only £1,600 of this sum. The evidence suggests that her appointed agent, John Robley, Joseph Robley's heir, had some responsibility for the disappearance of the balance.
137. Young MSS., History, 114. Not even the most spectacular of the French plans, for a great naval and perhaps military base at Man o'War Bay, produced any results.
138. C.O. 287/3, f. 52, Act No. 39b, 1 September 1803.
139. J.S. Watson, *The Reign of George III* (Oxford: Clarendon Press, 1960), 376; 412.
140. C.O. 288/6, M.L.C., 29 September 1804.
141. C.O. 288/6, M.L.C., 5 November 1804.
142. F.G. Spurdle, *Early West Indian Government* (Palmerston, N.Z.: The Author, [1962]), 77; 113; 151.
143. Nardin, op. cit., 204.
144. C.O. 288/6, M.L.C., 6 April 1804.
145. C.O. 288/6, M.L.C., 30 January 1805.
146. C.O. 287/3, f. 117, Act No. 50, 26 February 1805.
147. C.O. 287/3, f. 113, Act No. 49, 17 February 1805.
148. C.O. 288/6, M.L.C., 16 February 1805.
149. Laurence, "Tobago and British Imperial Authority, 1793-1802", in *Trade, Government and Society in Caribbean History, 1700-1920*, edited by B.W. Higman (Kingston: Heinemann, 1983), 40; 52.
150. C.O. 287/3, f. 125, Act No. 52a, 6 August 1806.
151. C.O. 285/12, Young to Windham, 25 April 1807; Young to Castlereagh, 2 June 1807.
152. C.O. 288/6, f. 215, M.H.A., 29 April 1807.
153. C.O. 285/12, Young to Castlereagh, 2 June 1807.
154. C.O. 288/7, ff. 154, 159, M.H.A., 12, 22 April 1808.
155. See for instance C.O. 285/17, Young to Bathurst, 7 August 1812.
156. C.O. 287/3, f. 161, Act No. 55b, 8 August 1807.
157. C.O. 288/6, f. 149, M.L.C., 6 August 1807.
158. C.O. 288/6, ff. 146, 149, M.L.C., 6 August 1807.
159. C.O. 285/12, f. 88, Young to Castlereagh, 1 September 1807, Separate.
160. C.O. 288/6, f. 247, M.H.A., 13 October 1807.
161. C.O. 288/6, f. 146, M.L.C., 6 August 1807.
162. C.O. 288/7, ff. 168A-169A, M.H.A., 22 July, 11 October 1808.
163. C.O. 288/7, ff. 166-169, M.H.A., 22 July 1808.
164. Ibid.
165. C.O. 288/7, f. 93, M.L.C., 13 July 1810.

166. C.O. 288/7, f. 168A, M.H.A., 22 July 1808.
167. C.O. 287/3, f. 261, Act No. 70, 31 July 1809. The poll tax on attached slaves was initially fixed at 12s. 6d., but raised to 16s. a few months later. C.O. 288/7, f. 67, M.L.C., 13 October 1809.
168. C.O. 288/8, f. 135, M.H.A., 14 January 1813.
169. C.O. 288/7, ff. 132-7, M.L.C., 12 August 1811. Protest by John Robley.
170. C.O. 285/15, f. 34, Young to Liverpool, 9 September 1810.
171. C.O. 288/7, f. 246, M.H.A., 14 July 1810.
172. C.O. 288/7, ff. 248-9, M.H.A., 14 July 1810.
173. C.O. 288/7, f. 251, M.H.A., 13 August 1810.
174. C.O. 288/7, F. 101, M.L.C., 15 August 1810. C.O. 285/15, f. 29, Young to Liverpool, 20 August 1810.
175. C.O. 288/7, f. 258, M.H.A., 16 August 1810.
176. C.O. 288/7, f. 104, M.L.C., 4 September 1810.
177. Ibid.
178. C.O. 285/15, ff. 29, 34, Young to Liverpool, 20 August 1810, 9 September 1810.
179. John Robley appears in other contexts to have been somewhat unscrupulous in pursuing his own economic gain. Although very wealthy in his own right (he owned at least six ships engaged in trade between Europe and Tobago in 1802), he was somehow involved in the disappearance of moneys designed for Mme. Sahuquet, whose agent he was, in 1803; while his personal financial dealings were such as to lead him to quarrel with Sir William Young. He had since 1798 been merchant consignee and mortgagee of Young's estates in St Vincent and Tobago and possibly elsewhere, and in 1814 he foreclosed on an old mortgage in circumstances which led Young to write that he "broke every promise of competent Supply to my Family". C.O. 285/19, f. 52, Young to Bathurst, 31 October 1814, Separate. See also D.J. Murray, *The West Indies and British Colonial Government, 1801-1834* (Oxford: Clarendon Press, 1965), 22.
180. C.O. 285/15, ff. 29-31, Young to Liverpool, 20 August 1810.
181. C.O. 285/16, f. 14, Young to Liverpool, 12 June 1811.
182. C.O. 288/6, f. 247, M.H.A., 13 October 1807.
183. C.O. 288/7, f. 103, M.L.C., 4 September 1810.
184. C.O. 288/7, f. 107, M.L.C., 6 September 1810.
185. C.O. 287/3, f. 291, Act No. 76, 8 September 1810.
186. C.O. 285/16, f. 44, Young to Liverpool, 30 July 1811.
187. C.O. 285/16, f. 47, Young to Liverpool, 28 August 1811.
188. C.O. 288/7, f. 129, M.L.C., 12 August 1811, Governor's message.
189. C.O. 285/16, f. 44, Young to Liverpool, 30 July 1811.
190. C.O. 288/8, ff. 131, 137, 145, M.H.A., 17 July 1812, 16 July

1813, 14 July 1814.
191. C.O. 288/8, f. 9, M.L.C., 16 July 1813.
192. C.O. 287/4, f. 37, Act No. 89, 17 July 1814.
193. C.O. 287/2, f. 41, Act No. 9, 17 August 1794.
194. C.O. 287/3, f. 9, Act No. 35, 8 February 1800.
195. C.O. 288/7, f. 159, M.H.A., 22 April 1808.
196. C.O. 286/4, f. 29, Portland to Campbell, 18 November 1796, Separate.
197. C.O. 285/9, f. 58, Campbell to Camden, 9 December 1804.
198. T.P.L., M.P.C., 27 November 1804.
199. C.O. 288/6, M.L.C., 6 December 1804.
200. C.O. 288/6, M.L.C., 6 December 1805.
201. C.O. 287/2, f. 29, Act No. 5, 15 April 1794.
202. See examples in C.O. 285/4, Minutes of Council, 14 August 1795. C.O. 288/5, M.P.C., 23 August 1800. T.P.L., M.P.C., 9 September 1806, 24 August 1811, 8 August 1814.
203. C.O. 288/6, f. 144, M.L.C., 3 August 1807.
204. C.O. 288/7, ff. 246, 248, M.H.A., 14 July 1810.
205. C.O. 288/8, f. 137, M.H.A., 13 July 1813.
206. C.O. 288/7, f. 125, M.L.C., 12 July 1811.
207. C.O. 288/8, ff. 144-6, M.H.A., 13, 15 July, 12, 13 October 1814.
208. T.P.L., M.P.C., 8 August 1814.
209. C.O. 288/7, ff. 164-5, 167, M.H.A., 19, 21 July 1808.
210. C.O. 288/8, f. 137, M.H.A., 14, 15 July 1813.
211. C.O. 288/8, f. 133, M.H.A., 12 13 November 1812.
212. C.O. 285/3, Minutes of Council, 4 March 1795.
213. C.O. 285/4, Portland to Governor, 15 April 1797, no. 1.
214. Buckley, *Slaves in Red Coats: the British West India Regiments, 1795-1815* (New Haven: Yale University Press, 1977), 2-8.
215. The word "ranger" is the usual English rendering of the German-derived "jager" or "ager" or "jaeger" which is commonly used in the contemporary sources.
216. Buckley, op. cit., 10; 13.
217. C.O. 318/12, Dundas to Bruce, 18 September 1793.
218. C.O. 285/3, Lindsay to King, 10 May 1795, Private; Lindsay to Portland, 7 June 1795, no. 7.
219. C.O. 285/3, Minutes of Council, 15 May, 9 June 1795.
220. C.O. 287/2, f. 88, Act No. 19, 12 May 1795.
221. C.O. 285/3, Lindsay to Portland, 3 August 1795, no. 9.
222. Buckley, op. cit., 10-20. Fortescue, *British Army*, Vol. 4, Part II, 410; 424; 431-38; 450-52.
223. Buckley, op. cit., 24-26.
224. Ibid., 88, 156-57.
225. Ibid., 36-42; 88; 156-57. See also Fortescue, *British Army*, Vol. 4, Part II, 450-52.
226. Buckley, op. cit., 38.
227. C.O. 285/3, Lindsay to Portland, 1 July 1795, no. 8, and encs.
228. C.O. 285/3, Lindsay to

Notes to pages 81-86 / 243

228. Portland, 3 August 1795, no. 9.
229. C.O. 285/3, Portland to Lindsay, 9 October 1795, no. 4.
230. C.O. 285/4, Minutes of Council, 25 January 1797.
231. C.O. 285/3, Minutes of Council, 15 August 1795. Later the demand was raised to 400 men (C.O. 285/3, Lindsay to Portland, 6 September 1795, Private).
232. C.O. 285/4, Minutes of Council, 15 August 1795. Address of the Council and General Assembly of the Island of Tobago to His Excellency the ... Governor in Chief.
233. C.O. 285/3, Lindsay to Portland, 3 September 1795, no. 12.
234. C.O. 285/3, Lindsay to Portland, 6 Sept, 1795, Private.
235. C.O. 286/4, f. 21, Portland to Lindsay, 17 November 1795, no. 5.
236. C.O. 285/4, Minutes of Council, 19, 30 October 1795.
237. Buckley, op. cit., 167, no. 93.
238. C.O. 285/4, Lindsay to Portland, 16 Jan, 1796, no. 21.
239. C.O. 285/4, Lindsay to Portland, 27 April 1796, no. 24.
240. Buckley, op. cit., 167, no. 95.
241. Ibid., 53.
242. Fortescue, op. cit., 542. C.O. 285/4, Minutes of Council, 11 April, 10 July 1797.
243. C.O. 285/4, Campbell to Portland, 19 February 1797, no. 6, and encs.
244. C.O. 287/2, f. 145, Act No. 30, 15 August 1797.
245. C.O. 285/4, Lindsay to King, 9 March 1796, Private.
246. C.O. 285/4, Minutes of Council, 15 April 1796.
247. C.O. 285, Minutes of Council, 9, 10 March 1797. Buckley, op. cit., 14.
248. C.O. 285/4, M.P.C., 28 March 1797.
249. C.O. 285/5, De Lancey to Cuyler, 25 September 1797, enc. in De Lancey to Portland, 2 April 1798, Separate.
250. C.O. 285/4, Minutes of Assembly, 7, 9, 10 August 1797.
251. C.O. 285/5, M.P.C., 23 December 1797; M.H.A., 16 January 1798.
252. C.O. 285/5, M.H.A., 16, 17 May 1799.
253. C.O. 285/6, M.H.A., 7 January 1800.
254. C.O. 285/6, Minutes of Council, 9 January 1800.
255. C.O. 288/5, M.H.A., 22, 23 September 1801.
256. C.O. 285/5, De Lancey to Portland, 2 April 1798, Separate.
257. C.O. 285/5, Minutes of Council, 1 November 1797.
258. C.O. 285/6, Minutes of Council, 28 June 1798.
259. C.O. 285/5, De Lancey to Portland, 2 April 1798, Separate.
260. C.O. 286/4, f. 34, Portland to De Lancey, 10 July 1798, Separate.
261. C.O. 285/6, Encs. in Master to Portland, 5 February 1800, no. 1.
262. J. Holland Rose, *William Pitt*

263. *and the Great War* (London: Bell, 1912), 276; 287.
263. C.O. 285/4, Memorial of Planters, Merchants and Others interested in the Island of Tobago to Portland, 5 November 1796.
264. Holland Rose, op. cit., 230.
265. C.O. 285/10, f. 33, Campbell to Camden, 15 March 1805, Private.
266. C.O. 285/4, Minutes of Council, 26 January 1797.
267. *Cambridge History of British Foreign Policy* (Cambridge: Cambridge University Press, 1922-23), Vol. 1: 573: Grenville to Eden, 18 April 1797, Most Secret.
268. *Cambridge History of British Foreign Policy*, Vol. 1: 276-78.
269. C.O. 285/4, Minutes of Council, 13 June 1797.
270. N.L.S., MS. 5039, f. 116, Thomas Ruddack to Charles Steuart, 16 March 1797.
271. Ibid., f. 126-7, Ruddack to Steuart, 8 July 1797.
272. C.O. 285/5, M.H.A., 4 September 1797.
273. C.O. 285/5, M.H.A., 1 November 1797.
274. Holland Rose, op. cit., 325.
275. J. Holland Rose, *Life of Napoleon I* (London: Bell, 1916), Vol. 1: 310.
276. C.O. 288/5, M.L.C., 14 October 1800.
277. C.O. 285/6, Portland to Master, - November 1800, no. 4,
278. C.O. 288/5, M.P.C., 14 July 1801.
279. C.O. 285/7, Memorial from Council and Assembly, enc. in Robley to Portland, 22 November 1800, no. 4.
280. C.O. 285/12, f. 136, Enc. in Young to Windham, 4 February 1807.
281. C.O. 285/8, Enc. in Carmichael to Hobart, 20 March 1802.
282. E.E. Williams, *History of the People of Trinidad and Tobago* (Port of Spain: PNM Publishing, 1962), 63-64.
283. Holland Rose, *Napoleon*, Vol. 1: 311.
284. *Cambridge History of British Foreign Policy*, Vol. 1: 305.
285. Holland Rose, *Napoleon*, Vol. 1: 333.
286. Holland Rose, *Napoleon*, Vol. 1: 313. *Cambridge History of the British Empire*, Vol. 2: 79.
287. F.O. 27/59, Cornwallis to Hawkesbury, 10 January 1802, Private. Holland Rose, *Napoleon*, Vol. 1: 341.
288. *Correspondence of Charles, First Marquis Cornwallis*, edited by Charles Ross (London: Murray, 1859), Vol. 111: 402, Cornwallis to Hawkesbury, 10 January 1802.
289. *The Political History of England*, edited by R.L. Poole and W. Hunt (London: Longman, 1905-14), Vol. XI, 11.
290. *Cornwallis Correspondence*, Vol. 111: 435, Cornwallis to Hawkesbury, 10 January 1802.
291. *Cornwallis Correspondence*, Vol. 111: 431, Addington to Cornwallis, 2 January 1802.
292. *Confidential Correspondence of Napoleon Bonaparte with his brother Joseph* (London: Murray, 1855), Vol. 1: 49, Napoleon to Joseph, 7 March

1802.
293. *Cornwallis Correspondence*, Vol. 111: 431, Addington to Cornwallis, 2 January 1802.
294. Holland Rose, *Napoleon*, Vol. 1: 333.
295. C.O. 285/7, John Robley to Hobart, 19 October 1801.
296. C.O. 285/7, Robley to Hobart, 1 December 1801, no. 8.
297. C.O. 285/8, Elphinstone Piggott to Hobart, 7 December 1801.
298. C.O. 285/7, Robley to Hobart, 1 December 1801, no. 8.
299. *Confidential Correspondence of Napoleon*, Vol. 1: 48, Napoleon to Joseph, 6 January 1802.
300. C.O. 318/21, Secretary of State to Grinfield, 16 May 1803, Most Secret.
301. C.O. 285/9, f. 128, Memorial of Council and Assembly to the King, September 1803.
302. C.O. 285/9, f. 57, Campbell to Camden, 9 December 1804.
303. C.O. 285/11, f. 32, Balfour to Windham, 31 July 1806.
304. C.O. 285/11, f. 94, John Robley to Windham, 5 August 1806.
305. C.O. 285/18, f. 138, Memorial to Bathurst from Council and Assembly, 25 December 1813.
306. C.O. 285/19, f. 60, Planters of Tobago to Bathurst, 6 January 1814.
307. C.O. 288/8, f. 142, M.H.A., 27 April 1814.
308. C.O. 288/8, f. 48, M.L.C., 12 July 1814.
309. C.O. 288/8, f. 50, M.L.C., 13 July 1814.
310. C.O. 288/8, f. 53, M.L.C., 15 July 1814.
311. C.O. 285/19, f. 41, Young to Bathurst, 29 July 1814.
312. C.O. 288/8, f. 145, M.H.A., 14, 15 July 1814.
313. C.O. 288/8, f. 62, M.L.C., 12 October 1814.
314. C.O. 285/9, Memorial enc. in Macdonald to Grinfield, 20 September 1803.

CHAPTER FOUR

1. C.O. 287/1, f. 103, Act No. 19.
2. Goveia, *Slave Society in the British Leeward Islands at the end of the Eighteenth Century* (New Haven: Yale University Press, 1965), 152-58.
3. C.O. 285/16, ff. 123-24, Return on Matters of Enquiry ..., 1 October 1811.
4. Though in 1775 in Grenada a white slave owner, one Bacchus Preston, was executed for murdering a slave, there had been no special law on the subject. It seems probable, however, that Preston only suffered thus because as a very efficient bailiff he was unpopular with the white population and without influence. E.V. Goveia, *The West Indian Slave Laws in the Eighteenth Century* (Bridgetown: Caribbean Universities Press, 1970), 34n., 30. Marshall, "Slave Society and Economy in the British Windward Islands, 1763-1823" (Ph.D. thesis, UWI, 1972), 323.
5. Marshall, op. cit., 265.
6. Goveia, *Slave Society*, 173.
7. Ibid., 160-65.
8. C.O. 287/2, f. 32, An Act for establishing Regulations

9. C.O. 287/3, f. 22, No. 39a, 2 March 1802.
10. C.O. 287/3, f. 63, No. 41b, 6 October 1803.
11. Goveia, *Slave Society*, 185.
12. Ibid., 195.
13. Ibid., 200-202.
14. D.H. Porter, *The Abolition of the Slave Trade in England, 1784-1807* (New York: Archon Books, 1970), 95-98.
15. C.O. 152/78, ff. 221 et seq. Young to the Leeward Islands' Assembly, cited in Porter, op. cit., 98-99.
16. G.R. Mellor, *British Imperial Trusteeship, 1783-1850* (London: Faber, 1951), 61.
17. Quoted in T. Southey, *Chronological History of the West Indies* (London: Longman, 1827), Vol. III: 173.
18. Marshall, op. cit., 324-26. Goveia, *Slave Society*, 327-28.
19. Mellor, op. cit., 61.
20. Goveia, *Slave Society*, 329-30.
21. Porter, op. cit., 101.
22. Goveia, *Slave Society*, 191-200.
23. C.O. 285/4, Minutes of Council, 10 July, 29 August 1797.
24. C.O. 285/4, Minutes of Council, 29 August 1797.
25. C.O. 285/5, Minutes of Council, 25 June 1798.
26. Mellor, op. cit., 61. Marshall, op. cit., 326-27.
27. C.O. 285/5, Minutes of Council, 5 September 1798.
28. C.O. 285/5, M.H.A., 1 October 1798.
29. E.E. Williams, *History of the People of Trinidad and Tobago* (Port of Spain: PNM Punblishing, 1962), 61.
30. The Report may be found in C.O. 285/5, enc. in Agent Petrie to Portland, 4 March 1799.
31. C.O. 285/5, Portland to Robley, 1 May 1799, no. 2; 8 August 1799, no. 3.
32. C.O. 285/6, Minutes of Council, 25 March 1800.
33. Woodcock, *History of Tobago* (Port of Spain: Columbus Publishers Ltd., rep. n.d.), 63; 65. C.O. 285/3, Lindsay to Portland, 6 September 1795, Private; C.O. 285/6, Master to Portland, 20 April 1800, no. 3. Deerr, Vol. 2: 350.
34. Cited in Marshall, op. cit., 260.
35. C.O. 285/6, Master to Portland, 20 April 1800, no. 3.
36. C.O. 285/6, M.H.A., 9 April 1800.
37. C.O. 285/6, Minutes of Council, 9 April 1800.
38. C.O. 285/6, Portland to Master, 11 July 1800, no. 2; M.H.A., 9, 14 October 1800.
39. E.V. Goveia, *Slave Laws*, 34n.
40. Goveia, *Slave Society*, 197.
41. Mellor, op. cit., 62.
42. The slave population of Tobago is given as 10539 in 1787, 14,170 in 1790 and 16190 in 1797 despite a significant tendency to natural decrease. In two years to 1 July 1797, 1533, or 10 per cent of the slave population were imported. See Sir William Young, *The West India Common-Place Book* (London: Phillips/Macmillan,

42. 1807) and C.O. 285/5, Report of the [Tobago] Committee of both Houses..., enc. in Agent Petrie to Portland, 4 March 1799. Cf. P. Curtin, *The Atlantic Slave Trade, A census* (Madison: University of Wisconsin Press, 1969), 65.
43. K.O. Laurence, "The Tobago Slave Conspiracy of 1801", *Caribbean Quarterly,* Vol. 28, no. 3: (September 1982).
44. C.O. 287/3, f. 19, Act no. 38a, 2 March 1802.
45. C.O. 287/3, f. 27, Act no. 40a, 3 March 1802.
46. C.O. 285/12, f. 115, Young to Castlereagh, 16 November 1807.
47. C.O. 318/29, Rattray to Beckwith, 16 January 1806, enc. in Beckwith to Castlereagh, 2 February 1806, no. 36.
48. T.P.L., M.P.C., 23 December 1805.
49. C.O. 285/11, f. 2, Mitchell to Castlereagh, 5 January 1806, no. 2.
50. C.O. 318/29, Rattray to Beckwith, 16 January 1806, enc. in Beckwith to Castlereagh, 2 February 1806, no. 36.
51. Ibid.
52. C.O. 285/11, f. 2, Mitchell to Castlereagh, 5 January 1806, no. 2.
53. C.O. 288/6, M.P.C., 25 December 1805, 3 January 1806.
54. C.O. 318/29, Rattray to Beckwith, 16 January 1806, enc. in Beckwith to Castlereagh, 2 February 1806, no. 36.
55. C.O. 285/11, f. 2, Mitchell to Castlereagh, 5 January 1806, no. 2.
56. C.O. 285/12, f. 45, Young to Castlereagh, 23 July 1807.
57. C.O. 285/12, ff. 114-5, Young to Castlereagh, 16 November 1807.
58. C.O. 285/12, f. 45, Young to Castlereagh, 23 July 1807.
59. C.O. 285/16, f. 114, Return on Matters of Enquiry ..., 1 October 1811. Two versions of this return exist in the Public Record Office, one in C.O. 285/16, the other in C.O. 285/18. They do not always give the same information and the former has generally, but not always, been preferred as it appears to be statistically the more up to date.
60. C.O. 285/12, ff. 114-5, Young to Castlereagh, 16 November 1807.
61. C.O. 285/12, f. 114, Young to Castlereagh, 16 November 1807.
62. Ibid.
63. C.O. 288/6, f. 257, M.H.A., 28 October 1807.
64. C.O. 288/6, f. 261, M.H.A., 4 November 1807.
65. C.O. 287/3, f. 180, Act No. 57b.
66. C.O. 285/12, f. 115, Young to Castlereagh, 16 November 1807.
67. C.O. 285/12, f. 126, Castlereagh to Young, 20 February 1808.
68. C.O. 285/13, f. 44, Young to Castlereagh, 27 March 1808.
69. C.O. 288/6, f. 151, M.H.A., 14 October 1807.
70. Ibid.

71. C.O. 285/12, f. 45, Young to Castlereagh, 23 July 1807.
72. C.O. 288/6, f. 255, 257, M.H.A., 28 October 1807.
73. C.O. 287/3, f. 229, Act No. 65, 18 October 1808.
74. C.O. 287/3, f. 252, Act No. 68, 16 January 1809.
75. C.O. 288/7, f. 68; 138, M.L.C., 13 October 1809, 10 October 1811. C.O. 288/8, f. 133, M.H.A., 13 November 1812.
76. C.O. 288/8, f. 139, M.H.A., 12 October 1813.
77. C.O. 288/8, f. 147; 155; 158, M.H.A., 15 October 1814, 13, 14 January 1815.
78. C.O. 287/4, f. 48, Act No. 92, 14 January 1815.
79. C.O. 383/86, 35-6, Annotation on Tobago Chain Gang Amendment Act, No. 92 of 1815.
80. C.O. 285/21, f. 70, P.C. Committee for Trade to Goulbourn, 1 July 1816 and minutes.
81. C.O. 288/7, f. 263, M.H.A., 10 July 1811.
82. C.O. 383/86, 35, Annotation on Tobago Chain Amendment Act, No. 92 of 1815.
83. C.O. 285/16, f. 124, Return on Matters of Enquiry ..., 1 October 1811.
84. Marshall, op. cit., 256-57.
85. Ibid., 262.
86. Ibid., 262
87. Higman, *Slave Populations of the British Caribbean, 1807-1834* (Baltimore and London: Johns Hopkins University Press, 1984), 183.
88. Marshall, op. cit., 258-60.
89. C.O. 285/16, f. 114, Return on Matters of Enquiry ..., 1 October 1811.
90. C.O. 285/12, f. 129, Young to Castlereagh, 25 December 1807. C.O. 285/16, f. 144, Young to Liverpool, 30 December 1811.
91. C.O. 285/13, f. 124, Young to Castlereagh, 8 December 1808.
92. B.L., Add. MS. 37888, f. 170, Young to Windham, February 1810.
93. Marshall, op. cit., 265.
94. Higman, op. cit., 251-52.
95. Marshall, op. cit., 267.
96. C.O. 285/12, f. 42, Young to Castlereagh, 23 June 1807.
97. C.O. 285/12, f. 92, Young to Castlereagh, 10 October 1807, Separate. C.O. 285/13, ff. 41; 97, Young to Castlereagh, 2 March 1808, Private and enc.; 1 June 1808.
98. C.O. 285/20, ff. 52, 59, Balfour to Bathurst, 11 October, 25 November 1815.
99. S.O.A.S.-L.M.S., Folder 3, Jacket A, Letter from Elliot, 28 July 1810.
100. Marshall, op. cit., 269.
101. Ibid., 273.
102. Ibid., 274-75.
103. Higman, op. cit., 223-25; 257.
104. Marshall, op. cit., 271.
105. Ibid., 272.
106. Woodcock, op. cit., 65.
107. Higman, op. cit., 99; 222; 255.
108. C.O. 285/18, f. 27, Return on Matters of Enquiry ..., 1 October 1811.
109. Higman, 262.
110. In 1811 there were ten doctors to about 16500 slaves. C.O. 285/16, f. 105, Return on Matters of Enquiry ..., 1 October 1811.

111. Higman, op. cit., 261-66; 376. See also R.B. Sheridan, *Doctors and Slaves, A Medical and Demographic History of Slavery in the British West Indies, 1680-1834*, (Cambridge: Cambridge University Press, 1985), 41; 70.
112. Marshall, op. cit., 408-11.
113. Higman, op. cit., 272.
114. Ibid., 242.
115. Ibid., 257-58.
116. Marshall, op. cit., 389.
117. Ibid., 391-92.
118. C.O. 285/18, ff. 95-98, Young to Bathurst, 31 October 1813.
119. Ibid.
120. C.O. 285/18, ff. 99ff., Encs. in Young to Bathurst, 31 October 1813.
121. C.O. 285/18, ff. 96-7, Young to Bathurst, 31 October 1813. Traynor died in prison before news of the reprieve reached her.
122. C.O. 288/7, f. 24, M.L.C., 11 October 1808.
123. C.O. 288/6, f. 220, M.H.A., 1 May 1807. C.O. 288/7, f. 146, M.H.A., 9 December 1807.
124. C.O. 287/3, f. 207, An Act for the better protection of Slaves, 21 January 1808, no. 62.
125. C.O. 288/7, f. 207, Privy Council to Cooke, 28 August 1809, entered in M.H.A., 9 January 1810.
126. C.O. 285/13, f. 2, Young to Castlereagh, 29 January 1808.
127. Marshall, op. cit., 239-40.
128. C.O. 285/16, ff. 119-20, Return on Matters of Enquiry ..., 1 October 1811.
129. C.O. 285/18, ff. 30-35, Return on Matters of Enquiry ..., 1 October 1811.
130. C.O. 285/16, ff. 107-10, Return on Matters of Enquiry ..., 1 October 1811. Higman, op. cit., 331-32.
131. Higman, op. cit., 331-32; 652.
132. C.O. 285/16, f. 119, Return on Matters of Enquiry ..., 1 October 1811.
133. Ibid, f. 120.
134. C.O. 288/7, f. 172, M.H.A., 13 October 1808.
135. C.O. 285/16, f. 126, Return on Matters of Enquiry ..., 1 October 1811.
136. B.W. Higman, *Slave Population and Economy in Jamaica, 1807-1834* (Cambridge: Cambridge University Press, 1976), 223-24.
137. G.G. Findlay & W.W. Holdsworth, *The History of the Wesleyan Missionary Society* (London: Epworth Press, 1921), Vol. II: 221.
138. C.O. 285/18, f. 44, Report on Matters of Enquiry ..., 1 October 1811.
139. C.O. 285/16, f. 125, Return on Matters of Enquiry ..., 1 October 1811.
140. C.O. 285/13, f. 46, Young to Castlereagh, 25 April 1808.
141. C.O. 285/13, f. 118, *Tobago Gazette*, Governor's Speech to Legislature, 11 October 1808.
142. C.O. 285/16, f. 125, Return on Matters of Enquiry ... , 1 October 1811.
143. Higman, op. cit., 243.
144. Cited in Marshall, op. cit., 264.

145. C.O. 285/16, f. 123, Return on Matters of Enquiry ..., 1 October 1811.
146. Ibid, f. 119.
147. Ibid, f. 121.
148. Goveia, *Slave Society*, 189.
149. C.O. 285/116, f. 121, Return on Matters of Enquiry ..., 1 October 1811.
150. Ibid, ff. 122-3.
151. Marshall, op. cit., 294; 299-301.
152. Goveia, *Slave Society*, 190.
153. C.O. 285/116, f. 121, Return on Matters of Enquiry ..., 1 October 1811.
154. Goveia, *Slave Society*,168; 171-72.
155. Higman, op. cit., 691.
156. C.O. 288/7, f. 255, M.H.A., 14 August 1810.
157. Higman, op. cit., 691.
158. Marshall, op. cit., 382-85.
159. Ibid., 282.
160. B.L. Add. MS. 37888, f. 167, Returns of Negroe Population in Tobago, 1807., by Sir William Young.
161. C.O. 285/18, f. 29, Return on Matters of Enquiry ..., 1 October 1811.
162. Ibid, 38.
163. Marshall, op. cit., 284.
164. T.P.L., M.P.C., 28 October 1812.
165. Marshall, op. cit., 265.

CHAPTER FIVE
1. C.O. 285/2, Ricketts to King, 17 July 1793.
2. C.O. 285/3, f. 3, [Secretary to State] to Ricketts, January 1794. C.O. 285/3, f. 143, Minutes of Council, 19 May 1794.
3. C.O. 285/3, f. 260, Lindsay to Portland, 21 April 1795.
4. C.O. 285/3, f. 262, Lindsay to Portland, 22 April 1795, Private.
5. C.O. 285/3, f. 267, Portland to Lindsay, 23 July 1795, no. 2.
6. C.O. 285/4, Minutes of Council, 14 November 1796. C.O. 285/5, M.P.C., 24 January, 21 March 1798; 11 February 1799; 9, 25 January 1800.
7. C.O. 288/5, M.P.C., 23 August 1800.
8. C.O. 285/7, Robley to Portland, 22 November 1800, no. 3; 30 April 1801, no. 19. C.O. 288/5, M.P.C., 14 July 1801.
9. C.O. 288/5, M.P.C., 2 February 1801. C.O. 285/14, f. 22, Enc. in Young to Castlereagh, 25 May 1809. T.P.L., M.P.C., 9 February 1811.
10. See Introduction, p. 5.
11. C.O. 288/8, f. 130, M.H.A., 14 April 1812.
12. Deerr, *History of Sugar* (London: Chapman & Hall, 1949-50), Vol. I: 202. No figures are available for the period of French rule. A hogshead is reckoned as containing an average of 13 cwt.
13. See D.B. Davis, *The Problem of Slavery in the Age of Revolution, 1770-1823* (Ithaca: Cornell University Press, 1975), 54n.
14. Sir William Young sometimes gives statistics for the "produce" of Tobago which are usually somewhat higher than those cited here for

"exports". These figures have been taken from Sir William Young, *Tobago Almanack, 1810* (B.L., Stowe 923, f. 31) (1799-1809) which gives figures for sugar very close to those in Noel Deerr, *History of Sugar*, or calculated from statistics in C.O. 290/3 (1810-1815). Young gives the average hogshead as 13 cwt. 12 lb., the tierce as 9¼ cwt., slightly smaller than elsewhere. In calculating these figures the hogshead has been taken at Noel Deerr's usual figure of 13 cwt.

15. Marshall, "Slave Society and Economy in the British Windward Islands, 1763-1823" (Ph. D. thesis, UWI, 1972), 217.
16. C.O. 285/14, f. 57, Young to Castlereagh, 10 September 1809.
17. C.O. 285/12, f. 139, Enc. in Young to Windham, 4 February 1808. Woodcock, *History of Tobago* (Port of Spain: Columbus Publishers Ltd., n.d.), 190.
18. Marshall, op. cit., 96.
19. C.O. 285/16, f. 138, Enc. in Young to Liverpool, 7 December 1811.
20. C.O. 285/16, f. 135, Young to Liverpool, 7 December 1811.
21. J. R. Ward, "The Profitability of Sugar Planting in the British West Indies, 1650-1834." *Economic History Review*, Vol. 31, no. 2 (1978): 205-07; 213.
22. C.O. 285/17, f. 8, Young to Liverpool, 4 April 1812.
23. C.O. 288/8, f. 142, M.H.A., 27 April 1814.
24. Marshall, op. cit., 258-60.
25. D.G. Hall, "Incalculability as a Feature of Sugar Production during the Eighteenth Century," *Social and Economic Studies*, Vol. 10, no. 3 (1978): 305-18.
26. C.O. 285/18, f. 89, Young to Bathurst, 29 September 1813. C.O. 285/16, f. 32, Young to Liverpool, 6 December 1811.
27. C.O. 287/4, f. 13, Act No. 81 of 3 December 1811.
28. N.L.S., MS 5038, f. 51, Thomas Ruddack to Charles Steuart, 30 September 1793.
29. N.L.S., MS 5038, f. 107, Thomas Ruddack to Charles Steuart, 17 March 1794.
30. N.L.S., MS 5038, f. 134, Thomas Ruddack to Charles Steuart, 26 June 1794.
31. N.L.S., MS 5038, f. 176, Thomas Ruddack to Charles Steuart, 13 October 1794.
32. N.L.S., MS 5038, f. 238, Thomas Ruddack to Charles Steuart, 17 July 1795.
33. N.L.S., MS 5039, f. 105, Thomas Ruddack to Charles Steuart, 18 January 1797.
34. N.L.S., MS 5039, ff. 64, 126, Thomas Ruddack to Charles Steuart, 4 May, 8 July 1797.
35. C.O. 285/9, f. 84, Joseph Robley to Chapman, 11 July 1803.
36. C.O. 285/9, f. 63, Fawkener to Sullivan, Council Office, 19 May 1803.
37. C.O. 285/9, f. 64, D.K. Rucker & John Robley to Hobart, 2 June 1803.
38. C.O. 285/9, f. 68, Joseph Robley to Hobart, 3 July 1803.

39. C.O. 285/9, ff. 93, 95, John Robley to Hobart, 16, 19 August 1803.
40. C.O. 285/9, f. 109-11, Joseph Robley to Hobart, 16 October 1803.
41. C.O. 285/9, f. 115, Petition from Planters, Merchants etc., 18 October 1803.
42. C.O. 288/6, M.L.C., 26 February 1805.
43. S.R.O., GD51/1/517/2, Address from Council and Assembly to Dundas, 3 June 1796.
44. S.R.O., GD51/1/517/1, Petrie to Dundas, 21 July 1796.
45. R.G. Anstey, *The Atlantic Slave Trade and British Abolition, 1760-1810* (London: Macmillan, 1975), 332-4; 347-8.
46. C.O. 324/103, f. 51, Castlereagh to Governors of Tobago etc., 21 August 1805.
47. C.O. 285/12, f. 121, Young to Castlereagh, 28 November 1807.
48. C.O. 285/21, Campbell to Bathurst, 17 August 1816, no. 2.
49. Anstey, op. cit., 371-72.
50. Ibid., 373-76.
51. Ibid., 376-98.
52. C.O. 288/6, f. 11, M.H.A., 13 January 1807.
53. C.O. 285/11, f. 14, Memorial enc. in Mitchell to Windham, 26 May 1806.
54. Ibid.
55. C.O. 285/12, Balfour to Windham, 24 April 1807.
56. Anstey, op. cit., 369.
57. C.O. 285/12, f. 25, Young to Castlereagh, 2 June 1807.
58. Young MSS, University of the West Indies Library, St Augustine, "An Historical, Statistical and Descriptive Account of the Island of Tobago, Introductory to an Essay on the Commercial and Political Importance of the Possession to Great Britain," 119.
59. C.O. 285/18, f. 111. Statistical Returns 1807-13, enc. in Young to Bathurst, 20 December 1813.
60. C.O. 285/16, f. 127-8, Return on Matters of Enquiry ..., 1 October 1811.
61. C.O. 285/21, f. 39, Enc. in Campbell to Bathurst, 28 October 1816. A return of slave population was made in October each year for tax purposes. Slightly different figures may be found in other sources but the trend remains the same.
62. C.O. 285/16, f. 126, Return on Matters of Enquiry, 1 October 1811.
63. Goveia, *Slave Society in the British Leeward Islands at the End of the Eighteenth Century* (New Haven: Yale University Press, 1965), 254-55.
64. Young MSS, "An Historical, Statistical, Descriptive Account ..." 94.
65. *Encyclopedia Britannica*, 1854 edn. cited in Woodcock, 188. C.O. 285/7, Enc. in John Robley to Hobart, 5 October 1801.
66. C.O. 285/4, Lindsay to Portland, 27 April 1796, no. 25.
67. B.L. Stowe 923, f. 31, *Tobago Almanack, 1810*, ed. Sir William Young.

68. Marshall, op. cit., 212.
69. C.O. 285/13, f. 66, Statistical Returns, 22 April 1808. Shrub was a liquor made of lime juice, sugar and rum, the equivalent of a rum punch.
70. Sir William Young, *Prospectus on Proposal for the Institution of an Agricultural Society in Tobago*, Grenada, 1807 (enc. in C.O. 285/12, f. 92, Young to Castlereagh, 10 October 1807, Separate.
71. C.O. 285/12, f. 75, Young to Castlereagh, 27 August 1807.
72. C.O. 285/12, f. 92, Young to Castlereagh, 10 October 1807, Separate.
73. C.O. 285/12, f. 118, *Tobago Gazette*, 13 November 1807, enc. in Young to Castlereagh, 16 November 1807.
74. C.O. 286/5, f. 120, Castlereagh to Young, 7 Jan, 1808, Private.
75. C.O. 285/13, f. 41, Young to Castlereagh, 2 March 1808, Private.
76. C.O. 285/16, f. 48, Young to Liverpool, 28 Aug 1811.
77. L.J. Ragatz, *The Fall of the Planter Class in the British West Indies 1763-1834* (New York: Octagon Books, 1962), 69.
78. C.O. 285/13, ff. 97, 107, 117, Young to Castlereagh, 1 June, 30 July, 1 November 1808.
79. C.O. 285/14, f. 66, Young to Castlereagh, 14 November 1809. S.O.A.S., LMS, Folder 3, Jacket A, Letter from Elliot, 28 July 1810.
80. C.O. 285/16, f. 47, Young to Liverpool, 28 August 1811. C.O. 285/17, f. 27, Young to Liverpool, 17 June 1812.
81. C.O. 285/20, f. 52, Balfour to Bathurst, 11 October 1815, no. 22,
82. T.P.L., M.P.C., 8 May 1815, Deposition of George Wightman.
83. C.O. 285/14, f. 16, Young to Castlereagh, 27 April 1809.
84. C.O. 285/18, f. 2, Young to Bathurst, 10 January 1813.
85. T.P.L., M.L.C., 8 May 1815, Deposition of George Wightman.
86. C.O. 285/14, f. 2, Young to Castlereagh, 20 Jan, 1809.
87. T.P.L., M.P.C., 8 May 1815, Deposition of John Anderson.
88. C.O. 285/20, f. 39, Memorial of Council and Assembly to Bathurst, 15 July 1815.
89. C.O. 285/5, M.H.A., 12 October, 12 November 1798.
90. Ibid.
91. C.O. 285/6, M.H.A., 15 May 1800.
92. C.O. 285/16, f. 114, Return on Matters of Enquiry ... 1 October 1811.
93. C.O. 287/3, f. 184, An Act to amend an Act for the better regulating of the Police .. and ... Markets, 6 November 1807, no. 59.
94. C.O. 285/12, f. 115, Young to Castlereagh, 16 November 1807. C.O. 285/13, f. 30, Young to Castlereagh, 2 March 1808.
95. C.O. 285/16, f. 116, Return on Matters of Enquiry ... 1 October 1811.
96. S.O.A.S., LMS, Folder 2, Jacket C, Purkis to Bogue, 1 November 1809.
97. C.O. 288/7, f. 23, M.L.C., 11 October 1808.

98. C.O. 288/7, ff. 178-9, 225, M.H.A., 14 January 1809, 16 April 1810.
99. C.O. 288/8, f. 12, M.L.C., 12 October 1813.
100. C.O. 287/3, f. 184, An Act to amend an Act ... for the better regulating of the Police ... and ... Markets, 6 November 1807, no. 59.
101. C.O. 287/4, f. 66, An Act to alter and amend an Act for regulating Trespasses.
102. C.O. 285/5, De Lancey to Portland, 1 May 1798, no. 10.
103. C.O. 285/4, M.H.A., 8 August 1797.
104. C.O. 287/2, f. 148, An Act ... to restrain all persons not licensed from selling by Retail Rum, Wine or any other Spirituous or Fermented Liquors ... 5 September 1797, no. 31.
105. C.O. 287/3, f. 82, An Act to restrain persons not licensed from selling by Retail Rum, Wine or any other Spirituous or Fermented Liquors ... 5 November 1804, no. 45.
106. C.O. 287/3, f. 277, An Act to amend an Act to restrain persons not licensed from selling by retail ... 15 July 1810, no. 74.
107. C.O. 288/8, f. 131, M.H.A., 16 July 1812, 13 January 1813.
108. C.O. 288/8, f. 6, M.L.C., 16 July 1813.
109. C.O. 285/18, f. 81, Young to Liverpool [sic], 31 July 1813.
110. C.O. 285/13, f. 76, Memo. by Young on Trade of Tobago, 20 April 1808.
111. C.O. 324/103, King to West India Governors, 17 January 1798, Circ.
112. C.O. 324/103, King to West India Governors, 26 May 1798, Circ.
113. C.O. 285/5, M.P.C., 23 July 1798.
114. C.O. 285/5, De Lancey to Portland, 30 July 1798.
115. C.O. 285/5, Minutes of Council, 14 September 1798.
116. C.O. 287/3, An Act to Establish and Regulate a Small Coinage for this Island, 5 November 1798, no. 34. The value of the stamped coins was fixed at 4 estampees or 6 black dogs to one bit.
117. C.O. 286/4, King to Robley, 8 April 1799.
118. C.O. 285/5, M.P.C., 23 August 1798.
119. C.O. 285/5, M.P.C., 17 September 1798.
120. C.O. 285/5, Enc. in Robley to Portland, 4 February 1799, no. 10.
121. C.O. 288/6, M.L.C., 25 June 1806.
122. C.O. 288/8, ff. 167-168, M.H.A., 11, 14, July 1815.
123. C.O. 285/12, f. 69, Castlereagh to Young, 10 October 1807.
124. C.O. 285/13, f. 76, Memo by Young on Trade of Tobago, 20 April 1808.
125. C.O. 285/18, f. 80, Young to Liverpool [sic], 31 July 1813.
126. C.O. 285/12, f. 49, Memo. enc. in Young to Castlereagh, 23 July 1807. C.O. 285/13, f. 79, Memo. by Young on Trade of Tobago, 20 April 1808.
127. Ibid.
128. C.O. 285/18, f. 80, Young to Liverpool [sic], 31 July 1813.
129. C.O. 285/15, f. 55, Young to

Liverpool, 4 December 1810.
130. C.O. 285/12, f. 49, Memo., enc. in Young to Castlereagh, 23 July 1807.
131. C.O. 285/11, f. 25, Balfour to Windham, 19 June 1806, no. 3. C.O. 285/10, ff. 60-64, Encs. in Campbell to Camden, 16 August 1805, no. 16.
132. C.O. 285/13, ff. 76-8, Memo. by Young on Trade of Tobago, 20 April 1808.
133. C.O. 288/7, f. 118, M.L.C., 9 July 1811.
134. C.O. 285/16, f. 38, Young to Liverpool, 17 July 1811.
135. C.O. 285/18, f. 4, Young to Bathurst, 22 January 1813.
136. C.O. 285/18, f. 127, C.T.P. to Harrison, 26 April 1813.
137. C.O. 285/18, f. 80, Young to Liverpool [sic], 31 July 1813.
138. C.O. 288/8, f. 36, M.L.C., 29 April 1814; f. 142, M.H.A., 29 April 1814.
139. C.O. 285/19, f. 37, Enc. in Young to Bathurst, 21 May 1814.
140. T.P.L., M.P.C., 14 March 1815.
141. C.O. 285/19, f. 30, Young to Bathurst, 21 May 1814.
142. C.O. 285/2, Ricketts to King, 17 July 1793.
143. C.O. 285/3, f. 114, Robley to Dundas, 11 September 1794.
144. C.O. 285/3, f. 199, Ricketts to Robley, 13 [misdated 30] December 1794, postscript by Ricketts, 15 December
145. C.O. 285/5, Robley to Portland, 16 December 1798, no. 2; 23 April, 16 June 1799, nos. 13, 16.
146. C.O. 285/6, Master to King, 6 April, 1 June 1800.
147. C.O. 288/5, M.L.C., 28 August 1801.
148. C.O. 318/23, 523, GPO to Hobart, 18 July 1803.
149. C.O. 285/14, f. 12, Young to Castlereagh, 24 March 1809.
150. C.O. 285/14, f. 68, Young to Liverpool, 15 December 1809. C.O. 285/15, f. 2, Young to Liverpool, 13 February 1810.
151. A schedule of arrivals for 1808 and 1809 is given in Sir William Young, *Tobago Almanack*, 1810 (B.L., Stowe MSS, 923, f. 27).
152. C.O. 285/3, Minutes of Council, 28 March, 2, 3, 9 April 1794.
153. C.O. 285/3, f. 184, Minutes of Council, 13 November 1794.
154. C.O. 287/2, f. 112, An Act to Ascertain, Repair Alter and Improve the Public Roads ..., 4 November 1795, no. 25.
155. C.O. 288/7, f. 125, M.L.C., 12 July 1811.
156. C.O. 285/5, Minutes of Council, 5, 6, September 1798. C.O. 285/6, M.H.A., 2 October 1799.
157. C.O. 288/6, f. 194, M.H.A., 14 October 1806.
158. C.O. 288/6, M.L.C., 6 December 1805.
159. C.O. 287/3, f. 133, An Act to continue and amend an Act ... to ascertain alter and amend the Public Roads ..., 16 December 1806, no. 51b.
160. C.O. 288/7, f. 112, M.L.C., 9 January 1811.
161. C.O. 285/5, M.H.A., 16 Jan, 10 May 1798.
162. C.O. 288/6, M.L.C., 16 May 1806.
163. C.O. 288/8, ff. 3, 82, 89, M.L.C., 15 July 1813; 14

164. January, 16 March 1815. C.O. 288/7, ff. 151, 155, M.H.A., 14 January, 12 April 1808.
165. C.O. 288/7, f. 70, M.L.C., 13 January 1810. C.O. 288/8, f. 16, 19, M.L.C., 13 October 1813; 12 January 1814.
166. E. Peters-Roberts, "Printing in Tobago: An Historical Perspective." *Working Papers on West Indian Printing, No. 22* (UWI, Department of Library Studies, Mimeo. 1984), 2-3.
167. C.O. 288/6, f. 198, M.H.A., 15 October 1806.
168. C.O. 285/12, f. 76, Young to Castlereagh, 27 August 1807.
169. C.O. 285/12, Young to Castlereagh, 10 October 1807, Separate.
170. C.O. 318/12, Cuyler to Dundas, 23 April 1793.
171. I. Dookhan, "War and Trade in the West Indies: A Preliminary Survey, 1783-1815", *Journal of the College of the Virgin Islands* no. 1 (May 1975): 35.
172. C.O. 285/3, Memo. by Agent J. Petrie, 7 January 1794.
173. Ragatz, op. cit., 232.
174. C.O. 290/1, ff. 7-12.
175. C.O. 285/2, Ricketts to King, 17 July 1793.
176. C.O. 285/3, ff. 31-2, Address of Council and Assembly to Dundas, 8 March 1794.
177. C.O. 285/4, Minutes of Council, 11 July 1796.
178. F. Armytage, *The Free Port System in the British West Indies* (London: Longman, Green & Co., 1953), 5.
179. C.O. 285/5, Robley to Portland, 16 December 1798, no. 2.
180. Armytage, op. cit., 98-103.
181. C.O. 286/4, King to Robley, 12 March 1799.
182. Armytage, op. cit., 103.
183. C.O. 285/6, Portland to Master, 22 March 1800, no. 1.
184. C.O. 285/6, Master to Portland, 10 July 1800, no. 5, and enc.
185. C.O. 285/9, f. 146, Robley to Cooke, 14 June 1804.
186. Ibid.
187. T.P.L., M.P.C., 30, 31 January 1805.
188. C.O. 285/10, f. 12, Camden to Campbell, 6 April 1805.
189. C.O. 285/10, f. 68, Campbell to Camden, 1 September 1805, no. 25.
190. C.O. 285/10, f. 83, Note from John Robley, 11 February 1805.
191. C.O. 285/10, f. 71, Castlereagh to Campbell, 21 October 1805, no. 2, and enc.
192. C.O. 285/13, f. 74, Statistical Return for Tobago, 22 April 1808. C.O. 285/11, f. 30, Enc. in Balfour to Windham, 4 July 1806, no.4.
193. C.O. 285/13, ff. 32, 124, Young to Castlereagh, 2 March, 8 December 1808. C.O. 285/13, f. 74, Statistical Return for Tobago, 22 April 1808. C.O. 285/14, f. 6, Young to Castlereagh, 20 February 1809.
194. Dookhan, op. cit., 41.
195. C.O. 285/13, f. 74, Statistical Return for Tobago, 22 April 1808.
196. B.L., Stowe 923, f. 31, *Tobago Almanack for 1810*, edited by

Sir William Young.
197. C.O. 285/3, Ricketts to Dundas, 28 April 1794, and enc. No sugar was exported to the USA. C.O. 285/4, Campbell to Portland, 19 February 1797, no. 5. C.O. 285/5, Robley to Portland, 21 August 1799, no. 22.
198. S.F. Bemis, *Jay's Treaty: A Study in Commerce and in Diplomacy* (New York: Macmillan, 1923).
199. C.O. 285/3, f. 116, Address to Council and Assembly from President Robley [c. July 1794].
200. C.O. 285/3, Robley to Dundas, 11 September 1794.
201. C.O. 285/3, Portland to Robley, 18 November 1794, no. 3.
202. Ragatz, op. cit., 230.
203. C.O. 285/3, Robley to Portland, 21 February 1795, no. 13; Lindsay to Portland, 3 August 1795, no. 9.
204. Dookhan, op. cit., 35.
205. The relaxation proclaimed in 1795, initially for six months, was still being regularly renewed at the end of 1800. C.O. 285, Robley to Portland, 22 December 1800, no. 5.
206. In the year ended 5 January 1795, 43 American vessels brought the following items to Tobago: 2071 bbl. beef or pork; 3381 bbls. flour; 10609 bushels Indian corn; 135 bales corn; 2700 bushels peas or beans; 1,258 casks rice; 25 bbl. potatoes; 302 kegs butter; 150 boxes salt fish; 1305 ft planks; 479 shingles; 136360 wooden hoops; 507,581 staves; 640 hooks; 79 sheep and hogs. Compiled by Marshall op. cit., 75, from C.O. 285/11, no. 15.
207. C.O. 285/11, f. 54, Enc. in Balfour to Windham, 16 December 1806, no. 16.
208. C.O. 285/7, Robley to Portland, 22 December 1800, no. 5.
209. C.O. 285/7, Proclamation enc. in Robley to Portland, 22 December 1800, no. 5.
210. C.O. 285/7, Council and Assembly to President, 10 December 1800, enc. in Robley to Portland, 22 December 1800, no. 5.
211. M.M.S., Tobago Letters, Account of the Moravian Mission in Tobago with James Crooks, 20 January 1803.
212. C.O. 285/20, f. 16, Returns enc. in Balfour to Bathurst, 3 May 1815, no. 9; Memorial from Council and Assembly to Bathurst, 15 July 1815.
213. Marshall, op. cit., 82-84.
214. C.O. 285/5, Minutes of Privy Council, 9 December 1797.
215. T.P.L., M.P.C., 2 March 1804.
216. C.O. 285/10, f. 102, Fawkener to Cooke, 21 October 1805.
217. T.P.L., M.P.C., 11 July 1803.
218. Ragatz, op. cit., 298.
219. C.O. 324/103, f. 35, Camden to West Indian Governors, 5 September 1804, Circular.
220. C.O. 324/103, f. 45, Camden to West Indian Governors, 16 January 1805, Circular.
221. C.O. 285/13, f. 73, Statistical Returns.
222. C.O. 285/10, ff. 60-64, Encs. in Campbell to Camden,

16 August 1805.
223. Marshall, 77-8; F.L. Benns, *The American Struggle for the British West Indian Carrying Trade, 1815 - 1830.* Indiana University Studies, no. 56 (Bloomington, Indiana, 1923), 22; Ragatz, op. cit., 300.
224. C.O. 285/11, f. 55, Memo. enc. in Balfour to Windham, 16 December 1806, no. 15.
225. C.O. 285/10, ff. 66-7, Campbell to Camden, 1 September 1805, no. 25.
226. C.O. 285/13, f. 3, Young to Castlereagh, 29 January 1808.
227. Ibid.
228. C.O. 324/103, f. 67, Windham to West Indian Governors, 21 March 1806, Circular.
229. C.O. 285/16, f. 12, Young to Liverpool, 3 May 1811.
230. C.O. 287/3, f. 176, An Act to provide a Bounty on Fish ..., 6 November 1807, no. 55b.
231. C.O. 285/10, f. 108, Cottrell to Cooke, 13 December 1805.
232. C.O. 285/12, f. 161, Fawkener to Cooke, 29 October 1807.
233. C.O. 324/103, f. 82, Windham to West Indian Governors, 21 September 1806, Circular.
234. C.O. 324/103, f. 85, Windham to West Indian Governors, 3 October 1806, Circular.
235. C.O. 288/6, M.P.C., 6 January 1807.
236. C.O. 285/12, f. 43, Young to Castlereagh, 23 July 1807.
237. C.O. 285/18, f. 9, Enc. in Young to Bathurst, 31 March 1813.
238. C.O. 285/12, ff. 73, 87, Young to Castlereagh, 27, 31 August 1807.
239. Dookhan, op. cit., 43.
240. Ibid.
241. C.O. 290/1, 2, 3, Returns of Shipping Entering Tobago, 1793 et seq.
242. C.O. 285/13, ff. 67-70, Import Statistics, 1805-07.
243. Marshall, op. cit., 99. These figures are more than doubtful since the official shipping returns took no notice of American shipping while the war of 1812-14 lasted.
244. Ragatz, op. cit., 321-22.
245. C.O. 285/12, f. 74, Young to Castlereagh, 27 August 1807.
246. C.O. 285/12, f. 75, Minutes of Council, 3, 9 August 1807.
247. C.O. 285/12, f. 50, Enc. in Young to Castlereagh, 23 July 1807.
248. C.O. 285/12, f. 74, Young to Castlereagh, 27 August 1807.
249. T.P.L., M.P.C., 7 August 1807, Petition to Governor.
250. C.O. 285/14, f. 21, Young to Castlereagh, 20 February 1809.
251. C.O. 285/12, ff. 124, 129, Young to Castlereagh, 28 Nov, 25 December 1807.
252. C.O. 285/12, f. 3, Young to Castlereagh, 16 November 1807. C.O. 285/13, f. 115, Young to Castlereagh, 29 January 1808.
253. Dookhan, op. cit., 40. Marshall, op. cit., 99.
254. C.O. 290/2, ff. 18-41, Returns of Shipping Entering Tobago, 1807-08. C.O. 285/13, f. 113, Young to Castlereagh, 25 September 1808.
255. C.O. 285/13, f. 124, Young to Castlereagh, 8 December

256. C.O. 285/14, f. 62, Young to Castlereagh, 2 October 1809.
257. C.O. 285/14, f. 6, Young to Castlereagh, 20 February 1809.
258. S.O.A.S., LMS, Folder 2, Jacket A, Elliot to LMS, 25 March, 26 May, 19 June 1809.
259. B.M., Add. MS 37888, f. 166, Young to Windham, 27 July 1809.
260. C.O. 285/14, f. 21, Young to Castlereagh, 25 May 1809.
261. C.O. 285/14, f. 27, Young to Castlereagh, 27 July 1809.
262. C.O. 285/15, f. 2, Young to Liverpool, 13 February 1810.
263. Ibid.
264. C.O. 285/16, f. 4, Young to Liverpool, 1 February 1811.
265. The fluctuations of 1811 are shown by the arrival of twenty-two, three, eight and seventeen ships in the four successive quarters as against ten, eleven, eight and fourteen in 1810. C.O. 290/2, ff. 65-78; C.O. 290/3, ff. 1, 3: Returns of Shipping, 1810 and 1811.
266. T.P.L., M.P.C., 19 September 1809. C.O. 285/14, f. 66, Young to Castlereagh, 14 November 1809.
267. Ragatz, op. cit., 322.
268. C.O. 288/7, M.H.A., 28 June 1809, Order in Council, 12 April 1809.
269. C.O. 287/3, f. 257, An Act for laying a Duty upon Fish ... and to lay a Tax upon the tonnage of ... [neutral] Ships or Vessels, 30 June 1809, no. 69.
270. C.O. 285/14, f. 83, Fawkener to Cooke, 23 October 1809.
271. Ragatz, op. cit., 324.
272. C.O. 288/7, ff. 218-19, M.H.A., 10 April 1810.
273. C.O. 324/103, f. 117, Liverpool to West Indian Governors, 15 February 1810, Circular.
274. C.O. 288/7, f. 111, M.L.C., 11 October 1810. C.O. 287/3, f. 297, An Act to lay a Duty upon Staves, Lumber ... and Provisions of any Kind ..., 23 November 1810, No. 77.
275. Ibid.
276. C.O. 288/6, M.P.C., 24 March 1807.
277. C.O. 285/13, f. 81, Memo. by Young on Tobago Trade, 20 April 1808.
278. C.O. 285/12, Fawkener to Cooke, 29 October 1807.
279. C.O. 285/15, f. 23, Young to Liverpool, 30 June 1810.
280. C.O. 854/1, ff. 20 et seq., Memorial of the Committee of Merchants interested in the Trade and Fisheries of the British North American Colonies, 1810, and Appendices.
281. C.O. 854/1, f. 18, Fawkener to Peele, 1 March 1811.
282. C.O. 285/16, f. 12, Young to Liverpool, 3 May 1811.
283. C.O. 285/16, f. 16, Young to Liverpool, 12 June 1811. The figures were:

	USA	BNA
5/1/1809 - 5/1/1810		
dried fish (qtl)	2,570	3,796
pickled fish (bbl)	892	660
6/1/1810 - 5/1/1811		
dried fish (qtl)	4,293	4,248
pickled fish (bbl)	379	26

284. C.O. 285/16, f. 130, Young to Liverpool, 13 November 1811.
285. C.O. 854/1, f. 26, Order in Council, 6 September 1811.
286. C.O. 287/4, f. 19, An Act to lay a Duty upon Staves, Lumber, Horses ... and every other Species of Live Stock and ... every other kind of Provisions ..., 16 January 1813, No. 82.
287. Dookhan, op. cit., 40.
288. C.O. 324/103, f. 133, Bathurst to West Indian Governors, Circular, 14 Sept 1812.
289. Dookhan, op. cit., 43.
290. C.O. 290/3, ff. 8-26, Shipping Returns 1812-14.
291. C.O. 285/20, ff. 19, 39, Balfour to Bathurst, 15 July 1815; Memorial from Council and Assembly to Bathurst, 15 July 1815.
292. C.O. 288/8, f. 14, M.L.C., 12 October 1813.
293. C.O. 854/1, f. 36, Buller to Bunbury, 2 January 1815.
294. T.P.L., M.L.C., 27, 29 March 1815. C.O. 285/20, f. 12, Balfour to Bathurst, 30 March 1815, no. 6.
295. C.O. 286/5, f. 135, Bathurst to Balfour, 20 May 1815.
296. T.P.L., M.P.C., 8 May 1815.
297. C.O. 285/20, f. 15, Balfour to Bathurst, 3 May 1815, no. 9.
298. C.O. 285/20, f. 19, Balfour to Bathurst, 16 May 1815.
299. C.O. 285/20, f. 11, Balfour to Bathurst, 30 March, 1815, no. 6.
300. C.O. 285/20, f. 15, Balfour to Bathurst, 3 May 1815, no. 9.
301. T.P.L., M.L.C., 18 May 1815.
302. T.P.L., M.L.C., 5, 20 June 1815.
303. C.O. 285/20, f. 39, Memorial from Council and Assembly to Bathurst, 15 July 1815.
304. T.P.L., M.L.C., 12 August, 29 September 1815.
305. C.O. 286/5, ff. 135-6, Bathurst to Balfour, 20 May, 23 August 1815.
306. C.O. 285/20, f. 37, Balfour to Bathurst, 19 July 1815, no. 16.
307. C.O. 285/20, f. 72, Lack to Bunbury, 8 August 1815.
308. C.O. 286/5, f. 137, Bathurst to Balfour, 19 October 1815.
309. C.O. 288/8, f. 110, M.L.C., 13 July 1815.
310. C.O. 285/20, f. 76, Bathurst to Piggott.
311. C.O. 285/20, f. 82, Buller to Bunbury, 2 October 1815.
312. C.O. 285/20, f. 37, Balfour to Bathurst, 19 July 1815, no. 16.
313. C.O. 285/20, ff. 49, 52, Balfour to Bathurst, 24 August, 11 October 1815.
314. C.O. 290/3, f. 31, Returns of Shipping, 1815.
315. C.O. 285/20, ff. 49, 52, Balfour to Bathurst, 24 August, 11 October 1815.
316. B.M. Brereton, *A History of Modern Trinidad, 1783-1962* (Kingston: Heinemann, 1981), 45-47.

CHAPTER SIX
1. Marshall, "Slave Society and Economy in the British Windward Islands, 1763-1823" (Ph. D. thesis, UWI, 1972), 425; Ince, "Protestant Missionary Activity in Five South Caribbbean Islands During Slavery, 1765-1826" (D. Phil. thesis, University of Oxford, 1984), 279.
2. C.O. 285/13, f. 3, Young to

Notes to pages 182-184 / **261**

Castlereagh, 29 January 1808. BM. Add. MS. 37888, f. 165, Young to Windham, 27 July 1809. C.O. 285/6, M.H.A., 8 April 1800. N.L.S., MS. 3844, f. 3, Lindsay to Dundas, 6 May 1793, Private. C.O. 288/6, M.L.C., 17 April 1804, 25 June 1806. C.O. 285/6, Minutes of Council, 9 January, 5 February 1800.
3. C.O. 285/10, f. 96, Halkett to Cooke, 21 September 1805.
4. C.O. 285/16, f. 125, Sir William Young, Return on Matters of Enquiry ..., 1 October 1811.
5. Ince, op. cit., 281.
6. Woodcock, *History of Tobago*, 182. C.O. 285/3, f. 85, Minutes of Council, 19 February 1794.
7. N.L.S., MS. 3844, f. 3, Lindsay to Dundas, 6 May 1793, Private. Fulham Papers, Vol. XX, f. 160, The State of the Clergy and Churches of Grenada on the 25th of March 1796.
8. C.O. 285/3, Petrie to Portland, 20 March 1799. C.O. 285/6, M.H.A., 11 November 1799.
9. M.M.S., Tobago Letters, Printed extract from Schirmer's Diary, 26 July 1800.
10. C.O. 285/6, M.H.A., 25 March 1800.
11. C.O. 288/6, M.L.C., 16 August 1803.
12. C.O. 288/6, M.L.C., 17 April, 1804.
13. C.O. 285/13, f. 3, Young to Castlereagh, 29 January 1808.
14. C.O. 285/13, f. 31, Young to Castlereagh, 2 March 1808.
15. Ibid.
16. C.O. 285/3, ff. 49, 115, Young to Castlereagh, 25 April, 25 September 1808.
17. S.O.A.S., LMS, Folder 2, Jacket B, Elliot's Journal, 7 January 1809.
18. C.O. 288/7, M.L.C., 13 April 1810.
19. BM. Add. MS 37888, f. 165, Young to Windham, 27 July 1810.
20. C.O. 285/15, f. 9, Young to Liverpool, 14 April 1810.
21. T.P.L., M.L.C., 11 August 1812.
22. C.O. 288/8, f. 118, M.L.C., 14 July 1815.
23. C.O. 285/13, f. 3, Young to Castlereagh, 29 January 1808.
24. C.O. 285/3, f. 21, Governor's Address to Council and Assembly, 10 February 1794.
25. C.O. 285/14, f. 56, Young to Castlereagh, 10 September 1809. C.O. 288/7, f. 267, M.H.A., 13 August 1811.
26. C.O. 288/8, f. 146, M.H.A., 13 October 1814.
27. C.O. 287/4, f. 85, An Act to authorize the Building a Place of Divine Worship ..., 12 January 1816 (No. 102).
28. C.O. 285/16, f. 126, Sir William Young, Return on Matters of Enquiry ..., 1 October 1811.
29. S.O.A.S., LMS, Folder 2, Jacket C, Purkis to Bogue, 1 November 1809.
30. Ince, op. cit., 281.
31. C.O. 285/16, f. 142, Young to Liverpool 18 December 1811. Woodcock (op. cit., 182) claims that 410 slave children were baptized in 1800 alone.

32. A. Caldecott, *The Church in the West Indies* (London: Society for Promoting Christian Knowledge, 1898), 45-46.
33. B.A. Marshall, "Missionaries and Slaves in the British Windward Islands". Paper Presented at the Twelfth Conference of Caribbean Historians, University of the West Indies, St Augustine, 1980, 9.
34. Cited in Marshall, "Missionaries and Slaves", 9-10.
35. M.M.S., Tobago Letters, Letter from John Hamilton, 20 June 1798.
36. Ibid.
37. M.M.S., Tobago Diaries and Confidential Minutes, Diary of the Negro Congregation in Tobago, 2 July 1800.
38. M.M.S., Tobago Letters, Subscription Lists, 8 January 1800, 27 March 1801.
39. M.M.S., Tobago Letters, Printed Diary, 26 July 1800; Diary, 5 February 1801.
40. M.M.S., Tobago Letters, Diary, passim. M.M.S., Diary, Minutes, passim.
41. M.M.S., Tobago Letters, Printed extract from Schirmer's Diary, 26 July 1800.
42. M.M.S., Tobago Letters, Printed letter from Church, 26 July 1800.
43. M.M.S., Tobago Letters, Document signed Thos Wilson [et. al.], 27 March 1801.
44. M.M.S., Diary, 15 April 1802.
45. M.M.S., Diary, June, September, October, 1801; March, April 1802, passim.
46. J. Holmes, *Historical Sketches of the Missions of the United Brethren for Propagating the Gospel among the Heathen, from their Commencement to the Year 1817*. (London: The Author, 1827).
47. Ince, "Protestant Misionary Activity", 72.
48. M.M.S., Diary, 23 December 1800; April 1801, various.
49. M.M.S., Diary, 11 May 1801.
50. Marshall, "Missionaries and Slaves", 11.
51. M.M.S., Diary, 31 December 1801.
52. M.M.S., Dairy, 19 April, 2 June, 30 November, 1801.
53. M.M.S., Diary, February-April 1802, passim.
54. S.O.A.S., LMS, Folder 1, Jacket A, Letter from George Baines, 25 August 1807; Baines to LMS, 28 August 1807.
55. S.O.A.S., LMS, Folder 1, Jacket A, Memo. of a Conversation between G. Baines and J. Robley, December 1807.
56. S.O.A.S., LMS, Folder 1, Jacket A, Elliot to LMS, 28 June 1808; Folder 1, Jacket B, Elliot to LMS, 8 August, 7 December 1808.
57. S.O.A.S., LMS, Folder 1, Jacket B, Elliot's Journal 1808, passim.
58. Ince, "The LMS Mission", 3-4.
59. S.O.A.S., LMS, Folder 1, Jacket B, Elliot to LMS, 7 December 1808.
60. S.O.A.S., LMS, Folder 2, Jacket B, Elliot's Journal, 29 October, 12, 26 November 1809.

61. Ince, "The LMS Mission", 7.
62. Ibid., 8.
63. Ibid., 26.
64. Ibid. Also Ince, "Protestant Missionary Activity", 91.
65. Cited in Ince, "The LMS Mission", 9.
66. Ince, "The LMS Mission", 10-11.
67. S.O.A.S., LMS, Folder 3, Jacket A, Elliot to LMS, 12 April 1810.
68. S.O.A.S., LMS, Folder 4, Jacket A, Elliot to LMS, 28 March, 11 October 1811.
69. S.O.A.S., LMS, Folder 4, Jacket A. Elliot to LMS, 11 October 1811, 28 January 1812; LMS to Grimshaw, 18 February 1812.
70. S.O.A.S., LMS, Folder 4, Jacket B, Elliot to LMS, 17 June, 24 September 1813.
71. S.O.A.S., LMS, Folder 3, Jacket A. Elliot to LMS, 12 April 1810.
72. S.O.A.S., LMS, Folder 2, Jacket C, Purkis to Bogue, 1 November 1809.
73. Ince, "The LMS Mission", 12-16.
74. Ibid., 17.
75. S.O.A.S., LMS, Folder 1, Jacket B, Elliot to LMS, 7 December 1808.
76. S.O.A.S., LMS, folder 2, Jacket C, Purkis to Bogue, 1 November 1809.
77. S.O.A.S., LMS, Folder 2, Jacket C. Purkis to LMS, 7 August 1809. See also Ince, "The LMS Mission", 17-18.
78. Marshall, "Missionaries and Slaves", 12. M.M.S., Diary, 22 February 1801.
79. Ince, "Protestant Missionary Activity", 64-6.
80. Ince, "The LMS Mission", 19.
81. S.O.A.S., LMS, Folder 1, Jacket B, Elliot's Journal, 19 May 1808.
82. S.O.A.S., LMS, Folder 4, Jacket A, Elliot to LMS, 17 August 1811.
83. G.W. Johnston & F.J. Osborne, *Coastlands and Islands* (Kingston: United Theological College of the West Indies, 1972), 63.
84. Ince, "The LMS Mission", 22.
85. Ibid., 20.
86. Ibid., 20-21. Ince, "Protestant Missionary Activity", 170.
87. M.M.S., Diary, 24 October 1800.
88. M.M.S., Tobago Letters, Printed Diary, 26 July 1800; Dairy 11, 13 October 1801.
89. Ince, "The LMS Mission", 22.
90. Ibid., 22-23.
91. M.M.S., Diary, passim, esp. 14 February, 30 April, 30 June 1800, 15 January 1802.
92. Ince, "Protestant Missionary Activity", 238-39.
93. S.O.A.S., LMS, Folder 2, Jacket B, Elliot's Journal, 13 December 1808.
94. Higman, *Slave Populations of the British Caribbean, 1807-1834* (Baltimore and London: Johns Hopkins University Press, 1984), 369. It does not appear that the law explicitly prohibited the marriage of slaves, but it was commonly regarded as out of the question; the Leeward Islands law of 1798 deemed it "unnecessary and even improper" (Higman, op. cit., 351) and in Jamaica it

required the owner's consent, not often forthcoming (Turner, *Slaves and Missionaries: The Disintegration of Jamaican Slave Society, 1787-1834* [Urbana: University of Illinois Press, 1982], 345.)
95. Ince, "The LMS Mission", 23-24.
96. M.M.S., Minutes, 21 May 1802. Ince, "Protestant Missionary Activity", 117.
97. M.M.S., Diary, 3 December 1801.
98. Ince, "Protestant Missionary Activity", 64-66.
99. M.M.S., Minutes, 8 March 1801.
100. Ince, "Protestant Missionary Activity", 119; M.M.S., Diary, passim.
101. M.M.S., Minutes, 22 April 1802.
102. M.M.S., Diary, 17 May 1801.
103. Ince, "Protestant Missionary Activity", 117.
104. See Ince, "The LMS Mission", 28; "Protestant Missionary Activity, 200-202.
105. Ince, "Protestant Missionary Activity", 156-73.
106. M.M.S., Diary, 12 October, 28 November 1800.
107. M.M.S., Diary, 5 February 1801.
108. M.M.S., Diary, 24 May 1801.
109. M.M.S., Diary, 10, 15 February 1801.
110. M.M.S., Minutes, 23 November 1800.
111. M.M.S., Minutes, 28 December 1800.
112. Ince, "Protestant Missionary Activity", 71.
113. Ibid., 156-77.
114. Ibid., 184.
115. Ibid., 182.
116. Ibid., 115.
117. S.O.A.S., LMS, Folder 1, Jacket B, Elliot's Journal, 3 October 1808.
118. S.O.A.S., LMS, Folder 2, Jacket C, Purkis to LMS, 7 August 1809.
119. S.O.A.S., LMS, Folder 4, Jacket A, Elliot to LMS, 28 January 1812.
120. See Ince, "The LMS Mission", 30.

CHAPTER SEVEN
1. S.R.O., GD51/1/491/1, Petrie to Dundas, 2 April 1795.
2. C.O. 285/4, Campbell to Portland, 17 January 1797, no. 4.
3. S.R.O., GD51/1/497, Petrie to Dundas, 14 August 1795.
4. B. Marshall, "Slave Society and Economy in the British Windward Islands, 1763-1823" (Ph. D. thesis, UWI, 1972), 168.
5. C.O. 285/3, f. 320, Lindsay to Portland, 5 September 1795, no. 13.
6. C.O. 319/6, Précis of Secretary of State's Corres., West Indies, 1795-1801.
7. C.O. 318/21, Secretary of State to Grinfield, 16 May 1803, Most Secret.
8. C.O. 318/22, Grinfield to Hobart, 24 June 1803, nos. 87, 89; 1 July 1803, no. 91 and encs.
9. C.O. 285/12, f. 139, 36, 55, Enc. in Young to Windham, 4 February 1807; Young to Castlereagh, 2 June, 23 July 1807.

10. C.O. 285/13, f. 106, Young to Castlereagh, 30 July 1808.
11. Laurence, "Tobago and British Imperial Authority 1793-1802", 45-46. See also above, p. 142-49.
12. C.O. 319/6, Précis of Secretary of State's Correspondence, West Indies, 1795-1801.
13. N.L.S., MS3972, ff. 13, 18, 21, Macdonald to Prevost, 26 December 1803; Macdonald to Moncrieff, 12 February, 16 March 1804. See above, p. 32.
14. C.O. 285/3, Minutes of Council, 9, 23 December 1794; 5 January 1795.
15. S.R.O., GD51/1/491/2, Extract of letter from Tobago to J. Petrie, 21 December 1794.
16. C.O. 285/3, Lindsay to King, 18 April 1795, Private.
17. C.O. 285/8, Carmichael to Hobart, 20 March 1802.
18. C.O. 285/3, f. 202, Minutes of Council, 5 January 1795.
19. C.O. 319/12, Digest of the most material proceedings ... with respect to the West Indies and the North American Provinces ..., 7, 9 January 1793.
20. C.O. 288/6, M.H.A., f. 245, 13 October 1807. T.P.L., M.L.C., 13 October 1812.
21. C.O. 288/6, M.H.A., f. 194, 245, 14 October 1806, 13 October 1807. C.O. 288/7, M.H.A., 12 April, 12 October 1808; 10 July 1811. T.P.L., M.L.C., 1811-20, 29; M.L.C., 13 October 1812.
22. C.O. 285/3, Minutes of Council, 27 February 1795.
23. C.O. 285/4, Minutes of Council, 28 September, 23 November, 1796, 10 July 1797.
24. C.O. 285/4, Minutes of Council, 16, 17 May 1799. C.O. 288/5, M.H.A., 2, 3 November 1801.
25. C.O. 285/8, Carmichael to Hobart, 25 July 1802.
26. N.L.S., MS3972, f. 3, Macdonald to Grinfield, 5 November 1803.
27. C.O. 288/6, M.L.C., 17 April 1804, 6 August 1807.
28. C.O. 285/13, f. 55, Enc. in Young to Castlereagh, 27 April 1808.
29. C.O. 285/14, f. 68, Young to Liverpool, 15 December 1809.
30. T.P.L., M.L.C., 12 August 1812, Message from Council to Assembly.
31. C.O. 285/13, ff. 55 et. seq., Encs. in Young to Castlereagh, 27 April 1808.
32. C.O. 285/5, Minutes of Council, 15 January 1799.
33. C.O. 288/6, M.L.C., 20 October 1803. N.L.S., MS3972, f. 3, Macdonald to Grinfield, 5 November 1803.
34. C.O. 318/23, 361, Macdonald to Grinfield, 15 October 1803.
35. C.O. 288/6, M.L.C., 1 November 1803.
36. C.O. 288/6, M.H.A., 13 October 1807. C.O. 285/12, f. 105, Young to Castlereagh, 21 October 1807.
37. C.O. 288/8, f. 136, M.H.A., 15 January 1813.
38. C.O. 288/8, f. 131, M.H.A., 16, 17, 18 July 1812. T.P.L., M.L.C., 12 August 1812.
39. C.O. 285/18, Young to Bathurst, 10 January 1813.
40. C.O. 288/8, f. 18, M.L.C.,

41. 12 January 1814.
42. Laurence, op. cit., 46-52.
43. T.P.L., M.L.C., 11 August 1812.
44. T.P.L., M.L.C., 12 August 1812.
45. C.O. 285/3, Minutes of Council, 12, 29 May, 19 June 1795.
46. Laurence, op. cit., 50-52.
47. C.O. 285/3, Minutes of Council, 28 March, and 2, 3, 9 April 1794.
48. C.O. 286/4, Dundas to President of Council, 3 May 1794.
49. C.O. 287/3, An Act to continue the Establishment of a Militia in this Island ... (No. 14, 10 January 1795).
50. C.O. 287/3, f. 94, No. 47, 5 December 1804.
51. C.O. 287/2, f. 63, No. 14, 10 January 1795.
52. C.O. 287/3, f. 65, Act No. 42b, 14 November 1803.
53. C.O. 287/2, f. 63, Act No. 14, 10 January 1795.
54. Laurence, op. cit., 43-45.
55. C.O. 285/5, Encs. in De Lancey to Portland, 2 April 1798, Separate.
56. C.O. 285/6, M.H.A., 7, 9 January 1800.
57. C.O. 285/4, Minutes of Council, 29 August 1796; M.H.A., 20 April 1795.
58. C.O. 285/2, Campbell to Lords of Trade & Plantations, 17 January 1797.
59. C.O. 287/2, f. 127, An Act for establishing and regulating ... a Troop of Horse ...
60. N.L.S., MS3927, f. 3, Macdonald to Grinfield, 5 November 1803.
61. C.O. 287/3, f. 65, Act No. 42b, 14 November 1803. C.O. 288/6, M.L.C., 20 October 1803.
62. C.O. 287/3, f. 65, Act No. 42b, 14 November 1803.
63. C.O. 287/3, f. 94, Act No. 47, 5 December 1804.
64. C.O. 285/13, f. 55, Enc. in Young to Castlereagh, 27 April 1808.
65. C.O. 287/4, f. 35, Act No. 88, 17 October 1814.
66. C.O. 287/3, f. 279, Act No. 75, January 1810.
67. C.O. 287/4, f. 68, Act No. 98, 17 July 1815.
68. C.O. 319/4, Instructions to Governor Ricketts, 14 September 1793.
69. C.O. 287/2, f. 63, Act No. 14, 10 January 1795.
70. C.O. 285/4, M.H.A., 20 April 1795.
71. C.O. 287/2, Act. No. 17, 21 April 1795.
72. C.O. 285/3, f. 270, Lindsay to Portland, 10 June 1795, no. 7. C.O. 285/4, Minutes of Council, 15 August 1795, 20 November 1795, 1 March, 1 June, 27 September 1796.
73. Spurdle, *Early West Indian Government* (Palmerston: The author [1962]), 61-62.
74. Laurence, op. cit., 52.
75. C.O. 287/3, f. 94, Act No. 47, 5 December 1804.
76. O. Warner, *A Portrait of Lord Nelson* (Harmondsworth: Penguin, 1963), 319.
77. C.O. 285/10, f. 14, Campbell to Camden, 15 March 1805, no. 8 and enc.
78. T.P.L., M.P.C., 26 February 1805.
79. C.O. 285/10, f. 32, Campbell

to Camden, 15 March 1805, Private.
79. C.O. 285/10, f. 14, Campbell to Camden, 15 March 1805, no. 8.
80. C.O. 285/10, f. 44, Camden to Campbell, 20 June 1805, no. 2.
81. T.P.L., M.P.C., 6 June 1805.
82. C.O. 288/6, M.P.C., 23 December 1805.
83. C.O. 287/3, f. 279, Act No. 75, January 1810.
84. C.O. 285/3, f. 256, Lindsay to Portland, 21 April 1795, no. 2.
85. C.O. 285/4, Campbell to Portland, 28 August 1796, no. 6.
86. C.O. 285/5, M.P.C., 27 December 1798.
87. C.O. 288/6, M.P.C., 9 May 1804.
88. See for instance C.O. 285/5, Robley to Portland, 19 May 1799, Particular, and encs.
89. C.O. 285/16, f. 26, Young to Liverpool, 21 June 1811.
90. C.O. 285/7, Robley to Hobart, 30 November 1801 and encs.
91. C.O. 287/3, f. 136, Act No. 52b, 16 December 1806.
92. C.O. 287/3, f. 279, Act No. 75, January 1810.
93. C.O. 285/8, Carmichael to Hobart, 25 July 1802.
94. C.O. 285/13, f. 107, Young to Castlereagh, 30 July 1808.
95. See for instance C.O. 285/4, Campbell to Portland, 28 August 1796, no. 6.
96. C.O. 285/10, ff. 15, 53, Campbell to Camden, 15 March, 10 August 1805, nos. 8, 21.
97. C.O. 285/3, f. 220, Lindsay to Portland, 18 April 1794.
98. C.O. 285/12, f. 36, Enc. in Young to Castlereagh, 2 June 1807.
99. B.L., Stowe MS923, f. 21. *Tobago Almanack, 1810*, edited by Sir William Young.
100. C.O. 288/6, f. 194, M.H.A., 14 October 1806.
101. C.O. 285/5, M.P.C., 18 March 1798.
102. T.P.L., M.P.C., 11 August 1812.
103. A.T. Mahan, *The Influence of Sea Power upon the French Revolution and Empire*, (Boston: Little, Brown & Co., 1919), Vol. 2: 211.
104. C.O. 285/4, Campbell to Portland, 22 March 1796, no. 1., 24 July 1796, no. 5.
105. C.O. 324/103, Portland to West India Governors, 3 April 1799.
106. S.R.O., GD46/17/24, f. 177, Seaforth Papers, Hood to West India Governors, 16 July 1803.
107. C.O. 285/3, Minutes of Council, 13 February 1794.
108. C.O. 285/3, Minutes of Council, 27 February 1795.
109. C.O. 288/6, M.L.C., 20 October 1803.
110. C.O. 318/23, Macdonald to Grinfield, 15 October 1803.
111. Ibid. Also C.O. 318/23, 315, Grinfield to Hobart, 20 October 1803, no. 137. C.O. 285/9, ff. 138-42, Encs. in letter from Robley, 31 December 1803.
112. C.O. 285/9, f. 144, Robert Mitchell to Adam Walley & Co., 24 January 1804.
113. N.L.S., MS3946, f. 203, Council and Assembly to

Macdonald, 3 November 1803.
114. C.O. 285/9, Macdonald to Hobart, 30 December 1803.
115. C.O. 285/9, f. 143, Lewis to John Robley, 24 December 1803.
116. N.L.S., MS3972, ff. 10, 12, Macdonald to Prevost, 4, 6, December 1803.
117. C.O. 288/6, M.P.C., 9 May 1804. C.O. 285/9, Enc. in Montgomerie to Hobart, 10 June 1804.
118. C.O. 285/9, ff. 142-3, Charles Wightman to Simpson & Davison, 27 January, 25 February 1804. Letter from Sir William Young, 4 January 1804.
119. C.O. 285/9, f. 144, Robert Mitchell to Adam Walley & Co., 24 January 1804.
120. C.O. 288/9, M.L.C., 12, 28 September 1804.
121. C.O. 285/9, Campbell to Camden, 8 December 1804.
122. C.O. 287/3, f. 109, An Act to raise a Sum of Money ... for the peculiar protection of the coasting trade of this Colony.
123. C.O. 285/10, Campbell to Camden, 11, 17, 22 April 1805.
124. C.O. 288/6, M.L.C., 10 December 1806.
125. C.O. 285/12, f. 23, Young to Castlereagh, 2 June 1807.
126. C.O. 285/12, f. 129, Young to Castlereagh, 25 December 1807.
127. B.L., Add MS37889, f. 35, Young to Windham, 27 February 1810.
128. C.O. 286/5, f. 129, Bathurst to Young, 6 March 1813, no. 3.
129. C.O. 285/18, Enc. in F.O. to Bunbury, 20 May 1813. C.O. 286/5, f. 130, Bathurst to Young, 3 June 1813.
130. C.O. 285/18, f. 4, Young to Bathurst, 22 January 1813.
131. C.O. 285/18, Young to Bathurst, 6 March, 7 May, 6 July 1813.
132. C.O. 285/18, f. 82, Young to Bathurst, 1 August 1813. C.O. 285/19, f. 54, Young to Bathurst, 31 October 1814.
133. C.O. 319/12, Digest of the most material proceedings ... with respect to the West Indies and the North American Provinces, 7 January 1793.
134. Mahan, op. cit., 205. P. Crowhurst, *The Defence of British Trade, 1689-1815* (Folkstone: Dawson, 1977), 202.
135. Mahan, op. cit., 204. Crowhurst, op. cit., 191.
136. C.O. 288/6, M.P.C., 17 May 1804. C.O. 285/9, f. 43, Enc. in Montgomerie to Hobart, 10 June 1804.
137. C.O. 324/103, Liverpool to West India Governors, 7 March 1812, Circ.
138. B.L., Stowe MS923, f. 28, *Tobago Almanack, 1810*, edited by Sir William Young.
139. C.O. 285/11, f. 28, Balfour to Windham, 3 July 1806, no. 4. See also C.O. 285/14, f. 12, Young to Castlereagh, 24 March 1809.
140. Mahan, op. cit., 204.
141. C.O. 288/6, M.P.C., 17 May 1804. C.O. 285/11, f. 25, Balfour to Windham, 13 June 1806, no. 2. C.O. 285/15, f. 9,

Young to Castlereagh, 14 April 1810.
142. C.O. 285/4, M.P.C., 7 April 1797.
143. S.R.O., GD46/17/24, f. 195, Seaforth Papers, Hood to Seaforth, 25 August 1803.
144. W. Laird Clowes, *The Royal Navy, A History* (London: F. Lowe, Marston & Co., 1899), 200-202; 241.
145. C.O. 318/22, Grinfield to Hobart, 3 July 1803, no. 93, Secret.
146. C.O. 285/10, Piston to Camden, 5 February 1805.
147. C.O. 285/12, f. 27, Young to Castlereagh, 2 June 1807.
148. C.O. 285/15, f. 25, Young to Liverpool, 7 August 1810.
149. C.O. 285/15, f. 45, Young to Liverpool, 2 November 1810.
150. C.O. 285/16, f. 131, Young to Liverpoool, 13 November 1811.
151. C.O. 285/18, f. 14, Young to Bathurst, 9 April 1813.
152. C.O. 287/2, f. 43. An Act to regulate the conduct of Persons resorting to this Island ..., No. 10, 23 August 1794.
153. C.O. 285/4, Minutes of Council, 30 July 1795.
154. Laurence, op. cit., 40-42. See above, p. 19-21.
155. C.O. 288/6, M.L.C., 13 September 1803.
156. C.O. 287/3, f. 60, Act No. 40b, 21 September 1803.
157. C.O. 285/16, Young to Liverpool, 6 December 1811.
158. C.O. 287/4, f. 9, Act No. 80, 23 November 1811.
159. C.O. 288/8, M.H.A., 14, 15 January 1813.
160. C.O. 288/8, M.L.C., 14 July 1815; M.H.A., 14 July 1815.
161. C.O. 383/86, 37-8, Register of Acts, Annotation on Tobago Act No. 96 of 1815 by Stephen Junior.
162. C.O. 286/5, Bathurst to Balfour, 24 February 1816.
163. C.O. 285/21, Balfour to Bathurst, 12 April 1816, no. 6.
164. Ibid.

BIBLIOGRAPHY

A. Primary Sources
Manuscripts

Public Record Office, London
   Colonial Office Records, Tobago
      C.O. 285   Original Correspondences
                        Governor's Despatches and Miscellaneous
      C.O. 286   Entry Books of Correspondence
      C.O. 287   Minutes of Privy Council, Legislative Council, House of Assembly
      C.O. 288   Acts
      C.O. 290   Shipping Returns
   Colonial Office Records, West Indies
      C.O. 318   Despatches
      C.O. 319   Entry Books
   Colonial Office Records, Colonies (General)
      C.O. 323
      C.O. 324

British Library
   Add. MSS. Windham Papers
   Stowe, MSS. Correspondence of Sir William Young, 1807
   Historical, Statistical, Descriptive Account of the Island of Tobago... by Sir William Young, 1809

Scottish Record Office, Edinburgh
   Balfour-Melville Papers   1767-1823   GD126
   Melville Castle Papers   1795-96   GD51/1
   Seaforth Papers   1803   GD46/17

National Library of Scotland
   Melville Papers   1795   MS 3844
   Robertson-MacDonald Papers   MSS 3946-7, 3972
   Charles Steuart Papers   1773-1798   MSS 5028-40

Moravian Missionary Society, Muswell Hill, London
   Diary of the Negro Congregation at Tobago, 1801
   Tobago, Minutes of Conferences, 1800-1802
   Tobago Letters

School of Oriental and African Studies, University of London
   London Missionary Society Records
   Records of the Tobago Mission, 1808-1813

Lambeth Palace Library
  Fulham Palace Papers
  Records relating to West Indies (General), Windward Islands, Tobago
Tobago Public Library
  Minutes of the House of Assembly, 1794-1804, 1808-1815
  Minutes of the Legislative Council, 1794-95, 1811-20
  Minutes of the Privy Council, 1803-1816
University of the West Indies Library, St. Augustine
  "Diaries" of Sir William Young, Bart.
  An Historical, Statistical and Descriptive Account of the Island of Tobago, Introductory to an Essay on the Commercial and Political Importance of the Possession to Great Britain. By Sir William Young, Bart. 1812.

Printed Documents

Confidential Correspondence of Napoleon Bonaparte with his Brother Joseph (London: Murray, 1855).
F.L. Nussbaum (ed.), *Documents Relating to the Claims of the Tobago Creditors, 1792* (Commission de recherche et de publication des documents relatifs à la vie économique de la Révolution).
C. Ross (ed.), *Correspondence of Charles, First Marquis Cornwallis* (London: Murray, 1859).
Sir William Young (ed.), *Tobago Almanack, 1810*.

B. Secondary Sources

Books and Articles

Anstey, R. G. 1975. *The Atlantic Slave Trade and British Abolition, 1760-1810*. London: Macmillan.
F. Armytage, 1953. *The Free Port System in the British West Indies*. London: Longman Green & Co.
Bemis, S.F. 1923. *Jay's Treaty: A Study in Commerce and Diplomacy*. New York: Macmillan.
Benns, F.L. 1923. *The American struggle for the British West Indian Carrying Trade, 1815-1830*. Indiana University Studies no. 56. Bloomington, Indiana.
Brathwaite, E. 1971. *The Development of Creole Society in Jamaica, 1770-1820*. Oxford: Clarendon Press.
Brereton, B.M. 1981. *A History of Modern Trinidad, 1783-1962*. Kingston: Heinemann.
Buckley, R.N. 1979. *Slaves in Red Coats: the British West India Regiments, 1793-1815*. New Haven: Yale University Press.
Caldecott, A. 1898. *The Church in the West Indies*. London: Society for Promoting Christian Knowledge.
Cambridge History of British Foreign Policy. 1922-23. Cambridge: University Press.

Clowes, W. Laird. 1899. *The Royal Navy, A History*. London: F. Lowe Marston & Co.

Crowhurst, P. 1977. *The Defence of British Trade, 1689-1815*. Folkstone: Dawson.

Curtin, P. 1969. *The Atlantic Slave Trade*. Madison: University of Wisconsin Press.

———. 1989. *Death by Migration: Europe's Encounter with the Tropical World in the Nineteenth Century*. Cambridge: Cambridge University Press.

Davis, D.B. 1975. *The Problem of Slavery in the Age of Revolution, 1770-1823*. Ithaca: Cornell University Press.

Deerr, N. 1949-50. *History of Sugar*. London: Chapman & Hall.

Dookhan, I. 1975. "War and Trade in the West Indies: A Preliminary Survey 1783-1815". *Journal of the College of the Virgin Islands*, no. 1 (May).

Duffy, M. 1987. *Soldiers, Sugar and Sea Power: The British Expeditions to the West Indies and the War against Revolutionary France*. Oxford: Clarendon Press.

Findlay, G.G. and W.W. Holdsworth. 1921. *The History of the Wesleyan Missionary Society*. 5 vols. London: Epworth Press.

Fortescue, Sir John. 1899-1930. *History of the British Army*. 13 vols. London: Macmillan.

Goveia, E.V. 1965. *Slave Society in the British Leeward Islands at the End of the Eighteenth Century*. New Haven: Yale University Press.

———. 1970. *The West Indian Slave Laws in the Eighteenth Century*. Bridgetown: Caribbean Universities Press.

Hall, D.G. 1978. "Incalculability as a Feature of Sugar Production during the Eighteenth Century". *Social and Economic Studies* 10, no. 3: 305-18.

Herskovits, M.J. 1958. *The Myth of the Negro Past*. 2nd ed. Boston: Beacon Press.

Higman, B.W. 1976. *Slave Population and Economy in Jamaica, 1807-1834*. Cambridge: Cambridge University Press.

———. 1984. *Slave Populations of the British Caribbean, 1807-1834*. Baltimore and London: Johns Hopkins University Press.

Holmes, J. 1827. *Historical Sketches of the Missions of the United Brethren for Propagating the Gospel among the Heathen, from their Commencement to the Year 1817*. London: The Author.

Ince, A.C. 1985. "The London Missionary Society's Mission to Tobago, 1808-1812: A Case Study of Missionary Character and Conflict in a West Indian Slave Society". Seminar Paper, Department of History, UWI, St Augustine.

Johnston, G.W. & F.J. Osborne. 1972. *Coastlands and Islands*. Kingston: United Theological College of the West Indies. Mimeo.

Kiple, K.F. 1984. *The Caribbean Slave: A Biological History*. Cambridge: Cambridge University Press.

Klein, H.S. 1978. *The Middle Passage*. Princeton: Princeton University Press.

Laurence, K.O. 1982. "The Tobago Slave Conspiracy of 1801". *Caribbean Quarterly* 28, no. 3 (September).

———. 1983. "Tobago and British Imperial Authority, 1793-1802". In *Trade, Government and Society in Caribbean History, 1700-1920*, edited by B.W. Higman. Kingston: Heinemann Caribbean.
Mahan, A.T. 1919. *The Influence of Sea Power upon the French Revolution and Empire*. Boston: Little, Brown.
Marshall, B.A. 1980. "Missionaries and Slaves in the Windward Islands". Paper Presented at the Twelfth Conference of Caribbean Historians, UWI, St Augustine.
Mellor, G.R. 1951. *British Imperial Trusteeship, 1783-1850*. London: Faber.
Murray, D.J. 1965. *The West Indies and British Colonial Government, 1801-1834*. Oxford: Clarendon Press.
Nardin, J.C. N.d. "Tobago, Antilles Françaises (1781-1793)". *Annales des Antilles*, vol. 14. Fort de France: Société d'histoire de la Martinique.
———. 1969. *La mise en valeur de l'isle de Tobago (1763-1783)*. Paris: Mouton and Co.
Pares, R. 1963. *War and Trade in the West Indies, 1739-1763*. London: Cass.
Parrinder, G. 1980. "The African Spiritual Universe". In *Afro-Caribbean Religions*, edited by B. Gates. London: Ward Lock.
Poole R.L. & W. Hunt, eds. 1905-14. *The Political History of England*. Vol. XI. London: Longman.
Porter, D.H. 1970. *The Abolition of the Slave Trade in England*. New York: Anchor Books.
Ragatz, L.J. 1963. *The Fall of the Planter Class in the British West Indies, 1763-1834*. New York: Octagon Books.
Rose, J. Holland. 1912. *William Pitt and the Great War*. London: Bell.
———. 1916. *Life of Napoleon I*. London: Bell.
Sheridan, R.B. 1985. *Doctors and Slaves, A Medical and Demographic History of Slavery in the British West Indies, 1680-1834*. Cambridge: Cambridge University Press.
Southey, T. 1827. *Chronological History of the West Indies*. London: Longman.
Spurdle, F.G. [1962]. *Early West Indian Government*. Palmerston, N.Z.: The Author.
Turner, M. 1982. *Slaves and Missionaries: The Disintegration of Jamaican Slave Society, 1787-1834*. Urbana: University of Illinois Press.
Ward, J.R. 1978. *British West Indian Slavery 1750-1834: The Process of Amelioration*. Oxford: Clarendon Press.
———. 1978. "The Profitability of Sugar Planting in the British West Indies, 1650-1834". *Economic History Review* 31, no. 2.
Warner, O. 1963. *A Portrait of Lord Nelson*. Harmondsworth: Penguin.
Watson, J.S. 1960. *The Reign of George III*. Oxford: Clarendon Press.
Williams, E.E. 1962. *History of the People of Trinidad and Tobago*. Port of Spain: PNM Publishing Co.
Woodcock, H.I. N.d. *History of Tobago*. Rep. Port of Spain: Columbus Publishers Ltd.
Young, Sir William, 1807. *The West India Common-Place Book*. London: Phillips/Macmillan.

Unpublished Theses

Ince, A.C. 1984. "Protest and Missionary Activity in Five South Caribbean Islands During Slavery, 1765-1826". D. Phil. thesis, University of Oxford.

Marshall, B. 1972. "Slave Society and Economy in the British Windward Islands, 1763-1823". Ph.D. thesis, University of the West Indies.

INDEX

Absentee owners: attempts to tax, 61, 62, 104; growth in number of, 15-16; tax on slaves of, 67-68
Abolition Act: passage of, 143
"Act for the Good Order and Government of Slaves ..." (1774-5), 94
Adelphi estate: sugar crop of (1793-7), 140
Agricultural production: in Tobago, 1,2,3
Agricultural Society: formation of, 147-148; influence of, on use of local products, 148; sponsorship of, by Governor Young, 118-119
Amelioration: attitudes to, 100-102; circulation of guidelines for legislation on, 102-103; recommendations of bill regarding, 105-106; recommendations for, in Tobago, 103-106
Amerindians: in Tobago, 1
Amity Hope: signal post at, 214
Anglican church: authorization of construction of building for, 184; and coloured and slave population, 184; responsibility of clergy, 182-183; in Tobago, 182-184
Assembly: absences from sittings of, 51-52; activities of, 52-53; desire of, to shift taxation burden, 68; disagreement with Council over taxes, 67-68, 69-78; efforts of, to establish constitutional privilege, 76; election of, 46; and influence over appointments, 58; opposition of, to Governor De Lancey, 84-85; privileges of, 51; qualification for membership in, 50; voting qualification for, 50-51
Assembly, Colonial: establishment of, by French, 2, 3

Bacolet swamp: drainage of, 19
Balfour, John: as Agricultural Society president, 147; as Council President, 53-54; as first Chief Justice, 55; and warning to British Government, 11
Baptism: approach of missionaries to, 192-193; and relationship to status of slaves, 192-193
Batteries, coastal: condition of, 203-204
Birth rates: among slaves, 33, 125
Black Carolina Corps: drafting of, into West India Regiments, 80
Black Corps: creation of, 80; proposal for, 79-80; proposal to revive, 84; repeal of Act authorizing, 84; tax to finance, 61; use of, in defence, 207. *See also* Black troops
Black troops: failure of recruitment programme, 80-82; reasons for rejection of proposal for, by Tobago planters, 82; recruitment and use of, by Britain, 79
Brasnell, William: appointment of, to Council, 75
Bridges: building and repair of, 159-160
British navy: and responsibility for defence at sea, 214
British settlers: and desire for return to British rule, 7; emigration of, under French rule, 3; encouragement of, in Tobago, 2
Burnet, George: printing press of, 160

Campbell, James: claims on assets of, 139; as Council member, 48, 49
Chain Gang Act: amendment to, 114; disallowance of, 114, 115; effect of passage of, 113-115
Chief Justice: appointment of, 77; John Balfour as, 55
Church: in Tobago, 227. *See also* Missionaries
Church, John: arrival of as missionary, 186
Christmas: celebration of, by slaves, 117-118
Clothing: of slaves, 120
Coins: circulation of, in Tobago, 153; efforts to standardize value of, 153-154; shortage of, 152, 155-156; in use in Tobago, 153
Colony House, 55

275

Colour: importance of, among slaves, 44
Communications: internal, 157; for defence of Tobago, 213-214
Concubinage: between white men and coloured women, 29-30
Contraband trade: in American goods, 177
Convoy Act: passage of, 217-218
Convoys: organization of, 218-219; permission for ships to sail without, 218; scheduling of, 218; use of, 217
Cotton: decline in production of, 4, 146; increase in production of, 2
Council: absences from, 46-48; and attempts to amend money bills, 66-67; appointment of, in 1783, 45; and challenge to Assembly's taxation control, 72; disagreements between Assembly and, over taxes, 67-68, 73-76, 69-78; and executive business, 50; and legislation, 53; position of, on income tax, 66, 69-70; qualifications for membership in, 48
Courland Bay: as naval base, 219; as port of entry, 175
Court of Chancery: establishment of, 55
Court of Common Pleas: establishment of, 55
Court of Escheat, 27
Cultural practices: of whites in Tobago, 20-21
Cumine, Dr George, 14, 36; as Assistant Justice, 55; as council member, 48
Cuyler, Cornelius (Major General), 7; and appointment of Council, 1783, 45

Dancing: among slaves, 43
De Bruille, John: as Crown Surveyor, 13
De Lancey, (Governor): opposition to, by Assembly, 84-85
Death rates: among slaves, 33
Defence: efforts to improve, 197, 221-222, 227-228; imperial contribution to Tobago's, 222; taxes to meet expenditure on, 61
Deficiency laws: amendment of, 28; fines under, 62; passage of, 16; tax payable under, 17,
Delgré, Louis, 3
Dillon, Count: arrival of, in Tobago, 4
Disease: pattern of, among slaves, 37. *See also* Mortality
Duncan, John, 134
Duties: to protect British colonial trade, 174-175

Economic development: effect of war on stability, 140-141; efforts to promote, under French rule, 4, 5; land acquisition and, 133-134; progress of, 180-181, 226
Economic independence: of slaves, 119
Elliot, Roger (LMS missionary), 43; approach of, to slavery, 189-190; arrival of, in Tobago, 187; methods used in ministry of, 190-191
Ellis, Charles Rose: and proposals for amelioration, 101
Embargo Act (American): effect of, on trade with Tobago, 172
Escheator to the Crown: revival of office of, 27
Estate mortgages, 138-139
Europeans: and settlement of Tobago, 1
Exclusif system, 4, 134
Exports: under French rule, 4; of sugar, 181; in trade with Spanish colonies, 162-163; during the war years, 1794-1815, 136, 146

Fees: of public officials, 58-59
Fertility levels: of slaves, 34-35
Fevers: prevalence of, in West Indian garrisons, 18-19
Finance Acts: dependence on, for revenue, 60, 63-65
Fish: measures for dealing with problem of imports, 174; calls for prohibition of foreign, 175-176
Flogging: as most common punishment, 100; provision for, under slave law, 1802, 28
Food: supply of, 161
Food production: encouragement of local, 146-148; increase in, 135
Foreign Slave Trade Bill: passage of, 143
Foreigners: legislation aimed at protection against, 220-221
Fort King George (Fort Castries), 8; maintenance of, and its surroundings, 201, 203
Fortifications: maintenance of, 201;

neglect of, after 1805, 205
Franklyn, Charles, 48, 49
Franklyn, John, 12
Free coloureds: composition of, 21-22; cultural habits of, 27; distribution of, 22; health status of, 27; inheritance among, 26-27; and membership in the Assembly, 26; occupations of women among, 26; relationship between whites and, 28-30; restrictions affecting, 26; as slave owners, 28; women as hucksters, 149
Free port: arguments for establishment of, 162; establishment of, in Scarborough, 4, 162; re-establishment of, 163
Free Port Act: amplification of, 164
French Revolution: effect of, on Tobago, 6-8; impact of ideas of, on slave population, 11; impact of ideas of, on British colonies, 11
French settlers: departure of, from Tobago, 12; as political problem in Tobago, 11-12

Garrison, British: improvement in health of, 200; stationing of, in Tobago, 197, 199
Glanville, John, 49
Golden Grove: establishment of LMS mission at, 187
Government House, 55
Grâces du roi, 2
Great Britain: war between Revolutionary France and, 7
Grenada: slave uprising in, 12
Grenville, Charles, 57
Guardians of the Rights of Negroes: suggested appointment of, 103
Gunboats: capture of, by French, 216; proposal for use of, 214-215; use of, 216
Gunpowder: tax in, 60-61

Hamilton, John, 184, 186
Health: of free coloureds, 27; of military garrison, 17; factors affecting, of slaves, 36-37; of Tobago whites, 17
Holidays: fixing of, 99
Hood, Matthew, 51
Hooker, Stephen: and invention of the windmill, 138

Hours of work : of slaves, 117
Houses: of slaves, 120; of whites, 21
Hucksters: free coloured women as, 149; and retail trade, 26

Income: of proprietors, 137
Income tax: abandonment of, in money bill, 72; attempts to introduce, 66; disagreements within the Assembly over, 71; position of Council on, 69-70
Indigo: cessation of production of, 146
Imports: hindrances to the flow of, 167-168; into Tobago, 1805-1807, 171; obstacles to, from USA, 227

Jay Treaty: signing of, 164-165
Justice: administration of, 55, 57
Justices of the Peace: appointment of, 55; and "pluralism in office", 58; and powers of detention, 106, 220-221

Land acquisition: and economic development, 133-134
Leeward Islands: attitude to slave trade in, 102
Legislation: against slave gatherings, 98; aimed at protection against foreigners, 220-221; method of publicizing, 160; revival of, in post-French period, 59
Legislature: and work of committees, 54-55
Liquor: sale of, 151-152
Liquor Licensing Act: passage of, 59
Loans: commission to investigate, 5
London Missionary society (LMS): attitude of planters to, 188; approach of missionaries of, to baptism, 192-193; approach of missionaries of, to marriage, 191-192; closure of mission, 189; decrease in support for, 189; disagreement between missionaries of, 188-189
Lumber: scarcity of, 179, 180

MacDonald, David: and grant of monopoly of printing, 160
Mail service: to Tobago, 156-157
Man o' War Bay: potential of, as naval base, 219
Markets: control of, under Police Act, 149, 151; establishment of, in towns, 149.

See also Sunday markets

Marriage: approach of missionaries to, 191-192

Martial law: declaration of, 106-107, 110; trend towards decrease in powers of governor under, 210-211; empowerment of governor to declare, 209-210; rules governing declaration of, 209, 210

Matthews, Rev. John, 183

McKnaight, Thomas, 49

Medical care: of slaves, 120-121

Militia: calling out of, 211-213; service in, for all free men, 208; use of, in local defence, 205

Militia Act (1795): lapse of, 207; requirements under, 205-207

Militia Act (1803): requirements of, 207, 208

Militia Act (1804): requirements of, 208; and creation of company of free coloured men, 208

Missionaries: beginning of work of, in the West Indies, 184; effect of, on slaves, 194-196; and perception of African lifestyle, 195-196. *See also* London Missionary Society; Moravian Church.

Money: measures to raise, 62

Money bills: Council's standing regarding, 67; protest against, by John Robley, 72-73

Montgomery, James, 186

Moravian church: collapse of first mission of, 186; start of mission in Tobago, 184

Mortality: among slaves 35-36, 125-126; among troops, 17-20; and work regime of slaves, 125-126

Music: among slaves, 43

Myers, William (Lt Colonel): as Lieutenant Governor of Tobago, 45

Napier, Archibald, 51; appointment of, to Council, 75

Naval bases: in Tobago, 219

Navigation laws, British, 134; exemption from, 164

Non-Importation Act: and prohibition of British goods to USA, 176

Nutrition: of slaves, 37

Obeah: influence of, on slaves, 42

Obeahmen: use of, in medical treatment of slaves, 121

Occupations: of free coloured women, 26; of slaves, 37-39; of white and coloured males, 22-25

Ottley, Drury, 48

Peace of Amiens, 8; and end to exemptions and licenses, 166

Petrie, Gilbert, 7, 8, 45

Petrie, John: as Tobago's Agent in Britain, 59

Piggott, Elphinstone (Chief Justice), 58

Pioneer corps: conversion of, into regular troops, 82-83; implicated in 1805 conspiracy, 110; raising of, 82

Plantation finances: problems of, 138-140

Plymouth: efforts to develop, 134

Police Act: and control of stray animals, 151; and enforcement of trading laws, 151; of Scarborough, call for revision of, 113; of Scarborough, and regulation of markets, 149-150

Poll tax: approval of, 68; position of Council on, 71-72; on slaves, 63, 71-72; on slaves owned by absentees, 66; on "unattached" slaves, 65

Port Louis, 2, 6

Printing: in Tobago, 160

Provisions: efforts to ensure adequate: 164-166; imperial view on problem of, 170; scarcity of, 172

Public accounts: auditing of, 77; auditing of, by Committee, 77-78

Public officials: appointment of, 57-59; payment of, 58

Punishment: recommendations in Amelioration bill regarding, 105

Purkis, Isaac, 28; approach of, to slavery, 190; arrival of, in Tobago, 187; conduct of, 188-189

Raynar, Jonathan: on treatment of slaves, 126

Religious beliefs: of slaves, 41-42

Representative System: restoration of, 45

Ricketts, George, 46

Road Act: of 1795, 157; replacement of old, 159

Roads: construction and maintenance of, 157-159

Index / 279

Robertson, Richard, 47
Robley, John, 49; protest against money bill by, 72-73; and request for LMS missionaries in Tobago, 187
Robley, Joseph, 3; death of, 49; as President of Tobago Council, 45, 49; as producer of high quality cotton, 146; and request for oath of allegiance from French settlers, 11
Ruddack, Thomas, 140
Rum: as substitute medium of exchange, 154-155

St Laurent, Roume de: as ordonnateur of Tobago, 4
Salary: of Chief Justice, 77; of governors, 77
Salt fish: in slave diet, 168
Scarborough: efforts to develop, 134; naval base at, 219; plan to attack barracks at, 108; renaming of, 2
Schirmer, Charles: arrival of as missionary, 186
Seven Years War, 1
Sex ratio: among new consignments of slaves, 31
Signal Hill: reasons for closure of mission at, 186-187; signal post at, 214; as site of Moravian mission, 186
Signal posts: use of, for internal communication, 214
Slave breeding, 35
Slave conspiracy: in Tobago, 106-108; suspicion of, in 1805, 109-110
Slave culture: of Tobago, 40
Slave family: structure of, 40-41; types of households in, 41
Slave Act (1775): re-enactment of, 99
Slave "doctors": use of, 121
Slave evidence: admission of in courts, 129
Slave Law: (1774-5), 94; (1802), 28, 108
Slave laws: attempts to ameliorate, 101; changes in, in Leeward Islands, 102; characteristics of, 96-98; passage of new, 99-100; principles of, 96; revival of, 59; vagueness of, 100
Slave population: mortality among, 226; effect of abolition of slave trade on, 145; increase in, 6; nature of, 44; and sugar production, 30; of Tobago, 30-36

Slave trade: abolition of, 111; arguments by Tobago against abolition of, 143-144; British agitation against, 141-142, 143; effect of abolition of, on treatment of slaves, 126; effect of news of abolition on slaves, 111; proposal for abolition of, 101
Slave revolts: defence preparations against, 223
Slaves: attitude of elite, 44; belief of, in racial inferiority, 132; bill to prevent ill treatment of, 124; Christmas celebrations of, 117-118; clothing of, 120; compensation for damage/injury to, 98; dependence of West Indian society on, 131; deputation of, to Governor Young, 111-112; distribution of, 31-33; earning capacity of, 119; economic independence of, 119; establishment of chain gang of convicts, 113; feeding of, 118-119; field workers, 37; functioning of gang system of, 115-116; funeral practices of, 42; hiring of, 99; hours of work of, 117; laws restricting gathering of, 98, 109; legal controls over punishment of, 98; legislation against killing of, 123-124; level of supervision of, 121; manumission of, 130-131; medical care of, 120-121; music among, 43; occupations of urban, 39; provenance of Tobago's, 40; recruitment of, for West India Regiment, 83; religious beliefs of, 41-42; restrictions on hawking by, 99; significance of ownership of, 15; social contact among, 121, 123; specialists among, 37-38, 39; suppression of freedom of movement of, 112; tax on "unattached", 65; taxes on, 63, 65; theft among, 127; treatment of, 43, 125, 127-128; women as owners of, 33
Sovereignty: politics of, 68
Special Commission: to investigate old loans, 5; termination of, 5
Sugar: instability of, 139, 139, 140
Sugar mills, 137-138
Sugar production, 3; expansion of, 135; problems of, 137-141; in relation to slave population, 30; in Tobago, 135-137

Sunday markets: resistance to, by missionaries, 150. *See also* Markets

Taxes: challenge to Assembly's control of, by Council, 72; disagreement between Council and Assembly over, 73-76; imposition of, 61-62
Terrill, Rev. William, 48, 183
Thomas, Rev. Anthony, 183
Tippling Acts, 62, 151-152
Tobacco: allowance of, to slaves, 118
Tobago: abrogation of British constitution, 2; attack on, by British forces, 7, 8; under British colonial constitution, 1; under control of Martinique commissioners, 6; and determination of allegiance, 85-93; and European settlement, 1; preservation of British character of, 2; recapture of, by British, 8-9; restoration of British colonial constitution, 8, 9; strategic value of, 1; vulnerability of, 199
Tobago Gazette: printing of, 160-161
Tobago National Guard, 6
Tobago Rangers, 83-84
Trade: 161-180; between Tobago and Spanish colonies, 162-163; changes in pattern of, 134-135; efforts to maintain, with USA, 166; under French rule, 4; hindrances to free port, 164; termination of, with Spanish colonies, 163
Trafalgar, Battle of, 199
Treaty of Paris, 1
Treaty of Versailles: terms of, 2
Trespass Act: passage of, 59
Troop of Horse: raising of, 207
Turmeric: experiment with, 3
Turner, Coll, 48

War: and economic stability, 140-141; and effect on shipping, 140
War of American Independence: and capture of Tobago by the French, 2
West India Regiment: drafting of Black Carolina Corps into, 80; as part of garrison in Tobago, 200; provision of slaves by Tobago for seventh, 83
Whites: composition and status of, 14-17; distribution of, 22; under French rule, 6; maintenance of, in population, 16-17; and monopoly of professional jobs, 23; relationship between free coloureds and, 28-30; state of health of, 17, 20; in Tobago, 13, 225
Wightman, Charles, 49
Women: occupations of free coloured, 26; as owners of slaves, 33

Young, Sir William: on abolition of slave trade, 145; and appointment of justices, 55; approach to period of governorship by, 68-69; death of, 53; on effect of abolition of slave trade on Tobago, 145; efforts by, to resolve conflict in legislature, 75; governorship of, 53; on male population, 13, 14; position of, on money bill, 74; and proposals for amelioration, 101; views of, on admission of slave evidence in court, 129; views of, on treatment of slaves, 124

www.ingramcontent.com/pod-product-compliance
Lightning Source LLC
Chambersburg PA
CBHW022003160426
43197CB00007B/244